Red Hat® Linux®
Survival Guide

Red Hat® Linux® Survival Guide

Mohammed J. Kabir

Hungry Minds™

Best-Selling Books ■ Digital Downloads ■ e-Books
Answer Networks ■ e-Newsletters ■ Branded Web Sites ■ e-Learning
New York, NY ■ Cleveland, OH ■ Indianapolis, IN

Red Hat® Linux® Survival Guide
Published by
Hungry Minds, Inc.
909 Third Avenue
New York, NY 10022
www.hungryminds.com

Library of Congress Catalog Card Number: 2001118281

ISBN: 0-7645-3631-1

Printed in the United States of America

10 9 8 7 6 5 4 3 2 1

1O/QV/RS/QR/IN

Distributed in the United States by Hungry Minds, Inc.

Distributed by CDG Books Canada Inc. for Canada; by Transworld Publishers Limited in the United Kingdom; by IDG Norge Books for Norway; by IDG Sweden Books for Sweden; by IDG Books Australia Publishing Corporation Pty. Ltd. for Australia and New Zealand; by TransQuest Publishers Pte Ltd. for Singapore, Malaysia, Thailand, Indonesia, and Hong Kong; by Gotop Information Inc. for Taiwan; by ICG Muse, Inc. for Japan; by Intersoft for South Africa; by Eyrolles for France; by International Thomson Publishing for Germany, Austria, and Switzerland; by Distribuidora Cuspide for Argentina; by LR International for Brazil; by Galileo Libros for Chile; by Ediciones ZETA S.C.R. Ltda. for Peru; by WS

Computer Publishing Corporation, Inc., for the Philippines; by Contemporanea de Ediciones for Venezuela; by Express Computer Distributors for the Caribbean and West Indies; by Micronesia Media Distributor, Inc. for Micronesia; by Chips Computadoras S.A. de C.V. for Mexico; by Editorial Norma de Panama S.A. for Panama; by American Bookshops for Finland.

For general information on Hungry Minds' products and services please contact our Customer Care department within the U.S. at 800-762-2974, outside the U.S. at 317-572-3993 or fax 317-572-4002.

For sales inquiries and reseller information, including discounts, premium and bulk quantity sales, and for-eign-language translations, please contact our Customer Care department at 800-434-3422, fax 317-572-4002 or write to Hungry Minds, Inc., Attn: Customer Care Department, 10475 Crosspoint Boulevard, Indianapolis, IN 46256.

For information on licensing foreign or domestic rights, please contact our Sub-Rights Customer Care department at 212-884-5000.

For information on using Hungry Minds' products and services in the classroom or for ordering examination copies, please contact our Educational Sales department at 800-434-2086 or fax 317-572-4005.

For press review copies, author interviews, or other publicity information, please contact our Public Relations department at 317-572-3168 or fax 317-572-4168.

For authorization to photocopy items for corporate, personal, or educational use, please contact Copyright Clearance Center, 222 Rosewood Drive, Danvers, MA 01923, or fax 978-750-4470.

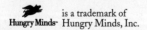 is a trademark of
Hungry Minds™ Hungry Minds, Inc.

Credits

Acquisitions Editor
Debra Williams-Cauley

Project Editor
James H. Russell

Technical Editors
Gregory W. Stephens,
Nancy Elizabeth Ellison

Editorial Managers
Kyle Looper,
Ami Frank Sullivan

Senior Vice President, Technical Publishing
Richard Swadley

Publishers
Mary Bednarek,
Joe Wikert

Project Coordinator
Nancee Reeves

Graphics and Production Specialists
LeAndra Johnson,
Kristin McMullan,
Jacque Schneider

Quality Control Technicians
Laura Albert,
Susan Moritz,
Charles Spencer

Proofreading and Indexing
TECHBOOKS Production Services

Cover Design
Michael J. Freeland

Cover photo
Hulton Getty

About the Author

Mohammed Kabir is the founder and CEO of Evoknow, Inc. His company specializes in CRM software development. When he is not busy managing software projects or writing books, he enjoys traveling around the world. Kabir studied computer engineering at California State University, Sacramento. He is also the author of *Red Hat Linux Server* and *Apache Server 2 Bible*. He can be reached at kabir@evoknow.com.

To the memory of my mother, Nazma Bathen.

Preface

Welcome to Red Hat Linux Survival Guide! Red Hat Linux is the most widely used Linux distribution in the world. Due to the enormous popularity of Red Hat Linux, there are many books about it. However, very few of these books focus on getting you up and running fast, focusing in on what you need to survive. This book — brought to you by the official Red Hat Press — is written to get you started on Red Hat Linux quick and easy. All topics are focused on practical Linux matters, things that a real-world Red Hat Linux administrator faces on a daily basis. So, if you're looking for a practical, to-the-point, and official Red Hat Linux book, then read on!

How This Book is Organized

The book has four parts. Short descriptions of each part follow.

Part I: Installation and Basic Configuration

In Part I, I show you how to install a fresh Red Hat Linux system, upgrade an existing Red Hat Linux system, dual-boot Red Hat Linux with other operating systems, configure the X Window System, and how to set up basic networking.

Part II: Getting Started

In Part II, I show you how to manage user accounts, work with files and directory permissions, run and control programs, use the GNOME desktop, and customize your Red Hat Linux kernel.

Part III: Configuring Services

In this part of the book you will learn to set up Apache Web server, Sendmail SMTP mail server, POP mail server, Wu-FTPD FTP server, BIND DNS server, and Samba file server.

Part IV: Appendixes

The appendixes introduce you to Red Hat Linux commands, basics of IP networking, and various Internet resources, such as USENET news groups, Web sites, and mailing lists that are available for Linux. You can also find help when you most need it: recovering from when your system crashes.

Conventions Used in This Book

You don't have to learn any new conventions to read this book. Just remember that when you are asked to enter a command, you need to press the Enter or the Return key after you type the command at your command prompt. A monospaced font is used to denote a configuration or code segment. Also, text in *italics* needs to be replaced with relevant information.

Also, pay attention to these icons.

The Note icon indicates that something needs a bit more explanation.

The Tip icon tells you something that is likely to save you some time and effort.

The Caution icon makes you aware of a potential danger.

The XREF icon points you to additional information about a topic in another chapter.

Tell Us What You Think of This Book

If you are interested in communicating with me directly, send e-mail messages to kabir@evoknow.com. I will do my best to respond promptly.

Acknowledgments

I want to thank both Red Hat Press and Hungry Minds teams, who together helped make this book a reality. It is impossible to list everyone involved, but I must mention the following kind individuals:

James Russell, the project development editor, who kept this project going. I don't know how I could have done this book without his generous help and suggestions every step of the way. Thanks James.

Debra Williams-Cauley, the acquisitions editor, who provided me with this book opportunity and made sure I saw it through to the end. Thanks, Debra.

Gregory W. Stephens and Nancy Elizabeth Ellison, the technical reviewers, who provided numerous technical suggestions, tips, and tricks — many of which have been incorporated in the book. Thanks, guys.

Razib Quraishi, a friend and co-worker, who helped me with various aspects of writing this book. Thanks, Raz.

Sheila Kabir, my wife, who had to put up with many long work hours during the few months it took me to write this book. Thank you, sweetheart.

Contents at a Glance

Contents

Part III: Configuring Services 279

Part I

Installation and Basic Configuration

Red Hat Linux is one of the easiest distributions of Linux to install and configure, which is one reason for its popularity (aside from the cool hat logo).

In this part, I show you how to install, get Linux up and running, and perform the basic configuration tasks that are required for a typical Red Hat system.

Chapter

Chapter 1

Installing a Fresh Linux System

IN THIS CHAPTER

- Selecting an installation source
- Understanding system requirements
- Installing from Red Hat CD-ROM

Unlike most Windows users, most Linux users actually prefer to go through the exercise of installing Linux on their systems. Although many major commercial hardware vendors, such as IBM, Dell, and Compaq, ship systems with Linux preinstalled, a true Linux user at some point will probably need to install Linux. I know quite a few Linux users who use Linux at work on workstations and servers and that eventually ended up installing Linux on their home machines, having become fond of this awesome operating system (thank you Linus Torvalds!).

In this chapter I show you how to install Red Hat Linux on your system as your workstation or server.

 If you are planning to dual boot your system with another operating system such as Windows, make sure you read Chapter 3 for details on what needs to be done before you install Linux. If you don't proceed carefully, you can disable or even delete other operating systems.

Choosing an Appropriate Installation Source

The most painless method of installing Red Hat Linux is from the official Red Hat Linux CD-ROM, although various other methods are available, such as from a hard disk partition or over the network via FTP or NFS-mounted file systems. In this chapter I assume that you're installing Red Hat Linux from the official, bootable Red Hat Linux CD-ROM distribution.

If you do not have the official Red Hat CD-ROM set and are installing by downloading Red Hat Linux distribution or via another method, you should be able to follow all of the instructions in this chapter, except for those that are specific to the CD-ROM.

Meeting the System Requirements

Before you attempt to install Red Hat Linux from the CD-ROM you must make sure that your system meets the minimal requirements. These requirements differ depending on what you want to use Linux for. Typically, Linux is installed on desktop PC workstations (at home or work), on servers, or on laptops.

In this section I discuss prerequisites for these three most typical types of Linux installations. Ensuring that the system that you're installing Linux on meets these requirements will help make your Linux experience worthwhile.

Most modern hardware far exceeds the minimum requirements for Linux, and so I do not discuss the minimum requirements in the following sections. Instead, I focus on configurations that will enhance your Linux experience. Although Linux can generally run on the most minimal, practical PCs, if you want to run older hardware you should probably review the minimum requirements at www.redhat.com.

Workstation hardware prerequisites

The term *workstation* usually refers to a PC that is used either at work or at home to perform various tasks via a desktop environment such as GNOME or KDE. To enable a desktop environment, you need to install the X Window System (often just called *X*) on your Linux workstation. To make sure that your X Window environment runs well, your system should meet the following requirements:

- **A 300 MHz or faster Intel Pentium-class CPU.** If your CPU meets at least these requirements, you won't need to worry about your CPU being a bottleneck in your system. Most U.S. retail stores don't even sell CPUs less than 500 MHz any more, so if you're buying a new system (or building your own), you'll probably wind up with a CPU that's at least 500 MHz anyway, which is absolutely a computing powerhouse.

- **At least 128MB RAM, but preferably 256MB or more.** While Linux can run on very little memory, the experience of running X with only a little memory is unacceptable to most users. Remember that RAM is the primary performance enhancement component in a computer, and that the more RAM you have on your system the better it performs. 128MB of RAM is enough to ensure a relatively smooth X window experience, but I recommend 256MB of RAM as an ideal amount of RAM for most users. If you use a lot of graphical applications such as GIMP or play 3-D games, you should probably consider installing even more memory for optimal performance.

- **A reasonably fast hard drive.** While SCSI hard disks are very fast, SCSI disks are much more expensive than EIDE disks. Today's EIDE disks are very reliable, fast, and quite cheap compared to SCSI or Fiber Channel disks.

- **A high-quality video card and monitor.** The best video card to get for Linux is one that is a recognized brand name and one that has a lot of memory. For example, 32MB of memory on a video card these days is not uncommon; such a card will be significantly instrumental in enhancing your experience with your X graphical environment.

- **A nice monitor.** You can buy the best video card in the world, but if your monitor is too old, you may not even be able to use the advanced functions and the higher settings that your video card allows. A good brand-name monitor with plenty of diagonal inches (i.e., size of the monitor) will be quite an eye pleaser (literally). I recommend at least a 17-inch monitor.

- **A high-quality sound card.** If you want to play any kind of sound on your system, be it music, video games, or whatever, get a brand name sound card. I highly recommend Creative Lab cards because they seem to work very well with Linux.

- **A quality mouse.** A good mouse, such as the Logitech scroll mouse or a brand-name optical mouse, can go a long way toward making your graphical environment experience seamless for Linux workstation users.

Server hardware prerequisites

Linux servers are typically used as Web, FTP, mail, NFS, or file servers. A server's hardware requirements depend on the expected load the server will bear. In this section I assume that you're building a Linux server for mid-range use (10–100 simultaneous user sessions). The following list describes each of the major hardware requirements for a typical server:

- **At least one 500 MHz or faster Intel Pentium-class CPU.** Having a dual or quad CPU setup may be helpful, depending on your server's needs. If you're not sure you need more than one CPU right away, but you're fairly certain (or at least hopeful) that your server load is likely to increase, you can always buy a system that can support dual or quad CPU setups and then install only a single CPU to begin with. As you monitor the system's performance over time you can add more CPUs as needed.

- **A minimum of 512MB of RAM per CPU.** RAM is the primary performance enhancer in a server system. Put simply, the more RAM you have on your system the better it performs. RAM price has dropped heavily in the last few years, and therefore many Linux servers are found with 1GB or more RAM.

Because most motherboards require all RAM sticks to be equivalent in size, you should buy RAM very carefully and in a planned manner. For example, if your motherboard has four slots for RAM, do not buy four 128MB RAM sticks to make 512MB of RAM; instead go for a single 512MB stick if available. This way you can drop in another three more 512MB memory sticks in the future as long as your system can make use of a maximum of 2 GB of RAM.

- **At least two hard drives (preferably SCSI).** If your server will do a great deal of disk I/O, such as serving a large amount of static Web pages, managing a great deal (say tens of thousands) of e-mail, or allowing hundreds of simultaneous FTP or NFS connections, then you need a very strong disk storage architecture. Minimally, a Linux server should have at least two disks. The operating system and all software should reside on one disk and the data (i.e., Web pages, e-mail, or FTP area) should reside on another.

If you have a great deal of traffic you should consider having more than two disks. Having a hard drive dedicated to logs and log activities such as Web access, FTP access, and so on can also help boost performance. You should also seriously consider using a blazing-fast SCSI hard drives, such as SCSI Ultra-160 disks. SCSI disks are much faster than current hard drive, and this only helps your server's performance. Note that SCSI drives are pretty expensive, so if you don't need SCSI you should go with EIDE drives instead.

- **A high-performance network interface card (NIC).** Your network cards can cause a big bottleneck if you do not buy high-performance cards from brand-name vendors such as 3COM or Intel.

TIP

Buying two cards for each server is a great way of dividing up traffic. For example, with two network cards you can create a backbone for your network servers using the second card and perform all system administration activity via that backbone network, isolating your system maintenance and file synchronization traffic from the actual intended Web, FTP, or other traffic. This configuration enhances both security and performance. Check out my Red Hat Linux Server 7 book (Hungry Minds, Inc.) for more details on how to create high-performance servers.

- **Inexpensive video hardware.** Because servers are typically not used as desktop systems you should not buy expensive video hardware. A minimal video card and monitor that handle VGA should be fine.

- **No sound card.** Again, because servers are not used as desktop systems, no sound card needs to be installed.

Laptop requirements

Laptop computers are very popular these days, in large part due to the significant price drop on laptop computers in recent years.

CAUTION

When buying a laptop to run Linux on, be careful because vendors might have specialized BIOS or tricky power-saving options that might get in the way of Linux. This is why you should really consider buying brand-name laptops to be used with Linux. Most brand-name laptop vendors such as IBM (Thinkpad), Dell, and Toshiba are quite well known for their Linux compatibility.

As far as the systems requirements, you should follow the workstation hardware prerequisites discussed earlier with the exception that your laptop monitor is going to be a TFT LCD display.

Installing from Red Hat CD-ROM

Red Hat Linux can be downloaded from the Red Hat FTP site (`ftp.redhat.com`) in your hard drive and installed from there using boot disks that you have to create. However, unless you have a very high-speed Internet connection and a great deal of time to download and create boot disks, etc., I highly recommend buying a copy of Red Hat Linux. The official Red Hat Linux distribution comes with bootable CD-ROM, which makes installing Red Hat Linux quite an easy task. In this section I assume that you are using a bootable Red Hat Linux CD-ROM.

To start the installation, insert the CD-ROM in your CD tray and boot (or reboot) the system. The following sections detail each step of the installation process.

Choosing an installation interface

The very first screen you see after booting your computer from the Red Hat CD-ROM is shown in Figure 1-1. You can choose to install using the default interface, which is a graphical interface, or you can enter **text** at the boot prompt to use menu-driven textual installation. If you choose the graphical installation but Linux doesn't automatically recognize how to work with your video card, you'll get the text installation anyway. The graphical installation is somewhat more user friendly, but this interface may not work for all systems due to video hardware issues. For this reason, I discuss the textual installation interface in this section. The choices in the graphical installation are similar to those of the text installation, though, and so the following sections are still useful if you're going with the graphical installation.

If you're an expert Linux user you can choose the expert installation. Also, if you're trying to fix an existing system you can enter rescue mode from this prompt. In the following sections I assume that you are installing a fresh copy of Red Hat Linux.

If you're upgrading from a previous version of Red Hat Linux, see Chapter 2; if you're setting up a dual-boot system so that you can run Linux alongside Windows, see Chapter 3 before starting the installation; if you need to recover from a file system error see Appendix D for details

```
              Welcome to Red Hat Linux 7.1!
  -  To install or upgrade Red Hat Linux in graphical mode,
     press the <ENTER> key.

  -  To install or upgrade Red Hat Linux in text mode, type: text <ENTER>.

  -  To enable low resolution mode, type: lowres <ENTER>.
     Press <F2> for more information about low resolution mode.

  -  To disable framebuffer mode, type: nofb <ENTER>.
     Press <F2> for more information about disabling framebuffer mode.

  -  To enable expert mode, type: expert <ENTER>.
     Press <F3> for more information about expert mode.

  -  To enable rescue mode, type: linux rescue <ENTER>.
     Press <F5> for more information about rescue mode.

  -  If you have a driver disk, type: linux dd <ENTER>.

  -  Use the function keys listed below for more information.

[F1-Main] [F2-General] [F3-Expert] [F4-Kernel] [F5-Rescue]
boot: text_
```

Figure 1-1 *Choosing an installation method.*

Choosing the installation language

After you've chosen your installation interface (again, the text installation is assumed here) then the installation process begins. You're then asked to choose the language of your installation, as shown in Figure 1-2.

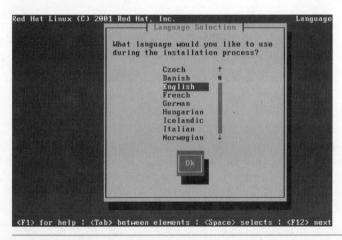

Figure 1-2 *Choosing the language that you want.*

Choose the language that's appropriate for you. The rest of the installation screen shots are displayed in English because I chose English as the installation language.

Choosing your keyboard

Next select the keyboard type from the list, as shown in Figure 1-3.

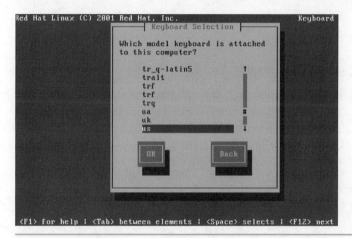

Figure 1-3 *Choose your keyboard type.*

If you do not know your keyboard type you can keep the default. After you've selected the keyboard type you see a welcome screen, as shown in Figure 1-4.

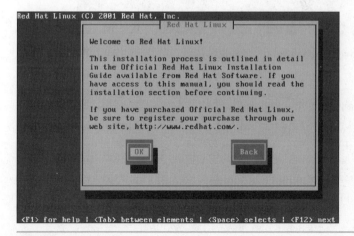

Figure 1-4 *The Red Hat Linux welcome screen.*

If you purchased Red Hat Linux, make sure to register at their Web site. This will allow you to get information on future updates and bug fixes via e-mail.

Choosing an installation type

The installer provides a few predefined installation types for you to choose from, such as Workstation, Server system, Laptop, Custom system, and Upgrade existing installation, as shown in Figure 1-5.

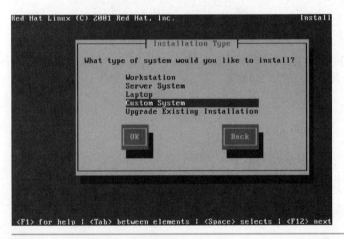

Figure 1-5 *Choose an installation type.*

The predefined installation types are supposed to make it easy for Linux newbies to install Red Hat Linux. For example, if you're installing Red Hat Linux for your workstation and choose the Workstation installation, the installer makes some assumptions about what software you need and installs that software. Similarly, if you choose the Server system installation, Linux makes assumptions about what software needs to be installed for your server and installs it.

If you're in a rush to install Linux and do not want to find out what is being installed, choose a type such as Workstation, Laptop, or Server. However, I highly recommend that you take the time (a few minutes at most) to install a custom system so that you know exactly what is going to be installed. In the following sections I assume that you have chosen to install a custom system.

Choosing the Server system installation will wipe your entire hard drive along with any other operating system that's residing on it!

Partitioning hard disks

Next you're asked to partition your hard drive(s). You're given the choice of two tools, as shown in Figure 1-6.

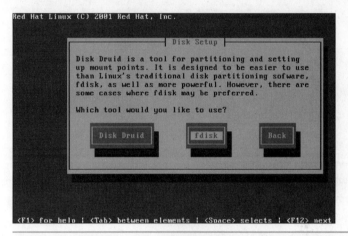

Figure 1-6 *Choose a disk partitioning tool.*

Disk Druid is a simple tool with a menu-driven interface. Disk Druid is easier than fdisk for novices but is less powerful than fdisk. Because fdisk is more versatile, I assume that you choose to use fdisk to partition your hard drive(s).

After you select fdisk as the partitioning tool, you're asked to choose which hard drive you wish to partition. If you have a single IDE hard drive, you'll see a list similar to that shown in Figure 1-7.

If you have a single hard drive, simply select the Edit button and press Enter. If you have multiple drives, the partitioning process is exactly the same as for a single drive. In such cases you partition one drive at a time and are given the chance to partition the other drives after you complete one. Simply select the drive that you want to partition and choose Edit.

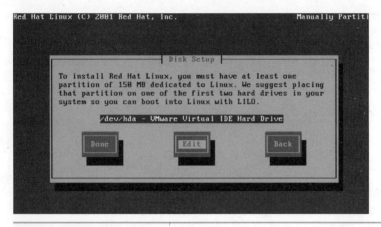

Figure 1-7 *Choose a disk to partition.*

fdisk displays the Command (m for help): command prompt from which you can enter **m** to get a help screen such as the following:

```
Command action
   a   toggle a bootable flag
   b   edit bsd disklabel
   c   toggle the dos compatibility flag
   d   delete a partition
   l   list known partition types
   m   print this menu
   n   add a new partition
   o   create a new empty DOS partition table
   p   print the partition table
   q   quit without saving changes
   t   change a partition's system id
   u   change display/entry units
   v   verify the partition table
   w   write table to disk and exit
   x   extra functionality (experts only)
```

To view your existing partitions in the selected disk, enter p, which displays all your current partitions in a table format such as the following:

```
Disk /dev/hda: 33 heads, 63 sectors, 1014 cylinders
Units = cylinders of 2079 * 512 bytes


    Device Boot     Start      End    Blocks   Id  System
/dev/hda1                1      505   524916   83  Linux native

/dev/hda2              506     1014   529105+   5  Extended

/dev/hda5              506      886   396018   83  Linux native

/dev/hda6              887     1011   129906   82  Linux swap
```

As you can see here, the /dev/hda disk has been divided into four partitions, where the first partition is /dev/hda1, which starts at block 1 and
ends at block 505. Each block is 1,024 bytes, or 1KB. So the first partition,
/dev/hda1, consists of 524,916 blocks, or 524,916KB, or approximately
512MB.

To remove all existing partitions one by one, use the d command and
enter the partition number you want to remove. If you are planning on dual
booting your system with Windows operating system, make sure you do
not delete the Windows partition and also make sure that Windows partition is bootable (see later in this section for information on how to turn
boot flag on for a partition). For example, Figure 1-8 shows a dual-boot
system with the first partition dedicated to Windows 2000 (NTFS) and
the rest of the three primary partitions dedicated to Linux.

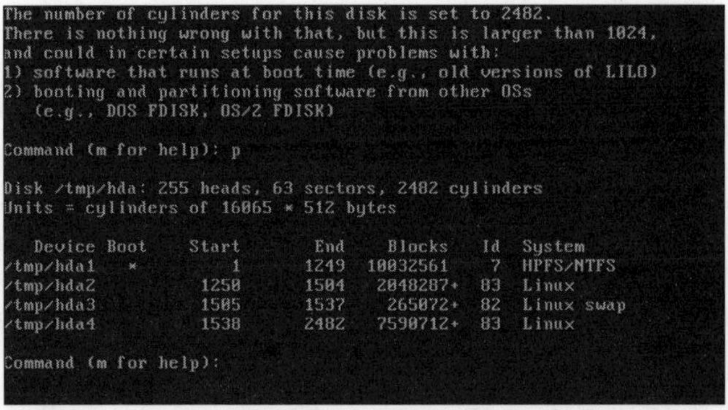

Figure 1-8 *Example partitions of a dual-boot system.*

After you have removed one or more partitions, you can create new
partitions as follows:

1. Enter n as shown here to add a new partition:

```
Command (m for help): n
Command action
    e   extended
    p   primary partition (1-4)
```

You get two choices, as shown here. You can create either an extended partition or a primary partition. You need extended partitions only if you want to create more than four partitions. Because you only need /, /usr, /home, and a swap partition to get things going under Linux, you really do not need to create extended partitions.

2. Create a primary partition by entering **p** at the prompt.

3. The next prompt asks you to select a partition number:

```
Partition number (1-4): 1
```

Enter 1 for the first partition, 2 for the second, and so on.

4. The next prompt asks you to select the starting block number. The range shown in the parentheses is the total blocks available for partitioning. If this is the first partition, you can choose 1 as the starting block as shown here:

```
First cylinder (1-1014): 1
```

5. To create a 512MB partition, you can enter the size in bytes, kilobytes, or megabytes. Because a value in megabytes is easy to deal with, I chose +512M for the last cylinder, as shown here:

```
Last cylinder or +size or +sizeM or +sizeK
([1]-1014): +512M
```

To create GB size partition use +nGB where n is the number of GB in this partition.

To see if the partition has been created as requested, use the p command to see the partition information:

```
Disk /dev/hda: 33 heads, 63 sectors, 1014 cylinders
Units = cylinders of 2079 * 512 bytes


  Device Boot    Start    End   Blocks   Id  System
/dev/hda1          1      505   524916   83  Linux native
```

As you can see, the first partition has been created as requested. The default partition type is Linux native; if you would like to change this, use the t command to toggle a partition's system ID flag. For example, to toggle a partition's system ID flag to Linux swap, you can use the following commands:

```
Command (m for help): t
Partition number (1-4): 1
Hex code (type L to list codes): 82
Changed system type of partition 1 to 82 (Linux swap)


Command (m for help): p


Disk /dev/hda: 33 heads, 63 sectors, 1014 cylinders
Units = cylinders of 2079 * 512 bytes


  Device Boot    Start    End   Blocks   Id  System
/dev/hda1          1      505   524916   82  Linux swap
```

As you can see, I have first entered the t command to toggle the system ID of a partition, selected the partition, and then entered **82** as the swap partition type. The l command can be used to list all the available partition types.

Note that if you use fdisk to create partitions, you must make a Linux native partition bootable. For example, to turn on /dev/hda1 as a bootable partition, I need to toggle the boot flag. At the prompt, I can enter the following commands to make the first partition bootable:

```
Command (m for help): a
Partition number (1-6): 1
```

Now if I display the existing partition table using the p command, I see the following:

```
Disk /dev/hda: 33 heads, 63 sectors, 1014 cylinders
Units = cylinders of 2079 * 512 bytes


  Device Boot    Start      End    Blocks    Id  System

/dev/hda1    *        1      505   524916    83  Linux native

/dev/hda2           506     1014   529105+    5  Extended

/dev/hda5           506      886   396018    83  Linux native

/dev/hda6           887     1011   129906    82  Linux swap
```

As you can see, /dev/hda1 has "*" in the Boot column, showing that this partition is bootable.

After you have created all the partitions you want and enabled at least one partition as bootable (using the a command) and created at least one Linux native (83) partition and one swap partition (82), you can use the verify command (v) to verify your partition layout. If you get a message stating that a very small number (62 or so) of blocks are unallocated then you are fine. In case you have lots of unallocated blocks, this means that your hard drive space is being wasted due to the improper sizing of partitions. To solve this, review your partition sizes by using the p command and if necessary delete them and recreate them. Do not leave empty spaces that are not partitioned. After you have verified that you have very little space left unallocated, write your new partition schema using the write (w) command.

You will be returned to the disk selection screen as shown in Figure 1-7 if you have multiple disks to partition. In such cases you will select the next disk and repeat the process. You do not have to partition each disk if you wish to keep them unavailable to Linux.

Assigning mount points to partitions

After you're done partitioning your drive(s) you'll be required to assign mount points to each of the Linux partitions. The partitions you created will be displayed as shown in Figure 1-9.

Select each partition that you want to mount under Linux and then click the Edit button. A screen similar to Figure 1-10 appears.

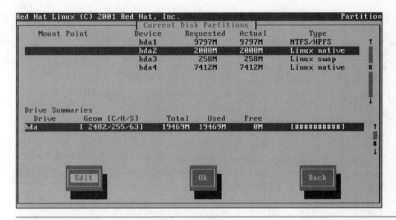

Figure 1-9 *Assigning mount points to partitions.*

You can install Linux on only two partitions: / (root) and swap. But you should have at least / (root partition), /usr, and swap partitions for server type installation. Here I will assume that you will create four partitions. Therefore you need to create at least / and /usr mount points. Note that if you place the / partition, which is where /boot directory will be stored, in a partition with more than 1024 cylinders you might get a warning message, as shown in Figure 1-11.

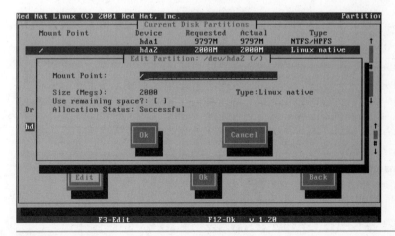

Figure 1-10 *Editing a mount point for a partition.*

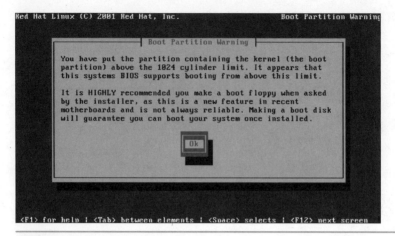

Figure 1-11 *A boot partition warning.*

If the warning message states that your BIOS supports such a boot partition then you can simply ignore it. However, if you later find yourself unable to boot from such partition, you will have to make your boot partition very small so that it does not exceed 1024 cylinders and then reinstall. Most modern motherboards BIOSes support booting from large boot partitions, so you should be fine.

Choosing which disk partitions to format

After you have assigned mount points to your partitions you can then format them. I highly recommend that you at least format the / and the /usr partition as shown in Figure 1-12. Formatting the / (root) and the /usr partition ensures that you do not have old files that might get mixed up with your installation.

If you are using a new disk you should elect to check for bad blocks while formatting. This slows down your installation significantly if you have a large hard disk (greater than 10GB), but it is worth doing at least for new hard drives.

Passing extra information to kernel during boot

If your system has some special hardware that requires that you tell the Linux kernel about it using a flag then you will have to enter it in the screen shown in Figure 1-13. Most systems do not need to pass anything.

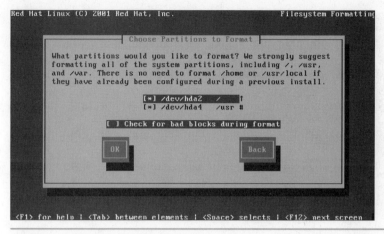

Figure 1-12 *Choosing disk partitions to format.*

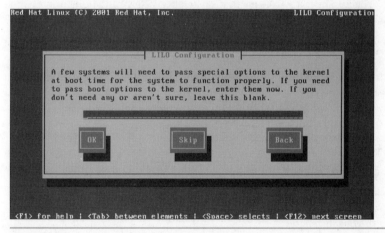

Figure 1-13 *Passing boot options to the kernel.*

Configuring LILO

Next you will be asked to select where you want to install the Linux boot loader program called LILO. You have two choices as shown in Figure 1-14.

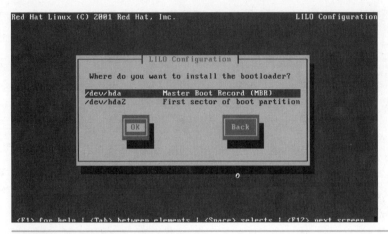

Figure 1-14 *Configuring LILO.*

You can install LILO on the Master Boot Record (MBR) only if you have no other operating system. In other words, if you are not going to dual boot Linux with another operating system such as Windows 2000 or Windows NT then MBR is a good choice.

However, if you do have another operating system installed, choose the first sector of the boot partition instead. This ensures that LILO is not installed on the MBR, which is where your other operating system, such as Windows, will have its own boot loader program.

See Chapter 3 for details on how to dual boot Linux and Windows 2000/NT and Windows 98 operating systems.

Next you will see a screen like that shown in Figure 1-15, which asks you to select which operating system you want to boot. In a single-boot system, as shown in the figure, there is nothing you need to do unless you wish to change the default boot label. If you do want to change the boot label from "linux" to something else, use the Edit button to modify it. Or continue forward by clicking the OK button.

Configuring your network

Next you will be asked to configure the network interface if you have one. If you do not have a network interface you can skip this section. The network interface configuration screen is shown in Figure 1-16.

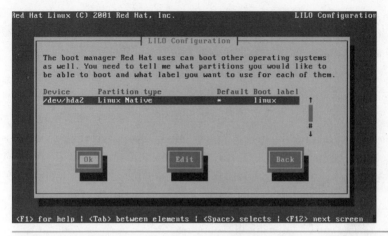

Figure 1-15 *Choosing the operating system to boot.*

Figure 1-16 *Configuring the network interface.*

If you want to use Dynamic Host Configuration Protocol (DHCP) or the BOOTP protocol to configure your network interface dynamically every time you boot your system then choose this option from this screen. On the other hand, if you have a static IP address, uncheck the Use bootp/dhcp option and enter the appropriate IP address, netmask, default gateway, and DNS server information and continue forward.

Next you need to give a host name to your computer. This host name is not arbitrary and therefore cannot be randomly picked up by anyone. This host name is associated with the IP address that you have assigned to the system in the earlier screen. If you do not have a host name and make up one here, this name will not be usable from other workstations or servers. In order for other users to find your system, the host name you enter here must have an A record in the domain to which it belongs.

For example, the Figure 1-17 shows that the host name of the machine being configured is called `hummer.evoknow.com`. The DNS server for `evoknow.com` must have an A record such as the following in the DNS configuration.

```
hummer.evoknow.com.    A   192.168.1.1
```

Enter an appropriate host name. If you use DHCP or BOOTP, the host name will be automatically configured for you upon system boot.

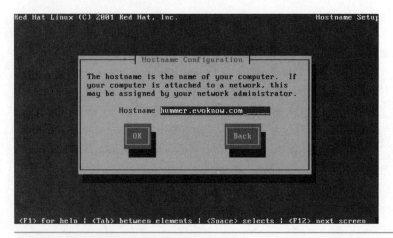

Figure 1-17 *Configuring the host name.*

Configuring firewall

The installation next allows you to enable and disable various services that are considered sensitive to attacks. Here, as shown in Figure 1-18, you are asked to choose from the following preset firewall configurations:

- **High:** Disables all incoming remote access to the system
- **Medium:** Allows remote access via secure protocols such as SSH but blocks FTP, Telnet, and services such as printing daemons that can print documents sent from remote systems
- **No firewall:** Allows all incoming traffic including Telnet and FTP

It is better to customize the firewall setup so you know what is being done. So choose the Customize option, and you will see a screen similar to Figure 1-18.

Figure 1-18 *Customizing firewall setup.*

You can configure the firewall setup to trust a network interface and/or you can choose certain network services to be enabled or disabled. By selecting the services that you want to enable, as shown in Figure 1-19, you ensure that they are available to you. If you know of a service that is not listed here you can add it using the Other ports option in the form of *service_name:protocol*. For example, if you wish to add the IMAP service then add `imap:tcp`.

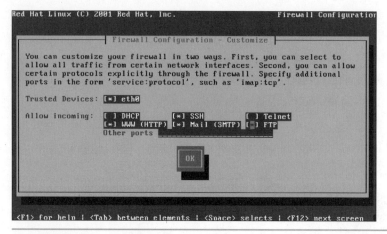

Figure 1-19 *Choosing your firewall options.*

Configuring mouse

If you have a mouse connected to your system you're next asked to select the mouse type, as shown in Figure 1-20.

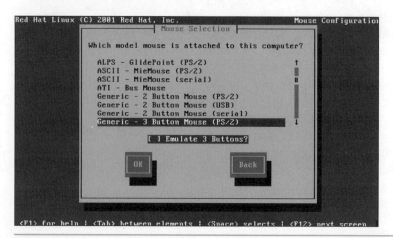

Figure 1-20 *Configuring the mouse.*

Select the mouse type that closely matches your mouse. If you do not have a three-button mouse, you can emulate the third button by selecting the Emulate 3 Buttons option. You will need to hold down both left and right mouse buttons to emulate the third button.

Configuring language of the operating system

When you started the installation process you were asked about the language of the installation. Now you have to select the language of the operating system. Select the appropriate language as shown in Figure 1-21.

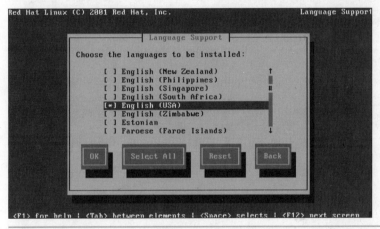

Figure 1-21 *Configuring your language.*

Configuring time zone

You need to tell the operating system about the time zone your computer will reside in so that it can keep appropriate time. Select time zone from the screen shown in Figure 1-22.

If your hardware clock is set to Greenwich Mean Time (GMT) then you can select the appropriate option in this screen to let the system know that.

Setting the root password and creating an ordinary user

Next you need to set the root password for the system as shown in Figure 1-23.

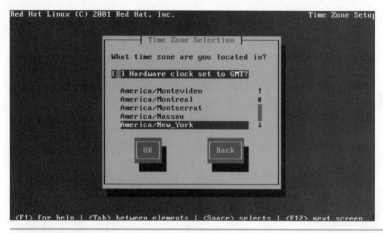

Figure 1-22 *Configuring your time zone.*

Figure 1-23 *Setting the root password.*

After you've completed the installation, you can always change the root password using the passwd command (while you are logged in as root).

After you've set the root password you can create an ordinary user so that you can log on to your system from a remote system via SSH, Telnet, or

FTP if you have enabled such access in the firewall configuration step earlier. Figure 1-24 shows a user called `kabir` being set up with a password.

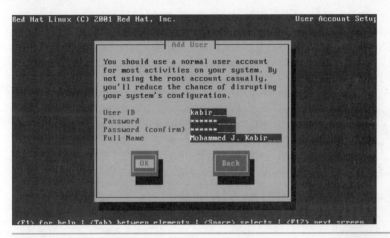

Figure 1-24 *Setting up an ordinary user.*

After you've added a new user, you can create more by clicking the Add button in the screen shown in Figure 1-25. You can create as many users as you want.

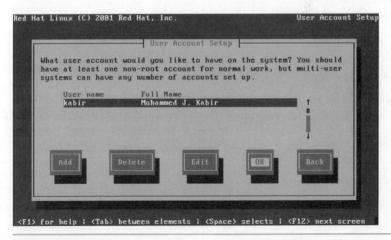

Figure 1-25 *A list of new users.*

Add as many users as you wish to have initially. Remember you can always add new users later. See Chapter 7 for details on how to create new users.

Configuring authentication options

Red Hat Linux can authenticate users using standard password file (/etc/passwd), or use shadow password files (/etc/passwd and /etc/shadow), or authenticate using remote authentication servers such as the Network Information System (NIS) server, Lightweight Directory Access Protocol (LDAP) server, or even Kerberos authentication server. Figure 1-26 shows your authentication configuration options.

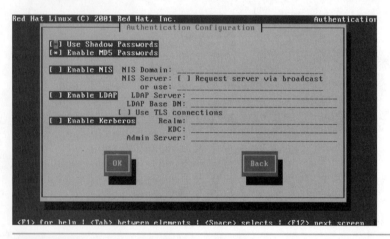

Figure 1-26 *Configuring authentication options.*

Unless you have existing remote NIS, LDAP, or Kerberos servers set up you should not enable them. You should definitely use the shadow password support and also enable MD5-based password support as shown in Figure 1-26.

Selecting package groups to install

Now you're ready to select the software package groups that you want to install on the system. The package selection is shown in Figure 1-27.

Select the packages you want to install. If you are installing Red Hat Linux on a workstation system, decide if you wish to install the X Window System, printing support, dialup support, and so on. When you select a package group one or more packages that are related will be installed. For example, if you select Graphics Manipulation package group then one or more graphics tools will be installed.

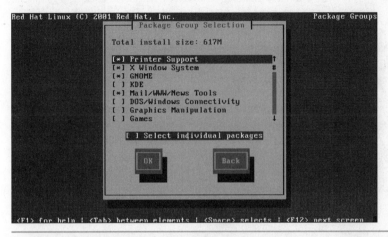

Figure 1-27 *Selecting package groups.*

If you wish to see or limit what exactly gets installed from within each package group, enable the Select Individual packages option. If you do, you'll then be asked to select each individual package from within each group. If you are new to Red Hat Linux you should not bother with this option if you want to find out what packages are out there and learn about them by playing with them for a bit. You can always get choosy later and uninstall what you don't like (or need).

Getting started with your coffee break

After you've managed to answer all the questions the installer had for you, you're told that a complete installation log will be created in /tmp/install.log so that you can review what got installed on your system. This message is shown in Figure 1-28.

Click the OK button to continue. The installer starts formatting selected hard drive partitions, as shown in Figure 1-29.

This process may take a long time depending on your hard drive size and depending on whether or not you've chosen to detect bad blocks. If you have a large hard drive (such as 30GB or above), you may want to take a coffee break (and maybe even a lunch break!).

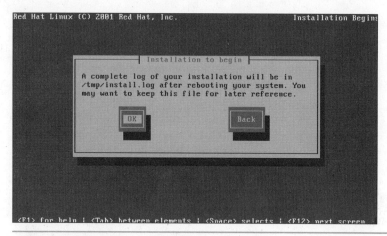

Figure 1-28 *Beginning the installation.*

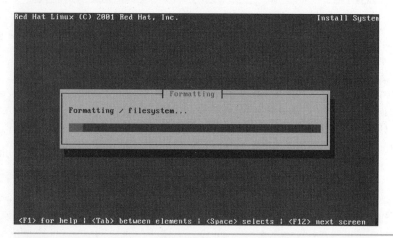

Figure 1-29 *Formatting selected hard drive partitions.*

After the formatting is completed, the software package installation begins and a status screen is displayed, as shown in Figure 1-30.

You can see how long the installation is estimated to take by looking at the information provided in this status screen.

Once the package installation is completed you will be asked to create a boot disk, as shown in Figure 1-31.

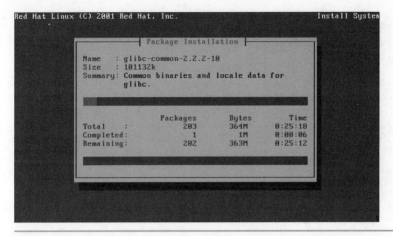

Figure 1-30 *The package installation status screen.*

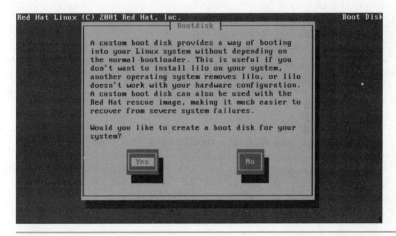

Figure 1-31 *Creating a boot disk.*

I strongly recommend that you create a boot disk by inserting a blank floppy disk in the drive and selecting the Yes option (the disk does not need to be formatted).

After you've created the boot floppy, you'll see an installation completion message, as shown in Figure 1-32.

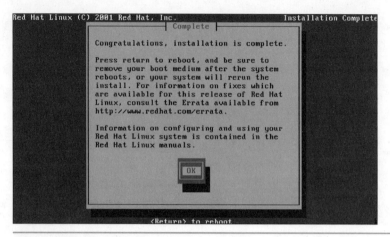

Figure 1-32 *Installation completion message.*

Press the Enter key to reboot the system. Make sure to remove your boot floppy or CD-ROM so that the system can boot from the hard drive. You should see a login prompt when the system has completed booting.

Congratulations! You are now a Linux user, and with this book you can soon become a power user. Enjoy!

Chapter 2

Upgrading Red Hat Linux

IN THIS CHAPTER

- Upgrading software using the command-line RPM command
- Upgrading software using Gnome RPM
- Upgrading software with the Red Hat Network Update Agent
- Upgrading the Linux kernel

Like most modern software, the software that ships with Red Hat Linux is updated often, and after a while certain packages need updating to remain compatible with the latest software. When upgrading Linux packages you have several choices of installation methods, the most popular being RPM binary packages and compiling binaries from source code.

In this chapter I show you how to use RPM tools (both command-line and graphical) to upgrade existing software components of the Red Hat Linux operating system, as well as how to upgrade your Linux kernel.

Upgrading Individual Software Package

Most applications and utilities that you use on your Red Hat Linux system are packaged using Red Hat Package Management (RPM) packages in either binary or source distributions. In this section I show you how to use both command-line and graphical RPM tools that are available to assist you when upgrading your software.

Upgrading using command-line RPM tool

The command-line RPM tool is very versatile in installing or upgrading RPM packages. This section shows you how to use it for the most common administrative tasks.

> **TIP**
>
> If you run rpm at a shell prompt or in an xterm terminal window you will see a lot of useful options that you can use with this tool. I strongly recommend that you read the man pages for the rpm command by using the man rpm command at the command prompt to learn more about this great tool.

Finding all the installed RPM packages on your system

To locate all the RPM packages installed on your system run the rpm -qa command. If you see lines scrolling past the screen you can use rpm -qa | more command to see a page at time by pressing the space bar key after reading each page.

Finding a specific RPM package

If you want to find out if a specific software RPM package is installed on your system, run the rpm -qa | grep *package_name* command. For example, to locate all the RPM packages for Perl run the following command:

```
rpm -qa | grep perl
```

A sample output of the preceding command is shown below:

```
perl-5.6.0-12
openssl-perl-0.9.6-3
perl-SGMLSpm-1.03ii-4
```

Finding information about a specific installed package

To find information about a package you can run the rpm -qip *package_ name* command. For example:

```
rpm -qip vlock-1.3-5.i386.rpm
```

This command produces the following information about the named package:

```
Name       : vlock    Relocations: (not relocateable)
Version    : 1.3      Vendor: Red Hat, Inc.
Release    : 5        Build Date: Thu 13 Jul 2000 11:25:38 AM BDT
Install date: (not installed) Build Host: porky.devel.redhat.com
Group      : Applications/System Source RPM: vlock-1.3-5.src.rpm
Size       : 8857     License: GPL
Packager   : Red Hat, Inc. <http://bugzilla.redhat.com/bugzilla>
Summary    : A program which locks one or more virtual consoles.
Description :
The vlock program locks one or more sessions on the console.  Vlock can lock the
current terminal (local or remote) or the entire virtual console system, which
completely disables all console access.  The vlock program unlocks when either
the password of the user who started vlock or the root password is typed.
```

 If you wish to know what files this package will install, run the `rpm -qlp` *package_name* command. For example:

```
rpm -qlp vlock-1.3-5.i386.rpm
```

This command shows the following output:

```
/etc/pam.d/vlock
/usr/bin/vlock
/usr/share/man/man1/vlock.1.gz
```

Finding out which package a file belongs to

To find out which package a particular file belongs to, run the following command:

```
rpm -qf path_to_file
```

Upgrading software

If you have the RPM package that you want to upgrade, run the following command to upgrade the software from within the directory where the file resides on your hard drive:

```
rpm -U package_name
```

Upgrading from an FTP site

If you've located a new version of a software package on an FTP site, you can use the following command to have rpm fetch it to upgrade the package:

```
rpm -U ftp://ftp_hostname/path_to_RPM_package
```

Forcing a software upgrade

Sometimes when you try upgrading a package by using the rpm -U package_name command, the package simply refuses to be upgraded. If you really want to upgrade no matter what, you can force the package to be upgraded by using the rpm -U --force package_name command.

Forcing an upgrade is not a good thing because you might break something else in the process. But, if you know exactly what you're doing it's good to know how to force a package upgrade.

You can also enable the -v and -h options to enable verbose mode and hash characters to ensure that you see some output during the upgrade process. For example, the following command forces an upgrade of gzip package version 1.3-12 on the system:

```
rpm -Uvh --force gzip-1.3-12.i386.rpm
```

The sample output from the above command looks as follows:

```
Preparing...   ################################### [100%]
   1:gzip        ################################### [100%]
```

Uninstalling before upgrading a software

If a software package requires that you uninstall a pervious version of the software before you install a new version, you can run the rpm -e *old_package_name* command to remove the current version and then run the rpm -ivh *new_package_name* command to install the new package.

Verifying that your packages are in good shape

If you're ever in doubt about an installed package and you want to verify that the package is installed properly, run the rpm -V *package_name* command. To verify the integrity of all packages in your system at the same time, run the rpm -Va command.

Upgrading using Gnome RPM tool

Gnome RPM (or GnoRPM) is a graphical interface for managing RPM packages that helps you easily install, upgrade, uninstall, verify, and query RPM packages. To run GnoRPM, click the GNOME Main Menu button and choose Programs ⇨ System ⇨ GnoRPM. The GnoRPM main window appears, as shown in Figure 2-1.

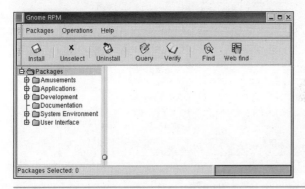

Figure 2-1 *The GnoRPM main window.*

To install an RPM package from the CD-ROM, insert the CD-ROM into the drive and then mount it if necessary (GNOME automatically mounts the CD-ROM unless you have disabled this option using the GNOME Control Center). Click the Install icon or choose the Install option from the Packages menu in the top left, and a screen like the one shown in Figure 2-2 appears.

GnoRPM reads the CD-ROM and locates packages. By default, GnoRPM only displays packages that are not already installed. If you click the Expand Tree button, all the packages are visible instead, as shown in Figure 2-3.

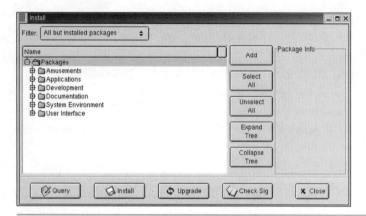

Figure 2-2 *Choosing new RPMs to install.*

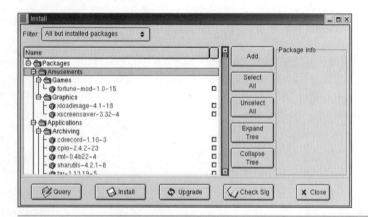

Figure 2-3 *Expanding the package tree.*

Select the appropriate packages and click the Install button to install selected packages. If you wish to upgrade existing packages using the current CD-ROM, simply change the filter rule (top left) to "All packages" or "Only newer packages" to make it easy for yourself to find appropriate packages. If you are upgrading from an older version of an installed package, use the Upgrade button instead of the Install button.

To verify that an existing package is intact, you can simply select the package and click the Verify button. For example, Figure 2-4 shows that GnoRPM has found six problems with the installed kernel package.

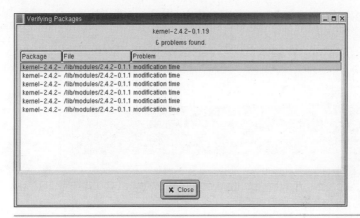

Figure 2-4 *Verifying a package.*

As you can see from the figure, because the only problem found is the modification date (which I know that I have changed myself), there is no need to reinstall this package. However, if GnoRPM reports files missing for a package that you have installed, it is best to reinstall it.

The Gnome RPM program can also find RPM packages that you need via the Web using the Web Find feature. This feature allows you to locate an RPM package on the Web and download it.

Using Red Hat Network Update Agent

Red Hat Network is the support and management service for Red Hat Linux. It offers these services primarily to paying customers (those who bought the Red Hat Linux package on CD-ROM) who want to update software and get support from Red Hat for a fee. Red Hat offers free access to their Software Manager service for a single machine per customer.

The Red Hat Update Agent is a tool that uses Red Hat Network to find out which packages on your system need to be updated and updates them automatically. To use the Red Hat Update Agent you first need to become a registered user of Red Hat Network, a process that I describe in the next section.

Becoming a registered user of Red Hat Network

To register for a trial free membership for a single machine, follow these steps:

1. Run the `rhn_register` command from an xterm in a GUI environment or from the command shell. (In this section I assume that you're using the GNOME desktop environment.) Figure 2-5 shows the first window displayed by this program in GNOME.

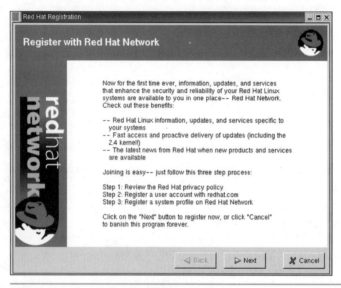

Figure 2-5 *The rhn_register intro screen.*

2. Click the Next button to continue. You're required to review the Red Hat Privacy Statement, as shown in Figure 2-6. Read the policy. If you agree to the policy, click the Next button again to continue.

3. Next you're asked to register or update an existing Red Hat Network account as shown in Figure 2-7. Enter information as requested and continue. You are then asked more questions, as shown in Figure 2-8. Fill in this information and click Next to continue.

4. Next you're asked to register your system's hardware profile. If you don't want to allow Red Hat to have this information, deselect the check box labeled "include information about hardware and network." Now if you wish to include installed package information, as shown in Figure 2-9, than leave the check box selected. Either way, click Next to continue.

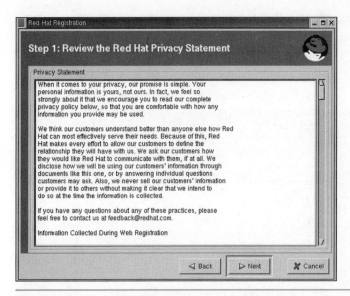

Figure 2-6 *The Red Hat Privacy Statement window.*

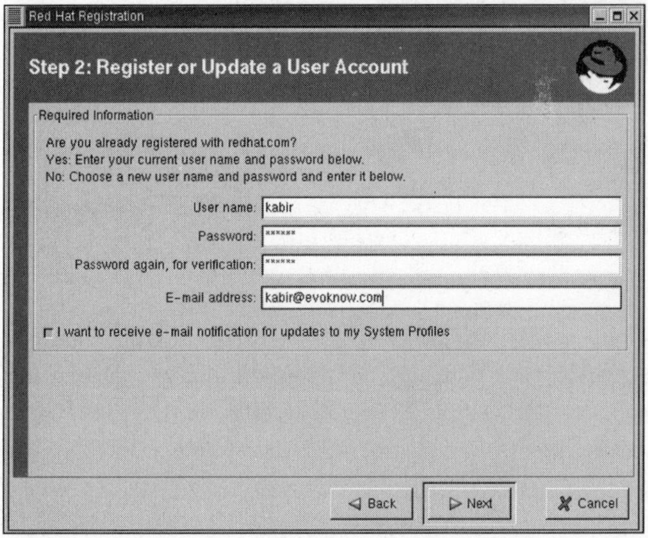

Figure 2-7 *Register or update a user account (Step 1).*

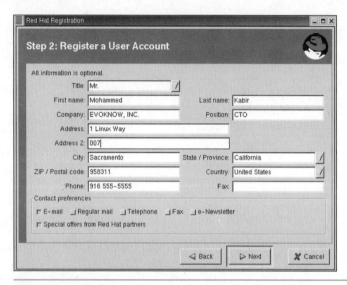

Figure 2-8 *Register or update a user account (Step 2).*

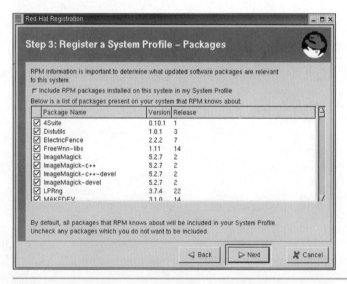

Figure 2-9 *Register or update a user account (Step 3).*

5. If you wish to send the system profile (hardware and installed package information) to Red Hat Network, click the Next button on the confirmation screen. After you have successfully registered, you see a status message as shown in Figure 2-10.

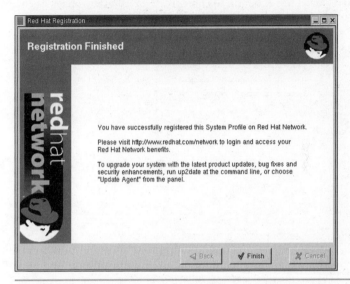

Figure 2-10 *Confirmation of a successful registration.*

Create a service level on Red Hat Network

Follow these steps to create a service level on the Red Hat Network:

1. Log on to www.redhat.com/network using your registered Red Hat Network user account information.

2. Create a service level for your system.

3. Click the Your Network link

4. Click the Assign Service Levels link

5. Locate your registered system in the unassigned system list (labeled "no service") and use the Upgrade button to move it to the Software Manager list on the right side.

6. Click the log out button on the top right corner. That's it; you've enabled the Software Manager service for the named host.

Configuring the Red Hat Update Agent

From the GNOME Main Menu, choose Applications ⇨ Systems ⇨ Configure Update Agent option to configure the Red Hat Update Agent. A window like Figure 2-11 appears.

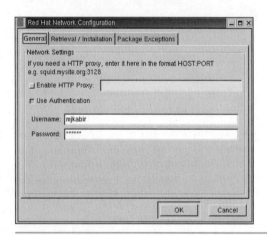

Figure 2-11 *Configuring general information.*

On the General tab you can configure network settings. If you need to access the Red Hat Network via a HTTP proxy, you can specify the proxy server name and port number here. Select the Use Authentication check box and enter your registered username and password so that the agent can authenticate to the Red Hat Network servers.

Click the Retrieval / Installation tab, and you will see a screen as shown in Figure 2-12.

If you do not wish to install packages after you retrieve them, you can disable that feature here. Also if you wish to retrieve the source RPM packages with binary packages when available you can enable that option here.

By default, binary RPM package files are not stored after they are installed; if you wish to keep them then enable this option in the Package Installation Options section. Make sure you keep the GNU Privacy Guard (GPG/GnuPG) package verification option turned on. You can also specify the directory name where packages are to be stored. The default should be fine for most users.

Click the Package Exceptions tab to see the screen shown in Figure 2-13.

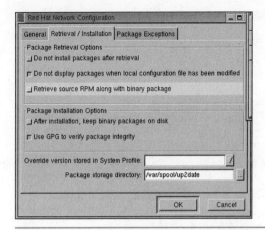

Figure 2-12 *Configuring retrieval and installation.*

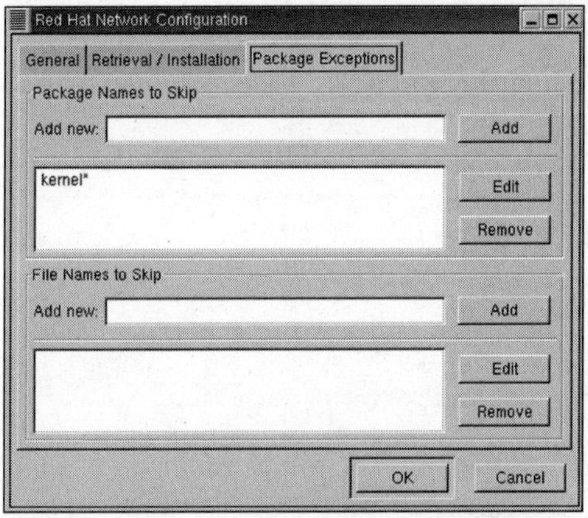

Figure 2-13 *Configuring package exceptions.*

If the automatic updating of certain packages could be very sensitive, or if you simply do not feel comfortable about Update Agent updating something automatically, you can add these packages in the exception list. By default, any kernel packages are considered an exception. After all, if a kernel update starts behaving in a bizarre fashion, you might not be able to access your system.

Running the Red Hat Update Agent

To run the Red hat Update Agent from the GNOME environment, click the Main Menu button and choose Applications ➪ Systems ➪ Update Agent.

When you run the Update Agent for the first time it displays a screen like that shown in Figure 2-14. This screen states that you do not have the Red Hat public key in your GPG key ring and therefore it needs to be added. You can click Yes to add it immediately. Next you will see a welcome screen as shown in Figure 2-15.

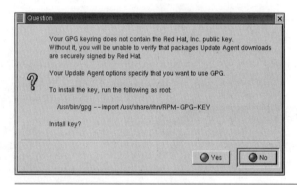

Figure 2-14 *Installing the public key.*

Click Next to continue. The Update Agent shows you the packages that are in your exception list, as shown in Figure 2-16.

If you wish to view an advisory on any of the packages shown, select the package and click the View Advisory button. A sample advisory is shown in Figure 2-17.

Depending on the severity of the advisory you might decide to update the package or not. You can also decide to include all the packages in the exception list by selecting the Select all packages check box. The installer retrieves packages that need to be updated, as shown in Figure 2-18.

You see an All Finished message after the updating is completed, as shown in Figure 2-19.

Figure 2-15 *The Update Agent welcome screen.*

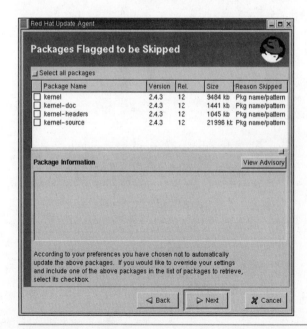

Figure 2-16 *Update Agent shows packages that will be ignored.*

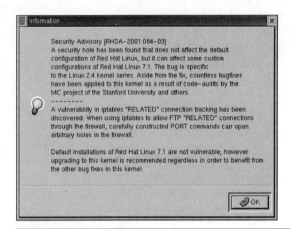

Figure 2-17 *The Update Agent shows an advisory on a package.*

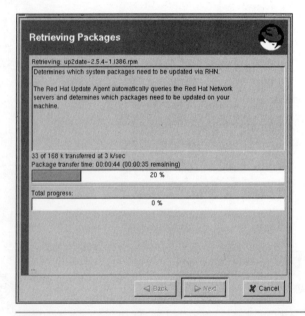

Figure 2-18 *Update Agent retrieving packages.*

Figure 2-19 *All finished!*

Upgrading the Linux Kernel

Updating the Linux kernel is a bit tricky of a process and should be done with care. If you mess things up, you may not be able to boot your system. Before you do anything, make sure you have a boot disk or a bootable CD-ROM such as the first (#1) Official Red Hat Linux CD-ROM. In this section I show you how to upgrade your Linux kernel.

Making a boot floppy

To create a boot disk for your current kernel, run the following command:

```
mkbootdisk --device /dev/fd0  version_number_of_current_kernel
```

For example, if your /boot/vmlinuz points to /boot/vmlinuz-2.4. 2-2, then your kernel version is 2.4.2-2. To create a boot disk for the 2.4.2-2 kernel you would run the following command:

```
mkbootdisk --device /dev/fd0  vmlinuz-2.4.2-2
```

Compiling a new upgrade kernel

I highly recommend that you download the latest kernel source from either www.redhat.com or www.kernel.org and compile the new kernel, as discussed in Chapter 11. Keep your old kernel image intact along with the modules. Install the new kernel as discussed in the Chapter 11.

Configuring LILO to boot the new and the old kernels

Edit your current /etc/lilo.conf file using a text editor such as vi. An example /etc/lilo.conf is listed below:

```
boot=/dev/hda
map=/boot/map
install=/boot/boot.b
prompt
timeout=50
message=/boot/message
linear
default=linux

image=/boot/vmlinuz-2.4.2-2
        label=linux
        read-only
        root=/dev/hda1
```

In the preceding, only one kernel (/boot/vmlinuz-2.4.2-2) is defined with a labeled called "linux," which is the default as well. Now add the following configuration lines in /etc/lilo.conf (remember to replace the *version_number* with appropriate version number of the new kernel you're installing and *device_partition* with the appropriate root device partition name).

```
image=/boot/vmlinuz-version_number
        label=newos
        read-only
        root=/dev/device_partition
```

For the previous `/etc/lilo.conf` and a new kernel at version 2.4.7-1, the full `/etc/lilo.conf` file would look as follows:

```
boot=/dev/hda
map=/boot/map
install=/boot/boot.b
prompt
timeout=50
message=/boot/message
linear
default=linux

image=/boot/vmlinuz-2.4.2-2
        label=linux
        read-only
        root=/dev/hda1

image=/boot/vmlinuz-2.4.7-1
        label=newos
        read-only
        root=/dev/hda1
```

Run the `/sbin/lilo` command to let LILO know of the changes to the `/etc/lilo.conf` file. At this point you have two kernels defined in the `/etc/lilo.conf`. By default, your system will still boot the original kernel because `default=linux` is still set to the original kernel. To boot the new kernel you have to enter or select "newos" at the LILO prompt.

Rebooting the system

To reboot the system, run the `shutdown -r now` command as root. When the LILO prompt appears select or enter the "newos" to boot using the new kernel. If you have compiled and installed the kernel properly, your system will boot the new kernel.

Verifying the running kernel's version

If the kernel version number matches the version number you just upgraded to then you have done it! You have upgraded your Linux kernel. Congratulations!

In case you booted to your old kernel and are seeing the old version, then you should recheck your kernel installation process and make sure that the links and files in /boot reflect the update. To verify which kernel was used to boot your system you can run the uname -r command. Also check to make sure that you have run the /sbin/lilo command. You can always run it again to make sure, reboot the system, and then choose the appropriate LILO label to boot the new kernel.

After you have gotten the new kernel to boot, modify the /etc/lilo. conf to make the new kernel label the default, which in our previous example would be default=newos. A better approach is to label the new kernel (using label=linux) and the old kernel (using label=old_ linux) and then run /sbin/lilo.

Chapter 3

Dual-Booting Red Hat Linux with Windows

IN THIS CHAPTER

- Dual-booting Linux with Windows NT/2000
- Dual-booting Linux with Windows 98
- Booting Windows within Linux by Using VMware

A *dual-boot system* is a computer that has two operating systems installed and can boot any one of the operating systems at any time. Dual-boot systems are most common among Linux users who want to use Windows-specific applications or games. In this chapter I show you how to dual-boot Red Hat Linux with Windows 2000, Windows NT, and Windows 98 operating systems, which are the most common dual-boot scenarios. I also discuss the commercial tool called VMware that lets you boot a second operating system within another!

Dual-Booting with Windows NT/2000

At the time of this book's writing, Windows 2000 is Microsoft's latest released version of their professional and server-class operating system. Windows 2000 is built on Windows NT technology. Dual-booting Linux with Windows 2000 or Windows NT (I just call it "Windows") requires the same process, which is discussed in the following sections of this chapter. In this book I use NT/2000 to mean Windows 2000 and Windows NT.

Windows XP Professional, which should be out by the time this book is released, is based on Windows 2000. Windows XP Professional users should be fine with the Windows NT/2000 instructions for the most part.

Prerequisites for dual-booting Linux and Windows NT/2000

You must have Windows NT/2000 installed on the first partition of your first hard disk.

In this section I assume that you are using a IDE hard disk (`/dev/hda`) and have at least two partitions (`/dev/hda1` and `/dev/hda2`). If you're using a SCSI hard disk, the instructions provided here will still apply, just replace all instances of hda with sda, which is the first SCSI hard disk in your system.

After you've installed Windows NT/2000 on `/dev/hda1`, the operating system is loaded by the Windows NT/2000 boot loader program called NTLoader. This program is installed on the Master Boot Record (MBR) of the first bootable hard disk on your system, which is `/dev/hda`.

There are two ways you can enable dual-booting on your system:

- Use LILO as a boot loader; you can use Linux boot loader program called LILO to boot either operating system. During this process you'll see a Linux-based LILO-generated boot options screen as shown in Figure 3-1. It is also much easier to implement than the other option.

You can also use GRUB, a GNU boot loader tool, to dual-boot Linux with Windows NT/2000. You can learn about GRUB at `www.gnu.org/directory/grub.html`.

Figure 3-1 *The LILO-generated boot options screen.*

■ You can also use a Windows NT/2000 boot loader called NTLoader to load either operating system. This process will display an NTLoader-generated boot options screen. This is appropriate for a Windows NT/2000-heavy environment, where users are more familiar with Windows than they are with Linux.

Dual-booting using LILO

To use LILO as a boot loader for booting to either Windows NT/2000 or Linux on system boot, you must perform the following tasks when installing Red Hat Linux on a system with a preexisting Windows NT/2000 installation:

■ If you are not using a bootable CD-ROM to install Red Hat Linux, you must create the boot floppy during the installation process.

You must select the custom installation class instead of either the Workstation, Server, or Laptop classes that are offered in the installation process. Choosing anything but the custom installation will overwrite the MBR that NTLoader resides on and will make it impossible for you to boot Windows NT/2000 without appropriate rescue or boot disks of that operating system.

> If you make a mistake and install the Linux boot loader on the
> MBR, you must reboot the system with Windows NT/2000
> recovery disks and select Recover. Next, switch to command-
> line mode, log on as Administrator, and run the `fixboot` and
> `fixmbr` commands to reinstall Windows NT/2000 boot
> loader on the MBR.

- During the installation process you're asked if you wish to install a boot loader on your system. A boot loader such as LILO or GRUB is only needed for a dual-boot system. A single-boot Linux system does not require such programs. Because you wish to dual-boot Linux with Windows NT/2000, you must choose to install a boot loader; in this case it will be LILO.

- Choose the first sector of the root disk partition, typically /dev/ hda2, as the location for LILO to avoid overwriting the Windows MBR.

- You will need to write a label name for the existing Windows NT/2000 operating system. Any name is fine; I usually use win2k or winnt as the label to identify the operating system in the boot menu, as shown in Figure 3-1.

- You're then asked to select one of the operating systems as the default. Choose Linux or Windows as necessary.

- Finally, install Red Hat Linux as usual.

  After you've installed Red Hat Linux, use the newly created Linux boot disk to boot Red Hat Linux. If you are using a bootable CD-ROM, use the `linux rescue` command at LILO prompt to boot Linux. Here I will assume that you are using a bootable CD-ROM and booting Linux in rescue mode. After you have booted Linux you need to fix the /etc/lilo.conf file.

  In rescue mode, the root file system is mounted on /mnt/sysimage, which can be accessed from the shell prompt. You can also mount it as / by running `chroot /mnt/sysimage` command. The /etc/ lilo.conf file for a dual-boot system using /dev/hda1 for Windows NT/2000 and /dev/hda2 for Red Hat Linux is shown in Listing 3-1.

Listing 3-1 *The /etc/lilo.conf file*

```
boot=/dev/hda
map=/boot/map
install=/boot/boot.b
prompt
timeout=50
message=/boot/message
linear
default=linux

image=/boot/vmlinuz-2.4.7-0.1.19
    label=linux
    read-only
    root=/dev/hda2

other=/dev/hda1
    optional
    label=win2k
```

The first line in the preceding tells LILO that the boot device is /dev/ hda (the very first IDE hard disk). The next line sets the map file path, and the following line sets the install file path. The prompt line tells LILO to prompt the user to select an operating system; without this line the default operating system specified by the default=*linux* line can be automatically loaded. The timeout=50 line sets the timeout value to be 5 seconds (it shows 50 because it's measured in tenths of a second). When a user does not manually select a different operating system at the LILO prompt, the default operating system, identified by the default=*label* line, is loaded (default=linux in the listing).

The image= line defines the Linux kernel image to boot when booting the operating system labeled linux as instructed by the label=linux line. The operating system boots from the root device, set by the root= line (such as root=dev/hda2 in the preceding listing), in read-only mode. The root partition is read-only only during boot, and later it goes in read-write mode.

The other=/dev/hda1 line states where to find the alternative operating system that is labeled win2k by using label=win2k.

If you're setting up a dual-boot system where /dev/hda1 contains the Windows NT/2000 operating system and /dev/hda2 contains the Linux operating system, make sure your /etc/lilo.conf looks like the above. After you've edited the lilo.conf file, make sure that you run /sbin/lilo to find out if LILO likes the configuration file.

If you get an error message stating a problem with the "liner" line, change that line to lba32, which is used to use logical block addressing to access disk, and then rerun /sbin/lilo. When LILO is happy it will show a line such as the following:

```
* Added linux
* Added win2k
```

Now you should reboot your system by running /sbin/shutdown -r now and choosing one of the operating systems from the boot menu. Make sure that you test-boot into both operating systems to ensure that you are able to successfully dual-boot your system to either Linux or Windows.

Dual-booting by using NTLoader

There is no technical advantage to dual-booting by using the Windows NT/2000 boot loader – NTLoader – over LILO. However, if you're using Linux as a secondary operating system and want to keep it under a low profile, you might want to use NTLoader instead of LILO. NTLoader is often used in Windows NT/2000 environments where users are already familiar with NTLoader. Before you can dual-boot Linux and Windows NT/2000 with NTLoader, you must ensure that the following prerequisites are met:

- Windows NT/2000 must be installed on the first partition of the first disk. Here I assume that you are using an IDE disk and that Windows NT/2000 therefore is installed on /dev/hda1 (for SCSI, the equivalent is /dev/sda1).

- Windows NT/2000 has installed the NTLoader in MBR, which is what the Windows NT/2000 installer does by default.

- You have Windows NT/2000 recovery disk set.

- Linux is installed on any partition of any disk other than the first partition of the first disk. Here I will assume that you have installed Linux on /dev/hda2. Note that you could also have Linux installed on a different hard disk partition, such as /dev/hdb1, the first partition of the second IDE hard disk, or wherever.

As mentioned before, it's extremely important that you do not install Linux on MBR. If you make a mistake and install Linux boot loader on MBR, then you must reboot the system with Window NT/2000 recovery disks or Windows NT/2000 bootable CD-ROM and select recover option and switch to recover console mode. Then, log on as Administrator and run the fixboot and fixmbr commands to reinstall Windows NT/2000 boot loader on MBR.

- You must have a Linux boot disk or a bootable Linux CD-ROM that provides the rescue option, which is available in the official Red Hat Linux CD-ROM #1.

- You need an MS-DOS formatted blank floppy disk. If you do not have a floppy drive, you will have to write access to a remote FTP site where you can temporarily keep a file. Or you'll need a valid e-mail account, to which you can send an attachment.

- Make sure that you've installed Linux with the MS-DOS or Windows connectivity option so that the mcopy program is installed. Note that you can ignore this requirement if you don't plan on using a floppy disk.

After you've ensured that the above prerequisites are met, you can follow these steps to dual-boot Linux and Windows NT/2000 using NTLoader:

1. Because NTLoader is not yet configured to boot Linux, you have to use the Linux boot disk to boot the system to Linux. If you do not have a boot disk, you can use the bootable Linux CD in rescue mode by entering linux rescue at the LILO prompt.

2. Copy the boot sector of your Linux installation using dd if=/dev/*linux_boot_device* bs=512 count=1 of=linux_bs. bin command. For example, if you've installed Linux on /dev/hda2 then this command will be as follows:

```
dd if=/dev/hda2 bs=512 count=1 of=linux_bs.bin
```

The dd command allows you to copy the first 512 bytes from the /dev/hda2 device to a file called linux_bs.bin.

3. The linux_bs.bin file needs to be in the Windows NT/2000 partition of your hard disk. If you have a floppy drive and a blank, MS-DOS-formatted floppy you can mount it under Linux using the mount —t msdos /dev/fd0 /mnt/floppy command. After you have the floppy disk mounted, change to the directory where you saved the file and copy the linux_bs.bin file to the floppy using the mcopy linux_bs.bin a: command. Skip the next step if you have this file stored on a floppy.

4. If you do not have a floppy drive or a floppy disk, you can FTP or e-mail the linux_bs.bin file to a remote FTP site or your e-mail account. This assumes that you have networking or Internet connectivity set up under Linux.

For more information on how to set up networking or Internet connectivity, see Chapter 6.

After you've stored the file in a remote FTP site or sent it to yourself via e-mail, you have to retrieve it from Windows NT/2000 side. This also assumes that you have Windows NT/2000 configured for networking and/or Internet connectivity. For information on how to set up networking and/or Internet connectivity on Windows, see an appropriate user's manual.

5. Restart your machine using the shutdown —r now command in Linux and log on to Windows NT/2000 as Administrator user.

6. Copy the linux_bs.bin file in the c:\ directory of your Windows NT/2000 installation either from the floppy, by getting it from the remote FTP site, or by downloading it from an e-mail attachment.

7. Run Windows Explorer (not Internet Explorer) by clicking Start ⇨ Run and entering explorer in the open location. Once Explorer has started, choose Tools ⇨ Folder Options and then click on the View tab of the Folder Options dialog window. Enable the Show hidden files and folders option under the Hidden Files and Folders

section and then click first Apply and then the OK button to activate your changes.

8. In the Explorer window, enter `C:\` as the address location or use the folder navigation tree to locate your Windows NT/2000 hard disk. You should see a file called `boot.ini` in the `C:\` directory. Double click this file to open it in your default text editor (Notepad), and the contents should be similar to the following:

```
[boot loader]
timeout=30
default=multi(0)disk(0)rdisk(0)partition(1)\WINDOWS
[operating systems]
multi(0)disk(0)rdisk(0)partition(1)\WINDOWS="Microso
ft Windows 2000 Professional" /fastdetect
```

The last two lines shown above are actually a single line that displays the Microsoft Windows 2000 Professional boot option.

9. Add a new line `c:\linux_bs.bin="Red Hat Linux"` in `c:\boot.ini` using the text editor and then save the file.

10. Using Windows Explorer, select the `linux_bs.bin` file and click the right mouse button and choose Properties from the context menu to view the file's properties. You can also click the file and then choose File ⇨ Properties in Explorer.

11. Turn the read-only flag on for the `linux_bs.bin` file in the file properties window by checking the appropriate check box under the attributes section of the file's Properties window.

12. Reboot Windows NT/2000 and you should see "Red Hat Linux" as a boot option in the boot menu displayed by NTLoader. Select that listing to boot Linux, or select the Windows option to boot Windows.

Dual-booting Linux with Windows 98

Booting Red Hat Linux alongside Windows 98 is less complicated than booting Linux and Windows NT/2000 systems. Unlike Windows

NT/2000, Windows 98 does not come with a boot loader such as NTLoader and therefore LILO or GRUB is necessary. Keep the following things in mind when setting up a dual-boot Windows 98 and Linux using LILO:

- Install Windows 98 on the first partition of your first hard disk before you install Red Hat Linux. Make sure that you have a second partition or a second disk to install Linux on.

- You have two choices of installing Linux: the Workstation class or the Custom class. If you install Linux using Workstation installation (see Chapter 1 for details), you have less that you need to do during Linux installation. If you do install by using a Custom installation, you must make sure that you install LILO on the MBR. The Workstation installation automatically installs LILO on MBR for you.

- After Linux is installed and LILO is installed on the MBR, you can boot either operating system from LILO when you next reboot.

Booting Windows within Linux by Using VMware

The VMware products are amazing virtual machine solutions that allow you to boot another operating system while you are running one. For example, you can be on Linux and run VMware for Linux to run Windows NT/2000 on your Linux desktop. Similarly you can run VMware on Windows NT/2000 and load Linux on your Windows desktop.

VMware virtual machines are commercial products that you can freely evaluate from www.vmware.com. A license file is necessary to evaluate the product, so when you download the evaluation make sure you also fill out the evaluation form to get a temporary license file sent to you by e-mail.

When you use VMware, you're practically setting up a machine within a machine. In other words, you are creating a virtual computer within a running computer. VMware requires that you click a button to switch on the power of the virtual computer, and then it even goes through the standard BIOS Power On Self Test (POST) process, hardware detection, and so on.

VMware is an interesting and potentially useful scenario where you need to have access to Linux applications from Windows, or if you require access to Windows applications while working within Linux. VMware uses terminology such as *host operating system*, which is the term meaning the operating system that's running the VMware product, and *guest operating system*, which is the term that refers to the operating system that's being run under VMware itself. VMware even allows you to run the guest operating system in full screen mode, as well as the ability to switch back to a windowed mode by pressing Ctrl+Alt+Esc.

Chapter 4

Booting and Shutting Down

IN THIS CHAPTER

- Understanding how the boot process works
- Understanding run levels and their role in the boot process
- Booting up your system
- Shutting down your system
- Rebooting your system
- Configuring the init process
- Managing `init` scripts

Red Hat Linux uses a highly configurable boot and shutdown process that needs to be understood by every Linux system administrator. There are many configuration options and files involved in the boot process that enable you to fine-tune which run level (single user, multiuser, graphical) the system boots to, what programs get started, how the network is configured, and so on. In this chapter you will get up to speed on the boot and shutdown processes.

Understanding the Boot Process

When you turn on your Linux system (or *boot* it) Linux looks to various files and programs — notably the `init` program and `/etc/inittab` file — for instructions on how to load your system, which services to start (and which not to), whether or not to start the X Window System, and so on. The init command is highly customizable; with init you can choose which programs and services run as part of the boot process. init is covered in detail in later sections of this chapter, but before you start looking hard at init you should have a basic understanding of how LILO and init work together to start your computer. The following list discusses the basic process that occurs whenever you boot up your Linux system.

1. The Red Hat Linux kernel (the *kernel* is the core operating system) is typically stored in a compressed file on your hard drive. When you first turn on your computer, the kernel is started by a boot loader program like LILO or GRUB.

2. After being started by LILO, the kernel uncompresses itself, initializes the display device, and starts checking other hardware attached to your computer.

3. As Linux finds your hard drives, floppy drives, network cards, and so forth, it loads the appropriate device driver modules. During this process it prints out text messages on your console screen.

If you are at the console when booting your system, you can press Shift+PageUp to scroll back the display to view boot messages. You can also view the boot messages at any time after system startup by running the dmesg program. The /var/log/messages files will also have many of the boot messages.

4. The kernel mounts the root file system (/) as read only and performs checks on the file system.

5. If everything checks out okay, the root file system is then typically mounted as read/write. If a problem arises and the kernel fails to mount the root partition or finds a severe problem with it, the kernel panics and halts the system. If the disk has become corrupt for some reason, the kernel might provide you an option to run a file system checker program such as fsck.ext2 from a restricted shell.

6. After the root file system is mounted, the kernel starts a program called init. init in turn starts all other programs required for the

user to log in to the system, including the login programs. After init has started all the necessary programs, the system is up and running and the boot process is complete.

Understanding Run Levels

At any given time a Linux system is running in a known state or level, which is called a *run level*. Table 4-1 shows the list of possible run levels. For example run level 0 refers to the state when the system is halted, run level 1 is the single-user state where none of the networking or multiuser capabilities of Linux are available.

Table 4-1 *Possible Run Levels in a Linux System*

Run Level	Description
0	Halt – used to halt the system. Never set the system default run level to this or else you won't be able to boot your system.
1	Single-user – used to set the system in a minimal configuration suitable for a single user.
2	Not used.
3	Multiuser – used to set the system in a configuration that supports multiple users.
4	Not used.
5	Used to start the X Window System and the **xdm**, **kdm**, or **gdmprograms** via /etc/X11/prefdm script.
6	Reboot – used to reboot the system.
S or s	Used internally by scripts that run in run level 1.
a, b, c	On-demand run levels – typically not used.

The init program allows you to switch from one run level to another. It is discussed in the "Configuring init" section later in this chapter.

Booting Up Your System

During the boot process, init first runs the rc.sysinit script and then runs the script for the default run level. You can set the default run level in /etc/inittab by changing the line in /etc/inittab file:

```
id:3:initdefault:
```

Here the default run level is set to 3, meaning that `init` runs the scripts needed to put the system in multiuser mode.

If you take a second look at `/etc/inittab`, you will notice that the following line specifies which `rc` script needs to be run for run level 3.

```
l3:3:wait:/etc/rc.d/rc 3
```

The `rc` script is run with an argument of 3. As mentioned before, this script runs all the scripts whose names start with "S" in the `/etc/rc.d/rc3.d` directory. It also supplies "start" as an argument to each of the "S"-prefixed scripts. When all the "S" scripts are run, the `rc` script finishes and the system becomes available in the default run level.

Booting to single-user mode

Booting to single-user mode is usually necessary in case of emergencies, such as when you need to fix a corrupt disk or reset a forgotten root password. Whatever the reason, you have two ways to boot in single-user mode.

If you're already logged into the system and want to switch to single-user mode, you can run the following command:

```
init 1
```

This tells `init` to switch run level to 1, which is the single-user mode. However, if you plan on getting access to the system in single-user mode when it is actually booting up, then at the LILO prompt enter:

```
linux single
```

This boots Linux to single-user mode.

If you are using graphical LILO prompt, you can press Ctrl+X to summon the text LILO prompt from which you can enter the above command.

Booting in rescue mode

If your Linux system does not boot for some reason and you wish to try and rescue the system, you can boot the system in rescue mode if you have the official Red Hat CD-ROM.

Follow these steps to do so:

1. Insert the Red Hat CD-ROM that you bought into the CD-ROM drive and make sure that your computer's BIOS has been set up to boot from CD-ROM first. If it hasn't been set up for this, simply reboot your system and go inside your BIOS utility and set the boot device option to boot from the CD-ROM first. Then reboot the machine with the official Red Hat CD-ROM inside the CD-ROM drive.

2. After the system displays the initial Linux installation screen in multicolored text, choose rescue mode by entering `linux rescue` at the LILO prompt.

3. You're then asked to select a language. Select English or whatever language you use and then press Enter to continue. The system will be mounted under `/mnt/sysimage,` and you can then press Enter to summon a shell prompt.

4. At the shell prompt you can use tools that are available in /sbin or /usr/bin directories to perform any necessary rescue operations. For example, if your password file (`/mnt/sysimage/etc/passwd`) was deleted by accident you can potentially rescue it from an older version by copying `/mnt/sysimage/etc/passwd` to `/mnt/sysimage/etc/passwd` or any other backup you have. If a disk problem caused your system to fail and you want to know how to access your disk partitions, first run `cat /etc/mtab` or `cat /proc/mounts` to see which partition of your disk is mounted at what directory under `/mnt/sysimage.` Then you can perform disk commands such as `fsck` on the appropriate partition. For example, if the `/usr` partition on your regular system caused the system to become unbootable, you can run `fsck /mnt/sysimage/usr` in rescue mode to isolate the problem with the disk and attempt to fix it.

5. After you exit the shell prompt by entering `exit` at the prompt, the system reboots automatically.

Shutting Down Your System

Shutting down a Linux system is simple but not as simple as powering down the computer. You should never turn off a computer running Linux without shutting down Linux itself. In this section I show you how to shut down properly.

Shutting down by using the shutdown command

The `shutdown` command is the most typical method of shutting down a system. `shutdown` broadcasts a warning message to all logged-in users that the system is changing run level. The `shutdown` command instructs `init` to change the current run level of the system to either halt (run level 0) or reboot (run level 6). For example, the following command tells `init` to switch the system to run level 0 (halt) immediately:

```
shutdown -h now
```

shutdown can also be used to reboot the system by substituting the -r option for the -h option in the preceding command. The -r option is discussed in the "Rebooting Your System" section later in this chapter.

The `shutdown` command also provides you with an option to schedule the `shutdown` event for a later time. For example, the following command halts the system in 10 minutes:

```
shutdown -h +10
```

All logged-in users receive a message saying that the system is going to halt shortly, allowing them to finish up and save their work.

When you use a delayed shutdown command, as described in this section, users who are logged in see a message warning them that the system will shut down soon. However, shutdown does not prevent anyone from logging in during the shutdown countdown period, and anyone who does log in during this period will not receive the warning. In order to prevent new logins when the shutdown command is pending, you can create a text file called /etc/nologin with an appropriate message stating that a system shutdown has already been scheduled and that people should try to log in at a later time. Do not forget to rename or delete the /etc/nologin file after you reboot. If you are rebooting a server remotely, be absolutely sure to remove or rename this file prior to the actual shutdown. No user accounts except root are allowed to log in when this file is present. In fact, you may want to add the rm —f /etc/nologin at the end of the /etc/rc.local script and make sure that init runs it at the end of run level 3.

Shutting down your system with init

You can run init to manually halt your system. For example, the following command halts the system immediately:

```
init 0
```

If you are running in a multiuser mode (run level 3), this command is not the best approach, because it does not inform the users on the system that the system is going to halt. Instead, you can use the shutdown command to halt the server, as described in the "Shutting down with the shutdown command" section earlier in this chapter.

Canceling a shutdown

The shutdown command enables you to schedule a shutdown event at a later time (as discussed in the "Shutting down with the shutdown command" section earlier in this chapter). However, before the system actually shuts down, a need might arise to cancel the shutdown event; in such a case you issue another shutdown command with a -c option to cancel any scheduled shutdown event as follows:

```
shutdown —c
```

Automatic shutdown on power failure

If you use a UPS (uninterruptable power supply) to provide backup power for your system and it uses a serial port-based UPS monitoring software (usually supplied by the UPS vendor), you can use init to shut down the system gracefully when your UPS power is nearly drained. The default /etc/inittab includes the following line:

```
pf::powerfail:/sbin/shutdown -f -h +2 "Power Failure; System Shutting Down"
```

This line tells init to run shutdown in case of a power failure. The powerfail action is activated when a UPS program or powerd (a power monitoring daemon) sends the SIGPWR signal to init. The default setting allows the system to run on UPS power for two minutes before it halts. If your UPS is capable of sustaining power for a greater or lesser amount of time, you should modify this value by changing +2 to a desired number of minutes. For example, to change it to five minutes, change +2 to +5.

If you restore your primary power source before your UPS power is totally drained, you can call init to cancel a previously scheduled shutdown event. You can do this by adding the following line in /etc/inittab:

```
pr:12345:powerokwait:/sbin/shutdown -c "Power Restored; Shutdown Cancelled"
```

When init receives a SIGPWR signal and a file called /etc/ powerstatus contains an "OK" string in it, the powerokwait action is activated and the shutdown is aborted.

Rebooting Your System

In addition to running the init command to halt your system (init 0), you can also run init manually to reboot your system with the following command:

```
init 6
```

Just as with using the init command to reboot, if you are running in a multiuser mode (run level 3), this command is not the best approach, because it does not inform the users on the system that the system is going to reboot. Instead, you can use the shutdown command to reboot the server. For example, to reboot immediately, you can run the following command:

```
shutdown -r  now
```

Or, you can schedule a reboot for some time in the future. For example, the following command reboots the server in 10 minutes:

```
shutdown -r +10
```

All logged-in users receive a message saying that the system is going to reboot shortly. This allows them time to finish up and save their work.

The `shutdown` command does not prevent new users from logging into the system while a reboot is pending. See the section "Shutting down with the shutdown command" earlier in this chapter for more information on how to (very carefully) use the `/etc/nologin` file to prevent users from logging in during this time.

Rebooting with Ctrl+Alt+Delete

If you are on the system console, you can use the traditional Ctrl+Alt+Del key combination to reboot your system. This is possible because of the following line in `/etc/inittab`:

```
ca::ctrlaltdel:/sbin/shutdown -t3 -r now
```

This line allows `init` to trap the Ctrl+Alt+Del key combination and call the `shutdown` script to reboot immediately.

Anyone who has physical access to your system console can shut down the system by pressing the Ctrl+Alt+Delete keys. To protect yourself from such a shutdown, you can create a file called `/etc/shutdown.allow` that will contain a list of users (one username per line) who are allowed to shut down the system. The root account does not need to be listed in this file.

Configuring init

As mentioned earlier in the chapter, `init` is the very first program that the kernel runs at the end of the boot sequence. There are two main versions of the `init` program: a UNIX System V-like `init` and a BSD-like `init`. The difference between the two flavors of `init` is that System V-ish `init` uses run levels and the BSD-ish `init` does not.

Red Hat Linux comes with the UNIX System V version of init, and so all discussion about init in this chapter is limited to this version.

/etc/inittab: The init configuration file

Because init is the first program that is run by the kernel at boot time, its process ID (PID) is 1. When init starts up, it reads a configuration file called /etc/inittab. Listing 4-1 shows the /etc/inittab file in a typical Red Hat Linux system.

Listing 4-1 *A typical /etc/inittab file*

```
#
# inittab - This file describes how the INIT
#           process should set up the system in
#           a certain runlevel.
#
# Author: Miquel van Smoorenburg,
#         <miquels@drinkel.nl.mugnet.org>
#
# Modified for RHS Linux by Marc Ewing and
# Donnie Barnes
#


# Default runlevel. The runlevels used by RHS are:
#    0 - halt (Do NOT set initdefault to this)
#    1 - Single-user mode
#    2 - Multi-user, without NFS (The same as 3, if you
#                                 do not have networking)
#    3 - Full multi-user mode
#    4 - unused
#    5 - X11
#    6 - reboot (Do NOT set initdefault to this)
#
id:3:initdefault:
```

```
# System initialization.
si::sysinit:/etc/rc.d/rc.sysinit

l0:0:wait:/etc/rc.d/rc 0
l1:1:wait:/etc/rc.d/rc 1
l2:2:wait:/etc/rc.d/rc 2
l3:3:wait:/etc/rc.d/rc 3
l4:4:wait:/etc/rc.d/rc 4
l5:5:wait:/etc/rc.d/rc 5
l6:6:wait:/etc/rc.d/rc 6

# Things to run in every runlevel.
ud::once:/sbin/update

# Trap CTRL-ALT-DELETE
ca::ctrlaltdel:/sbin/shutdown -t3 -r now

# When our UPS tells us power has failed, assume we have
# a few minutes of power left. Schedule a shutdown for
# 2 minutes from now.
#
# This does, of course, assume you have powerd installed and
your
# UPS connected and working correctly.
#
pf::powerfail:/sbin/shutdown -f -h +2 "Power Failure; \
System Shutting Down"

# If power was restored before the shutdown kicked in, cancel
it.
pr:12345:powerokwait:/sbin/shutdown -c "Power Restored; \
Shutdown Cancelled"
```

Continued

Listing 4-1 *Continued*

```
# Run gettys in standard runlevels
1:12345:respawn:/sbin/mingetty tty1
2:2345:respawn:/sbin/mingetty tty2
3:2345:respawn:/sbin/mingetty tty3
4:2345:respawn:/sbin/mingetty tty4
5:2345:respawn:/sbin/mingetty tty5
6:2345:respawn:/sbin/mingetty tty6


# Run xdm in runlevel 5
# xdm is now a separate service
 x:5:respawn:/usr/bin/X11/prefdm-nodaemon
```

The `/etc/inittab` file defines how `init` behaves during server startup or shutdown events. Let's take a closer look at the structure of this file.

The `init` program ignores all of the blank and comment lines (that is, lines that start with a "#" sign) in the `/etc/inittab` file. The lines with colon-delimited fields are the `init` configuration lines. The syntax for such a line is as follows:

```
ID:runlevels:action:process [arguments]
```

The first field *(ID)* is a unique label field to identify an entry in the file. An ID can be 2 to 4 characters long. The second field (*runlevels*) defines which run levels this line applies to. The third field *(action)* defines the action to be done, and the last field (*process*) defines the process to be run. You can optionally specify command-line arguments for the process in this fourth field.

Note that you can specify multiple run levels in a single `init` configuration line. For example, if you want `init` to run a process for both single-user and multiuser modes, you can specify a line such as:

```
id:13:action:process [arguments]
```

The action field states how init runs the process named in the process field. Table 4-2 shows possible actions. A process can be any program.

Table 4-2 *Possible Actions for a Specific Run Level*

Action	Description
Respawn	The process restarts whenever it terminates.
Wait	The process runs once and `init` then waits until it terminates.
Once	The process runs once.
Boot	The process runs during system boot and `init` ignores the run level field.
Bootwait	The process runs during system boot and `init` waits for the process to terminate.
Off	No action is taken. You can use off to disable a configuration line without removing it. However, you can also just comment out the line with a leading "#" character instead.
Ondemand	Useful only when the run level is a, b, or c. The process runs whenever `init` is called with any of the three on demand run levels. Typically not used.
initdefault	Sets the default run level for the system. The process field is ignored. Do not set default run level to 0 or 6.
sysinit	The process runs once during system boot. A `sysinit` action takes precedence over boot or `bootwait` actions.
powerwait	The process runs when `init` receives a `SIGPWR` signal. Typically Uninterruptible Power Supply (UPS) monitoring software detects a power problem and issues such a signal to `init`. In such a case `init` waits until the process terminates.
powerfail	Same as `powerwait`, but `init` does not wait for the process to complete.
powerokwait	The process runs when `init` receives a `SIGPWR` signal and a text file called `/etc/powerstatus` contains an "OK" string. Typically, a UPS monitoring program creates this file and sends the `SIGPWR` signal to `init` to indicate that the power problem has been fixed.
ctrlaltdel	The process runs when `init` receives a `SIGINT` signal.
kbrequest	The process runs when `init` receives a signal 1 from the keyboard handler.

The System V flavor of `init` (which is the version of `init` that Red Hat Linux uses) utilizes the following directory structure (explanations of each item are in parentheses):

```
/etc (dir)
 +-rc.d (dir)
    +-init.d (dir)
    +-rc0.d (dir)
```

```
+-rc1.d  (dir)
+-rc2.d  (dir)
+-rc3.d  (dir)
+-rc4.d  (dir)
+-rc5.d  (dir)
+-rc6.d  (dir)
+-rc.sysinit  (script)
+-rc.local     (optional script, supplied with Red
Hat Linux)
+-rc.serial    (optional script)
+-rc (script)
```

/etc/rc.d/rc.sysinit

As mentioned earlier in the chapter, when a Red Hat Linux system boots, the kernel runs the init program. init in turn runs the /etc/rc.d/ rc.sysinit script before processing any other scripts for the desired run level. init runs this script before anything else because of the following line in the /etc/inittab file:

```
si::sysinit:/etc/rc.d/rc.sysinit
```

 Notice that the run level field in the preceding line is empty. This is because init recognizes sysinit as a system initialization action.

The rc.sysinit script does many things, including setting the host name, enabling the swap partition, checking the file systems, loading kernel modules, and more. Typically, you do not need to modify this script.

/etc/rc.d/init.d

The init.d subdirectory stores all the scripts needed for all run levels. Keeping these scripts in one location makes it easier to manage them. Each script starts or stops a particular service — the Domain Name Service (DNS), the Web service, or the like. All of these scripts follow a special command-line argument syntax. For example, to start the Network File System (NFS) service, you can run the following script:

```
/etc/rc.d/init.d/nfs start
```

To stop the same service, you can run the same script as follows:

```
/etc/rc.d/init.d/nfs stop
```

As you can see, the `nfs` script takes `start` and `stop` as arguments. This is true for all the scripts in this directory, which are symbolically linked to the `rc[0–6].d` directories as needed.

/etc/rc.d/rc

When `init` changes run level it runs a script specified in one of the following lines in the `/etc/inittab` file:

```
l0:0:wait:/etc/rc.d/rc 0
l1:1:wait:/etc/rc.d/rc 1
l2:2:wait:/etc/rc.d/rc 2
l3:3:wait:/etc/rc.d/rc 3
l4:4:wait:/etc/rc.d/rc 4
l5:5:wait:/etc/rc.d/rc 5
l6:6:wait:/etc/rc.d/rc 6
```

As you can see, for each run level (0–6) a script called `/etc/rc.d/rc` is run with the run level number as the argument to the script. This script is responsible for starting and stopping all the services for the desired run level. For example, say that `init` is told to change the run level to 3. In this case, `init` runs the `/etc/rc.d/rc` script with an argument of 3 in a command line similar to this one:

```
/etc/rc.d/rc 3
```

This script primarily does the following things:

1. It checks to see if a subdirectory exists for the run level specified in the argument. In other words, if the script runs with an argument of 3, it checks to see if the `/etc/rc.d/rc3.d/` directory exists or not. If it exists, the script continues to the next step.

2. Next the script determines whether or not any of the programs (often called services) that are supposed to run in the new run level are already running. If a service is already running, the script kills the service so that it can restart it in the next step. To kill a running service, the script runs the necessary "K" script with the "stop" argument. K scripts are discussed in the next section.

3. In this final step the rc script runs all the "S" scripts with the "start" argument. S scripts are discussed in the next section.

/etc/rc.d/rc[0-6].d

The rc0.d to rc6.d subdirectories are used for run levels 0 to 6. These directories contain symbolic links to scripts in the /etc/rc.d/init.d directory. For example, if you look at the rc3.d directory in a Red Hat Linux system you will notice that scripts from the /etc/rc.d/init.d directory are linked in two ways. Some scripts are linked as:

```
K{two-digit_number}{script_name}
```

For example K99httpd is a script that is linked to the /etc/rc.d/init.d/httpd script. Other scripts are linked as:

```
S{two-digit_number}{script_name}
```

For example, S99httpd is a script that is linked to the /etc/rc.d/init.d/httpd script. All the scripts prefixed with a letter "K" run with the "stop" argument, and all scripts with a letter "S" run with the "start" argument. The two-digit number is used to set the execution order. Thus a script called S01foo runs before S10bar. The /etc/rc.d/rc script runs the "S" and "K" scripts.

After the rc script is finished, the processing done by init also finishes and the system becomes available in the new run level.

/etc/rc.d/rc.local

The rc.local script is typically executed once at the end of the run levels 2, 3, and 5. You can add anything that needs to be run once per boot in this file. Simply append whatever command you want to run at the end of this file using a text editor, and the command you add will be run once every time you boot your system.

/etc/rc.d/rc.serial

Like the `rc.local` script, `rc.serial` is typically run once at the end of run level 1 or 3 to initialize serial ports.

Managing init Files

The version of `init` that comes with Red Hat Linux uses a lot of files, symbolic links, and directories. This section discusses a few of the more commonly used tools that help to simplify management of `init` files.

Managing run levels with chkconfig

The `chkconfig` utility enables you to maintain the various symbolic links necessary for starting or stopping services in a run level. `chkconfig` can manage run level configuration for all the scripts in the `/etc/rc.d/init.d` directory. The following sections show you how to use `chkconfig`.

Listing manageable services

To view the services that will start or stop in each run level and see which run level they start or stop in, run the following command

```
chkconfig --list
```

This command lists all the services that you can manage with `chkconfig` and tells you which services are going to be started (turned on) or stopped (turned off) for each run level. You can also check the run level configuration for a particular service by specifying the service name (that is, the script name in `/etc/rc.d/init.d`) from the command line. For example:

```
chkconfig --list httpd
```

The preceding command shows the following output from my Red Hat Linux server:

```
httpd 0:off 1:off 2:off 3:on 4:on 5:on 6:off
```

As you can see, the `httpd` service is on for run levels 3, 4, and 5, and off for 0, 1, 2, and 6.

Adding a new service

If you just added a new script in the /etc/rc.d/init.d directory and want to make the service it offers available for a particular run level, you can run the chkconfig command as follows:

```
chkconfig --add service_name [--level runlevel]
```

For example, the following command adds a service called named to the current run level:

```
chkconfig --add named
```

In other words, the preceding command creates a symbolic link that has an S {two-digit number} prefix in the current run level directory pointing to the /etc/rc.d/init.d/named script. If you want to add the service to a run level other than the current one, you can specify the desired run level with the --level option. For example, the following command adds the named service to run level 4:

```
chkconfig --level 4 --add named
```

Deleting an existing service

To remove an existing service from a run level, use the following command:

```
chkconfig --del service_name [--level run_level]
```

For example, the following command removes the named service from the current run level:

```
chkconfig --del named
```

To remove the service from a run level other than the current one, use the --level option. For example, the following command removes the named service from run level 5:

```
chkconfig --del named --level 5
```

Managing run levels with ntsysv

The ntsysv utility enables you to turn various services in any run levels on or off by using a simple menu interface. When you run the command without any argument, it displays a menu screen. This scrollable menu screen shows the state of all the services in the current run level. To turn on a service, you need to select it; to turn off a service, you just deselect it. After you have made all the changes, you can either save your changes by clicking the OK button or abort your changes by clicking the Cancel button. If you want to work on a different run level configuration, just run the ntsysv command with both the run level with the --level option. For example, the following command lets you work on the run level 1 configuration:

```
ntsysv --level 1
```

Managing run levels with Linuxconf

You can also use the Linuxconf utility to configure run levels. To do so, follow these steps:

1. Select the Control ⇨ Control Panel ⇨ Control Service activity option.

2. Enable or disable one or more services.

3. Accept the changes.

4. Activate the changes before you quit Linuxconf.

Creating a new service for a run level

If you install server software packages from well-known vendors, most likely they will provide you with a nice RPM package that also includes the necessary service script that goes into the /etc/rc.d/init.d. Sometimes, however, you'll find useful software that doesn't come with an easy-to-use installer with all the bells and whistles, and you end up having to customize the software or at least modify how it works on your system. In such a case, you may need to create a service script for your new software.

In this section I show you how you can easily create a new service script to put in the /etc/rc.d/init.d directory. First, take a look at an existing service script from the /etc/rc.d/init.d directory. Listing 4-2 shows one such script called httpd, which is used to start and stop the Apache Web server.

Listing 4-2 *An example /etc/rc.d/init.d/httpd script*

```
#!/bin/sh
#
# Startup script for the Apache Web Server.
#
# chkconfig: 345 85 15
# description: Apache is a World Wide Web server.  \
#              It is used to serve HTML files and CGI.
# processname: httpd
# pidfile: /var/run/httpd.pid
# config: /etc/httpd/conf/httpd.conf

# Source function library.
. /etc/rc.d/init.d/functions

# See how we were called.
case "$1" in
  start)
     echo -n "Starting httpd: "
     daemon httpd
     echo
     touch /var/lock/subsys/httpd
     ;;
  stop)
     echo -n "Shutting down http: "
     [ -f /var/run/httpd.pid ] && {
        kill `cat /var/run/httpd.pid`
        echo -n httpd
     }
     echo
     rm -f /var/lock/subsys/httpd
     rm -f /var/run/httpd.pid
     ;;
  status)
     status httpd
     ;;
```

```
   restart)
      $0 stop
      $0 start
      ;;
   reload)
      echo -n "Reloading httpd: "
      [ -f /var/run/httpd.pid ] && {
          kill -HUP `cat /var/run/httpd.pid`
          echo -n httpd
      }
      echo
      ;;
   *)
      echo "Usage: $0 {start|stop|restart|reload|status}"
      exit 1
esac


exit 0
```

The preceding sh script is really a simple case (conditional) statement.

The following list shows you an example of how you can create a new service script from an existing service script. Assume that your new service is called webmonitor and that the executable is stored in /usr/sbin/ webmonitor. Change these values for your own scripts as necessary.

It is standard practice to use the same name for both the script and the executable program.

Here is how you create the /etc/rc.d/init.d/webmonitor script from an existing script in the /etc/rc.d/init.d directory:

1. Copy an existing script from /etc/rc.d/init.d as /etc/rc.d/ init.d/webmonitor. For simplicity and ease of understanding, I assume that you copied the /etc/rc.d/init.d/htttpd script shown in Listing 4-2.

2. Using your favorite text editor (such as vi), search and replace all instances of "httpd" with the string "webmonitor."

3. If you keep the executable in any directories other than /sbin, /usr/ sbin, /bin, or /usr/bin, change the daemon webmonitor line to reflect the path of the webmonitor executable. For example, if you keep the executable in the /usr/local/web/bin directory, you have to change the daemon webmonitor line to daemon /usr/ local/web/bin/webmonitor.

4. If /usr/sbin/webmonitor does not create a PID file (/var/run/ webmonitor.pid), you'll have to replace the kill `cat /var/run/ webmonitor.pid` line with killproc webmonitor and remove the rm -f /var/run/webmonitor.pid line.

5. Run chmod 750 /etc/rc.d/init.d/webmonitor to change the file permissions so that the root user can read, write, and execute the script.

6. Use the chkconfig, ntsysv, or Linuxconf utility to add this new service to a desired run level, as described in earlier sections of this chapter.

Chapter 5

Configuring the X Window System

The X Window System is a hardware-independent, client/server windowing system that provides the base platform for graphical user interfaces (GUIs) such as GNOME and KDE. Using a GUI, you can even run Microsoft Windows applications under X Window System using a software emulator such as WINE.

The X Window System is the end result of research and development in many prestigious computer research organizations such as Stanford University, Xerox, and the Massachusetts Institute of Technology (MIT). MIT released a version of the X Window System in 1984 as part of a project called Athena. The X Window System is currently developed and distributed by the Open Group. The X Window System is commonly referred to as X Windows, or just X. I use both of these terms throughout this chapter.

In this chapter, I discuss how you can set up X on a Red Hat Linux system. I also show you how to install and configure the XFree86, which is the most commonly used version of the X Window System and the version typically used with Red Hat Linux. I also show you how to customize and personalize the X Window environment using various tools.

What Is XFree86?

XFree86 is a freely distributable implementation of the X Window System. It is developed by the XFree86 Project, Inc., a nonprofit organization. Although XFree86 is based on the Open Group's X Window System, it has its own development goals. Traditionally, XFree86 was developed for the Intel x86 family of processors, but it now runs on other platforms, such as Compaq/Digital Alpha processors as well. The official Xfree86 Web site is located at `http://www.xfree86.org/`. The official Red Hat Linux comes with the latest XFree86 distribution, and so that's the version of X discussed in this chapter.

Preparing Your System for X

The XFree86 X Window package requires a lot of system resources to be comfortably usable. Although you can run XFree86 on an Intel 486 with a mere 4MB of RAM, the uses of such a system would be limited. The following sections discuss the system requirements that you need to consider before you install XFree86 on any system.

RAM requirements

RAM is a resource you can never have enough of. Having plenty of RAM helps just about everything you do on a multiuser system such as Red Hat Linux. My personal experience shows that having 64MB of RAM with 128MB of swap space provides a very comfortable user experience on a Red Hat Linux system running XFree86 on a regular basis. However, if you would like to run XFree86 while serving Web pages with the Apache Web server and providing NFS or Samba file sharing services, the amount of RAM you need depends on how loaded your server gets at peak hours. At the low end, I recommend that you install 128MB of RAM with 256MB of swap space; as your load increases, you can always add more and more RAM to improve your server performance.

Video card requirements

Not all video cards are supported by XFree86, so don't forget to check the XFree86 Web site for a list of supported video cards. I recommend a brand-name PCI video card with at least 4MB of video memory. In this day and age, such a card is practically the low end. The more video memory you have (some cards have up to 32MB and higher), the better your X experience will be.

In the spirit of getting the most recent hardware, you might consider buying the very latest in video cards. Don't. XFree86 developers may not have had a chance to tinker with the latest and the greatest video hardware as soon as it hits the market, and so it's a really good idea to stick to S3- or ATI-based video cards that are a bit older than it is to buy the one that was released yesterday.

Before installing XFree86, you should take note of the amount of video memory you have on your video card, along with the chipset it uses. You also need the brand and model information.

Monitor requirements

A good monitor and a good video card can make your XFree86 user experience superb. I recommend a large-screen, brand-name, high-resolution monitor. Although large monitors — 19-inch, 21-inch, or more — are quite expensive, they greatly enhance your day-to-day X experience. The more screen real estate you have, the better. Unfortunately, large brand-name monitors often cost more than a high-end PC.

Disk space requirements

Expect to use roughly 400-500MB of hard drive space for a full-blown XFree86 installation with all the goodies (applications, utilities, games, and so forth) that come with it.

Now that you know about the prerequisites, the next section gets you started with the installation.

Installing X

When you install Red Hat Linux from the official CD-ROM, you get a chance to install and configure XFree86. If you haven't done that already, you can install XFree86 quite easily using the RPM packages on your

CD-ROM. To install XFree86 from the RPMS directory of your Red Hat Linux CD-ROM, run the following command:

```
rpm -ivh XFree86*.rpm
```

This installs all the XFree86 packages from the CD-ROM. Now continue with XFree86 configuration.

Configuring X

Before you can configure XFree86 for your system, you need to know the following:

- How much video memory you have
- What kind of chipset your video card uses
- The maximum resolution your monitor supports
- Your monitor's make and model
- Your monitor's horizontal and vertical refresh rates

If you do not know the information for your video card, you can run the SuperProbe utility to determine it. SuperProbe is included with XFree86. You can run it with the following command:

```
/usr/X11R6/bin/SuperProbe
```

Following is a sample SuperProbe output:

```
WARNING - THIS SOFTWARE COULD HANG YOUR MACHINE.
         READ THE SuperProbe.1 MANUAL PAGE BEFORE
         RUNNING THIS PROGRAM.


    INTERRUPT WITHIN FIVE SECONDS TO ABORT!


First video: Super-VGA
        Chipset: S3 Trio64V+ (Port Probed)
        Memory:  2048 Kbytes
        RAMDAC:  Generic 8-bit pseudo-color DAC
            (with 6-bit wide lookup tables (or in 6-bit mode))
```

As the warning message in the output clearly indicates, this program can make your system unresponsive, and therefore you should read the SuperProbe man pages before you run it.

After you have information about your hardware, you need to decide how you want to configure XFree86. You have the following three choices of tools:

- Xconfigurator: A full-screen, menu-driven utility
- xf86config: A command line, prompt-oriented configuration utility
- You can manually create an XF86 configuration file.

The XF86Config file is the primary configuration file needed to create a usable X Window environment in XFree86, and all of the above-listed methods involve configuring this file. The XF86Config file usually resides in the /etc/X11 directory, and typically, a symbolic link (/usr/X11R6/lib/ X11/XF86Config) is pointed back to /etc/X11/XF86Config. Because Xconfigurator is the standard choice, I discuss only that tool in this chapter.

Creating an XF86Config file using Xconfigurator

The Xconfigurator utility enables you to create the XF86Config file quite easily. You can run the program by following these steps:

1. Run the following command to start Xconfigurator:

/usr/X11R6/bin/Xconfigurator

The utility appears with a screen like the one shown in Figure 5-1. As suggested in the opening screen, you should read the /usr/X11R6/lib/X11/doc/README.Config file to learn about the latest details on the structure of the file.

2. Click OK twice to continue. You will see the result of a PCI probe as shown in Figure 5-2.

AGP video cards are shown as PCI video cards.

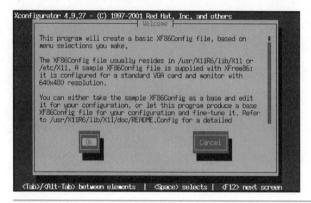

Figure 5-1 *The opening screen for Xconfigurator.*

3. Click OK again to continue. The utility probes your monitor, and the result of the probe will be displayed as shown in Figure 5-3.

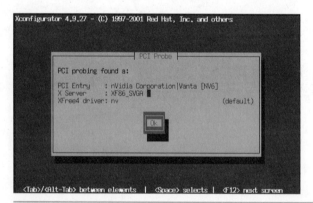

Figure 5-2 *The results of PCI probe.*

4. If your monitor is not detected properly you can select NO and manually choose your monitor. Use the up- and down-arrow keys to scroll back and forth to locate your monitor brand and model. If you find your monitor in the list, select it and press OK to continue. Figure 5-4 shows that I have selected Viewsonic PS775 as my monitor brand and model.

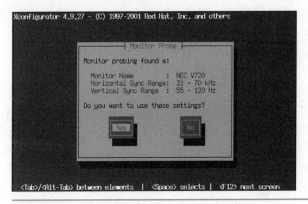

Figure 5-3 *The results of a monitor probe.*

However, it is quite possible that your monitor might not be listed here. In such a case you have to select the Custom monitor and press OK to continue. You then see a screen where you need to specify your monitor's vertical refresh rate and horizontal sync rate. You should first consult with your monitor's manual to find these numbers.

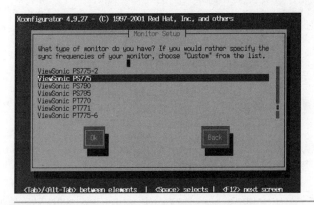

Figure 5-4 *Selecting a monitor by brand name.*

If you lost or have thrown away the monitor manual, you might be able to find information about your monitor on the vendor's Web site. If you still cannot locate information on your monitor, check the /usr/X11R6/share/Xconfigurator/

`MonitorsDB` file for information on your monitor. Most brand-name monitors are listed in this file.

5. Click OK to proceed with the monitor specification. A screen like that is shown in Figure 5-5 appears.

6. From the list, select the most appropriate resolution and horizontal refresh rate for your monitor. If you do not know what these settings should be, call your monitor or computer vendor to find this information.

Don't experiment with these settings unless you care very little about the health of your monitor. If you give XFree86 the wrong monitor settings, you may well harm your monitor.

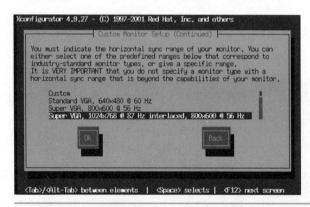

Figure 5-5 *Specifying the resolution and horizontal refresh rate for a monitor.*

7. After you've specified the resolution and the horizontal refresh rate, you can click OK to continue to specify the vertical refresh rate as shown in Figure 5-6.

If Xconfigurator cannot determine how much video memory your video card has, it asks you to specify the amount of video RAM you have, as shown in Figure 5-7. Also, Xconfigurator might ask you to specify the clock chip your video card uses. Use the recommended

"No clockchip setting" option unless you specifically know your video card clock chip information.

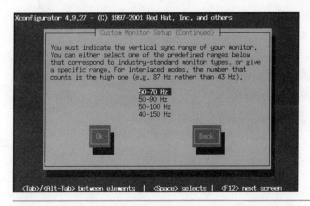

Figure 5-6 *Specifying the monitor's vertical refresh rate.*

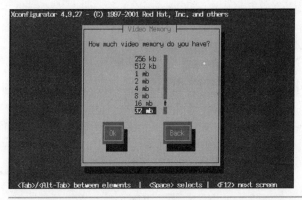

Figure 5-7 *Specifying your video RAM.*

8. Click OK again and you see a dialog box stating that Xconfigurator now probes your video card using the selected X server.

9. Click OK again to continue. If you have chosen Custom monitor then you will be asked to select video chipset as shown in Figure 5-8. The default setting "No clockchip setting" is recommended unless you know the setting and can find it in the supplied list.

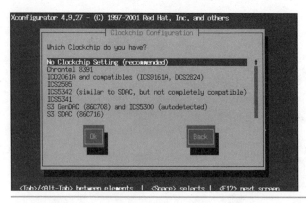

Figure 5-8 *Selecting chipset for custom monitor.*

10. Click OK again to continue and wait for the probing to complete. As warned by the previous dialog window, the screen might blink a few times as part of the probing procedure. After the probing is complete (hopefully without any problem), you see a screen as shown in Figure 5-9. This screen shows the manual default video mode selection options for 8-bit (256 colors), 16-bit (64,536 colors), and 24-bit (16,777,216 colors) modes.

11. Using the up- and down-arrow keys, select an appropriate resolution for each color mode by pressing the spacebar. You can also toggle a selection using the spacebar. After you have selected all the default video modes for each color mode, click OK to complete this step and continue to the next.

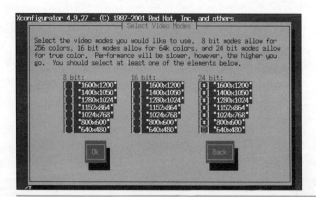

Figure 5-9 *Manually choosing default video modes.*

12. A dialog screen confirms the creation of the XF86Config file. Before you start the X server, you can take a look at the XF86Config file to understand the configuration. People who understand this configuration file can change settings in the file with a simple text editor, which is often a quicker hack then using a GUI tool such as the Xconfigurator. The next section helps you understand what you see.

Understanding the XF86Config file

Like any typical Unix configuration file, the XF86Config file ignores blank lines, as well as any lines that start with leading "#" characters (which are treated as comments). The XF86Config file is divided into multiple sections that each provide a particular type of information to the X server. Each section starts with the Section *"Name_of_the_section"* line and ends with an EndSection line. The following sections describe each section in the file.

Files section

This section is used to specify font and color database paths. Following is an example Files section:

```
Section "Files"



    RgbPath    "/usr/X11R6/lib/X11/rgb"
    FontPath    "/usr/X11R6/lib/X11/fonts/TrueType"
    FontPath    "unix/:7100"


EndSection
```

The following list describes the options shown in the preceding Files section:

- RgbPath: This option specifies the path to the rgb file. You do not need to change it.

- FontPath: If you add new fonts to your system, you can use this option to specify the directory for the fonts you installed.

Server flags section

This section is used to specify general options to the X server. Following is an example ServerFlags section:

```
Section "ServerFlags"

# Uncomment this to cause a core dump at the
# spot where a signal is received.  This may leave
# the console in an unusable state, but may provide
# a better stack trace in the core dump to aid in debugging
#NoTrapSignals

# Uncomment this to disable the <Crtl><Alt><BS>
# server abort sequence This allows clients to receive
# this key event.
#DontZap

# Uncomment this to disable the
# <Crtl><Alt><KP_+>/<KP_-> mode switching sequences.
# This allows clients to receive these key events.
#DontZoom

EndSection
```

The following list describes the options shown in the preceding Server-Flags section:

- NoTrapSignals: This option should be turned on by removing the leading "#" sign (that is, comment character) only if you are an X Window System developer and know what you are doing.

- DontZap: Disables the ability to terminate the X Window server using Ctrl+Alt+Backspace. If you have an X application that requires this key sequence, you can uncomment the DontZap line so that this key sequence can be passed to the application.

- DontZoom: Disables the ability to switch back and forth between different screen resolutions using Ctrl+Alt+Keypad-Plus and Ctrl+Alt+Keypad-Minus (that is, the + and - keys on the keypad to the right of your keyboard). If you have an X application that requires these key sequences, you can uncomment the DontZoom line so that these key sequences can be passed to the application.

Other commonly used options that you can add in this section are listed in Table 5-1.

Table 5-1 *Additional Options for the Files Section of XF86Config*

Option	Use
AllowNonLocalXvidtune	Allows the xvidtune program to connect from a remote host
DisableVidMode	Disables certain video mode extensions used by the xvidtune program
AllowNonLocalModInDev	Allows a remote X client to change keyboard and mouse settings
DisableModInDev	Disables certain input device extensions that can normally be set dynamically
AllowMouseOpenFail	Allows the X server to start without a mouse

Keyboard section

Use this section to set up keyboard devices. Following is an example Keyboard section:

```
Section "Keyboard"

  Protocol    "Standard"

  # when using XQUEUE, comment out the above line,
  # and uncomment the following line
  #Protocol    "Xqueue"

  AutoRepeat  500 5

  LeftAlt     Meta
```

```
RightAlt        Meta
ScrollLock      Compose
RightCtl        Control


XkbRules        "xfree86"
XkbModel        "pc101"
XkbLayout       "us"
```

EndSection

The following list describes the options shown in the preceding Keyboard section:

- **Protocol:** Specifies the keyboard option and should be set to Standard for all Linux systems.

- **AutoRepeat:** Sets the auto repeat delay (first argument) and rate (second argument).

- **LeftAlt, RightAlt, ScrollLock, and RightCtl:** These options enable you to map the Left Alt key, Right Alt key, Scroll Lock key, and Right Ctrl key to either Meta, Compose, or Control values.

- **XkbModel:** If you have a non-U.S. 102-key keyboard, you can use this option to set it to pc102. Similarly, if you have a Microsoft Natural Keyboard, you can set XkbModel to Microsoft.

- **XkbLayout:** If you use any language other than American English, you can set the language by using the two-digit language code with this option. For example, to set your keyboard language to French, you can use fr as the XkbLayout option. The default is us.

- **XkbOptions:** If you are used to Sun Microsystems keyboards, which have the Ctrl key in place of a regular keyboard's Caps Lock key, you can swap these keys (that is, Caps Lock becomes Ctrl) in a regular keyboard using this option. For example, the following option swaps Caps Lock with Ctrl:

XkbOptions "ctrl:swapcaps"

The default is to leave the keys as is.

■ XkbRules: You can specify this option to specify the keyboard rules file. The default rules file is xfree86.

Other commonly used options that you can add in this section are listed in Table 5-2.

Table 5-2 *Additional Options for the Keyboard Section of XF86Config*

Options	Explanation
XkbTypes	Sets keyboard type. The default is "default"; other possible values are basic, cancel, complete, iso9995, mousekeys, nocancel, pc.
XkbCompat	Sets keyboard compatibility. The default value is "default"; other possible values are accessx, basic, complete, group_led, iso9995, japan, keypad, misc, mousekeys, norepeat, pc, pc98, xtest.
XkbSymbols	Sets the keyboard symbol. The default value is "us"; the other possible values are amiga, ataritt, be, bg, ca, cs, ctrl, czsk, de, de_CH, digital, dk, dvorak, en_US, es, fi, fr, fr_CH, fujitsu, gb, group, hu, iso9995-3, it, jp, keypad, lock, nec, no, pc104, pl, pt, ru, se, sgi, sony, sun, th.
XkbGeometry	Sets the keyboard geometry parameters. The default value is "pc"; other possible values are amiga, ataritt, dell, digital, everex, fujitsu, keytronic, kinesis, Microsoft, nec, northgate, sgi, sony, sun, winbook.
XkbKeycodes	Sets the key codes for the keyboard. The default value is "xfree86"; other possible values are amiga, ataritt, digital, fujitsu, hp, ibm, sgi, sony, sun.

Pointer section

Use this section to set up the pointer device, which is typically a mouse. An example Pointer section follows:

```
Section "Pointer"


  Protocol    "Microsoft"
  Device      "/dev/mouse"


EndSection
```

The following list describes the options shown in the preceding Pointer section:

- `Protocol`: Sets the protocol for the pointer device. The protocol can be `Auto`, `BusMouse`, `GlidePoint`, `GlidePointPS/2`, `IntelliMouse`, `IMPS/2`, `Logitech`, `Microsoft`, `MMHitTab`, `MMSeries`, `Mouseman`, `MouseManPlusPS/2`, `MouseSystems`, `NetMousePS/2`, `NetScrollPS/2`, `OSMouse`, `PS/2`, `SysMouse`, `ThinkingMouse`, `ThinkingMousePS/2`, or `Xqueue`. If you do not know what protocol is appropriate for your late-model pointer device, try setting the protocol to `Auto`.

- `Device`: Specifies the device path. If you use a mouse as your pointing device and have it connected to serial port 1 (`cua0`) or serial port (`cua1`), you can specify `/dev/cua0` or `/dev/cua1`, respectively. However, the best method is to create a symbolic link called `/dev/mouse` that points to your serial port device (`cua0` or `cua1`) and have the device set to `/dev/mouse`. This way, if you change the port, all you need to do is readjust the link, not the configuration file as well.

Other commonly used options that you can add are listed in Table 5-3.

Table 5-3 *Additional Options for the Pointer Section of XF86Config*

Option	Explanation
BaudRate	Sets the baud rate for your pointer device.
Port	Same as Device option.
Button	Sets the number of buttons.
Emulate3Buttons	Emulates a three-button mouse with a two-button mouse. When you press both buttons together, you get the action the third button would give you.
Emulate3Timeout	Sets the time-out (in milliseconds) for three-button emulation. The X server waits for the specified number of milliseconds to decide whether or not a third button was pressed when you hold down both of the buttons.

Monitor section

The monitor section is the most commonly modified. Use this section to describe your monitor. Following is an example Monitor section:

```
Section "Monitor"

Identifier  "My Monitor"
VendorName  "Unknown"
ModelName   "Unknown"
HorizSync   31.5 - 82.0
VertRefresh 50-100

# This is a set of standard mode timings.
# Modes that are out of monitor spec
# are automatically deleted by the server
# (provided the HorizSync and VertRefresh lines
# are correct), so there's no immediate need to
# delete mode timings (unless particular mode timings
# don't work on your monitor). With these modes,
# the best standard mode that your monitor
# and video card can support for a given resolution
# is automatically used.

# 640x400 @ 70 Hz, 31.5 kHz hsync
Modeline "640x400" 25.175 640  664  760  800    400  409  411
450

# 640x480 @ 60 Hz, 31.5 kHz hsync
Modeline "640x480" 25.175 640  664  760  800    480  491  493
525

# 800x600 @ 56 Hz, 35.15 kHz hsync
ModeLine "800x600" 36      800  824  896 1024    600  601  603
625

# 640x480 @ 72 Hz, 36.5 kHz hsync
Modeline "640x480" 31.5 640 680 720  864 480 488 491 521
```

```
# 800x600 @ 60 Hz, 37.8 kHz hsync
Modeline "800x600" 40 800 840 968 1056 600 601 605 628 +hsync
+vsync

# 1024x768 @ 60 Hz, 48.4 kHz hsync
Modeline "1024x768" 65 1024 1032 1176 1344 768 771 777 806 -
hsync -vsync

# 1024x768 @ 70 Hz, 56.5 kHz hsync
Modeline "1024x768" 75 1024 1048 1184 1328 768 771 777  806 -
hsync -vsync

# 1024x768 @ 76 Hz, 62.5 kHz hsync
Modeline "1024x768"  85  1024 1032 1152 1360   768  784  787
823

# 1280x1024 @ 61 Hz, 64.2 kHz hsync
Modeline "1280x1024" 110 1280 1328 1512 1712  1024 1025 1028
1054

# 1280x1024 @ 74 Hz, 78.85 kHz hsync
Modeline "1280x1024" 135 1280 1312 1456 1712  1024 1027 1030
1064

# 1280x1024 @ 76 Hz, 81.13 kHz hsync
Modeline "1280x1024" 135 1280 1312 1416 1664  1024 1027 1030
1064

EndSection
```

The following list describes the options shown in the preceding section:

- `Identifier`: Sets a unique identifier for the monitor. Each monitor needs to have a unique identifier that can be referenced in the `Screen` section.

- `VendorName` and `ModelName`: Use these options to specify the vendor name and model of the monitor.

- **HorizSync**: Use this option to set the horizontal refresh (sync) rate in kilohertz (KHz). If you would like to specify this rate in megahertz or in hertz, use MHz or Hz at the end of the line.

- **VertRefresh**: Use this option to set the vertical refresh (sync) rate in hertz (Hz). If you would like to specify this rate in megahertz or in kilohertz, use MHz or KHz at the end of the line.

- **ModeLine** options: Use these options to specify video modes. Each ModeLine option has the following format:

```
ModeLine mode clk_rate Horizontal_timing
Vertical_timing Flags
```

Here, *clk-rate* is the rate of the pixel clock for this mode. This number is a single positive (integer) number. *Horizontal_timing* and *Vertical_timing* are a set of four timing (integer) numbers. Use the optional *Flags* to specify additional characteristics of the mode. You can write a ModeLine on a single line or in multiple lines using the mode option. For example:

```
ModeLine "1024x768i" 45 1024 1048 1208 1264 768 776
784 817 Interlace
```

is identical to the following:

```
Mode "1024x768i"
DotClock        45
HTimings        1024 1048 1208 1264
VTimings        768 776 784 817
Flags           "Interlace"
EndMode
```

Graphics Device section

The Graphics section is used to set options for the video card. Following is an example Graphics section:

```
# Device configured by Xconfigurator:

Section "Device"
    Identifier   "Trio32/Trio64"
    VendorName   "Unknown"
    BoardName    "Unknown"

EndSection
```

The following list describes the options shown in the preceding section:

- `Identifier`: Use this option to set a unique identifier for the monitor. Each monitor needs to have a unique identifier that can be referenced in the Screen section.

- `VendorName` and `BoardName`: These options specify the vendor name and name of the video card.

Screen section

Use the screen section to specify how the video hardware (monitor and video card) should be used by X server. Following is an example of a Screen section:

```
Section "Screen"
    Driver      "accel"
    Device      "Trio32/Trio64"
    Monitor     "My Monitor"

    Subsection "Display"
        Depth       8
        Modes       "640x480" "800x600" "1024x768" "1280x1024"
        ViewPort    0 0
        Virtual     1280 1024
    EndSubsection

    Subsection "Display"
```

```
        Depth       16
        Modes       "640x480" "800x600" "1024x768"
        ViewPort    0 0
        Virtual     1024 768
    EndSubsection

    Subsection "Display"
        Depth       32
        Modes       "640x480" "800x600"
        ViewPort    0 0
        Virtual     800 600
    EndSubsection

EndSection
```

The following list describes the options shown in the preceding section:

- `Driver`: This option sets the driver name. Supported driver names are `accel`, `mono`, `svga`, `vga2`, and `vga16`.

- `Device`: This option sets the name of the video card that is to be used.

- `Monitor`: Sets the name of the monitor that is to be used.

- `Display subsections`: The display subsection specifies a set of parameters for a particular display type. A screen section may have multiple display sections, each of which includes the following options:

  - `Depth`: Sets color depth

  - `Modes`: Sets video modes or resolutions

  - `ViewPort`: Sets the top-left corner of the initial display

  - `Virtual`: Specifies the virtual video resolution

You can cycle through various video resolutions while running an X Window session by pressing the Ctrl+Alt+ Keypad-Plus and Ctrl+Alt+Keypad-Minus keys.

Starting X

You can start X Window in one of several ways. The first method is to run xinit, which starts the X server and then runs the first X client application. The client application it runs depends on the .xinitrc script in a user's home directory. For example, if you run xinit as root, the ~root/.xinitrc script is used to determine which X client application needs to be started after the X server is up and running. If no client application is specified in the command line, or if the ~user_home_directory/.xinitrc file does not exist, xinit uses the following command as a default:

```
xterm -geometry +1+1 -n login -display :0
```

The above command starts an xterm session as the sole client application. When this client application exits, the X server also terminates.

In order to provide better user control on what gets started, an sh script called startx is distributed. You can run startx without any argument to start the X server. This script is really a front end for the xinit program.

By default, the startx script looks for .xserverrc in the user's home directory, and if such a file is not found, it looks for a system-wide xserverrc file in the /usr/X11R6/lib/X11/xinit directory. The ~user_home_directory/.xserverrc file or the /usr/X11R6/lib/X11/xinit/xserverrc file is used to determine which X server needs to be started. The script also looks for .xinitrc in the user's home directory, and if such a file is not found, it looks for a system-wide xinitrc file in the /usr/X11R6/lib/X11/xinit directory. The ~user_home_directory/.xinitrc or the /usr/X11R6/lib/X11/xinit/xinitrc file is used to determine which client applications are going to be run after the X server has been started.

You can provide command-line arguments to alter the default settings found in any of these files. However, if you keep overriding the defaults, you may as well put your chosen settings in these files so that you don't have to type them every time you want to run this script.

If you like, start you can start X in a different color mode by specifying the color mode in the command line. For example:

```
startx--bbp 8
```

This will start X Windows in 256-color mode. To start X Window in true color mode, use the following command:

```
startx--bbp 32
```

The double dashes are required to pass arguments directly to the `xinit` program.

When you run `startx` for the first time, your home directory is not likely to have a preinstalled .xinitrc file, and therefore the system-wide xinitrc file is used. To create your own .xinitrc file, run the `locate xinitrc` command to locate a copy of the file in /usr/X11R6/lib/X11/xinit or in /etc/X11/xinit. Copy this file to your home directory by renaming it with a period as the first character so that the final name is .xinitrc. The next section shows you how to configure this file to customize your X environment.

Configuring .xinitrc

As mentioned before, the .xinitrc script is used to launch client applications to suit a user's preference. When such a script is found in a user's home directory, `startx` runs it; when the .xinitrc script exits, it terminates the X Window server. Therefore you must call a client application in the script so that control does not fall through to the bottom of the script (causing it to exit) until you terminate that client application. Typically, you accomplish this by running all but the last client program in the background. The last client program is usually an X Window manager. Listing 5-1 shows an example .xinitrc file.

Listing 5-1 *An example .xinitrc file*

```
#
# Example .xinitrc
#


# start xclock (in the background)
xclock -geometry 50x50-1+1 &
```

Continued

Listing 5-1 *Continued*

```
# start two xterms (in the background)
xterm -geometry 80x50+494+51 &
xterm -geometry 80x20+494-0 &


#
# now start a window manager in
# the foreground
#


# If my favorite GNOME is there, start it
if [ -f  /usr/bin/gnome-session]; then
    exec gnome-session

# Ok, no GNOME, try KDE
elif [ -f  /usr/bin/startkde]; then
    exec startkde

# Ok, no GNOME or  KDE, try just  twm
else
    exec twm
fi
```

As you can see, instances of X applications such as xclock and xterm are executed in the background using the "&" operator. Only the X window manager application is run in the foreground. You should start with a simple .xinitrc file such as the preceding one and modify it to include X applications you need to start by default.

You can decide to run X Window without a window manager by running xinit directly; however, most people will find window managers must-have tools to work under X Window. The popular X Window managers are fvwm2, fvwm, afterstep, twm, wmaker, and wmx, among others. Each window manager has its own look and feel and thus provides a different appeal to different users. I recommend that you install the popular window managers by installing the necessary RPM files and try them out.

Because window managers are so numerous, taking full advantage of them requires knowledge of each package, which in turns require a great deal of time on your part. It almost seems as if you need a manager for the window managers.

Customizing the look and feel of client applications

When you run an X client application such as an xterm or a calculator (xcalc), the default look and feel of the application typically comes from a file in `/usr/X1R6/lib/X11/app-defaults`. For example, the default look and feel of the xcalc calculator comes from the `/usr/X1R6/lib/X11/app-defaults/XCalc` file. You can modify these defaults to provide a customized look and feel for you and/or your users. Be sure to back up each file you want to modify.

If you are interested only in changing the look and feel of a few applications for yourself, you can create an .Xresources file in your home directory and add lines using the following syntax:

```
application_and_resource_key: resource_value
```

For example, in the following example I have changed the default background color (black) of the digital display of the xcalc program by placing this line in my .Xresources file:

```
XCalc*bevel.Background:   red
```

To identify which resource is responsible for changing this particular color, I first looked at the `/usr/X1R6/lib/X11/app-defaults/XCalc` file. After I located the resource (`bevel.Background`), I created the above line in my .Xresources file that prefixed the resource name with the name of the application (XCalc). If you use an .xinitrc file in your home directory, you should put `xrdb -merge $HOME/.Xresources` in it before loading any client applications. Any time you add or modify resources in your .Xresources file, you can run this command from the command line to integrate the resource changes into your current X environment.

Using xdm, the X Display Manager

If you have installed Red Hat Linux and selected the appropriate check boxes to enable a graphical login you do not need to manually set up xdm. In such a case you can skip this section. If you would like to provide a GUI-based user authentication interface, X Display Manager, or xdm, is your answer. Using xdm you can authenticate users via a graphical login screen and take them straight to their X Window environment. The purpose of this program is to provide services similar to getty and login. You can start the display manager as follows:

```
xdm &
```

The xdm configuration files are located in the /usr/X11R6/lib/X11/xdm directory. The file xdm-config is for configuring how the login screen appears to users, and Xsetup_0 is used to tell xdm what programs should be launched when X is started. The default Xsetup_0 is shown here:

```
#!/bin/sh
# Xsetup for Red Hat Linux
# Copyright (c) 1999, 2000 Red Hat, Inc.


pidof -s kdm > /dev/null 2>&1
if [ $? -eq 0 -a -x /usr/bin/kdmdesktop ]; then
  /usr/bin/kdmdesktop
else
  /usr/X11R6/bin/xsetroot -solid "#356390"
fi


# only set the background if the xsri program is installed
if [ -x /usr/bin/xsri ]; then
    /usr/bin/xsri  -geometry +5+5 -avoid 300x250 -keep-aspect \
        /usr/share/pixmaps/redhat/redhat-transparent.png
fi
```

This file starts the xconsole and xbanner programs when a user is authenticated. These are practically useless for most users. Hence you should modify this to whatever is appropriate. For example, you might use the xv program to set the background of the X environment to something appropriate for your organization. Or perhaps you can start up a few applications that are typically run by most users, such as the xmailbox.

The xdm can be run automatically after boot by changing the default run level to 5. To change the run level of your system to 5, modify the following line in the /etc/inittab file:

```
id:3:initdefault:
```

To change the default run level, simply replace the 3 with 5. And make sure that you have the following lines in the same file:

```
# Run xdm in runlevel 5
# xdm is now a separate service
x:5:respawn:/etc/X11/prefdm —nodaemon
```

Chapter 6

Setting Up Networking

Chances are, if you want to use your Red Hat Linux system for connecting to any network, you need networking functionality. Your network could be a simple one, such as connecting one system to the Internet, or your network could be vast, covering multiple locations and hundreds of users. In this chapter, I show you how to get Linux up and running on a network.

Configuring a Network Interface

Most administrators are likely to have to connect a Linux computer to an Ethernet. Such an Ethernet can be your very own Local Area Network (LAN), or a LAN at an ISP (for examples, co-located servers). In this section I assume that you've already installed an Ethernet adapter card (that is, a network interface card, or NIC) that works with Red Hat Linux. To find out which NICs are compatible with your version of Red Hat Linux, see the hardware compatibility section of the Red Hat Web site. In general, though, most popular NIC cards work fine with Red Hat Linux.

You may already have configured your network during the Red Hat Linux installation phase, but I still recommend that you read this section because you may need to change your network configuration at a later time.

You can configure your network in several ways. First I will discuss the command-line method, as it is the most powerful (in the sense that you do not need to rely on any special tool other than your favorite text editor), and then I discuss the Network Configurator (or netcfg for short), a GUI tool you can use to more easily create a network interface.

When setting up the network interface by using either the traditional or the netcfg method, you must provide a default gateway IP address. In the following section, I discuss why you need a default gateway.

Configuring a network interface card manually

The traditional way of configuring your NIC is by doing it manually from the command-line interface. This is my favorite method of doing all types of configuration because it forces me to know exactly what is needed to configure something. My motto is: Once you know how to do things the "old-fashioned" way, you can do them any way you like.

Configuring a new network interface

Before you do anything, run the dmesg program (or view the /var/log/dmesg file) to find out if the current Linux kernel recognizes your network card. If it does not, read the module configuration section in Chapter 2. If the Linux kernel does recognize your card, you should see some lines in the dmesg output pertaining to the kernel's discovery of your network device. For example, when I run the dmesg | grep -I eth command on a Red Hat Linux system with a generic (NE2000 compatible) Ethernet card, I get the following output:

```
NE*000 ethercard probe at 0x340: 00 c0 f6 98 37 37
eth0: NE2000 found at 0x340, using IRQ 5.
```

This output tells me that the kernel has found my NE2000-compatible network card and is using Interrupt Request Line (IRQ) 5 for it, and that the I/O address space starts at 0x340. Also note that this device is called eth0 (that is, Ethernet device 0).

After you've confirmed that the kernel is recognizing your network device, you're ready to configure it. In this example, I assume that you want to configure the first Ethernet device, eth0, and that you want a persistent configuration. A *persistent configuration* is a configuration that you use every time you start your computer. You can do this with the help of the /etc/rc.d/init.d/network script. When this script is symbolically linked (where the name of the link is Sxxnetwork, *xx* being any number) from the default run level directory (which could be /etc/rc.d/rc3.d), the /etc/rc.d/init.d/network script runs at boot time. This script loads the network interfaces by using files stored in the /etc/sysconfig directory. The next section shows you how to configure eth0 so that it automatically starts up at system boot.

Configuring eth0 to start at system boot

The very first file you have to modify to configure eth0 to start upon system boot is the /etc/sysconfig/network file. Listing 6-1 shows an example of this file.

Listing 6-1 *An example /etc/sysconfig/network file*

```
NETWORKING=yes
FORWARD_IPV4=yes
HOSTNAME=picaso.evoknow.com
DOMAINNAME=evoknow.com
GATEWAY=206.171.50.49
GATEWAYDEV=eth0
```

The NETWORKING=yes line states that you want to enable networking support.

The FORWARD_IPV4=yes should be set to yes if you would like to allow forwarding of IP packets to and from your Red Hat Linux server. This is required only if a Red Hat Linux computer is going to act as a gateway or router (discussed in a later section) for a network. For example, if you are planning on installing proxy server software on your computer to allow Web access for other computers on your LAN, you should set the FORWARD_IPV4 option to yes. On the other hand, if you are just planning on using this computer as a co-located Web server on an ISP network, you can turn IP forwarding off by setting this option to no.

The next two lines specify the host name of the computer and the domain name of your network. The host name you specify here must include the domain name you specify in the DOMAINNAME line. In other words, don't specify a host name that uses a different domain name from the name you state in the DOMAINNAME line.

The next two lines specify the information that you need to determine the default gateway for a computer. A default gateway is a computer (or a router) that transfers packets to and from your computer. For example, if you intend to connect your Red Hat Linux computer to your LAN, where you have an ISDN router that connects the LAN to the Internet, specify the IP address of the ISDN router's network interface as the default gateway.

GATEWAYDEV is important when you have multiple network interfaces. If you have only one Ethernet device, you should always set this to eth0. If you have multiple Ethernet devices (eth0, eth1, and so on), you have to use the interface name connected to the default gateway.

After you configure the /etc/sysconfig/network file, you are ready to create the network interface file in the /etc/sysconfig/network-scripts directory. The network interface file uses ifcfg-interface as the naming convention. For example, the network interface filename for eth0 is ifcfg-eth0. An example of this file is shown in Listing 6-2.

Listing 6-2 *An example /etc/sysconfig/network-scripts/ifcfg-eth0 file*

```
DEVICE=eth0
IPADDR=206.171.50.50
NETMASK=255.255.255.240
NETWORK=206.171.50.48
BROADCAST=206.171.50.63
ONBOOT=yes
BOOTPROTO=static
```

Before you can configure the information in this file, you have to obtain the network address, the network mask, the IP address for the network interface on the host, and the broadcast address from your Internet service provider. (I discuss the network mask and broadcast address further in a later section.)

The first line in this file specifies the device name. The second line specifies the network mask (netmask) number. The third line specifies the

IP address of the network. The fifth line specifies the broadcast address. Set the ONBOOT option, which is shown in the sixth line, to yes if you want the network interface to be "up" (that is, started) after boot. The BOOT-PROTO line can be either set to static (for a network card with static IP address), dhcp (network interface that gets IP from a DHCP server), or bootp (network interface that gets its IP address from a BOOTP server).

Bringing up the network

After you configure /etc/sysconfig/network and /etc/sysconfig/network-scripts/ifcfg-eth0 files, you are ready to bring up the network. The easiest way to bring up the interface you just configured is to run the following command:

```
/etc/sysconfig/network-scripts/ifup eth0
```

The ifup script takes the device name as the argument and starts it, and also creates a default route for the network. After you've run this command, you can use the ifconfig program to see if the interface is up and running. To see if device eth0 is up, run:

```
ifconfig eth0
```

You should see output similar to the following:

```
eth0 Link encap:Ethernet HWaddr 00:C0:F6:98:37:37
inet addr:206.171.50.50  Bcast:206.171.50.63
Mask:255.255.255.240
UP BROADCAST RUNNING MULTICAST  MTU:1500  Metric:1
RX packets:9470 errors:0 dropped:0 overruns:0 frame:0
TX packets:7578 errors:0 dropped:0 overruns:0 carrier:0
collisions:0
Interrupt:5 Base address:0x340
```

In the preceding, ifconfig reports that network interface device eth0 has an Internet address (inet addr) of 206.171.50.50, a broadcast address (Bcast) of 206.171.50.63, and a network mask of 255.255.255.240. The rest of the information shows the following: how many packets this interface has received so far (RX packets); how many packets this interface has transmitted so far (TX packets); how many errors of different types have occurred so far; what interrupt address line this device is using; what I/O address base is being used; and so on.

You can run `ifconfig` without any arguments to get the full list of all the up network devices. Note that the `ifup` script uses `ifconfig` to bring an interface up. For example:

```
ifconfig eth0 206.171.50.50 netmask 255.255.255.240 \
broadcast 206.171.50.63
```

The preceding command starts `eth0` with the IP address 206.171. 50.50. You can also quickly take an interface down by using the `ifconfig` command. For example, the following command takes the eth0 interface down:

```
ifconfig eth0 down
```

Testing the interface

After you've got the interface up and running, you should try to contact a computer in your network. You can use the `ping  IP_address` command to determine if you can use your new interface to contact a host on the same network.

If your `/etc/resolv.conf` file was not set up properly during installation, you will not be able to successfully `ping` a host by using its host name. The `/etc/resolv.conf` file looks like the following:

```
search evoknow.com
nameserver 206.171.50.50
```

This file is set up during Red Hat Linux installation. If you have specified an invalid IP address for the name server, your computer is not able to contact the name server. So, if you have your network interface up but you are unable to successfully `ping` a host by using the host name, try using the IP address of the host (that is, the network interface address). If you can `ping` the other host on your network, your interface is set up properly; just correct the `nameserver` line by fixing the IP address of the name server.

However, if you cannot successfully `ping` a host by using either the IP address or the host name, you might have a routing problem. If you have not used the `ifup` script as shown earlier and instead have used `ifconfig` to bring up the interface, you need to create a default route to your network and a default gateway manually. To create a default route for your network, use the route command as follows:

```
route add -net network_address netmask device
```

For example, to create a default route for the 206.171.50.48 network with a 255.255.255.240 `netmask` and `eth0` as the interface, you can run the following command:

```
route add -net 206.171.50.48 255.255.255.240 eth0
```

To set the default gateway, you can run the `route` command as follows:

```
route add default gw gateway address device
```

For example, to set the default gateway address to 206.171.50.49, I can run the following command:

```
route add default gw 206.171.50.49 eth0
```

You can verify that your network route and default gateway are properly set up in the routing table by using the following command:

```
route -n
```

Here is an example of output of the preceding command:

```
Kernel IP routing table
Destination    Gateway        Genmask            Flags Metric Ref Use Iface
206.171.50.48  0.0.0.0        255.255.255.240    U     0      0   6   eth0
127.0.0.0      0.0.0.0        255.0.0.0          U     0      0   5   lo
0.0.0.0        206.171.50.49  0.0.0.0            UG    0      0   17  eth0
```

At this point, you should use the `ping` program to ping hosts inside and outside your network. If you are successful, your network is up. If you still do not get any replies from your `ping` attempts, you should go back to the beginning of this section and ensure that you have followed all steps as suggested.

Aliasing multiple IP addresses with a single network interface

In the preceding sections I discuss how to configure a network interface so that a single IP address is associated with it. As I mention earlier, each interface must have its own unique IP address, but you can associate multiple IP addresses to the single interface by using the IP alias module for the Linux kernel. So what can you do with an IP alias? Here are few practical uses of IP aliases.

- Say that you have two machines providing Web services and all of a sudden one of the machines becomes unavailable because of some problem. Or, perhaps you want to take the machine down for a couple of days for some upgrade work. In either case, you can use an IP alias to service the unavailable machine's IP address. You can simply add virtual Web sites to service the Web sites you hosted on the broken or unavailable system until the system is functional again.

- Many older Web browsers do not use the name-based virtual hosting feature (see Chapter 12). In such a case, you can use IP aliases to create virtual IP-based Web sites.

Follow these steps to create an alias for the eth0 device:

1. Copy your existing /etc/sysconfig/network-scripts/ ifcfg-eth0 file to /etc/sysconfig/network-scripts/ ifcfg-eth0:0. This creates an alias device named eth0:0.

2. Modify the file so that the lines are similar to the ones in Listing 6-3. Of course, your network, netmask, and IP address will vary. Make sure that you change only the DEVICE and IPADDR lines. You should set the DEVICE line to eth0:0 and IPADDR to the IP address you want to use as an alias to what you have assigned for eth0.

Listing 6-3 *An example /etc/sysconfig/network-scripts/ifcfg-eth0:0 file*

```
DEVICE=eth0:0
USERCTL=no
ONBOOT=yes
BOOTPROTO=
BROADCAST=206.171.50.63
NETWORK=206.171.50.48
NETMASK=255.255.255.240
IPADDR=206.171.50.58
```

3. To start the alias device, run ifconfig eth0:0 and you should see output similar to the following:

```
lo Link encap:Local Loopback

    inet addr:127.0.0.1  Bcast:127.255.255.255  Mask:255.0.0.0

    UP BROADCAST LOOPBACK RUNNING  MTU:3584  Metric:1

    RX packets:501 errors:0 dropped:0 overruns:0 frame:0

    TX packets:501 errors:0 dropped:0 overruns:0 carrier:0

      collisions:0


eth0 Link encap:Ethernet  HWaddr 00:C0:F6:98:37:37

    inet addr:206.171.50.50 Bcast:206.171.50.63 Mask:255.255.255.240

    UP BROADCAST RUNNING MULTICAST  MTU:1500  Metric:1

    RX packets:2 errors:0 dropped:0 overruns:0 frame:0

    TX packets:2 errors:0 dropped:0 overruns:0 carrier:0 collisions:4

    Interrupt:5 Base address:0x340


eth0:0 Link encap:Ethernet  HWaddr 00:C0:F6:98:37:37

    inet addr:206.171.50.58  Bcast:206.171.50.63 Mask:255.255.255.240

    UP BROADCAST RUNNING  MTU:1500  Metric:1

    RX packets:9 errors:0 dropped:0 overruns:0 frame:0

    TX packets:9 errors:0 dropped:0 overruns:0 carrier:0 collisions:0
```

As you can see from the preceding output, the eth0:0 device is up
and running. You can create an alias of any other Ethernet device in
the same way.

Configuring a network interface
card using netcfg

You need to have the X Window System working on your machine in
order to use the Network Configurator, or netcfg. This program allows
you to configure all aspects of the basic network configuration.

Although using netcfg may be easy compared to the steps
in the manual method described in the previous section, I
highly recommend learning about the manual method – a
network administrator must know how things work from the
inside out.

Adding a network interface with netcfg

You must run `netcfg` as a superuser (such as root) from within a graphical environment such as GNOME. The initial window, shown in Figure 6-1, displays the current host name, domain name, and name server configuration.

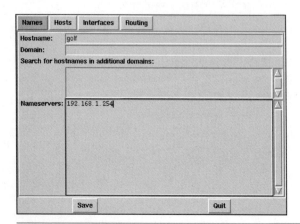

Figure 6-1 *The Names tab of the Network Configurator.*

To change the host name, the domain name, or the name servers, click the Names tab. Simply modify the values and click Save.

The program does not display any status message when you click Save, and this can be a bit confusing at first. Also note that the domain name displayed in the program comes from the search list (the first entry in the list) in the /etc/resolv. conf file. If you do not have any search list set up in this file, netcfg does not display a domain name.

To add, modify, or remove a network interface, click the Interfaces tab. This tab, shown in Figure 6-2, displays the current network interfaces.

To add a new network interface using the Network Configurator, follow these steps:

   1. Click Add to bring up a dialog box like the one shown in Figure 6-3.

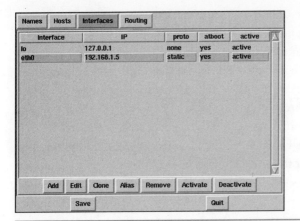

Figure 6-2 *The Interfaces tab of the Network Configurator.*

2. Click Ethernet to create a new Ethernet network interface configuration. Click OK and you'll see a dialog box like the one shown in Figure 6-4.

Figure 6-3 *Adding a new network interface.*

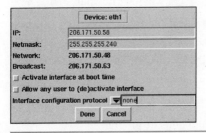

Figure 6-4 *Entering information about a new interface.*

3. Enter the IP address and netmask for the new device. The `netcfg` program automatically calculates the network and broadcast address from the information you provide. If you would like this interface to be active at boot, select the Activate interface at boot time option. You should leave the Allow any user to (de)activate interface option unchecked because allowing just anyone to activate/deactivate your network interfaces is really a bad idea for security reasons. If you're not using DHCP or BOOTP servers to dynamically assign IP addresses for this interface, select none as the interface configuration protocol. Click Done to complete the configuration; you are asked to confirm that you want to save the configuration. Save the configuration by clicking OK. The new interface appears in the interface list in the next screen.

4. If you would like to activate the interface right away, click Activate. The screen should update the status of the interface to be active. However, `netcfg` might show the interface as active when it is really not. This happens when you try to configure a nonexistent network card. One of the easiest ways to check the interface is to run the `ifconfig interface_name` command from the command line to see which interfaces are up and running.

Setting the default gateway

After you've activated a new interface, you need to set up a default gateway (which is discussed in a later section) by following these steps:

1. Click Routing to bring up the window shown in Figure 6-5.

2. Enter the default gateway IP address. The gateway device name should be the device you just configured.

3. If you would like to set this device up to forward IP packets to and from computers on your network, set the Network Packet Forwarding (IPV4) option.

4. Save the new settings and quit the program.

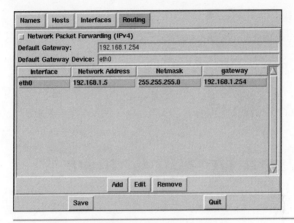

Figure 6-5 *Configuring a default gateway.*

Testing the interface

After you've configured a new interface, you have to set up a default gateway. Test your new interface by pinging a computer on your network by using the `ping IP address` command. If you can `ping` a remote host, you have successfully configured the new interface.

To modify an existing network interface, follow these steps:

1. Click the Interfaces tab. Double-click the existing network interface line. Make changes as appropriate.

2. After you've made and saved the changes, deactivate the interface first and then reactivate it.

If you are using the X Window System on a remote terminal to run the `netcfg` program, do not deactivate the interface used for providing network connectivity to your terminal. In other words, if you deactivate the interface needed for your remote X connection, your X session will not work and you will not be able to activate the interface without local access.

Deleting an interface

To delete an existing network interface, follow these steps:

1. Click Interfaces. Select the existing network interface.

2. Click Delete to complete the process. The statements in the preceding Caution apply here.

Why Use a Default Gateway?

Take a look at Figure 6-6. It shows two networks: network A (192.168.1.0) and network B (192.168.2.0).

Network A 192.168.1.0

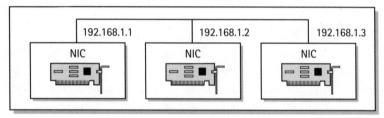

Network B 192.168.2.0

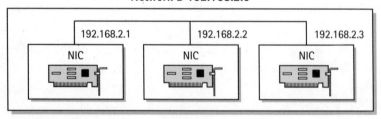

Figure 6-6 *Two distinct IP networks.*

These two networks are completely separate. The computers in either network can see the hosts in the same network just fine. A user using the 192.168.1.1 computer in network A can ping the other two computers by using their network interface IP addresses. However, he or she cannot access any of the host computers on network B. Why? There is no way for the packets in network A to go to network B. How can these two networks be joined? You guessed right — by using a gateway computer or a router. Figure 6-7 shows how we can do this.

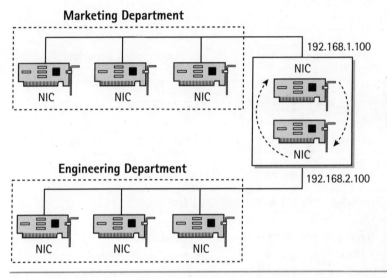

Figure 6-7 *Two distinct IP networks joined by a gateway.*

The new computer in the network is the gateway computer. It has two network interfaces. The network interface attached to the A network has an IP address 192.168.1.100, and the interface attached to the B network has an IP address of 192.168.2.100. The computer is set up to forward IP packets between these two networks. For example, when the 192.168.1.1 computer wants to send a packet to 192.168. 2.1, it forwards the IP packet to the 192.168.1.100 gateway computer. This gateway machine places a modified version of the packet on its other interface (192.168.2.100), which becomes available to the destination computer. When the destination computer wants to respond, it follows a similar process so that the gateway computer is able to send the packet to the source computer on network A.

You need the gateway computer only if you want to communicate with two different networks. Note that the gateway computer need not be a PC or a workstation; it can be a specialized computer hardware such as a router.

Now that you know how to join two different networks by using a gateway, the next section shows you how to split networks by creating subnetworks or subnets.

Dividing a Network into Subnetworks

Take a look at the network in Figure 6-8.

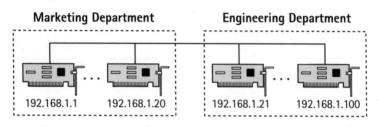

Network/netmask: 192.168.1.0/255.255.255.0

Figure 6-8 *A large network shared by 100 users.*

This network has 100 host computers connected to a single network, 192.168.1.0. Because all computers share the same physical network cable, the traffic load is likely to be quite heavy at peak hours. For example, if all marketing people start using the network at the same time as the engineers in the engineering department, things become very slow, as every host has to share the network bandwidth. So what's the solution? Subnetworks. Now take a look at Figure 6-9.

Here we divide the 192.168.1.0 network into two networks — 192.168. 1.0 and 192.168.1.128. Both of these subnetworks are connected to each other using a gateway (or router) with two network interfaces. When we configure each host computer on each of these two networks properly, we separate the network traffic between these networks. For example, when a user in the marketing department wants to communicate with another computer in the same department, the network traffic between these two computers remains in their network. The same is true for the engineering side. However, when users from different departments want to communicate with each other's computers, it is allowed. The gateway computer forwards such inter-network traffic to and from these networks. The result is a speedier network because not all users are on the same, large network anymore. Now see how you can implement such a solution.

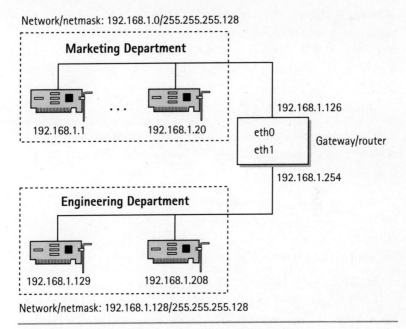

Network/netmask: 192.168.1.0/255.255.255.128

Marketing Department

192.168.1.1 ... 192.168.1.20

eth0
eth1

192.168.1.126

Gateway/router

192.168.1.254

Engineering Department

192.168.1.129   192.168.1.208

Network/netmask: 192.168.1.128/255.255.255.128

Figure 6-9 *Splitting a large network into subnetworks.*

When a full network such as 192.168.1.0 needs to be divided into subnets, the computer needs a way to determine which IP address belongs to which network. For example, the computer with the network interface 192.168.1.1 in the marketing department needs to know if 192.168.1.129 is in the same network or if it should send packets destined for 192.168.1.129 to the gateway computer for further forwarding tasks. The way it can determine if an IP address belongs to its own subnet is by using a mask called a network mask, or *netmask*.

Before you can create a subnet from a network, you need to understand how to create a netmask. For example, say you want to determine the network mask for the network 192.168.1.0. This address in binary format looks like:

11000000.10101000.00000001.00000000

Because this is a class C address, the network bits are the first 24 bits (3 bytes). To create the mask, you must set these bits to 1s and the remaining (host interface) bits to 0s. So the netmask looks as follows:

11111111.11111111.11111111.00000000

In decimal format, this looks like 255.255.255.0. When creating a netmask, all you need to remember is that the network bits are all 1s and the host bits are all 0s. For example, the netmask for the class A network 10.0.0.0 is 255.0.0.0, and, similarly, the netmask for the class B network 129.1.0.0 is 255.255.0.0.

In a TCP/IP network, when a computer wants to send a packet to an IP address, it determines whether the IP address is local by performing a bitwise AND operation. For example, to determine if 192.168.1.1 is local to a network with subnet mask 255.255.255.0, a host computer does the following:

```
    Binary.                           Decimal
    11000000.10101000.00000001.00000001 => 192.168.1.1
AND 11111111.11111111.11111111.00000000 => 255.255.255.0

    _____

    11000000.10101000.00000001.00000000 => 192.168.1.0
```

As you can see, a bitwise AND operation returns the network address (192.168.1.0) of the IP address 192.168.1.1. Because a host computer knows to what network it belongs, it can very easily determine how to handle packets for such an IP address.

Because you are likely to deal with class C networks a lot, I use this class in all examples in this section.

When a class C network is left in its entirety, the netmask is 255.255.255.0. To divide the network into subnets, you need to create a new netmask. You can do this by setting one or more bits in the host interface part of the default class netmask (255.255.255.0) to 1s. Consider the ongoing example class C network — 192.168.1.0. By setting the most significant bit in the host interface number part of the address to 1, we get the following:

```
11111111.11111111.11111111.10000000 => 255.255.255.128
```

This is a new netmask that splits the class in half. All IP addresses from 192.168.1.0 to 192.168.1.127 belong to the 192.168.1.0 network, and the rest of the IP addresses, 192.168.1.128 to 192.168.1.255, belong to the 192.168.1.128 network. Both networks use the 255.255.255.128 netmask. For example, to determine which network an IP address called 192.168.1.10 belongs to, we can perform the following bitwise AND operation:

```
Binary                                 Decimal
    11000000.10101000.00000001.00001010 => 192.168.1.10
AND 11111111.11111111.11111111.10000000 => 255.255.255.128

    - - - - - - - - - - - - - - - - - - - - - - - - - -

    11000000.10101000.00000001.00000000 => 192.168.1.0
```

As you can see, the netmask 255.255.255.128 tells us that the given IP address belongs to the 192.168.1.0 network. Now see which network an IP address called 192.168.1.200 belongs to:

```
Binary                                 Decimal
    11000000.10101000.00000001.11001000 => 192.168.1.200
AND 11111111.11111111.11111111.10000000 => 255.255.255.128

    - - - - - - - - - - - - - - - - - - - - - - - - - -

    11000000.10101000.00000001.10000000 => 192.168.1.128
```

As you can see again, the same netmask gives us a different network address (192.168.1.128) for the given IP address. Using this netmask, you have effectively separated the 192.168.1.0 networks into two subnets — 192.168.1.0 and 192.168.1.128.

Because a full class C network has 256 possible IP addresses, the separate subnets have 128 IP addresses. However, not all of them are ever usable as host (interface) IP addresses. In a full class C network such as 192.168.1.0 (with netmask 255.255.255.0), we use 192.168.1.0 as the network address and 192.168.1.255 as the broadcast address. We use a broadcast address to communicate with all host computers in the network, so these two addresses are in a sense reserved. Therefore, in a full class C network, you have 254 (255 – network IP address – broadcast IP address) possible IP addresses. Similarly, when a network is subdivided, each subnet gets a network address and a broadcast address; therefore, when a class C network is divided into two subnets, four IP addresses become unusable for host addressing. In our example, this looks like the following:

```
Network: 192.168.1.0
Netmask: 255.255.255.128
First usable host IP address: 192.168.1.1
Last usable host IP address: 192.168.1.126
Broadcast address: 192.168.1.127
```

```
Network: 192.168.1.128
Netmask: 255.255.255.128
First usable host IP address: 192.168.1.129
Last usable host IP address: 192.168.1.254
Broadcast address: 192.168.1.255
```

You might wonder how many subnets you can create out of a full class A, B, or C network. The formula is as follows: number of subnets = $2^{(host\ bits\ -\ 1)}$.

For example, the number of host bits in a class C network is 8 (the last byte), so technically, you can create 2^7 (128) equal-sized subnets from a single class C network. However, because of the loss of IP addresses (as network and broadcast addresses), most network administrators do not make more than 16 subnets out of a class C network.

If you are new to the subnetting concept, you might find the `ipcalc` tool quite useful. For example, say you want to make sure your subnet calculations are as expected. You can use this tool to reassure yourself that your numbers are right. Say you want to confirm that the subnets used in Figure 6-9 are correct. You can supply any IP in the 192.168.1.1–254 range to `ipcalc` along with the subnet mask to determine which network the IP address belongs to. Here are two examples:

```
ipcalc --broadcast --network 192.168.1.1 255.255.255.128
BROADCAST=192.168.1.127
NETWORK=192.168.1.0


ipcalc --broadcast --network 192.168.1.129  255.255.255.128
BROADCAST=192.168.1.255
NETWORK=192.168.1.12
```

In the first example, the `ipcalc` program is told to display the broadcast address (using the --broadcast argument) and the network address (using the --network argument) of an IP address 192.168.1.1 using the 255.255.255.128 netmask. It returns the broadcast address as 192.168.1.127 and the network address as 192.168.1.0. This is correct. In the second example, the program is asked to display the same information for an IP that belongs to the other half of the network, and it displays the correct addresses.

Now that you know a great deal about how to create subnets, take a look at what's involved in creating the example subnets in Figure 6-9.

Gateway computer configuration

The gateway computer in Figure 6-9 must have two network interfaces. One of the interfaces has to be connected to each of the subnets. The /etc/sysconfig/network file for this computer is shown in Listing 6-4.

Listing 6-4 *An example /etc/sysconfig/network file*

```
NETWORKING=yes
FORWARD_IPV4=yes
HOSTNAME=gateway.nitec.com
DOMAINNAME=nitec.com
```

The most important setting here is FORWARD_IPV4=yes, which enables IP forwarding in the kernel.

You must have IP forwarding support built into the kernel. You can use the cat /proc/sys/net/ipv4/ip_forward command to see if IP forwarding is enabled in a running kernel. If the output is 1, then IP forwarding is set; a value of 0 signifies that IP forwarding is off. You can also turn it on or off by pushing a value of 1 or 0 by using the echo *n* > /proc/sys/net/ipv4/ip_ forward command, where *n* is either 1 or 0.

Listings 6-5 and 6-6 show the two interface (eth0 and eth1) files.

Listing 6-5 *An example /etc/sysconfig/network-scripts/ifcfg-eth0 file*

```
DEVICE=eth0
IPADDR=192.168.1.126
NETMASK=255.255.255.128
NETWORK=192.168.1.0
BROADCAST=192.168.1.127
ONBOOT=yes
```

Listing 6-6 *An example /etc/sysconfig/network-scripts/ifcfg-eth1 file*

```
DEVICE=eth1
IPADDR=192.168.1.254
NETMASK=255.255.255.128
NETWORK=192.168.1.128
BROADCAST=192.168.1.255
ONBOOT=yes
```

After you configure these files and the interfaces are up and running (either via a reboot or using the `ifup` command), you need to create two default routes for the two networks by using the following route commands:

```
route add --net 192.168.1.0    255.255.255.128 eth0
route add --net 192.168.1.128 255.255.255.128 eth1
```

Both of the preceding route commands make sure that packets destined for the named network are transmitted via the named interface device.

Host computer configuration

You must configure the host computer on each subnet so that each host computer knows the network address, the local subnet mask, and the gateway information. For example, assuming that all host computers are also Linux workstations and each has a single Ethernet interface device (`eth0`), the `/etc/sysconfig/network` file on any of the host computers on the 192.168.1.0 network will look like the one shown in Listing 6-7.

Listing 6-7 *The /etc/sysconfig/network file*

```
NETWORKING=yes
FORWARD_IPV4=yes
HOSTNAME=marketing-1.nitec.com
DOMAINNAME=nitec.com
GATEWAY=192.168.1.126
GATEWAYDEV=eth0
```

The interface file on this computer looks like the example in Listing 6-8.

Listing 6-8 *The /etc/sysconfig/network-scripts/ifcfg-eth0 file*

```
DEVICE=eth0
IPADDR=192.168.1.1
NETMASK=255.255.255.128
NETWORK=192.168.1.0
BROADCAST=192.168.1.127
ONBOOT=yes
```

In a similar fashion, you need to set up the computers in the 192.168.1.128 network. Each computer in this network includes the GATEWAY=192.168.1.254 line in the /etc/sysconfig/network file and uses NETWORK=192.168.1.128 and BROADCAST=192.168.1. 255 in its /etc/sysconfig/network-scripts/ifcfg-eth0 files.

Of course, if any of these computers are non-Linux systems such as Windows 9*x*/2000 or NT systems, you have to use the appropriate network configuration tool to set these values.

After you have the gateway computer and at least one host set up in each network, you are ready to test the subnets. The easiest way to test subnets is to use the ping program. Following is a simple testing and troubleshooting process.

To remove all DNS-related issues from the testing, I recommend you use only IP addresses during a network test as follows:

1. First, use the ping program to ping a host computer in the same subnet. For example, run ping 192.168.1.2 from the 192.168.1.1 computer. If you do not get ping replies, check the network configuration files (/etc/sysconfig/network and /etc/sysconfig/ network-scripts/ifcfg-eth0). Correct any problems that you notice and restart the interface by first taking it down using the ifconfig eth0 down command and then bringing it up using the /etc/sysconfig/network-scripts/ifup eth0 command. Once you are able to ping a host in the same subnet, proceed to the next step.

2. After you have ensured that you can `ping` a host from another computer in the same subnet for both subnets, `ping` the gateway computer from each subnet. If you cannot perform this operation, check the gateway computer's network configuration files and correct any errors or typos. Once you can `ping` the gateway computer from each subnet, proceed to the next step.

3. Now try to `ping` a host in the other subnet. If you can't `ping` the host in the other subnet, try using the `traceroute IP address` command to determine if the packets are even making it to the gateway machine. If `traceroute` shows that the packets are making it to the gateway but not being forwarded to the destination, the problem is at the gateway. You should ensure that IP forwarding is on. Run `cat /proc/sys/net/ipv4/ip_forward` on the gateway computer to see if the returned value is 1 or 0. If it is not 1, IP forwarding is either off in the `/etc/sysconfig/network` file or not enabled in the kernel. In such a case, fix the problem and retry.

At this point, you should be able to send `ping` requests from any of the two subnets. Once this is true, you have two working subnets.

Part II

Getting Started

In this part of the book you will learn how to manage user accounts, work with files and directory permissions, run and control programs, use the GNOME desktop, and customize your Red Hat Linux kernel.

Chapter 7

Managing Users

Typically, Red Hat Linux systems are used as multiuser servers. There are different types of users: root (or other superusers) and ordinary users. User administration is a big part of managing a Linux system. This chapter introduces you to various tools that allow you to manage both the root user (and other superusers) or ordinary users.

Becoming Root

There are two ways you can log on to a Red Hat Linux system to become root (also known as the *superuser*): you can either log in to the Linux machine as that user or use the su command to change your current (non-root) user ID to root when logged into the Linux system.

When logging in as root, you simply enter **root** as the username and then enter the appropriate password for this account at the log in screen.

For security reasons, it is not a good idea to allow direct root logons via Telnet or other insecure remote access methods. The preferred method is to log on to the system as an ordinary user and then run the su command to become root. Also, you should only become root for tasks that require root privileges.

Using su to become root

Whenever you are logged onto the system as an ordinary user you can run the su command to become another user. For example, running the su *username* command allows you to change your user ID (UID) and group ID (GID) to the account indicated by the username argument. If you are not the root user and you run the su command with a username argument, you will be asked to enter the password for the named account. After you supply the appropriate password you will then become that user.

When the su command is used without a username, the program assumes that you want to become the root user and prompts you for the root account's password. After successfully entering the appropriate password you can become root.

If you run the su command with the – argument, such as su – or su – *username*, than you can even load the user's default shell settings.

Creating multiple superusers

Many novice system administrators think that the root user is the only root or superuser account, but this is not true at all. The username "root" is not what makes an account into a superuser; the user ID and group ID together perform this function. Take a look at the following lines from an example /etc/passwd file:

```
root:dcw12Y6bSUfyo:0:0:root:/root:/bin/tcsh
bin:*:1:1:bin:/bin:
daemon:*:2:2:daemon:/sbin:
kabir:.HoiviYBP4/8U:0:0:Mohammed
sheila:gTwD/qLMFM9M.:501:501::/home/sheila:/bin/tcsh
apache:!!:502:502::/usr/local/apache:/bin/false
```

The `/etc/passwd` file has the following format:

```
username:password:UID:GID:fullname:home-dir:shell
```

In the preceding password file, the UID (user ID) and GID (group ID) fields of the root account are both set to 0. If you look at the line for the otherwise ordinary-looking user `kabir`, you see that his UID and GID are also set to 0. This is what turns a user into a superuser; in other words, any user with a UID and GID of 0 is equivalent to the root user.

As you can see, you can easily turn any ordinary user account into a superuser account. Multiple superuser accounts are sometimes used in organizations that have multiple system administrators working on the same systems to help ensure accountability in a multiadministrator environment. For example, if the `kabir` and root accounts in the password file just described are for two different system administrators, it will then be a bit easier to tell who did what as the superuser by looking at various log files than it would be if the two system administrators were to share the default root account.

In most situations, though, you shouldn't have multiple superuser accounts, because multiple superuser accounts can mean additional security risks. The next section discusses the main risk in using multiple superusers: hackers.

Getting hacked by false superusers

Multiple superuser accounts can be used by people with ill intent to hack into your system. In such a case, the hacker creates a regular user account and then makes that account a superuser account by setting the account's UID and GID values to 0 in the `/etc/passwd` file. This account, which looks just like an ordinary account except for its UID and GID values, allows the hacker to log back in and become a superuser without knowing the root user's password.

Realistically, no system administrator has the time (in the context of a real for-profit organization) to monitor for hackers on a daily basis, so you might want to employ some scripts as your helpers in such a case. For example, the following small script uses a few standard commands to check the `/etc/passwd` file for users with UID and GID values set to 0:

```
/bin/grep '0:0' /etc/passwd | \
awk 'BEGIN {FS=":"} {print $1}' | \
mail -s "`date +"%D %T"`" root
```

If you place this script in `/etc/cron.daily` to run it once a day, you will get an e-mail message from it every day with a list of all users with superuser access. You can check the daily e-mail the `cron` utility sends you to make sure only valid accounts have superuser privileges. Of course, a smart hacker will be able to change the script to feed you fake information. However, most hacking is done by thrill-seekers who just find a hacker program on the Internet, compile it, and run it to get access; these so-called hackers often lack the skills to punch through security measures such as this script that a careful system administrator might have put in place.

Now, just because any user account can be turned into a superuser account doesn't mean a hacker can log on to a Red Hat Linux system without some effort. The Red Hat Linux system by default uses the Pluggable Authentication Module (PAM) for logon authentication, which requires that superuser access be allowed only from terminals that are considered secure. By default, the PAM configuration file for logon, `/etc/pam.d/login`, contains a line such as the following:

```
auth       required      /lib/security/pam_securetty.so
```

This line states that the security restrictions enforced by the `pam_securetty.so` module need to be satisfied before a logon can be permitted. This particular module considers a superuser logon attempt satisfactory only if the logon is being attempted from a TTY (or terminal) listed in the `/etc/securetty` file. So, even if a hacker turns an ordinary user into a superuser and attempts to log on via Telnet (which will use a pseudo-TTY device), they will not be able to log on because in this case Telnet is not considered a secure terminal. If you really want to, you can easily change this by adding the pseudo-TTY devices (typically, `ttyp1` to `ttyp12`) to the `/etc/securetty` file. This is not recommended, however, because it creates a security risk. Instead, if you must use multiple superuser accounts for administrative and accountability reasons, do the following:

1. Create multiple superuser accounts.
2. Create one ordinary user account per superuser.
3. Instruct each superuser to log on to the system as an ordinary user and then change to their superuser account by using the `su` command.

Remember that superusers (UID = 0, GID = 0) have access to everything in the system, and thus these are very sensitive accounts that should only be used when necessary.

Using sudo to perform root tasks by ordinary users

The sudo command enables ordinary users to execute commands that are typically run by a superuser. As an example of how this could be useful, suppose that you are the chief system administrator for your organization and have just been blessed with two new assistant system administrators, to whom you want to delegate some of your routine administrative tasks. While you could create two new superuser accounts with UIDs and GIDs set to 0 for the new administrators, whether you do so or not depends on how confident you are in their ability to be as careful as you are when working as the ultimate user. Because confidence is something that requires a certain amount of time to build, you would probably want to allow these new administrators access only to what they need to have access to. To do this, you need to configure the sudo command, which allows users specified in the /etc/sudoers file to run superuser commands. For example, an ordinary user who is permitted to run superuser commands via sudo can run the following to modify the /etc/passwd file:

```
sudo vi /etc/passwd
```

The sudo program is very configurable, so you can custom-tailor what an ordinary user who is listed in /etc/sudoers can or cannot do. The /etc/sudoers files have the following types of lines:

- **Blank and comment lines (starting with #).** This information is for humans only. The sudo program ignores these lines.

- **Optional host alias lines.** These are used to create short names for the list of hosts. A host alias line must start with the Host_Alias keyword, and the hosts in the list must be separated by commas. For example, in the following line, wormhole and blackhole are two hosts that can be called REDHAT:

```
Host_Alias REDHAT=wormhole,blackhole
```

- **Optional user alias lines.** Used to create short names for the list of users. A user alias line must start with the `User_Alias` keyword, and the users in the list must be separated by commas. For example:

  `User_Alias ASSISTANTS=mike,brian`

- **Optional command alias lines.** Used to create short names for the list of commands. A command alias must start with the following:

  `Cmnd_Alias CMDS=/bin/rm,/bin/chmod,/bin/chown`

- **Optional run-as alias lines.** Used to create short names for the list of users. Such an alias can be used to tell `sudo` to run commands as one of the aliased users. For example:

  `Runas_Alias OP=root,operator`

- **Required user access specification lines.** The syntax for the user access specification is as follows:

  `user host=[run_as_user]  command_list`

  You can specify a real username as *user* or use the `User_Alias` to specify a list. Similarly, you can use a real host name or a `Host_Alias` for *host*. By default, all commands executed via `sudo` are run as root. If you want to run a command using a different user, you can specify the username (or a `Runas_Alias`). You also can specify a command (or a `Cmnd_Alias`); for example, the following command allows user `kabir` to run the `/sbin/shutdown` command on a host called `wormhole`:

  `kabir  wormhole=/sbin/shutdown`

You can insert a ! (exclamation sign) in front of a command or a command alias to deny (or turn off) the command or command alias.

It is possible to define multiple aliases in a single line; for example:

`UserAlias ASSISTANTS=mike,brian:INTERNS=joe,`

`robert,steve`

defines two aliases (ASSISTANTS and INTERNS) in a single line, where the alias definitions are separated by a colon. This same syntax also applies to the other alias types.

Two special keywords exist for sudo: ALL and NOPASSWD. ALL is used to mean "everything," and NOPASSWD is used to state that no password should be required.

Listing 7-1 shows an example /etc/sudoers file.

Listing 7-1 *An example /etc/sudoers file*

```
# sudoers file.
#
# This file MUST be edited with the 'visudo'
# command as root.
#
# See the man page for the details on how to
# write a sudoers file.
#


# Host alias specification

# User alias specification
User_Alias   SENIORADMIN=kabir
User_Alias   ASSISTANTS=mike,john
# User privilege specification

SENIORADMIN ALL=ALL
ASSISTANTS  ALL=ALL
```

This /etc/sudoers file defines two user aliases, SENIORADMIN and ASSISTANTS, where the former has only one user (kabir), and the latter has two users (mike and john). The user privilege specification states the following:

■ The users listed in user alias SENIORADMIN can run sudo on all hosts as root and can run all commands. Because user kabir is the only one in this group, this effectively states that kabir can run all commands via sudo. In other words, the user kabir can do anything the user root can do.

- The second user specification states that users listed in the ASSISTANTS user alias are allowed the exact same access privileges as those in the first specification.

Returning to the first example scenario, where you have two assistants who don't yet need full superuser access, suppose that you (user ID = yourid) want these two users (sysad1, sysad2) to have privileges to run only the shutdown command. In such a case, your /etc/sudoers file might look like the following:

```
# User alias specification
User_Alias   SENIORADMIN=yourid
User_Alias   ASSISTANTS=sysad1,sysad2


# User privilege specification
SENIORADMIN ALL=ALL
ASSISTANTS  ALL=/sbin/shutdown
```

In this same scenario, suppose that after a while you become confident that these two users can handle other superuser privileges in a responsible manner, so you want to give them full access *except* for the privilege to run the su command. The /etc/sudoers file would then look as follows:

```
# User alias specification
User_Alias   SENIORADMIN=yourid
User_Alias   ASSISTANTS=sysad1,sysad2


# User privilege specification
SENIORADMIN ALL=ALL
ASSISTANTS  ALL=ALL,!/bin/su
```

As you can see from the user specifications for the ASSISTANTS, they are allowed to run ALL commands via sudo except for the /bin/su command.

Managing Ordinary Users and Groups

Red Hat Linux comes with a set of command-line and graphical tools that you can use to create, modify, and delete ordinary users. These tools are discussed in the following sections.

This section shows you the traditional way of managing users with various command-line tools. As with any command-line tools you can run these tools via a simple text-based remote shell such as a Telnet or ssh connection.

 Graphical tools require support for the X Window System, as well as a window manager.

Creating a new user account

Creating a new user account is quite easy from the command line: simply run the `useradd` command. For example, to create a user called `newuser`, run the following command:

```
useradd newuser
```

where *newuser* is the name of the user you want to add. This adds a new entry for user `newuser` in the `/etc/passwd` file (and in `/etc/shadow` if you use shadow passwords) using system defaults. After running the preceding command on a Red Hat Linux system, for example, the `/etc/passwd` file shows a new line like the following:

```
newuser:!!:506:506::/home/newuser:/bin/bash
```

If you remember the `/etc/passwd` fields from the earlier discussion (see the Note icon in the "Creating multiple superusers" section earlier in this chapter), you will see that the password (second) field is set to `!!`. This means that this password is not set and *newuser* cannot log on yet. So, you need to create a password for this user by running the `passwd` command as follows:

```
passwd newuser
```

You are asked to enter the password twice. After your password is accepted, it is encrypted and added to the user's entry in the `/etc/shadow` file.

The UID and the GID values will be selected automatically by `useradd`. Basically, `useradd` just increments the last UID in `/etc/passwd` by 1 and the last GID in `/etc/group` by 1 to create the UID and GID, respectively, for the new user. You can also set the UID and the GID manually by using the command-line switches `-u` and `-g`, respectively. The home directory for *newuser* is created in the default top-level home directory (usually /home) and the login shell is similarly selected from a system default. The processes for changing these defaults once the account has been created are explained in the "Modifying an existing user account" section later in this chapter.

Run the man useradd command to learn more about the available, not so frequently used command-line options.

If you want to override a system default while creating the account, specify a command-line option. To override the default home directory, you use the -d   new_directory option (where new_directory is the name of your directory). For example, the following command creates a new user (called *newuser*) and sets the user's home directory to /www/ *newuser*:

```
useradd newuser -d /www/newuser
```

useradd will create only the final directory, not the entire path. For example, if you specify -d /some/new/dir/ myuser as the option, useradd will create myuser only if /some/new/dir/ already exists.

When the new home directory is created, files contained in the /etc/skel directory are copied to the new home directory. These files are typically the dot configuration files for the default shell. For example, if the default shell is /bin/bash, you should have default versions of .bashrc, .bash_profile, and .bash_login in the /etc/skel directory so that the new user's home directory can be automatically set up with these files.

The useradd utility that comes with Red Hat Linux creates a private group for the user with the same name as the username. For example, if you run useradd kabir, then a new user named kabir is created in the /etc/passwd file and a new group called kabir is created in the /etc/group file. This method allows the new user to be totally isolated from other users and therefore ensures greater privacy for the user. Whenever the new user creates a new file, by virtue of this private group, the file is accessible only by the new user. The user has to change the file permissions explicitly to allow someone else to see the file.

However, if your user account philosophy clashes with this kind of private group idea, you can override it by using the -g *group* option (where *group* is the name of your group). For example, the following command forces useradd to create the user kabir with the default group set to the users group:

```
useradd kabir -g users
```

> **TIP**
>
> You can use the groups *username* command to find out which user belongs to what group.

If you want to make the new user a member of additional groups on your system, use the -G comma-separated list of groups option. For example, the following command adds the user kabir to the wheel and admins groups in the /etc/group file:

```
useradd kabir -G wheel,admins
```

Creating a new group

To create a new group, use the groupadd command. For example, the following command adds a new group called mygroup in the /etc/group file (and in the /etc/gshadow file if you are using shadow passwords):

```
groupadd mygroup
```

By default, the groupadd program creates the group with a GID above 499, because 0 through 499 are (sort of) reserved for system-level accounts such as root, bin, and mail. So if your /etc/group file has the last group GID set to 511, the new group you create with this program will have a GID of 512, and so on. If you want to set the GID of your new group specifically, use the -g *GID* option. Also, if you want to create a group with a GID in the 0 to 499 range, use the -r option with the -g *GID* option to force groupadd to create the new group as a system group. Note that if the group or GID you are trying to use with the program is already in use in /etc/group, you will get an error message and the command will fail.

Modifying an existing user account

Dealing with forgotten user passwords is the most common task a system administrator performs. This section explains how to change various details of a user account.

Changing a password

To change or set a user's password, use the `passwd` command. For example, the following enables you to change user `kabir`'s password:

        passwd kabir

You are then asked to enter the password twice to confirm it.

 Choose good passwords for your users, or train them to choose good passwords for themselves. Do not use simple-to-remember passwords that use common dictionary words.

The `passwd` program can also be run by a user to change his or her own password. When ordinary users run the `passwd` program, no username argument is required, because the program allows them to change only their own passwords.

Changing the shell

If the default shell is not appropriate for a user, you may change it to any shell you list in `/etc/shells`. Use the `chsh` command to change a user's shell. For example, the following command enables you to change user `brian`'s current shell:

chsh brian

You will be asked to prodive the new shell path. If you specify any shell or program name that is not in `/etc/shells`, the user will not be able to log in. Note that users can change their own shell by using this command. Ordinary users do not need to specify the username as an argument, because the only shells they can change are their own.

 You can also use the `usermod` command to modify the shell information, as follows:

usermod -s *new_shell_path* *username*

where *new_shell_path* and *username* are the correct values.

Changing the home directory

To change the home directory of an existing user, run the usermod command as follows, where *new_home_directory* and *username* are the correct values:

```
usermod -d new_home_directory username
```

For example, if a user called keller has /home/keller as her home directory, and you want to move it to /home2/keller, you would run the usermod command as follows:

```
usermod -d /home2/keller keller
```

This sets the new directory as keller's home directory.

If you want to move the contents of a user's existing home directory to the new location, use the -m option. For user keller, the command would be as follows:

```
usermod -d -m /home2/keller keller
```

Changing a UID

To change the UID of a user, run the usermod command as follows, where *UID* and *username* are the correct values:

```
usermod -u UID username
```

For example, the following command changes the UID for user mrfrog to 500:

```
usermod -g 500 mrfrog
```

All the files and directories owned by the user within mrfrog's home directory will automatically reflect the UID change. However, if the user owns files outside her own home directory, you will have to manually change the ownership using the chown command.

Changing a default group

To change a user's default group, run the usermod command as follows, where *group_name_or_GID* and *username* are the correct values:

```
usermod -g group_name_or_GID username
```

For example, the following changes the default group for user `mrfrog` to 777:

```
usermod -g 777 myfrog
```

Changing an account expiration date

If you are using shadow passwords, you can change the expiration date of a user account using the `usermod` command as follows:

```
usermod -e MM/DD/YY username
```

where `MM/DD/YY` and `username` are the correct values.

For example, the following resets the account expiration date for user `kabir` to 12/31/99:

```
usermod -e 12/31/99 kabir
```

Changing finger information

If you allow your users to use the `finger` program to locate one another or to run a `finger` daemon for people outside to finger your user accounts, you can also change the `finger` information, such as the full name and phone numbers. Run the `chfn` command to change a user's finger information. For example, the following allows you to change user `jennifer`'s finger information, which is stored in the `/etc/passwd` file:

```
chfn jennifer
```

A user can change his or her own `finger` information by using this program, as well. A user can also create a text file called `.plan` file in their home directory that will be appended to the information shown by the `finger` program.

Modifying an existing group

To modify an existing group name or GID, use the `groupmod` command. To rename a group to a new name, use the following syntax:

```
groupmod -n new_group_name current_group_name
```

For example, the following renames the existing `novices` group to `experts`:

```
groupmod -n experts novices
```

To change the GID, use the -g *new_GID* option. For example, the following changes the current GID of the troublemakers group to 665:

```
groupmod -g 665 troublemakers
```

Deleting or disabling a user account

To delete an existing user, use the userdel command. For example, the following deletes the user called snake:

```
userdel snake
```

If you want to remove the user's home directory and all of its contents, use the -r option. Note that userdel will not delete anything if the user is currently logged on. Ask the user to log out by sending her a write message (write *username*), and if asking isn't an option, use the killall *username* command to terminate all processes associated with the user, and then run the userdel command.

If you want to temporarily disable a user account, you can do one of the following:

- Use the usermod -s *new_shell username* command to change the shell to /bin/false (make sure the new shell is listed in the /etc/shells file). This disallows the user from logging on to the system. Edit the /etc/shells file to add the new shell in a new line in that file.

- If you are using the shadow passwords, use the usermod -e *MM/DD/YY username* command to cause the user account to expire. You can later go back and extend the expiration date to re-enable the account.

If you want to disable all user account access temporarily, you can create a file called /etc/nologin with a message explaining why you are not allowing access. The login program will not allow any nonroot account to log on to the system as long as this file is in place.

If you administer the server via Telnet or any other remote means, such as secure shell (ssh) access, do not create /etc/nologin, because you will not be able to log on to your system. This is because, by default, root or other superuser accounts are not allowed to log on directly from a nonsecured TTY (that is, any TTY not specified in /etc/securetty), so you can't log on as an ordinary user first and then su to a privileged user account.

Creating default user settings

The default settings for creating new users using useradd come from /etc/default/useradd. An example of this file is shown in Listing 7-2.

Listing 7-2 *An example /etc/default/useradd file*

```
# useradd defaults file
GROUP=100
HOME=/home
INACTIVE=-1
EXPIRE=
SHELL=/bin/bash
SKEL=/etc/skel
```

The following are explanations of the entries in this file:

- **GROUP=100.** Specifies that the default GID is 100. This value is used only when you disable (using the -n option) the default private group (the group with the same name as the new user). You can specify a group name instead of the numeric value, as well. The value you specify in this line must exist in /etc/group. You can change this value as follows, where *new_group_name* and *GID* are the proper values:

  useradd -D -g new_group_name or GID

- **HOME=/home.** Specifies the default top-level home directory for new users. For example, when you create a new user called joe, the default home directory is /home/joe. You can change this setup to fit your needs. Make sure that the directory already exists. You can change this value with the following command:

  useradd -D -d *directory*

- **INACTIVE=-1.** Specifies when (in days) the account will become inactive after the password expires. This is useful only if you are using shadow passwords. The default value of -1 states that accounts are never inactive. You can change this value as follows:

```
useradd -D -f number_of_days
```

■ **EXPIRE=.** Specifies when an account should be disabled. This is useful only if you are using shadow passwords. By default, accounts never become disabled. You can change this value as follows:

```
useradd -D -e MM/DD/YY
```

The defaults used in creating new users come from the /etc/login.def file. (Listing 7-3 shows an example of this file.)

■ **SHELL=/bin/bash.** Specifies the default login shell path. You can change this value as follows:

```
useradd -D -s /bin/tcsh
```

Note that the useradd program does not check whether the path you specify is a valid shell, or even whether it exists. So, make sure that the path you specify is a valid shell and listed in /etc/shells file.

■ **SKEL=/etc/skel.** Specifies the directory where various user configuration files are kept, such as dot files for shells, the X Window System, and so forth. The files in this directory are copied to the new home directory of a new user account. Normally, you do not want to change this path to some other directory. On the other hand, if you do want to change it, you have to modify the /etc/default/useradd file by using a text editor, or simply create a symbolic link /etc/skel that points to the desired directory.

If you are using shadow passwords, another default configuration file called /etc/login.defs is used in creating user accounts. Listing 7-3 shows an example of this file.

Listing 7-3 *An example /etc/login.defs file*

```
# *REQUIRED*
#    Directory where mailboxes reside, _or_ name
#    of file, relative to the home directory.
#    If you _do_ define both, MAIL_DIR takes precedence.
#    QMAIL_DIR is for Qmail
#
```

Continued

Listing 7-3 *Continued*

```
#QMAIL_DIR   Maildir
MAIL_DIR  /var/spool/mail

#MAIL_FILE    .mail
# Password aging controls:
#
#  PASS_MAX_DAYS  Maximum number of days a
#                 password may be used.
#
#  PASS_MIN_DAYS  Minimum number of days allowed
#                 between password changes.
#
#  PASS_MIN_LEN   Minimum acceptable password length.
#
#  PASS_WARN_AGE  Number of days warning given before
#                 a password expires.
#
PASS_MAX_DAYS  99999
PASS_MIN_DAYS  0
PASS_MIN_LEN   5
PASS_WARN_AGE  7

#
# Min/max values for automatic uid
# selection in useradd
#
UID_MIN  500
UID_MAX  60000

#
# Min/max values for automatic gid
# selection in groupadd
#
GID_MIN  500
GID_MAX  60000
```

```
#
# Require password before chfn/chsh can make
# any changes.
#
CHFN_AUTH   yes


#
# Don't allow users to change their "real name"
# using chfn.
#
CHFN_RESTRICT   yes


#
# If defined, this command is run when removing a user.
# It should remove any at/cron/print jobs etc. Owned by
# the user to be removed (passed as the first argument).
#
#USERDEL_CMD   /usr/sbin/userdel_local


#
# If useradd should create home directories for
# users by default on RH systems, we do. This option is
# ORed with the -m flag on useradd command line.
#
CREATE_HOME   yes
```

Because the comments in this file are sufficient to explain the configuration details, they are not discussed any further here.

Saving Disk Space with Disk Quotas

Disk space on a multiuser system can be quite a scarce resource. My experience has been that as soon as you plug in a new drive with lots of space, users tend to use it up quite rapidly. So, the more space you add, the more space you need! The best way to ensure that you have enough disk space for your system is to enforce disk quotas. The following sections explain how.

Installing disk quota software

The official Red Hat CD-ROM comes with quota software. For example, to install the quota software for an Intel-compatible *x*86 machine, run the following command from the CD-ROM's /RedHat/RPMS directory:

```
rpm -ivh quota-version.i386.rpm
```

After the quota software is installed, you are ready to configure it. If you do not have the official Red Hat CD-ROM, you can download the quota software RPM from an RPM Web site such as www.rpmfind.net.

Configuring your system to support disk quotas

To configure your system for disk quotas, first decide which partitions you want to bring under disk quotas. Typically, these are the partition(s) for user home directories and Web space. You also must decide whether you want to enforce quotas per user, per group, or both. This discussion assumes that you want to enable disk quotas for the /home and /www partitions and that you want to enforce only the per-user disk quota for the /home partition and the per-group disk quota for the /www partition. It also assumes that you have an /etc/fstab file that looks like the following:

```
/dev/sda1    /home  ext2    defaults  1 2
/dev/sda5    /www   ext2    defaults  1 2
```

To enforce user-level disk quotas on /home, modify the first line as follows:

```
/dev/sda1    /home  ext2    defaults,usrquota  1 2
```

The new option in the mount option field in the preceding line is needed to enable disk quotas for users. Similarly, to enable group-level disk quotas on /www, modify the second fstab line as follows:

```
/dev/sda5    /www   ext2    defaults,grpquota  1 2
```

TIP

You can also use both usrquota and grpquota for a single partition if you plan to enforce quotas for both users and groups.

After you complete these modifications, add the following lines in the /etc/rc.d/rc.local script:

```
# Check quota and then turn quota on.
if [ -x /sbin/quotacheck ]; then
      echo "Checking quotas. This may take some time..."
      sbin/quotacheck -avug
      echo " Done."
   fi
if [ -x /sbin/quotaon ]; then
      echo "Enabling disk quota .."
      /sbin/quotaon -avug
      echo " Done."
   fi
```

When this script is run after the file systems have been loaded, it enables quota checking and then turns on the disk quota feature.

Next, you need to create quota files for each file system you have placed under quota control. You create the quota files as follows:

```
touch /home/quota.user
touch /www/quota.group
```

 Make sure that these two files have read and write permissions for the root user only.

Now you have completed the system-level quota configuration; before you continue with the quota assignments for users and groups as described in the next section, reboot the system. This will run the quotacheck program, which creates disk usage information in the quota files.

Assigning disk quotas to users and/or groups

After you reboot the system with the new quota configuration, you are ready to assign disk quotas for each user. To assign disk quotas per user, use the edquota command. For example, to allocate a disk quota for a user named kabir, run edquota as follows:

```
edquota -u kabir
```

This brings up the default text editor (such as vi or whatever editor is set in the $EDITOR environment variable) with contents similar to the following:

```
Quotas for user kabir:
/dev/sda5: blocks in use: 0, limits (soft = 0, hard = 0)
           inodes in use: 0, limits (soft = 0, hard = 0)
```

Here, the user kabir has so far used 0 blocks (in K) on disk partition /dev/sda5 (under usrquota control), and the limits (soft or hard) are not set yet. Similarly, this user has not yet owned any files (inodes), and no limit (soft or hard) has been set yet.

As you can see, you can simultaneously set limits for the amount of space (in blocks) a user can consume and control how many files can be owned by the user. The soft limit specifies the maximum amount of disk space (blocks) or files (inodes) a user can have on the file system. The hard limit is the absolute amount of disk space (in blocks) or files (inodes) a user can have.

For example, suppose you want to allow user kabir to have a soft limit of 1MB (1,024K) and a hard limit of 4MB (4,096K) for disk space. Also, suppose that you want to allow this user a soft limit of 128 files/directories (inodes) and a hard limit of 512 files/directories. Set the quota limit using edquota -u kabir as follows:

```
Quotas for user kabir:
/dev/sda5: blocks in use: 0, limits (soft = 1024, hard = 4096)
           inodes in use: 0, limits (soft = 128, hard = 512)
```

After you save the configuration, the user can no longer exceed the hard limits. If the user tries to go over any of these two (disk space and inode count) limits, an error message will be displayed. For example, in the following, user kabir tries to create a new directory in /home, but the quota limit for this quota has been exceeded, so the error message is displayed:

```
[kabir@picaso /home]$ mkdir eat_space
mkdir: cannot make directory `eat_space': Disc quota exceeded
```

If you have many users to assign quotas to, the preceding method could be quite time-consuming. To aid you in such a situation, the edquota program includes a -p *prototype user* option that allows you to copy the prototype user's disk quota configuration for others. For example, suppose you want to use the quota configuration you just created for user kabir to set the identical configuration for three other users (sheila, jennifer, and mrfrog). To do so, run the following command:

```
edquota -p kabir  -u sheila jennifer mrfrog
```

Now, all three of these users have the same quota configuration as user kabir.

Placing groups under disk quota control is very similar to the process for users. The edquota syntax for configuring group quota requirements is as follows:

```
edquota -g group_name
```

To enforce the soft limit for either user or group quotas, you need to configure the grace period by using the edquota -t command. When you run this command, your editor will display output similar to the following:

```
Time units may be: days, hours, minutes, or seconds
Grace period before enforcing soft limits for users:
/dev/sda5: block grace period: 0 days, file grace period: 0 days
```

You can specify the grace period in days, hours, minutes, or even seconds. For example, in the following, the grace period for the disk space limit (in blocks) is 7 days, and the grace period for the number of files (inodes) is only 5 hours:

```
Time units may be: days, hours, minutes, or seconds
Grace period before enforcing soft limits for users:
/dev/sda5: block grace period: 7 days, file grace period: 5 hours
```

Monitoring disk usage

To find out how much of your disk space a particular user is using, run the quota command with the -u option (u meaning user). The quota command's syntax is as follows:

```
quota -u username
```

The following example shows the command and resulting output for a quota check on user kabir:

```
quota -u kabir
Disk quotas for user kabir (uid 500):
Filesystem blocks quota limit grace files quota limit    grace
/dev/sda5  0      1024  4096         1     128   512
```

You can run the same command to monitor disk usage of a group by using the -g (g for "group") option as follows:

```
quota -g group
```

When you find users or groups that are over the limit, you can work with them (perhaps by e-mail) to ensure that disk usage is brought down to acceptable limits.

Chapter 8

Working with Files and Directories

IN THIS CHAPTER

- Understanding the Linux File Hierarchy Structure
- Accessing files and directories
- Setting file and directory permissions

When you work on a computer, you work with files. Some of these files are executable programs, some are data files needed by the programs, and some files are storage for the data that the user creates. Files and directories are the most commonly used objects within a computer. In Linux, these objects can be manipulated only by those who have privileges to do so. Therefore, it is very important to understand the way files and directories work under Linux. In this chapter I discuss working with the Linux file system, as well as how to control access to who has what on a network: permissions.

Understanding the Linux File Hierarchy Structure

A file structure refers to a schema that defines where files are stored. Red Hat Linux complies with the File Hierarchy Structure (FHS) standard developed by the FHS Group. The FHS standard is maintained in a collaborative document that mandates the standard names and locations of many files and directories of an operating system such as Red Hat Linux. The benefit of the FHS standard lies in compatibility with other FHS-compliant systems. For example, if a software developer wishes to support both Red Hat Linux and another FHS compliant Linux distribution, he or she can simply make the installation program use a standard directory for installing the software. This makes life easier for both developers and users of the software. The details of the FHS standard are available at **www. pathname.com/fhs**.

The top directories of a FHS system are shown in Table 8-1.

Table 8-1 *Top Directories of an FHS System*

Directory	Purpose
/	The root directory.
/bin	Contains essential command binaries.
/boot	Contains boot loader files.
/dev	Contains device files.
/etc	Contains system configuration files.
/lib	Contains kernel modules and shared library files.
/mnt	Usually used for storing mount point directories for removable media such as CD-ROM, floppy drive, etc.
/opt	Contains third-party applications.
/sbin	Contains system binaries.
/tmp	Temporary space for all users.
/usr	This is a separate directory structure of its own. It is discussed in Table 8-2.
/var	Variable data space used by programs to store logs, spools, etc.

The /usr directory structure is very important because it is (usually) available throughout the entire file system for all users. The /usr directory structure is shown in Table 8-2.

Table 8-2 *The /usr Directory Structure*

Directory	What's in It
/usr/bin	User executable programs are kept here.
/usr/doc	Miscellaneous. documentation for /usr/bin programs.
/usr/etc	Configuration files for programs in /usr/bin.
/usr/games	Silly games.
/usr/include	C header (include) files that are needed to compile other software.
/usr/kerberos	Kerberos authentication related binaries and other files.
/usr/lib	Library files that are required by many programs.
/usr/libexec	Small programs that are needed by many programs.
/usr/local	This directory is a hierarchy of its own. It is dedicated to locally compiled or developed programs. Usually it has the following subdirectories: /bin (for binaries), /doc (for documentation), /etc (for configuration), /lib (for library files), /src (for source code).
/usr/man	Online manual pages for many programs.
/usr/sbin	System administration programs.
/usr/share	Shared documentation and other files that are not architecture specific.
/usr/src	Source code for many programs in the /usr hierarchy.
/usr/X11R6	X Window System-specific files and directories.

Accessing Files and Directories

This section shows you how to work with a few commonly used file and directory commands that are available on your Red Hat Linux system. You can access these commands from a shell prompt or an xterm session if you're using a GUI.

Changing directories with cd

The cd command is really a built-in shell command. To use the cd command, simply run the command as follows, where *directory* is the name of the directory you want to change to:

```
cd directory
```

Note that if the directory you want to change to is not a subdirectory of your current working directory, you'll need to specify the full path to the directory. One exception to this is the cd .. command, which moves you up one directory.

> **TIP**
>
> If you don't provide a directory name as an argument, the cd command returns you to the home directory of the user account you are currently using. Any time you are in doubt about where you are in the file system, use the pwd command, which displays your current directory name.

Listing files in a directory with ls

The ls program probably is the most widely used program on any Unix or Unix-like platform. ls is often used as a standalone command, with no options. However, you can customize the output of the ls command easily by using options. The most common options for ls are listed in Table 8-3.

Table 8-3 *Commonly Used ls Options*

Option	Purpose
-l	Long listing which shows the file permissions, last modification date and time, owner name, group name, etc.
-a	All files including filenames that start with a period (these are often called hidden dot files)
-1	Single-column, filenames-only listing
-R	Recursive listing

Creating new directories with mkdir

Use the mkdir command to create new directories. The syntax of the mkdir command is mkdir *new_directory_name*. For example, to create a new directory called newsoftware, run the following command:

```
mkdir /newsoftware
```

If you want to create a directory path such as /dir1/dir2/dir3 in a single command, run a command like the following (replacing the names of the directories with your own):

```
mkdir -p /dir1/dir2/dir3
```

This creates all the three directories if they do not exist already.

Finding files and directories

You can use various commands to locate a file. The following sections briefly discuss the more popular file-locating commands: which, locate, and find.

Locating the path of a program with which

To locate the exact path of a program, use the which command. For example, the following command shows you the fully qualified path name of the httpd program if it is available in a directory that is included in the $PATH environment variable:

```
which httpd
```

Some shells have a built-in which command, and others use /usr/sbin/which instead.

Locating a file or directory with locate

You can locate a file or directory with a partial or full name using the locate program. For example, the following command queries the updatedb filename database and returns all occurrences of the netpr.pl file:

```
locate netpr.pl
```

For locate to work properly, you must have a cron job set up to run updatedb on a daily basis so that the database is up to date when you query it. The default Red Hat installation sets up such a job automatically.

Finding a file or directory with find

You can also use the find program to locate files or directories. For example, to locate all of the HTML files in the current directory and all of its subdirectories, run find as follows:

```
find . -type f -name "*.html"
```

Accessing common removable devices

Files and directories that are stored in removable media such as CD-ROM or floppy drives can only be accessed after the device is mounted by the operating system. In this section I show you how to mount common devices such as CD-ROM or floppy drives and access their contents.

Mounting a CD-ROM from the command line

Mounting a CD-ROM is quite simple. If you are working in a text mode environment (i.e., using a remote shell or console) you can do the following to mount a CD-ROM:

1. Insert a CD-ROM in the CD-ROM drive.

2. As root, run the mount /mnt/cdrom command to mount the CD-ROM. You should now be able to access the inserted CD-ROM from the /mnt/cdrom directory.

The mount /mnt/cdrom command should work by default because Red Hat Linux comes with the following configuration line in the /etc/fstab file to mount CD-ROMs by using the above command.

```
/dev/cdrom /mnt/cdrom iso9660 noauto,owner,kudzu,ro 0 0
```

In case this command does not work for you, you can use mount -t iso9660 /mnt/cdrom /dev/cdrom command instead.

3. When you need to eject the CD-ROM, you should unmount it using `umount /mnt/cdrom` command and then run the `eject /mnt/cdrom` command to eject it.

Mounting a CD-ROM from a graphical environment

If you're using the X Window System, you should be able to access the CD-ROM after you have inserted it in the CD-ROM drive. Click the CD-ROM icon on the desktop to access the contents. You can eject the CD-ROM at any time by right-clicking the CD-ROM icon and selecting the Eject device option, which will automatically unmount the CD-ROM.

If X does not automatically mount your CD-ROM (like when you are root) when inserted in the drive, you need to do the following:

1. Run the GNOME Control Center program by clicking the tool box icon on the Panel or by clicking the Main Menu button and choosing Programs ⇨ Settings ⇨ GNOME Control Center and then choosing Peripherals ⇨ CD Properties from the left-hand tree menu.

2. Select the Automatically Mount CD When Inserted option under the Data CDs section.

TIP
If you wish to mount a CD-ROM only when needed, you can disable the automatic mount option and simply right-click the CD-ROM icon on the desktop to mount it by choosing the Mount Device option.

3. Select the Run Command When CD is Inserted option under the Audio CDs section if you wish to play your audio CDs automatically. You can also specify an audio CD player command in the command-line entry box if you want, although the default `gtcd` player works quite well.

Mounting a floppy disk

Mounting a floppy disk is quite simple. If you're running a remote shell or terminal window, insert the floppy disk and run the `mount /mnt/floppy` command to mount it. You should be able to access the floppy from the /mnt/floppy directory. If you're using the X Window System and are utilizing a graphical environment such as GNOME, simply insert the disk into the disk drive and double-click the floppy disk icon to view the contents of the floppy disk.

Determining a file's type with file

Unlike Windows, Linux does not rely on file extensions to determine file types. In Linux, you use the file command to determine a file's type. For example, the following command shows what type of file /usr/bin/file (itself) is:

```
file /usr/bin/file
```

Here is an example of the output of this command:

```
/usr/bin/file: ELF 32-bit LSB executable, Intel 80386, \
version 1, dynamically linked, not stripped
```

Viewing the access statistics of a file or directory with stat

You can use the stat command to get statistics on a file or directory. The syntax for the stat command is stat *file_or_directory_path*. For example, the following command shows statistics on the /tmp directory:

```
stat /tmp
```

Here is an example of its output:

```
File: "/tmp"
  Size: 2048    Filetype: Directory
  Mode: (1777/drwxrwxrwt)    Uid: ( 0/ root) Gid: ( 0/ root)
Device: 3,0  Inode: 16321   Links: 22
Access: Sun Feb  7 02:00:35 1999(00000.00:01:11)
Modify: Sun Feb  7 02:01:01 1999(00000.00:00:45)
Change: Sun Feb  7 02:01:01 1999(00000.00:00:45)
```

Copying files and directories with cp

Use the cp command to copy files from one location to another. For example, the following command copies a file called important.txt from the /some directory to the /new/place directory:

```
cp /some/important.txt /new/place/
```

TIP

You can also specify a new destination filename, if necessary, by adding a new filename to the end of the destination path in the command.

To copy a file to a location where another file exists with the same name, you can force cp to copy over the existing file with the -f option. For example, the following command copies the important.txt file even if a file by that name is already in the /new/place directory:

```
cp  -f /some/important.txt /new/place/
```

To copy a directory along with all of its files and subdirectories, use the -r option to copy the directory recursively. The syntax of the command is cp -r *source_directory destination_directory*. For example, the following command copies the /tmp/foo directory along with the contents of the directory itself and all of its subdirectories to the /zoo/foo directory:

```
cp -r /tmp/foo /zoo/foo
```

Moving files and directories with mv

To move files or directories, use the mv command. The syntax for mv is mv *original_path new_path*. For example, the following command moves /file1 to /tmp/file2:

```
mv /file1 /tmp/file2
```

Similarly, you can move a directory recursively along with all of its contents. To do this, use cp with the -r option to copy the directory to the new file system, and then remove the directory (see the next section) from the current location.

mv does not move directories across different file systems. When you need to move a directory from one file system to another, copy the directory by using the cp command with -r flag, as discussed above, and then you can remove the old directory using the rm command, as discussed below.

Deleting files and directories with rm

To delete a file or directory, use the rm command. The syntax for the rm command is rm *file_or_directory_name*. For example, the following removes a file called letter.txt:

```
rm letter.txt
```

To remove a directory's contents recursively, you need to specify the -r option. You can use the -f option to force a removal. For example, the following command removes all the files and subdirectories within the specified directory:

```
rm -rf directory
```

 You may set an alias called rm as follows:

```
alias rm rm -i
```

In such a case, the -i option tells the command to prompt you before actually deleting anything.

Working with Permissions

Permissions allow for security on multiuser systems. In this section I discuss the basics of permissions and some of the common tools with which you can change permissions. I also give you a few sample permission policies that you can either use as-is or customize as you require.

Understanding file and directory permissions

Linux associates a file or directory with a user and a group, just as all other Unix and Unix-like operating systems do. The term *permissions* refers to the aspects of a file that determine who has access to read it, write to it, and execute it (for executable files).

By default, the permissions of the file belong to the file's owner. When a new file is created, the file owner is the file creator, and the group is the owner's default group. In Red Hat Linux, when a user creates a file or directory, its group is also set as the default group of the user, which happens to be a private group with the same name as the user.

As a regular user, you cannot reassign a file's or a directory's ownership to someone else. For example, I cannot create a file as user `kabir` and reassign its ownership to a user called `sheila`. The reason for this strict permission structure is security. If a regular user were allowed to reassign file ownership to others, someone could create a nasty program that deleted files, change the program's ownership to the superuser, and then wipe out the entire file system. So, only a superuser (such as the root user) can reassign file or directory ownership.

You can check the permissions of a file or directory with the `ls -l` command. For example, to check the permissions for the `milkyweb.txt` file you would use the `ls -l milkyweb.txt` command. For example, if user `sheila` logs into a Red Hat Linux system and uses the `ls -l milkyweb.txt` command, the following output (or similar) appears:

```
-rw-rw-r--  1 sheila   intranet    512 Feb 6 21:11 milkyweb.txt
```

You can see the following from the preceding output:

- The `milkyweb.txt` file is owned by a user called `sheila`.
- As the file's owner, `sheila` is the only regular user who can change the access permissions of this file. The only other user who can change the permissions is the superuser.
- The group for this file is `intranet`.
- Any user who belongs to the `intranet` group can access (that is, read, write, or execute) the file based on what current group permission is set (by the owner).

Check out how Table 8-4 breaks down the output above piece by piece.

Table 8-4 *Output of an Example ls -l Command*

ls Output	Information Type
-rw-rw-r--	File access permissions
1	Number of links
sheila	User (file owner)
intranet	Group
512	File size (in bytes)
Feb 6	Last modification date
21:11	Last modification time

Managing file and directory permissions

The following sections show you how to use some of the more common command line tools to easily manage permissions.

Changing file or directory ownership

As root (or as another superuser), you can change the ownership of a file or directory by using the chown command. To change the ownership of a file or directory, run the command as follows:

```
chown newuser file_or_directory
```

For example, the following command makes user sheila the new owner of the file kabirs_plans.txt

```
chown sheila kabirs_plans.txt
```

As root (or another superuser), you can change the group for a file or directory with the chown command at the same time as you change the ownership of the file or directory, as follows:

```
chown newuser.newgroup file_or_directory_name
```

For example, the following not only makes sheila the new owner but also resets the group of the file to be admin:

```
chown sheila.admin kabirs_plans.txt
```

To change the user and/or group ownership of all the files or directories under a given directory, a superuser (such as root) can use the -R option to run the chown command in recursive mode. For example, the following command changes the user and group ownership of the /home/kabir/plans directory and all the files and subdirectories within it:

```
chown -R sheila.admin /home/kabir/plans/
```

Changing group ownership of file or directory

Although you have to be the superuser to change the ownership of a file, you can still change a file's or directory's group as a regular user by using the chgrp command. The chgrp command lets you change the owner of a file or directory as long as you are also part of the new group.

In other words, you can change groups only if you belong to both the old and new groups or if you are a superuser. For example, if you run the following command to change the group for all the HTML files in a directory, you must also be part of the httpd group:

```
chgrp httpd *.html
```

You can find out what groups you belong to by using the groups command without any argument.

 Like the chown command, chgrp also uses -R to recursively change group names of one or more files or directories.

Using octal numbers to set permissions

Although using octal numbers is my favorite method for setting file or directory permissions, I must warn you that it involves 1s and 0s. If you feel you are mathematically challenged, skip to the next section, which explains how to set the same permissions using a much simpler access string.

Although the octal-number-based permissions may seem a bit hard at the beginning, with practice, their use can become second nature.

The *octal number system* uses eight digits as opposed to the commonly used ten digits of the decimal system. The octal digits are 0 through 7, and each digit can be represented by 3 bits (in binary system). Table 8-5 shows the binary equivalent for each octal digit.

Table 8-5 *Octal to Binary Conversion*

Octal	Binary
0	000
1	001
2	010
3	011
4	100
5	101
6	110
7	111

After you determine the permissions that you need, to construct each octal digit, you can use the numbers in Table 8-6.

Table 8-6 *Octal Numbers*

Octal Number	What It Represents
1	Execute permissions. A user with this permission can execute the file, if it's executable. The su command, for example, typically only has executable permissions for the root user, because su allows a regular user to become root, which is a dangerous capability.
2	Write permissions. A user with write permissions can write to, that is alter, the file and save it. Without these permissions, the user cannot change the file in any way.
4	Read permissions. A user with read permissions can do just that: read the file. Without also having write or executable permissions, the user can do nothing more than read the file.

Octal Number	What It Represents
3, 5, 6, 7	Combinations of permissions. For example, the number 3 grants executable plus write permissions (1 + 2), 5 grants execute and read permissions (1 + 4), 6 grants read and write permissions (4 + 2), and 7 grants read, write, and executable permissions (4 + 2 + 1).

Octal permission values are based on numbers containing four octal digits. Figure 8-1 shows how you can visualize the permissions as four octal digits. Here, the first octal digit is the leftmost or most significant one.

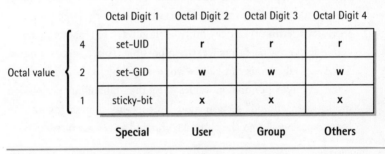

Figure 8-1 *A permission diagram using four octal digits.*

As Figure 8-1 demonstrates, the first octal digit is used for setting special permissions, the second digit is used for setting permissions for the file owner, the third digit is used for setting permissions for the group, and the fourth digit is used for setting permissions for everyone else. Owner and group permissions are discussed in earlier sections of this chapter, and "everyone else" just means everyone other than the file's group or owner. Special permissions are a little strange, though; choosing special permissions involves deciding whether the set-UID, set-GID, or sticky bit is necessary. Each of these concepts is explained in the following list.

- **set-UID (set user ID):** When an executable file with set-UID permission is run, the process runs as the file owner. In other words, if a file is set-UID and owned by the user gunchy, any time it is run, the running program enjoys the privileges of the user gunchy. So, if a file is owned by root, and is also set to be set-UID, anyone who can run the file essentially has the privileges of the superuser.

If a set-UID root file can be altered by anyone but root, this is a major security hole. Be very careful when setting the set-UID bit.

- **set-GID (set group ID):** Similarly to set-UID, when an executable file with set-GID is executed, it essentially has all the privileges of the group of the file.

- **The sticky bit:** This infrequently used feature tells the OS to keep an executable program's image in memory even after it exits. This is an external attempt to reduce the startup time of a large program. Instead of setting the sticky bit, you should try to recode the application for better performance, when possible. To see some examples of how octal permission values work, see Table 8-7, which shows some example permission values. See the "Changing permission modes with chmod" section a bit later in this chapter for info on how to use octals and the chmod command to set permissions.

When any of the four digits of a permission value are omitted, it is considered to be a 0. For example, 400 is equivalent to 0400.

Table 8-7 *Example Permission Values*

Permission Value	Explanation
0400	Grants Only read (r) permission for only to the file owner. This is equivalent to 400, where the missing octal digit is treated as a leading 0.
0440	Read (r) permission for both the file owner and the users in the group. This is equivalent to 440.
0444	Read (r) permission for everyone. This is equivalent to 444.
0644	Read (r) and write (w) permissions for the file owner. Everyone else has read-only access to the file. This is equivalent to 644; the number 6 is derived by adding 4 (r) and 2 (w).

Permission Value	Explanation
0755	Read (r), write (w), and execute (x) permissions for the file owner, and read (r) and execute (x) permissions for everyone else. This is equivalent to 755; the number 7 is derived by adding 4 (r) + 2 (w) + 1 (x).
4755	Same as 755 in the last example, except that this file is set-UID.
2755	Similar to 755, but also sets the set-GID bit.
1755	Similar to 755, but also sets the sticky bit, formally known as the save text mode.

Using access strings to set permissions

The access string method of setting permissions is (supposedly) simpler than the numeric method discussed in the preceding section. Figure 8-2 shows the access string version of the permissions diagram.

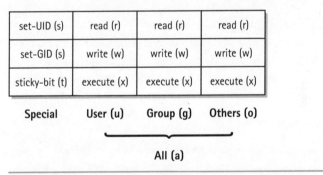

Figure 8-2 *The permissions diagram using access strings.*

With this method, each type of permission is represented with a single character (in parentheses). To create a permission string, you need to specify the following:

- **Who it affects.** Your choices are u (user), g (group), o (others), or a (all).

- **The type of permission that needs to be set.** Your choices are r (read), w (write), x (execute), s (set-UID or set-GID), or t (sticky bit). For more info on these choices and what they mean, see the previous section.

■ **The action type.** Indicate whether you're setting the permission or removing it. When setting the permissions, you need to specify + to specify an addition, and – to specify a removal.

For example, to allow the file owner read-access to the file, you need to specify a permission string such as u+r. To allow everyone to read and execute a file, you need a permission string such as a+rx. Similarly, to make a file set-UID, you need u+s; to set it as set-GID, you need g+s. See the next section for info on how to use this method to change permissions by using the chmod command.

Changing permission modes: chmod

The chmod utility allows you to *ch*ange permission *mod*es and hence is called chmod. You can use either the octal or the string method with this nifty utility. For example, the following command changes permissions for files ending with extension .pl:

```
chmod 755 *.pl
```

Each of the perl (.pl) files is set as read, write, and execute (7 = 4 [read] + 2 [write] + 1 [execute]) by the owner. The files are also set to be readable and executable (5 = 4 [read] + 1 [execute]) by the group and others.

You can accomplish the same result by using the string method as follows:

```
chmod a+rx,u+w *.pl
```

In this command, a+rx is used to allow read (r) and execute (x) permissions for all (a), and u+w is used to allow the file owner (u) to write (w) to the file. Note that when multiple access strings need to be used, each pair of strings needs to be separated by a comma, as in the preceding example. Also, note that no space is allowed between the permission strings.

If you want to change permissions for all the files and subdirectories within a directory, use the -R option to perform a recursive permission operation. For example, the following command applies the 750 octal permission to all the files and subdirectories of the /www/mysite directory.

```
chmod -R 750 /www/mysite
```

Be very careful when using the -R option with chmod. You could change permissions for subdirectories and potentially create security problems.

Some notes on directory permissions

The permission settings for a directory are similar to those for regular files, but not identical. Following are some things that you should note about directory permissions:

- Read-only access to a directory doesn't allow you to cd into that directory; to do that, you need execute permission.

- Execute-only permission allows you to access the files inside a directory as long as you know their names and have permission to read the files.

- To list the contents of a directory by using a program such as ls, or to cd into a directory, you need both read and execute permissions.

- If you have write permission for a directory, you can create, delete, or modify any files or subdirectories within that directory, even when the file or subdirectory is owned by someone else.

Overriding the default file permission mask

A permission mask, called a umask, is a number that your shell uses to set the default file permission. The system administrator can set a default permission mask in a global resource file for the shell you are using. For example, if you are using the /bin/tcsh shell, the system administrator can set default file permissions for you in the /etc/csh.cshrc file by using the umask command.

If you are using bash shell (bash is the default shell in Red Hat Linux), modify /etc/profile instead of the /etc/csh. cshrc file.

If you want to override the default permission mask, however, run umask from the command line to change the default mask. For example, the following command sets the default permission mask to read-only for everyone:

```
umask 222
```

In other words, it turns off the write permission for user, group, and others. This also overrides whatever the system default was for your shell. However, this change is temporary; when you log out and log back in, the system default will be effective again. If you dislike the system's permission mask, put the appropriate umask command in your shell's resource file. For example, if you prefer the mask to be 222 all the time and use /bin/tcsh as a shell, you can put this command in your ~/.cshrc file so that every time you log on, the umask command overrides the system's default.

Protecting your files with chattr

The ext2 file system (used in Red Hat Linux) allows you to make a file immutable — or unchangeable — for even the root user to protect against accidents involving files. To do this, you use the chattr command with the -i option. For example, the following command sets the i attribute of a file in an ext2 file system:

```
chattr +i filename
```

When this attribute is set for a file, that file cannot be modified, deleted, or renamed by anyone, nor can any links be added to point to this file. This attribute can be set or cleared only by the root user. When you need to clear the attribute, run the following command:

```
chattr -i filename
```

Because this attribute does not show up in ls output, it can be pretty easy to forget that you had previously set the immutable attribute of a file using chattr. To see which files have what ext2 attributes, simply run the lsattr command with the filename as the argument.

Managing permissions for symbolic links

Apart from the regular files and directories, you will quite frequently encounter another type of file — *links*. Links are files that point to other files. A link allows you to create multiple names for a single file or directory. The two types of links are hard and soft (symbolic) links, which are often called *symlinks*. This section discusses the special permission issues that arise from the use of links.

Changing permissions or ownership of a hard link

If you change the permission settings or ownership of a hard link, you also change the permission of the original file. For example, take a look at the following ls -l output:

```
-rw-r--r--    1 root            21 Feb  7 11:41 todo.txt
```

Now, if the root user creates a hard link (using the command line ln todo.txt plan) called plan for todo.txt, the ls -l output looks as follows:

```
-rw-r--r--    2 root            21 Feb  7 11:41 plan
-rw-r--r--    2 root            21 Feb  7 11:41 todo.txt
```

As you can see, the hard link, plan, and the original file, todo.txt, have the same file size (shown in the fourth column) and also share the same permission and ownership settings. Now, if the root user runs chown sheila plan to give the ownership of the hard link to a user called sheila, will it work as usual? Take a look at the ls -l output after this command:

```
-rw-r--r--    2 sheila   root   21 Feb  7 11:41 plan
-rw-r--r--    2 sheila   root   21 Feb  7 11:41 todo.txt
```

The chown command changed the ownership of plan, but the ownership of todo.txt (the original file) has also changed.

Changing permissions or ownership of a soft link

Changing the ownership of a soft (symbolic) link does not work the same way as changing the ownership of a hard link. For example, take a look at the following ls -l output:

```
lrwxrwxrwx   1 sheila    root      8 Feb  7 11:49 plan -> todo.txt
-rw-r--r--   1 sheila    root     21 Feb  7 11:41 todo.txt
```

The plan file is a symbolic link to todo.txt. Now, suppose the root user changes the ownership of the symbolic link as follows:

```
chown kabir plan
```

The ls -l output shows:

```
lrwxrwxrwx   1 kabir     root      8 Feb  7 11:49 plan -> todo.txt
-rw-r--r--   1 sheila    root     21 Feb  7 11:41 todo.txt
```

As you can see, the permissions of the plan symlink have changed from user sheila to user kabir, but todo.txt is still owned by sheila. As a result, kabir cannot write to todo.txt using the plan symbolic link unless the directory where these files are stored is owned by user kabir. However, if you change the permission settings of a soft link, the file that the soft link points to inherits the new settings. For example, the following command changes the todo.txt file's permission:

```
chmod 667 plan
```

Executing the ls -l command after executing the above permissions command results in the following output:

```
lrwxrwxrwx   1 kabir     root      8 Feb  7 11:49 plan -> todo.txt
-rw-rw-rwx   1 sheila    root     21 Feb  7 11:41 todo.txt
```

Creating a permission policy

Most problems that users encounter on Unix and Unix-like systems are related to file permissions. If something that was working fine yesterday suddenly stops working, you should first suspect a permission problem. The following section discusses a few permission policies that you might want to implement, especially if you have many users on a single system, to keep permission snafus to a minimum.

One of the most common causes of permission problems involves misuse of the root account. Many inexperienced system administrators often access files and programs via the root account. When a program is run using the root user account, the files that this program creates often are set with root ownership, effectively disallowing any use of the program by non-root users.

Setting users' configuration file permissions

Each user's home directory houses some partially hidden files with filenames that start with a period (or dot). These files, often referred to as *dot files*, are often used to execute commands at user login. For example, all the shells (csh, tcsh, bash, etc.) available to a user read their settings from a dot file, such as those with the extension .cshrc or .bashrc. If a user is not careful to keep file permissions set properly, another not-so-friendly user can cause problems for the naive user. For example, if one user's .cshrc file is writable by a second user, the latter can play a silly trick like putting a logout command at the beginning of the .cshrc file so that the first user will be logged out as soon as she logs in. Of course, there are worse silly tricks that the malevolent-minded could use to harm your system. To avoid privacy problems of this nature, you should make sure to keep watch for such situations on a multiuser system. Here are a couple ways that you can do so:

- If you have a lot of users, you can run the COPS program, a security analysis tool (www.fish.com/cops/), to detect many permission problems.

- If you have only a handful of users, you can also quickly perform simple checks, such as the following:

```
find /home -type f -name ".*rc" -exec ls -l {} \;
```

This command generates a list of permissions for all the dot files ending in rc (.cshrc, .bashrc, and so on) in the /home directory hierarchy. If your users' home directories are kept in /home, this quickly shows you which users might have a permission problem. For example, a sample output of the above command is shown below:

```
-rw-r--r-- 1 kabir    kabir  124 Jul 4 18:02 /home/kabir/.bashrc
-rw-r--r-- 1 kabir    kabir 3728 Jul 4 18:02 /home/kabir/.screenrc
-rw-r--r-- 1 webcam   httpd  124 Aug 7 20:57 /home/webcam/.bashrc
-rw-r--r-- 1 webcam   httpd 3728 Aug 7 20:57 /home/webcam/.screenrc
```

Setting default file permissions for users

As a system administrator, you can define the default permission settings for all the user files on your system. To set the default permissions for new files, use the umask command, as follows:

umask *mask*

As an example of how umask works, suppose that umask is set to 022. When a new file is created, typically a permission setting of 0666 is requested by the file creation function — open. However, in such a case, the final permission settings for the file are derived by the system, as shown in Figure 8-3.

As Figure 8-3 shows, the requested permission, 0666, is ANDed with the complement of the current mask (that is, 022 becomes 755) so that the result is 0644, which allows the file owner read- and write-access but gives everyone else read-access only.

To create a default mask for file permissions, you can embed the umask command in a global shell resource file in /etc so that when a user logs in and runs a shell, the global resource file for that shell is executed. This in turn executes the umask command and provides a default mask for the user session. For example, if your users use the /bin/csh or /bin/tcsh shell, you can put a desirable umask command in the /etc/csh.cshrc file for this purpose. For bash users, the umask is set in /etc/profile file.

Setting executable file permissions

Program files that can be run by regular users should never have write permission set for anyone but the owner. For example, the program files in /usr/bin should have permission settings such that only root can read, write, and execute, and everyone else can only read and execute these files. Allowing others to write into a program file can create serious security holes. As an example of such a hole, if someone other than the root user is allowed to write to a program such as /usr/bin/zip, a malicious user can replace the real Zip program with a Trojan-horse program that compromises system security and damages files and directories as it pleases.

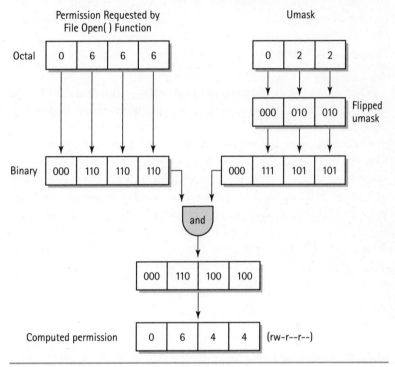

Figure 8-3 *How umask is used by the system.*

To avoid security issues of this nature, always check to make sure that the program files on your systems have proper permissions. Run COPS frequently to detect permission-related problems.

Setting default file permissions for FTP

If many of your users FTP their files on the server, you can control the default umask setting for the FTP server to ensure that one user's file is not accessible by another. For example, if you want to set permissions so that only the user and her group can read a file uploaded on a Web server via FTP, you can modify the server_args line in the /etc/xinetd.d/ wu-ftpd file. This line by default looks as follows:

```
server_args            = -l -a
```

To set a default umask for all files uploaded via FTP, you need to add a -u argument with the appropriate umask value. For example, to set 640 (rw-r-----) permission for each file uploaded, you can set the umask to 026. To do so, change the preceding line as follows:

```
server_args            = -l -a -u026
```

Then restart the inetd server (killall -USR1 xinetd) and FTP a file via a user account to see whether the permissions have been set as expected. This can be very handy for systems that act as Web servers for many different clients. If you do not want one client to see another client's files, you can use this option along with a special ownership setting. For example, suppose you keep all of your Web client files in the /www partition or directory, where each client site has a directory of its own (for example, /www/myclient1, /www/myclient2, and so on). You have probably already given each client an FTP account with which to upload files to these directories. To stop a client from seeing another client's files, use umask with the FTP server as described above and then reset the ownership of each client site as follows:

```
chown -R client.Web server user /www/client dir
```

For example, if you run your Web server as httpd and have a client user called myclient, then the preceding command will look like this:

```
chown -R myclient.httpd /www/myclient
```

This changes the ownership of the /www/myclient directory along with all of its subdirectories and files to the myclient user and to the httpd group, allowing the client user to own, modify, and delete her files and the Web server to read the files in the directory. To disallow everyone else, you must change the permissions as follows:

```
chmod -R 2770 /www/client dir
```

For the current example, the actual command is as follows:

```
chmod -R 2770 /www/myclient
```

This sets all the files and subdirectory permissions for /www/myclient to 2770, which allows the files and directories to be readable, writable, and executable by the owner (myclient) and the Web server user (httpd) and also ensures that when new files are created, they have their permissions set to allow the Web server user to read the file. This is done using the set-GID (2) digit.

Chapter 9

Running Programs

IN THIS CHAPTER

- Learning Linux from the command line
- Starting a program from the command line
- Stopping a running program
- Changing a program's priority
- Monitoring and logging running programs
- Scheduling programs using at and cron

Linux is primarily a command-line operating system, which is also capable of running a very rich Graphical User Interface (GUI) called X Window system. However, like most Unix systems the power of Linux lies within the commands themselves. Therefore knowing how to run, monitor, log, and schedule commands is very important in becoming an expert in Linux. In this chapter you will learn how to do just that.

Working from the Linux Command Line

Much of your work with Linux will consist of entering and executing commands one after another. These commands follow established rules commonly known as *command-line syntax*. If you do not follow the syntax correctly, a command may execute incorrectly, and problems can result.

Commands are entered at a Linux command prompt, which can be found either when you're logged in to Linux and not running X or a graphical interface, or from a terminal window within a graphical environment (often called an xterm). When you type a command, you type the name of the command, possibly followed by other information. The items that follow the name of the program are called *arguments*. The program carries the responsibility of determining how to use the arguments.

The general syntax of a Linux command is:

```
command_name options parameters
```

In the following command, for example, there are two arguments, −1 and doc.txt:

```
wc −1 doc.txt
```

When entering commands at the command line, remember the arguments are case sensitive just as filenames in Unix are.

There are two types of arguments: *options* and *parameters*. Options come right after the program name and are usually prefixed with a dash (-). The parameters follow the options. In the preceding example, −1 is an option telling the wc command to count the number of lines in the doc.txt file (the parameter).

Most commonly, you use commands one at a time. However, you can stack multiple commands into one command line by separating the commands with a semicolon. For example, you can clear the screen and then list the contents of the current directory with one command line with the following command:

```
clear; ls
```

Saving typing with wildcards

When you use directory and file commands, you can use special characters called wildcards to specify patterns of filenames. Wildcards make selecting multiple items easy. For example, to list all of the files in the current directory that end in .c, you would use the following command:

```
ls *.c
```

In this command, the shell interprets the * symbol as a wildcard and lists all of the filenames that end in .c.

You can also use wildcards to avoid typing long filenames. For example, a current version of Mozilla (the open-source project based on Netscape's Communicator code) has the filename embed-gcc295-i68-pc-llinux-gnu.tar.gz. No one wants to have to type out that entire filename. Using the * wildcard, if only one file in the directory starts with the letter e, you can get away with substituting e*.tar.gz for the preceding filename in your commands. If there are two files in your directory that start with the same letter, term, or other combination of characters and you want to specify one of them using the * wildcard, you'll have to type enough of the filename as required to tell the shell which file in the directory you're specifying. For example, if there are two files in your directory that start with e, say email_to_mother.txt and email_to_sister.txt, you'd have to at least type e*m*.txt.

Table 9-1 shows the most commonly used wildcards, and Table 9-2 shows a few examples of wildcard usage.

Table 9-1 *Commonly Used Wildcard Characters*

Wildcard	Meaning
*	Match any sequence of one or more characters
?	Match any single character
[ ]	Match one of the enclosed characters or range

Table 9-2 *Examples of Wildcard Usage*

Example	Meaning
Jo*	Files that begin with Jo
Jo*y	Files that begin with Jo and end in y
Ut*l*s.c	Files that begin with Ut, contain an l, and end in s.c
?.h	Files that begin with a single character followed by.h
Doc[0-9].txt	Files with the names Doc0.txt, Doc1.txt, . . . , Doc9.txt
Doc0[A-Z].txt	Files with the names Doc0A.txt, Doc0B.txt, . . . , Doc0Z.txt

Specifying patterns using regular expressions

Regular expressions provide a convenient and consistent way of specifying patterns to be matched. Regular expressions are similar to wildcards, but are much more powerful, providing a wider scope of pattern selecting. Several different Linux commands use regular expressions, including ed, sed, awk, grep, and, to a limited extent, vi and emacs.

The special characters in Table 9-3 are typical of regular expressions in general. Once you understand these special characters, you need to learn only a few variations as they arise.

Table 9-3 *Special Characters for Regular Expressions*

Symbol	Meaning
.	Matches any single character except newline.
*	Matches zero or more of the preceding characters.
^	Matches the beginning of a line.
$	Matches the end of a line.
\<	Matches the beginning of a word.
\>	Matches the end of a word.
[ ]	Matches one of the enclosed characters or range of characters
[^]	Matches any characters not enclosed
\	Take the following symbol literally

Within a regular expression, any character that does not have a special meaning stands for itself. For example, to search for lines that contain the word "foo" in the file data.txt, you would use the following command:

```
grep foo data.txt
```

To search only for lines in data.txt that begin with the word "foo," you would use the following command instead:

```
grep '^foo' data.txt
```

The use of single quotes tells the shell to leave these characters alone and to pass them to the program. Single quotes are necessary whenever using any of the special characters.

The dollar sign indicates that you want to match a pattern at the end of the line. In the following command, for example, any lines ending with the word "hello" result in a match using the preceding regular expression:

```
grep 'hello$' data.txt
```

To look for a pattern that begins a word, use \<. For example, the following command searches for words that begin with "ki" in the file data.txt:

```
grep '\<ki' data.txt
```

To find the pattern "wee," but only at the end of a word, use:

```
grep 'wee\>' data.txt
```

In Table 9-3, notice that the period matches any single character except the newline character (i.e., ASCII character value x10). This comes in handy if, for example, you're searching for all the lines that contain the letter "C" followed by two letters and end in "s"; in this case, the regular expression is:

```
grep 'C..s' data.txt
```

This expression matches patterns such as "Cats," "Cars," and "Cris" in the file data.txt.

If you want to specify a range of characters, use a hyphen to separate the beginning and end of the range. When you specify the range, the order must be the same as in the ASCII code. For example, to search for all lines that contain a "B" followed by any single lowercase letter, use the following command:

```
grep 'B[a-z]' data.txt
```

You can also specify more than one range of characters in the same pattern. For example, the following command selects all lines that contain the letter "B" that are followed by an uppercase or lowercase letter.

```
grep 'B[A-Za-z]' data.txt
```

Running Programs

In most cases, when you run a process from a console, shell, or xterm, the program runs in the foreground. When a process is running in the foreground, you have to wait for it to finish before you can do something else. Instead of waiting for a process to finish, however, you can run the process in the background by specifying an "&" character at the end of the command line. This ability comes in very handy when you're running a process that takes a long time to finish and you'd rather do something useful while it works. For example, say you want to use the du command to get an idea of which files are taking up the most disk space in your system. You can run du in the background with the following command:

```
du &
```

If you don't want the output from du interrupting you while you're working on something else, you can redirect the command's output to a file so that you can check it at your convenience. To redirect the output of the preceding du command to a temporary file called du.out, for example, the command would be as follows:

```
du > /tmp/du.out  &
```

TIP   If you would like to leave a program running in the background after you log off from a shell session, you can use the nohup program, which immunizes a command from the SIGHUP signal (i.e., hup or interrupt request) and allows the process to continue without a login shell. See the nohup man page for details.

Terminating a Running Program

Like all Unix-like systems, Linux provides a way to send various signals to processes. A *signal* is an exception that is typically used to tell the process to do something other than what it usually does. For example, if you need to kill a process, you can send it a signal to terminate. The command to signal a process is called kill.

kill is a confusing name for this function because you can use kill to send any valid signal, not just to send a signal to kill the process.

Using kill to terminate a running program

kill is a built-in shell command for many popular shells, such as bash, csh and tcsh. However, there is also an external kill program, which typically resides in the /bin directory. Both versions work the same way. This command can be run as follows:

```
kill [-numeric_signal_number] [ -short_signal_name] PID
```

You can either use a numeric signal number or a short name for a signal to send to the named process ID (PID). For example:

```
kill -1 12345
```

This sample kill command sends signal 1 (SIGHUP) to a process with ID 12345. Similarly, kill -HUP 12345 sends the same signal to the same process. Table 9-4 shows a list of available signals. The most commonly used signals are SIGHUP and SIGKILL.

Table 9-4 *Available Signals*

Signal	Name (short name)	Description
1	SIGHUP (HUP)	Hang up. This signal is often used to instruct a process to reload configuration files.
2	SIGINT (INT)	Interrupt.
3	SIGQUIT (QUIT)	Quit.
4	SIGILL (ILL)	Illegal instruction.
5	SIGTRAP (TRAP)	Trace trap.
6	SIGIOT (IOT)	IOT instruction.
7	SIGBUS (BUS)	Bus error.
8	SIGFPE (FPE)	Floating-point exception.

Continued

Table 9-4 *Continued*

Signal	Name (short name)	Description
9	SIGKILL (KILL)	Kill. This signal cannot be caught (that is, handled in a process), blocked, or ignored. When this signal is sent to the process, it is terminated immediately. This signal should be used wisely in case of emergency.
10	SIGUSR1 (USR1)	User-defined signal 1.
11	SIGSEGV (SEGV)	Segmentation violation.
12	SIGUSR2 (USR2)	User-defined signal 2.
13	SIGPIPE (PIPE)	Write on a pipe with no one to read it.
14	SIGALRM (ALRM)	Alarm clock.
15	SIGTERM (TERM)	Software termination signal. This is often sent before a KILL signal is issued. This allows a process to catch this signal and to prepare to exit.
16	SIGSTKFLT	Stack fault on coprocessor.
17	SIGCHLD (CHLD)	Child status has changed.
18	SIGCONT (CONT)	Continue after STOP signal. This signal cannot be blocked.
19	SIGSTOP (STOP)	Stop. This signal cannot be caught (that is, handled in a process), blocked, or ignored.
20	SIGTSTP (TSTP)	Stop signal generated from keyboard, typically by using Ctrl+Z.
21	SIGTTIN	Background read attempted from control terminal.
22	SIGTTOU	Background write attempted to control terminal.
23	SIGURG	Urgent condition present on socket.
24	SIGXCPU	CPU time limit exceeded. See man setrlimit (2).
25	SIGXFSZ	File size limit exceeded. See man setrlimit (2).
26	SIGVTALRM	Virtual time alarm. See man setitimer (2).
27	SIGPROF	Profiling timer alarm. See man setitimer (2).
28	SIGWINCH	Window size change.

Signal	Name (short name)	Description
29	SIGIO	I/O is possible on a descriptor. See man fcntl (2).
30	SIGPWR	Power failure.
31	UNUSED	Not used.

Using killall to terminate all instances of a command

This nifty utility lets you kill a process by name. For example, if you have a process called infiniteloop.pl and want to kill it without typing its PID, you can run the killall command as follows:

```
killall --KILL infiniteloop.pl
```

When you do not provide a signal name, killall automatically sends the SIGTERM signal. However, be careful when using killall; it kills all instances of the named command. In this light, sometimes the convenience of not having to know the PID can go sour. For example, look at the following ps output:

```
PID   TTY  STAT TIME COMMAND
1246  p8   S    0:00 -tcsh
2160  p6   S    0:00 -tcsh
2365  p1   S    0:00 -bash
2459  p6   S    0:00 vi bar.txt
2460  p8   S    0:00 vi foo.txt
2463  p1   R    0:00 ps
```

Say that for some reason you want to kill the vi process used for editing the foo.txt file. If you run killall vi foo.txt expecting it to terminate only this instance of vi, you will be surprised to find that *all* of your vi sessions have terminated. This occurs because killall expects command names as arguments and sends signals to all instances of a named program. So, if you know that you have more than one process using the same command running, you'll have to use the PID if you want to stop only one instance of that command.

Be extremely cautious when running the `killall` command as root (or another superuser) because it removes every instance of the named command from the entire system, which includes all users.

Prioritizing Programs

Linux has two priority numbers associated with each process. For example, if you run `ps -l`, you see two fields, PRI and NI. The PRI field shows the actual process priority, which the operating system dynamically computes. Among other factors, the operating system takes the NI number into account when it computes and updates the PRI number. The NI number is usually called the *nice number* or the *requested process execution priority number*. The owner or the superuser can set this number to influence the actual execution priority number (PRI). You can use the /bin/nice utility to change the NI number. The valid range of process priority is from -20 to 20, where -20 is the highest NI priority, and 20 is the lowest. The functionality of the `nice` utility is often built into popular shells such as /bin/ bash, /bin/csh, /bin/tcsh, and others.

 By default, the `nice` utility allows a user to decrease process priority only. Only a superuser such as root is allowed to increase the priority of a process.

Before you can set the priority of a process, run `which nice` to determine if you are going to run the built-in shell version of nice or the /bin/nice utility. This is necessary because the syntax varies between these two versions. For example, suppose you want to run a Perl script called `foo.pl` at the lowest priority (20). The shell version of the appropriate `nice` command is:

```
nice +10 foo.pl
```

but the /bin/nice version of the same command is:

```
/bin/nice -10 foo.pl
```

To ensure that your priority changes are taking effect, you can run ps −l to determine the value of NI field.

As another example, if you're a superuser and want to increase the priority of the foo.pl script to -10, the built-in shell version of the command is:

```
nice -10 foo.pl
```

whereas the /bin/nice version of the same command is:

```
/bin/nice−10 foo.pl
```

If nice is too confusing to you, you can use the snice utility to handle process priority upgrades or downgrades. Before you use snice, first use the ps command to find the PID of the process whose priority you want to change.

Just as with nice, any user can lower priority of the processes he or she owns, but only a superuser can increase the priority of a process.

Use ps to find the PID of the process whose priority you want to change. To upgrade the priority of a command with snice, the command syntax is snice −n PID, where *n* is the new priority number. For example, the following command increases the priority of process 1234 (the process' PID) by 5:

```
snice −5 1234
```

To downgrade the priority of a process with snice, the command syntax is snice +n PID, where *n* is the new priority number. For example, the following command decreases the priority of process 1234 (the process's PID) by 5:

```
snice +5 1234
```

As with snice, you can use the renice utility to change the priority of a process. The preceding instructions for snice also apply to renice.

Monitoring and Logging Programs

A great number of tools are available for Linux that can help you measure and monitor system performance. In this section I discuss a few of these tools that are easy to use and ideal for getting started.

Running ps to monitor system performance

The ps utility allows you to monitor the processes that are running on your system and allows you to see how much memory or CPU bandwidth each process is using, which user owns each process, and other information. A sample output of the ps command is shown below:

```
PID  TTY          TIME CMD
4406 pts/1    00:00:00 su
4407 pts/1    00:00:00 bash
4480 pts/1    00:00:00 ps
```

In the above output, ps reports that there are three programs running under the current user ID: su, bash, and ps (yes, ps even tracks itself). If you want to get a list of all the processes running on the system, you can run ps aux and all the processes will be listed. A shortened sample of the output of this command follows:

USER	PID	%CPU	%MEM	VSZ	RSS	TTY	STAT	START	TIME	COMMAND
root	1	0.1	0.1	1324	532	?	S	10:58	0:06	init [3]
root	2	0.0	0.0	0	0	?	SW	10:58	0:00	[kflushd]
root	3	0.0	0.0	0	0	?	SW	10:58	0:00	[kupdate]
root	4	0.0	0.0	0	0	?	SW	10:58	0:00	[kpiod]
root	5	0.0	0.0	0	0	?	SW	10:58	0:00	[kswapd]
root	6	0.0	0.0	0	0	?	SW<	10:58	0:00	[mdrecoveryd]
root	45	0.0	0.0	0	0	?	SW	10:58	0:00	[khubd]
root	349	0.0	0.1	1384	612	?	S	10:58	0:00	syslogd -m 0
root	359	0.0	0.1	1340	480	?	S	10:58	0:00	klogd
rpc	374	0.0	0.1	1468	576	?	S	10:58	0:00	portmap

[Additional lines deleted]

Table 9-5 explains the meaning of the common output fields for ps.

Table 9-5 *Output Fields for ps*

Field	Explanation
USER or UID	The process owner's username.
PID	Process ID.
%CPU	CPU utilization of the process. Because the time base over which this is computed varies, it is possible for this to exceed 100 percent.
%MEM	Percentage of memory (in kilobytes) that the process is using.
SIZE	Size (in kilobytes) of virtual memory that the process is using.
RSS	Resident Set Size – size of real memory (in kilobytes) the process is using.
TTY	Terminal (called `tty`) that is associated with the process. Usually, the `tty` name is shortened. For example, p7 is displayed to represent `/dev/ttyp7`.
STAT	State of the process. Process states are represented by characters such as D (disk wait); I (idle); N (lowered priority by nice); P (page wait); R (running or ready to run); S (sleeping); T (terminated); W (swapped out); Z (zombie); < (execution priority raised by superuser), and so on.
START	Process start time or date.
TIME	Total CPU time the process is using.
COMMAND	Command line being executed.
NI	The `nice` priority number.
PRI	The process's priority number.
PPID	The process ID (PID) of the parent process.
WCHAN	The name of the kernel function where a process is sleeping. This name is retrieved from the `/boot/System.map` file.
FLAGS	A numeric flag associated with the process.

The ps utility also accepts a number of command-line arguments. Table 9-6 shows commonly used options.

Table 9-6 *Commonly Used ps Options*

Options	What It Shows
A	Processes belonging to all users.
E	Displays process environment information.
L	Displays output in long format.
U	Displays user name and process start time.
W	Displays the output in wide format. If you don't use this option, the output is truncated if it cannot fit on a line.
Txx	Displays processes associated with xx terminal (`tty`) device.
X	Displays processes without controlling the terminal (`tty`).

To help you really see how versatile `ps` can be, the following sections discuss some examples of how to use some of the more common `ps` options together.

Customizing your process display

Using the −a and −u options with `ps` tells that command to display all processes (excluding the one not associated with any controlling `tty`). For example, to find out what processes a particular user owns, you can run the following command, substituting *username* for the name of the actual user:

```
ps au | grep username
```

For example, the `ps au | grep sheila` command shows all the interactive processes (that is, processes associated with a `tty`) that are being run by user `sheila`. Typically, normal users are not allowed to run daemon processes or processes not associated with a tty. However, if you just want to find if any such processes exist for any user, you can run the following command:

```
ps aux
```

Adding the −x option to the −a and −u options tells `ps` to list processes detached from terminals. You can identify these processes by looking at the TTY field, which displays a "?" character instead of the shortened name of a tty device such as p7 (`/dev/ttyp7`).

Finding the PID of a process's parent

To find the PID of a process's parent, you can run the following command, where PID is the process ID:

```
ps l PID
```

For example, if you want to find the parent of a process with PID 123, you can run the ps l 123 command. The parent's PID will be listed in the PPID field of the report.

Displaying environment information

Knowing a program's environment information is often a great way to determine bugs and also configuration problems. To determine what initial environment variables are available to processes, you can run the following command, which appends the environment information to the COMMAND field of the resulting ps report:

```
ps e
```

A regular (non-superuser or root) user cannot use the -e option to see the environment information of another user's processes. This is a security feature. Only root or other superusers can view environment information of all the processes.

Monitoring a process over time

At times you find that you need to run ps to monitor a specific process for a certain amount of time. For example, say that you installed a new sendmail mail server patch and want to make sure the server is up and running and determine whether it is using an excessive amount of system resources. In such a case you can combine a few Linux commands as follows:

```
watch --interval=n  "ps auxw | grep process_you_want_to_monitor"
```

For example, you can run watch --interval=30 "ps auxw | grep sendmail" to see how much resource sendmail is using by running the ps program every 30 seconds.

Viewing processes in a tree structure

You can run pstree to display a tree structure of all processes running on
your system. A sample output of the pstree command is shown below.

```
init-+-apmd
     |-atd
     |-crond
     |-identd---identd---3*[identd]
     |-kflushd
     |-khubd
     |-klogd
     |-kpiod
     |-kswapd
     |-kupdate
     |-lockd---rpciod
     |-lpd
     |-mdrecoveryd
     |-6*[mingetty]
     |-named
     |-nmbd
     |-portmap
     |-rhnsd
     |-rpc.statd
     |-safe_mysqld---mysqld---mysqld---mysqld
     |-sendmail
     |-smbd---smbd
     |-sshd-+-sshd---bash---su---bash---man---sh---sh-+-groff---
grotty
     |     |                                          `-less
     |     `-sshd---bash---su---bash---pstree
     |-syslogd
     |-xfs
     `-xinetd
```

You can tell the following from the above output:

- The parent of all processes is init. This does not change.

- One branch of the tree is created by safe_mysqld, which has itself spawned three mysqld daemon processes.

- Another branch of the tree is the sshd branch. The sshd daemon has forked two child daemon processes that have then opened bash shells and launched other processes down the road. Notice that the pstree output was generated by one of the subbranches of the sshd daemon.

- The output shows that I used sshd to connect to my Linux system, switched to bash as my shell after I logged in, used su to switch users to root (instead of logging in directly as root, which is both risky and usually unnecessary), and then ran the pstree command.

Running top to monitor system activity

The top utility allows you to monitor system activity in an interactive manner. When you run top from a shell window or an xterm it displays all the active processes and updates the screen by using a user-configurable interval. A sample top session is shown in Listing 9-1.

Listing 9-1 *An example top session*

```
12:13pm  up  1:15,  2 users,  load average: 0.05, 0.07, 0.01

48 processes: 47 sleeping, 1 running, 0 zombie, 0 stopped

CPU states:  1.1% user,  2.1% system,  0.0% nice, 96.7% idle

Mem:    387312K av,   96876K used,  290436K free,   27192K shrd,   36040K buff

Swap: 265064K av,        0K used,  265064K free                   34236K cached


  PID USER      PRI  NI  SIZE  RSS SHARE STAT %CPU %MEM   TIME COMMAND

 6748 kabir      15   0  1032 1032  832 R    0.9  0.2   0:00 top

    1 root        0   0   532  532  468 S    0.0  0.1   0:06 init

    2 root        0   0     0    0    0 SW   0.0  0.0   0:00 kflushd

    3 root        0   0     0    0    0 SW   0.0  0.0   0:00 kupdate

    4 root        0   0     0    0    0 SW   0.0  0.0   0:00 kpiod
```

Continued

Listing 9-1 *Continued*

5	root	0	0	0	0	0	SW	0.0	0.0	0:00 kswapd
6	root	-20	-20	0	0	0	SW<	0.0	0.0	0:00 mdrecoveryd
45	root	0	0	0	0	0	SW	0.0	0.0	0:00 khubd
349	root	0	0	612	612	512	S	0.0	0.1	0:00 syslogd
359	root	0	0	480	480	408	S	0.0	0.1	0:00 klogd
374	rpc	0	0	576	576	484	S	0.0	0.1	0:00 portmap
390	root	0	0	0	0	0	SW	0.0	0.0	0:00 lockd
391	*root*	*0*	*0*	*0*	*0*	*0*	*SW*	*0.0*	*0.0*	*0:00 rpciod*
401	rpcuser	0	0	768	768	656	S	0.0	0.1	0:00 rpc.statd
416	root	0	0	524	524	460	S	0.0	0.1	0:00 apmd
470	nobody	0	0	720	720	608	S	0.0	0.1	0:00 identd
477	nobody	0	0	720	720	608	S	0.0	0.1	0:00 identd
478	nobody	0	0	720	720	608	S	0.0	0.1	0:00 identd
480	nobody	0	0	720	720	608	S	0.0	0.1	0:00 identd
482	nobody	0	0	720	720	608	S	0.0	0.1	0:00 identd
489	daemon	0	0	576	576	500	S	0.0	0.1	0:00 atd
504	named	0	0	1928	1928	1152	S	0.0	0.4	0:00 named
535	root	0	0	1040	1040	832	S	0.0	0.2	0:00 xinetd
550	root	0	0	1168	1168	1040	S	0.0	0.3	0:00 sshd
571	lp	0	0	888	888	764	S	0.0	0.2	0:00 lpd
615	root	0	0	1480	1480	1084	S	0.0	0.3	0:00 sendmail
650	root	0	0	744	744	640	S	0.0	0.1	0:00 crond
657	root	0	0	912	912	756	S	0.0	0.2	0:00 safe_mysqld
683	mysql	0	0	1376	1376	1008	S	0.0	0.3	0:00 mysqld
696	xfs	0	0	2528	2528	808	S	0.0	0.6	0:00 xfs
704	mysql	0	0	1376	1376	1008	S	0.0	0.3	0:00 mysqld

By default, top updates its screen every second. You can change this interval by using the d *seconds* option. For example, to update the screen every 5 seconds you would run the top d 5 command. If you let top update the screen every second, the program will show up as the main resource consumer in its own output. So, it's a good idea to use a 5- or 10-second interval for the screen update interval.

top also allows you to perform interactive tasks on processes. For example, if you press the H key while top is running you will see the following output screen:

```
Proc-Top Revision 1.2
Secure mode off; cumulative mode off; noidle mode off


Interactive commands are:


space    Update display
^L       Redraw the screen
fF       add and remove fields
oO       Change order of displayed fields
h or ?   Print this list
S        Toggle cumulative mode
i        Toggle display of idle processes
I        Toggle between Irix and Solaris views (SMP-only)
c        Toggle display of command name/line
l        Toggle display of load average
m        Toggle display of memory information
t        Toggle display of summary information
k        Kill a task (with any signal)
r        Renice a task
N        Sort by PID (Numerically)
A        Sort by age
P        Sort by CPU usage
M        Sort by resident memory usage
T        Sort by time / cumulative time
u        Show only a specific user
n or #   Set the number of process to show
s        Set the delay in seconds between updates
W        Write configuration file ~/.toprc
q        Quit


Press any key to continue
```

Using the keyboard options listed in the preceding output you can control how top displays its output and even kill a process (or task) as long as you have permission to do so.

Monitoring I/O activity with vmstat

The vmstat utility also provides interesting information about processes, memory, I/O, and CPU activity. When you run this utility without any arguments, the output looks similar to the following:

```
procs        memory           swap    io system    cpu
r b w  swpd free  buff cache si so bi bo in  cs us sy id
0 0 0     8 8412 45956 52820  0  0  0  0 104 11 66  0 33
```

The fields in the first line of the above are described in Table 9-7.

Table 9-7 *vmstat Fields*

Field	What It Displays
System	The number of interrupts (in) and context switches (cs) per second.
Procs	The number of processes waiting for run time (r), the number of processes blocked (b), and the number of processes swapped out (w).
Memory	The amounts of swap, free, buffered, and cached memory in kilobytes.
Swap	The amount (in kilobytes per second, or Kbps) of memory swapped in (si) from disk and the amount of memory swapped out (so) to disk.
Io	The number of blocks sent (bi) and received (bo) to and from block devices per second.
Cpu	The percentage of total CPU time in terms of user (us), system (sy), and idle (id) time.

TIP

If you would like vmstat to update information automatically, you can run it as vmstat *nsec*, where *nsec* is the number of seconds you want vmstat to wait before another update.

Logging program-generated messages

A process log is a system administrator's best friend. Log files can provide many clues about what's going on with a certain process. Almost all widely used server software packages—sendmail, Apache, named, and so on—write logs. There are two trends when it comes to writing logs. Some server programs write custom log files, and some use a facility called syslog, a logging facility provided by the syslogd daemon itself. Typically, init starts syslogd at run level 3 (the multiuser state). The syslog facility provides a centralized logging environment for processes that wish to write logs.

Configuring syslog

Typically, syslog is already configured on most systems. The default Red Hat installation installs syslogd and its /etc/syslog.conf configuration file, which is shown in Listing 9-2. The default syslogd configuration writes the log files to the /var/log directory.

Listing 9-2 *An example /etc/syslog.conf file*

```
# Log all kernel messages to the console.
# Logging much else clutters up the screen.
kern.*    /dev/console


# Log anything (except mail) of level info or higher.
# Don't log private authentication messages!
*.info;mail.none;authpriv.none  /var/log/messages


# The authpriv file has restricted access.
authpriv.*  /var/log/secure


# Log all the mail messages in one place.
mail.* /var/log/maillog


# Everybody gets emergency messages.
*.emerg *
```

Continued

Listing 9-2 *Continued*

```
# Save mail and news errors of level err and
#higher in a  special file.
uucp,news.crit  /var/log/spooler
```

`syslog.conf` is actually quite simple. The blank lines and the lines starting with "#" are ignored. The structure of a `syslogd` configuration line is as follows:

```
facility.priority   destination
```

where *facility* can be one of the following keywords: auth, Authpriv, cron, daemon, kern, lpr, mail, news, syslog, user, uucp, and local0–local7. *priority* can be one of the following keywords in ascending order of severity: debug, info, notice, warning, err, crit, alert, emerg, none. You can also use "*" as a wildcard for either *facility* or *priority* to indicate all facilities or all priorities, respectively. You can use a comma-separated list of multiple facilities with the same priority in a line. For example:

```
uucp,news.crit  /var/log/spooler
```

Here, log entries (often called *messages*) of critical (crit) priority from the uucp and news facilities are written to `/var/log/spooler` file.

You can also use a semicolon-separated list of multiple facility and priority pairs to assign a single destination to each pair. For example, with the following command, all informative (info) log entries from all facilities are written to the `/var/log/messages` file except for the informative messages from the mail and authpriv facilities:

```
*.info;mail.none;authpriv.none  /var/log/messages
```

Monitoring logs with tail

If you are experiencing problems with a server process, find out if that process writes log files. If it writes log files of its own or uses the syslog facility, you can monitor the log files by using the tail utility as the process runs. tail allows you to monitor growing log files by viewing the last part of a file. For example, to monitor the `/var/log/messages` file, you can run the following command:

```
tail -f  /var/log/messages
```

This command allows you to view the file as new entries are written to it. If you would like to limit the number of lines you see, use the --line number option. For example, to view only the last three lines of the same file as the last example, you can run `tail -f —line 3 /var/log/messages`.

Note that `syslogd`-produced log files can grow very large in an active system. Therefore, it is important to rotate your log files by using the `logrotate` facility. In fact, by default, the RPM package for `syslogd` installs a `logrotate` configuration file called `syslog` in the `/etc/logrotate.d` directory. The `logrotate` setup rotates the log files on a weekly basis and keeps compressed backups of backup logs as well.

Scheduling Programs

Like all other forms of Unix and other Unix-like operating systems, Red Hat Linux provides you with two popular process-scheduling facilities: `at` and `cron`. In the following sections I show you how to use both of these services.

Queuing commands with at

The `at` utility allows you to queue a command for execution "at" a later time. For example, to run the disk usage summary generator utility called du at 8:40 p.m., you can run `at` as follows:

```
at 20:40
```

The at command displays an `at>` prompt where you can enter the du command as follows:

```
at> du -a > /tmp/du.out
```

Here, the output of du is directed to a file. After you enter the command (the du command in this example), `at` displays the prompt again. You can press Ctrl+D to exit. After you exit, you will see a message similar to the following:

```
at> <EOT>
warning: commands will be executed using /bin/sh
job 1 at 2001-12-06 20:40
```

This means that at has scheduled the at daemon *(atd)* to run du —a > /tmp/du.out job at 8:40 p.m., 12/06/2001. Note that you can use a variety of time formats to specify the time of execution. For example, instead of using at 20:40, you can use at 8:40 p.m.. You can also specify the date with the time. For example, 8:40 p.m. feb 23, 10 a.m. + 5 days, 12:30 p.m tomorrow, midnight, and noon are all valid time specifications.

To verify that your job is in the job queue, run the atq command, which displays the currently scheduled job in the queue. All scheduled jobs are stored in /var/spool/at directory.

TIP   If you are the root user on a system, you see commands that are scheduled to be run by examining the files in the /var/spool/at spool directory.

If you want to stop the scheduled job, you can run the atrm command to remove your job. You need to know the job sequence number to remove a job with atrm. To find what jobs you have scheduled, run the atq command, and then you can delete any job by using atrm *job#*. For example, to remove job #1, you would specify atrm 1.

The scheduled job is run via the atd daemon process, which init starts for run level 3 (multiuser mode). If you would like to restrict use of the at facility, you can create a /etc/at.allow file and list all users that you want to allow to run it (the file needs to include only a single username per line). Any user not in this allow file will not have access to the at utility. On the other hand, if you want to deny only a few users but allow the rest, you can create a similar file called /etc/at.deny. All usernames in this file will be denied access to at.

Although at provides you with process-scheduling capabilities, another utility called cron is more widely used than at, as it offers a more structured way for creating unattended process execution schedules for repetitive tasks. cron is discussed in the next section.

Using cron to schedule tasks

As a system administrator, you will likely need to schedule many tasks (processes) in a Linux system for unattended execution on a regular basis.

For example, to rotate the log files `syslogd` creates, or to remove old files from the `/tmp` directory, you can choose to run a process daily or weekly. The `cron` facility allows you to create a recurring task schedule. In fact, it was not so long ago that there was no `atd` daemon, and all `at` jobs were run via a program called `atrun`, which in turn was run via the `cron` facility.

The `cron` facility includes the `crond` daemon, which the `init` process launches. `crond` reads task schedules from `/etc/crontab` and from files in the `/var/spool/cron` directory. The latter directory stores schedule files (often called `crontab`, or *cron table*) for normal users allowed to run cron jobs. As a superuser, you can specify a list of users that are allowed to run cron jobs in an `/etc/cron.allow` file. Similarly, you can explicitly deny cron access to users by specifying their names in an `/etc/cron.deny` file. Both files use a simple, one username per line format. If you allow users to run cron jobs, they can use the `crontab` utility to create job schedules; for example, they can run `crontab -e` to create and edit their cron job entries. A cron job specification has the following format:

```
minute(s) hour(s) day(s) month weekday username command argument(s)
```

Table 9-8 describes the first five time-specification fields.

Table 9-8 *cron Time-Specification Fields*

Fields	Description	Range
Minutes(s)	One or more minutes in an hour. You can specify a comma-separated list of minutes.	0–59
Hour(s)	One or more hours in a day. You can specify a comma-separated list of hours.	0–23, where 0 is midnight
Day(s)	One or more days in a month. You can specify a comma-separated list of days.	1–31
Month(s)	One or more months in a year. You can specify a comma-separated list of months.	1–12
Weekday(s)	One or more days in a week. You can specify a comma-separated list of days.	1–7, where 1 is Monday

For any of the fields in Table 9-8, you can use "*" as a wildcard. For example, the following command states that `/some/script` runs every first minute of every hour, every day, every month, and every weekday:

```
01 * * * * root /some/script
```

The preceding script runs as the root user. To run this script every 10 minutes, you can define a `cron` job such as the following:

```
0,10,20,30,40,50 * * * * root /some/script
```

To run the same script only once a month, you can schedule a `cron` job as follows:

```
01 1 1 * * root /some/script
```

In this command, the script runs at 1:01 A.M. on the first day of every month.

The default `cron` job for the system is `/etc/crontab`, which includes a few interesting `cron` job entries such as the following:

```
SHELL=/bin/bash
PATH=/sbin:/bin:/usr/sbin:/usr/bin
MAILTO=root


# run-parts
01 * * * * root run-parts /etc/cron.hourly
02 4 * * * root run-parts /etc/cron.daily
22 4 * * 0 root run-parts /etc/cron.weekly
42 4 1 * * root run-parts /etc/cron.monthly
```

You use these `cron` jobs to run the `run-parts` script in the `/usr/bin` directory. This script runs every hour, every day, every week, and every month using the four `cron` job specifications in the preceding listing. The `run-parts` script takes a directory name as an argument and runs all scripts or programs in the specified directory. For example, consider the first `cron` entry in the preceding listing, which states that the `run-parts` script should run at the first minute of every hour for the `/etc/cron.hourly` directory. Because the script runs all the files in this directory, the entire process effectively works as if all the files in the `/etc/cron.hourly` directory are set up as `cron` jobs. This trick allows you to put new files in the `/etc/cron.hourly` directory and have it automatically scheduled to run hourly. Similarly, the other three `cron` entries allow you to run any program on a daily, weekly, or monthly basis by just placing them in the `/etc/cron.daily`, `/etc/cron.weekly`, or `/etc/cron.monthly` directories. This makes it easy to create cron jobs for almost everything without having to configure a cron entry.

For example, say you want to synchronize your system time with a remote time server on a daily basis. You decide to use the rdate utility to set the time via the Internet. The command to run is:

```
/usr/bin/rdate --s  time.server.host.tld
```

Because the default /etc/crontab contains a cron entry that allows you to schedule daily cron jobs by simply placing the script or program in the /etc/cron.daily directory, you can create a simple shell script such as the following and place it in the /etc/cron.daily directory to run the rdate utility:

```
#!/bin/sh
/usr/bin/rdate --s time.server.host.tld
```

Your job is done. Every day at 4:02 a.m., your script runs with all other scripts and programs in the /etc/cron.daily directory.

As you can see, setting up cron jobs is much more systematic than using at commands to queue repetitive tasks, and, therefore, cron is preferred over at when you need to run something on a set schedule over and over again. I recommend using at for one-time scheduling jobs only.

Chapter 10

Using the GNOME Desktop

The primary purpose of the GNOME project is to provide a complete, user-friendly desktop environment using only open source, freely distributed software. The official Web site for this project is located at www. gnome.org.

In this chapter I show you how to install GNOME if you didn't install it during the installation process, how to use the GNOME desktop environment, and how to use some of the more common GNOME administration tools.

Installing GNOME

The official Red Hat Linux CD-ROM comes with the software required for using the GNOME desktop environment. You can also download the latest RPM packages from www.gnome.org or one of its mirror sites near you. Because GNOME is being developed rapidly, I highly recommend that you visit the Web site to find out about the latest version and download it.

You can install GNOME during Red Hat Linux installation by selecting X Windows and later choosing GNOME as part of your installation options. However, if you have not installed GNOME during Linux installation, you can still install GNONE manually.

Before you can install the GNOME-related RPM packages, you need to ensure that you have already installed the umb-scheme, xscreensaver, and guile packages from your Red Hat Linux CD-ROM. To find out if you have already installed the umb-scheme package, run the following command:

```
rpm -q umb-scheme
```

If one or more of these prerequisite packages are not installed, you can install them from the Red Hat Linux CD-ROM. After you have installed these packages, you can install the GNOME software by running the following command from the gnome directory of your Red Hat Linux CD-ROM:

```
rpm -ivh gnome-*.rpm
```

If you do not have the Red Hat Linux CD-ROM then download the RPM packages from the GNOME Web site at www.gnome.org.

Using the GNOME Desktop Environment

After you've installed the GNOME packages, you can run your favorite window manager and load the GNOME desktop by running the following command:

```
gnome-session &
```

If you prefer to load the GNOME desktop by default, modify your .xinitrc file and add the following line just before you load the window manager:

```
exec gnome-session
```

When you start GNOME for the first time, the Help Browser window and the GNOME Panel appear, as shown in Figure 10-1.

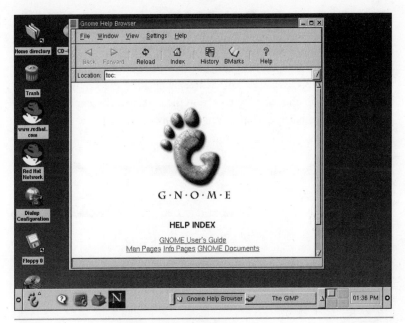

Figure 10-1 *The GNOME environment.*

The stylized foot icon you see on the bottom-left corner of the figure is the Main Menu button. This menu is embedded in the Panel, which is the heart of the GNOME interface. The Panel houses applications, applets, and the Main Menu. You can start any of the preloaded applications by clicking the Main Menu button and selecting what you want. Figure 10-1 shows the first-level menu options, which can be expanded by selecting one of the menu options.

TIP

The left arrow button next to the foot icon (the Main Menu button) or the right arrow button in the bottom-right corner of the Panel enables you to reduce the Panel to the button itself. You can also configure the Panel to hide itself automatically or move itself to a different edge of the screen by using the middle mouse button.

The Panel can be configured by using the options available under the Panel menu in the Main Menu. You can also add new panels to your desktop, if you wish. The more you use GNOME, the more you find it highly configurable and user-friendly. The next section shows you how to do just that.

Configuring GNOME

To configure your GNOME environment per your needs, you need to run the Control Center program (`/usr/bin/wm-properties-capplet`). You can open the GNOME Control Center by clicking the GNOME Main Menu button and choosing its item from the Settings submenu of the Programs menu of the Main Menu. When you open it, you should see a screen as shown in Figure 10-2.

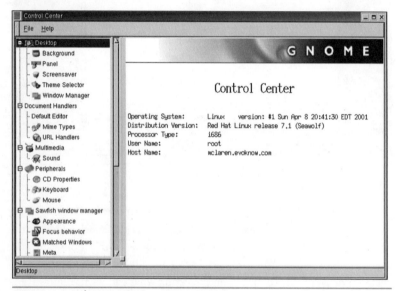

Figure 10-2 *The GNOME Control Center.*

The GNOME Control Center enables you to customize your desktop, document handlers, multimedia, peripherals, window manager, and user interface. The following sections show you how to configure various aspects of your desktop by using the GNOME Control Center.

Choosing a window manager

By default GNOME uses the Sawfish window manager as shown in Figure 10-3. You can install other window manager such as fvwm95, fvwm, AnotherLevel, or other window managers by using an appropriate RPM package found in the Red Hat CD-ROM or by downloading it from the Internet. To choose a new window manager program, click on the Window

Manager option under Desktop in the tree menu on the left side of the GNOME Control Center window. A list of available window manager programs appears, as shown in Figure 10-3.

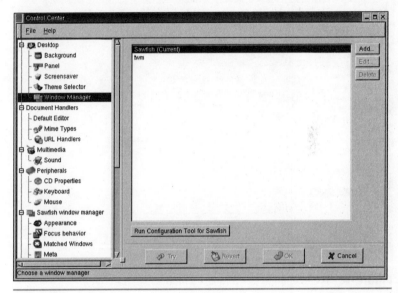

Figure 10-3 *Choosing a window manager.*

The other window manager found in the default installation of Red Hat Linux is TWM, which is a very old style window manager that I personally do not recommend. However, you can always experiment with other window managers and find the one you like.

Configuring your window manager

The Sawfish window manager can be configured from within the GNOME Control Center. Click on the Sawfish window manager option in the tree menu to expand all the options as shown in Figure 10-4.

You can configure various look-and-feel related features of the window manager by clicking on the appropriate option. Because customizing a window is a matter of personal taste, there is no right or wrong approach in changing them. Try out different options and find out what you like. However, one of the features, workspace, might be a new concept for you if you migrated from the world of Microsoft Windows. A *workspace* is a very powerful feature that enables you to create virtual "desktops" called work-spaces on a single monitor screen.

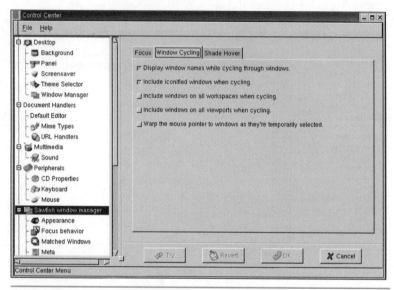

Figure 10-4 *Configuring the Sawfish window manager.*

Figure 10-5 shows the main GNOME Panel of a typical X Window System desktop. Notice the four rectangles on the bottom-right side of the screen. Each of these rectangles represents a workspace window. If you click on any of these rectangles, you automatically switch to that workspace. In a workspace, you can run a number of client programs such as Netscape Navigator, xterms, etc. to organize your screen space in the way you like.

Figure 10-5 *The GNOME Panel.*

If six workspaces are not enough, you can create more workspaces using the GNOME Control Center application as follows:

1. Click the Workspace option under the Sawfish window manager option from the tree menu. You see a window similar to the one shown in Figure 10-6.

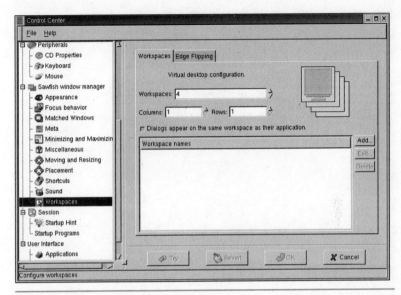

Figure 10-6 *Configuring your workspace.*

2. Enter the desired number of workspaces, and even assign a name for each workspace if you wish.

3. Click OK, and you should see the workspaces appear in the bottom-right panel as rectangles. Clicking on any of these rectangles takes you to the appropriate workspace.

Setting session options for expert mode

As you use GNOME Control Center more and more, you become an expert at it. One of the side effects of becoming an expert user is that a few routine things such as startup splash screen, tips or hints, starting the same programs again and again, "Are you sure" types of prompts, etc., become very boring. You can remove these irritations using the session configuration options available under the Session subtree. In this section I show you the session settings I use.

Click on the Session option in the tree menu, and you notice the options Startup Hints, Startup Programs, etc. Click on the Startup Hints option, and you see a screen like the one in Figure 10-7.

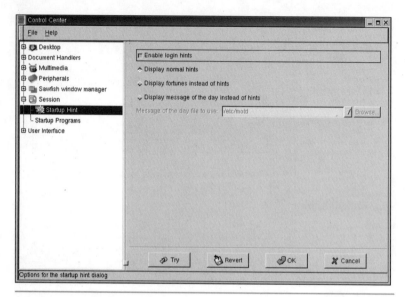

Figure 10-7 *Disabling startup hints.*

To disable possibly annoying startup hints, ensure that the "Enable login hints" option is not checked.

Now click on the Startup Programs option in the tree menu, and you see a screen as shown in Figure 10-8.

Now make sure that "Show splash screen on login" option is disabled. If you do not want to be prompted for logout confirmation, ensure that the "Prompt on logout" option is disabled. You can also choose to save session-related changes automatically by enabling "Automatically save changes to session" option.

If you wish to start a program every time you start GNOME, you can add it using the Add option under the Non-session-managed Startup Programs option. For example, to run a terminal window whenever you start GNOME, simply add "xterm" using the Add button. If you wish to run multiple programs at startup, you can control the run order using the priority numbering scheme available during the add operation.

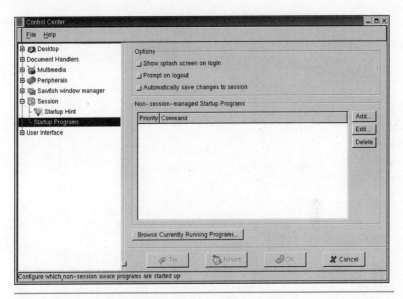

Figure 10-8 *Disabling splash screens and prompts.*

Using X Window for Administration

Some X Window applications can make it a bit easier to perform some system administrative tasks. I discuss a few very interesting ones in the following sections.

Using Gnome RPM

GnoRPM is really a graphical interface for managing RPM packages that enables you to install, upgrade, uninstall, verify, and query RPM packages quite easily. To run it, click the Main Menu button and choose the Programs ➪ System option ➪ GnoRPM. GnoRPM appears, as shown in Figure 10-9.

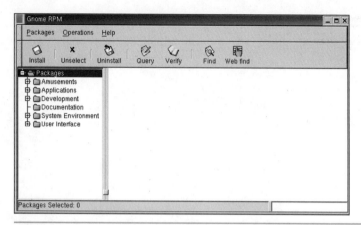

Figure 10-9 *The GnoRPM screen.*

To install an RPM package from a CD-ROM, insert the CD-ROM and mount it (GNOME automatically mounts the CD-ROM unless you disable this option using GNOME Control Center). Click the Install icon or select the Install option under the Packages menu (top left). The window should look like that shown in Figure 10-10.

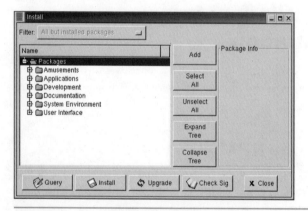

Figure 10-10 *Installing new RPMs.*

GnoRPM reads the CD-ROM and locates packages. By default, GnoRPM only displays packages that aren't installed already. If you click the Expand Tree button, all of the packages are visible, as shown in Figure 10-11.

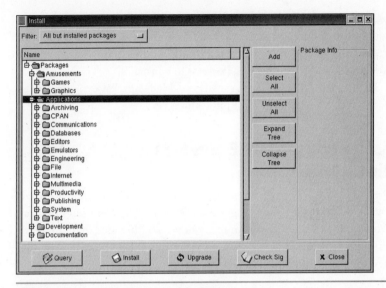

Figure 10-11 *Expanding the package tree.*

Select the appropriate packages and click the Install button to install selected packages.

If you wish to upgrade existing packages using the current CD-ROM, simply change the filter rule (top left) to "All packages" or "Only newer packages" to make it easy for yourself to find appropriate packages. If you are upgrading from an older version of an installed package, use the Upgrade button instead of the Install button.

To verify that an existing package is intact, you can simply select the package and click the Verify button. For example, Figure 10-12 shows that GnoRPM has found six problems with the installed kernel package.

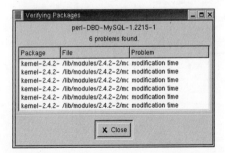

Figure 10-12 *Verifying a package.*

As you can see in the figure, because the only problem found is the modification date that I already know I have changed, there is no need to reinstall this package. However, if GnoRPM reports files missing for a package that you have installed, it is best to reinstall it.

The Gnome RPM program can also find RPM packages that you need via the Web by using the Web Find feature.

Using the GNOME System Monitor (Gtop)

The GNOME System Monitor or Gtop enables you to feel the heartbeat of your system. Gtop is a very glorified version of the top utility that can be quite a treat for a system administrator who is interested in finding how her system spends resouces such as CPU time, disk usage, and RAM. Figure 10-13 shows a sample window of a system running Gtop.

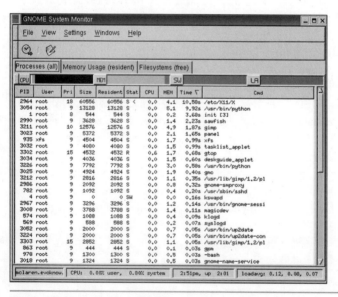

Figure 10-13 *Running Gtop.*

Gtop enables you to sort by any column. For example, you can sort all the running processes by their CPU usage by simply clicking on the CPU column header, or sort by owner (user) by clicking on the User column. The resident memory usage information is displayed separately. Click the Memory Usage (resident) tab to view a screen similar to the one shown in Figure 10-14.

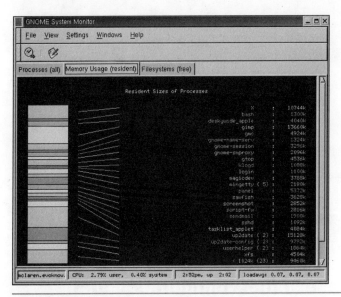

Figure 10-14 *Viewing resident memory usage.*

Using Time Tool

To set system time and date use the Time Tool. This is a very simple tool that enables you to change the system's time or date. The interface is shown in Figure 10-15.

Figure 10-15 *The Time Tool.*

Using netcfg

See Chapter 6 for details on using netcfg.

Using printtool

See Chapter 15 for details on using printtool.

Using the kernel configuration tool

See Chapter 11 for details on using the kernel configuration tool.

Using the help search tool

The help search tool that the control panel runs is called helptool, which searches online documents including man pages, info files, and random documents in the /usr/doc and /usr/local/doc directories to locate matches for keywords you specify.

Using Red Hat Network Update Agent

The Red Hat Update Agent is a graphical tool that uses Red Hat Network to find out which packages on your system needs to be updated and updates them automatically. See Chapter 2 for details.

Chapter 11

Configuring the Kernel

IN THIS CHAPTER

- Understanding the need for kernel upgrades
- Preparing for a kernel upgrade
- Installing a new kernel
- Compiling a custom kernel from the source
- Patching a kernel's source code
- Setting up the kernel with `kernelcfg`

Linux is probably the only operating system that develops a new kernel fairly often. Generally speaking, you can expect a new kernel from Red Hat every two to three months. This should tell you how heavy developmental efforts are in this platform. In this chapter, you learn to upgrade, configure, compile, and install custom kernels.

Linux runs on many hardware architectures, such as *x*86 (Intel), Power-PC, Alpha, and Sparc, among others. It is practically impossible to discuss kernel issues for all platforms in a single chapter, and therefore I assume that, like a majority of Red Hat Linux users, you have an *x*86 (Intel)-based system. However, if you are running Red Hat Linux on a system based on the mighty Alpha processor, you can find useful kernel-related information at `www.alphalinux.org/`. Also, for all architectures, you can go to `www.kernel.org/`.

Why Do You Need a Newer Kernel?

The most common reason to upgrade a kernel is to take advantage of new device drivers to handle specific devices. For example, suppose that you have a fancy SCSI controller that has a bare-bones driver and you find that a vendor has released a new module or that a driver guru has written one that allows you to customize your SCSI controller more, or use features that you couldn't with the bare-bones driver. Another reason you might want to upgrade your Linux kernel is to plug security holes in the kernel or in a module. You should monitor the following Web site for availability of updated packages:

`www.redhat.com/corp/support/errata/index.html`

Of course, many people (perhaps those with lots of time) want to upgrade just to be on the cutting edge of the Linux revolution. If you are such a Linux disciple, my only recommendation is that you keep the latest and the greatest Linux kernel away from any of your production servers. Playing with the latest development-grade Linux kernel on a personal workstation can be quite an amusing task for people who "dig it." This chapter shows you how to upgrade and customize your kernel.

Finding Out Which Linux Kernel You Have

Before you do anything else, determine the version of the current kernel in your system. For example, you can run the following command:

```
rpm -q kernel \
      kernel-headers \
      kernel-ibcs \
      kernel-pcmcia-cs \
      kernel-source > /current-kernel-pkgs.txt
```

The `current-kernel-pkgs.txt` file has version information for kernel-related packages. You also need to know the version numbers for mkinitrd (used to create initial ramdisk images), SysVinit (the init package), and the initscripts (the /etc/rc.d scripts) packages that often change with the new kernels. You can run the following command to add version information for these packages to the current-kernel-pkgs. txt file.

```
rpm -q mkinitrd SysVinit initscripts > /current-kernel-pkgs.txt
```

By running the preceding rpm commands, you have placed version information for all the typical packages you need for a full kernel upgrade. Table 11-1 lists the names and RPM descriptions of these packages.

Table 11-1 *Typical Packages Needed for Kernel Upgrades*

Package	Description Found in the RPM
kernel-2.x.xx-x. i386.rpm	This package contains the Linux kernel used to boot and run your system. It contains few device drivers for specific hardware. Modules loaded after booting support most hardware.
kernel-headers- 2.x.xx- x.i386.rpm	These are C header files for the Linux kernel, which define structures and constants that you need to build most standard programs under Linux, as well as to rebuild the kernel.
kernel-ibcs-2.x. xx-x.i386.rpm	This package allows you to run programs in the iBCS2 (Intel Binary Compatibility Standard, version 2) and in related executable formats. You can download this package from www. rpmfind.net.
kernel-pcmcia-cs-2. x.xx-x.i386.rpm	Many laptop machines (and some others) support PCMCIA cards for expansion. Also known as "credit card adapters," PCMCIA cards are small cards for everything from SCSI support to modems. They are hot-swappable (you can exchange them without rebooting the system) and quite convenient. This package contains support for PCMCIA cards of all varieties and supplies a daemon that allows you to hot-swap them.
kernel-source-2.x.xx-x. i386.rpm	This is the source code for the Linux kernel. It is required to build most C programs, as C programs depend on constants defined here. You can also build a custom kernel that is better tuned to your hardware. The source code is shipped in the second CD-ROM of the official Red Hat Linux distribution.

Continued

Table 11-1 *Continued*

Package	Description Found in the RPM
mkinitrd-x.x-x.rpm	You can build Generic kernels without drivers for any SCSI adapters that load the SCSI driver as a module. You use an initial ramdisk to solve the problem of allowing the kernel to read the module without being able to address the SCSI adapter. The operating system loader (such as LILO) loads the ramdisk and is available to the kernel as soon as it is loaded. That image is responsible for loading the proper SCSI adapter and allowing the kernel to mount the root file system. This program creates such a ramdisk image using information in /etc/conf.modules. The source code is shipped in the second CD-ROM of the official Red Hat Linux distribution.
SysVinit-x.xx-x.rpm	SysVinit is the first program the Linux kernel starts when the system boots, controlling the startup, running, and shutdown of all other programs.
initscripts-x.xx-x.rpm	This package contains scripts used to boot a system, change run levels, and shut the system down cleanly. It also contains the scripts that activate and deactivate most network interfaces.

To find out which kernel you are using to boot the system, take a look at your /etc/lilo.conf file. For example, my /etc/lilo.conf on a Red Hat Linux 7 system has the following lines:

```
boot=/dev/hda
map=/boot/map
install=/boot/boot.b
prompt
timeout=50
message=/boot/message
linear
default=linux

image=/boot/vmlinuz-2.2.16-21
        label=linux
        read-only
        root=/dev/hda2
```

As you can see, I am using a single Linux kernel image (/boot/ vmlinuz-2.2.16-21) labeled "linux," and my current kernel is /boot/ vmlinuz-2.2.16-21. If you have upgraded your Linux kernel, you might have multiple labels defined in your /etc/lilo.conf file. In such a case, you need to identify the kernel (image=/boot/vmlinux-2.x.xx-x.x) that you use to boot your system. Simply locate the LILO label you use to boot the system, and find the corresponding image=/boot/vmlinux-2.x.xx-x.x line. Note the version number of your kernel, which you need in a later section to create an emergency boot disk.

Preparing for a Kernel Upgrade

Before you can upgrade your kernel you need to get necessary RPM packages and also create a boot disk with your existing kernel on it. These tasks are discussed in the following sections.

Getting new packages

The official FTP site for the Red Hat Linux updates is ftp://updates. redhat.com/. I can never get into this site unless it is a very odd time such as 3 a.m. or later. Your best choice is to locate a mirror site near you. You can find a mirror near your area at www.redhat.com/mirrors.html.

After you have located a mirror site for the updated kernel RPM packages, connect to the site and compare versions of the packages you have stored in the /current-kernel-pkgs.txt file earlier.

Download the new packages to replace the packages in the /current-kernel-pkgs file created previously. If you do not see a new package for one of the packages in the /current-kernel-pkgs.txt file, just ignore it; a new package is not yet available.

Making a boot disk

I highly recommend that you create an emergency boot floppy at this point in case something goes wrong with the kernel upgrade. After you have created the boot disk, reboot your system by using this disk to ensure that the emergency boot disk actually works.

To create a standalone boot floppy, insert a formatted floppy disk in your floppy drive, and run the following command:

```
mkbootdisk 2.x.xx-x.x
```

Don't forget to replace 2.*x.xx-x.x* with your current kernel version. Also, if you have multiple floppy drives and do not want to use the default floppy device (/dev/fd0), you can use the --device option to specify your floppy device of choice. For example, the following command creates the emergency boot floppy on /dev/fd1 by using kernel image version 2.0.36-0.7:

```
mkbootdisk—device /dev/fd1 2.0.36-0.7
```

Installing the New Kernel

After testing the emergency boot disk, you are ready to install a new kernel. Using rpm, install all the packages you have downloaded. I typically download all new packages to a new directory in a temporary space such as /tmp/new-kernel-pkgs and run the following command:

```
rpm -ivh /tmp/new-kernel-pkgs/*.rpm
```

> **TIP**
>
> If you do not plan to compile the kernel, you may skip the kernel-headers-2.*x.xx-x*.i386.rpm and kernel-source-2.*x.xx-x*.i386.rpm packages, as you need them only to compile custom kernels.

After you've upgraded the new kernel and related packages, you need to create the initial ramdisk image file the kernel needs to boot the system. The initial ramdisk image file allows a kernel to access modules such as disk drivers, which you need, in turn, to access the rest of the modules residing on the root file system.

Creating the initial ramdisk

You use the mkinitrd command to create the initial ramdisk. Replacing 2.*x.xx-x* with the version number of your new kernel, run the following command:

```
mkinitrd /boot/initrd-2.x.xx-x.img 2.x.xx-x
```

This creates the /boot/initrd-2.x.xx-x.img initial ramdisk image file. Using the ls utility, confirm that this file is in the /boot directory.

After you've created the initial `ramdisk`, you need to modify the `/etc/lilo.conf` file to configure LILO for the new kernel.

Configuring LILO

Configuring LILO is critical to your kernel installation, and you must not reboot the system until you have reconfigured LILO as discussed here. Using your favorite text editor, add a new configuration segment such as the following to your `/etc/lilo.conf` file:

```
image=/boot/vmlinuz-2.x.xx-x
        label=new-linux
        root=/dev/hda1
        initrd=/boot/initrd-2.x.xx-x.img
        read-only
```

Remember to replace *2.x.xx-x* with the appropriate kernel version number for both the `image=` and `initrd=` lines. The `label=` line should be set to an arbitrary string of your choice. The `root=` line should point to your root disk partition. For example, if your current root partition is `/dv/sda1`, you should make sure the `root=` line is set to that partition. After you've modified and saved the `/etc/lilo.conf` file, run the following command:

```
/sbin/lilo
```

This makes LILO read the new configuration file and updates the boot sector of the appropriate root partition. You can use the –v option with the preceding command to make LILO a bit more verbose. After you've run LILO, you're ready to reboot the system.

Booting with the new kernel

Use the `shutdown –r now` command to reboot your system as usual. At the LILO prompt, press the Tab key to see your choices. The labels you enter (in the `label=` lines) for your old and new kernels appear on the screen. Enter the label for your new kernel (in the example in the previous section, this label is `new-linux`) at the LILO prompt to boot the system with the new kernel.

The next step mostly depends on your facial expression after you tell LILO to start the new kernel. If you find yourself smiling, your new kernel is up and running. On the other hand, if you find yourself not smiling but screaming because your system will not boot, don't panic. You still have the old kernel on floppy disk, remember?

If the system locks up, press Ctrl+Alt+Del, or do a hard reboot. After you get the LILO prompt again, enter the label name for your old kernel. The system should boot up as usual. In such a case, you need to check the steps you have taken, especially the /etc/lilo configuration file. Make sure that you have the new configuration set up correctly. Then rerun /sbin/lilo and try to boot the system with the new kernel. If the problem persists, you need to post the details of your problem (such as what appears on the console when you attempt to boot the new kernel) to a comp.linux newsgroup specific to Linux. If your software license permits, you may also contact Red Hat for help.

In most cases, the new installation should go smoothly without incident. To make sure you are running the new kernel, run the following command:

```
uname -a
```

This displays the kernel version number with other information. After the new kernel is up and running, you should create a new boot disk by using the mkbootdisk command as described earlier in this chapter.

Customizing the Kernel

The only way you can customize a kernel to your liking is via custom compilation. To compile a kernel on your Red Hat Linux server system, you need the kernel header and source RPM packages. If the kernel you are trying to customize is not production grade, there might not be an RPM version available. In such a case, you have to download the source in compressed tar format (.tar.gz). Check the official Red Hat Web site for availability of the kernel source and header RPM packages. If you can't find the RPM packages, download the .tar.gz distribution from the official www.kernel.org/ site (or any of its mirrors). In this section, I assume that you want to customize the latest 2.2.2 kernel and have downloaded the linux-2.4.7.tar.gz source distribution from the site just mentioned.

Installing Linux kernel source

Extract the linux-2.4.7.tar.gz distribution in the /usr/src directory by entering the tar xvzf linux-2.4.7.tar.gz command. The source distribution is stored in a subdirectory called `linux-2.4.7` in `/usr/src`. The Linux kernel is traditionally stored in `/usr/src/linux` (actually, `/usr/src/linux` is a symbolic link to the `/usr/src/linux-x.x.xx` directory). Remove the symbolic link by using rm `/usr/src/linux`; then create a new symbolic link by using the following command:

```
ln -s /usr/src/linux-2.4.7 /usr/src/linux
```

The series of commands you have to run to arrive at this stage might look as follows:

```
cd /usr/src
tar xvzf linux-2.4.7.tar.gz
rm -f /usr/src/linux
ln -s linux-2.4.7 linux
```

When I extracted the source distribution in the `/usr/src` directory, it created a `linux` subdirectory, and therefore the symbolic link was unnecessary. However, if you plan to experiment with various kernels, I recommend that you keep a particular source distribution in the `/usr/src/linux-x.x.xx` directory and always point a symbolic link (`linux`) to the kernel you are currently working on.

Although a freshly downloaded source distribution is not going to have stale object files, it is wise to run the following command to clean up such files just in case:

```
make mrproper
```

Now you are ready to configure (customize) the kernel. You have multiple choices as to how you can customize the kernel.

Configuring the kernel the old-fashioned way

To configure the kernel the old-fashioned way, from the command line, you need to run the following command from the `/usr/src/linux` directory:

```
make config
```

Using make config to configure the kernel is quite a long process, and also a bit cumbersome; however, it is quite appropriate if you happen to be configuring the kernel via a Telnet connection on a remote server. The line-based interface may not be elegant, but it works for most scenarios, and you should consider it the default method of configuration when the following two methods (make menuconfig and xconfig) are unusable.

make config is the simplest way to configure a kernel; however, it might not be the most suitable for beginning kernel hackers. In this section and the following subsections I discuss a sample kernel configuration session using the make config method. However, you should know that as features and support for various devices are added on an ongoing basis to Linux, the exact steps that make config shows also change. Therefore, what you see in the following section might not be exactly what you see when you run make config on your system. I discuss the major decision points here. If you find a new configuration question when you run make config, you can simply find more about it by entering ? at the prompt, or you can choose to go with the default.

You can choose the default answer by pressing the Enter key. Also note that the default answer is always represented as a capital letter.

Code maturity-level options

In this section, you're asked if you want to be prompted for experimental features. You can choose to see (and perhaps use) these experimental features if you are configuring the kernel for a system where experimentation or downtime and crashes are part of the fun and not a burden. The prompt appears as follows:

```
Prompt for development and/or incomplete code/drivers (CONFIG_EXPERIMENTAL)
[Y/n/?]
```

The default answer (Y) is fine.

Loadable module support

The Linux kernel uses an innovative method for keeping a low profile: it uses features and drivers implemented as external modules. These modules are dynamically loaded and unloaded on an as-needed basis. This allows the kernel to require less memory and to become more hardware independent. Typically, you load the modules by using a program called `kerneld`, which, in turn, uses another program called `modprobe` to manage available modules. Modules can be device drivers, file systems, binary executable formats, and so on. In this section, you're asked if you want module-related support or not. The first question is as follows:

```
Enable loadable module support (CONFIG_MODULES) [Y/n/?]
```

This really should not be an option — you definitely want to have loadable module support for almost all scenarios. The default is fine.

```
Set version information on all symbols for modules (CONFIG_MODVERSIONS) [Y/n/?]
```

When you compile modules with version information, you can reuse them with new kernels without needing to compile them from scratch. However, the preferred method is to compile the modules along with the new kernel to eliminate compatibility problems. Hence the preferred answer is no (i.e., enter **n**).

```
Kernel module loader (CONFIG_KMOD) [Y/n/?]
```

Linux can load modules using the `kerneld` daemon. This prompt asks you if would like to use a kernel module loader inside the kernel itself to avoid using the `kerneld` daemon. Because `kerneld` \is written using System V Interprocess communication (SysV IPC) code, which is not considered very solid by many programmers, it is better to avoid using `kerneld` and have a kernel module as a replacement. The default answer (Y) is sufficient.

Processor type, memory model, and features

In this section, you are asked about the processor family, the memory model, the math coprocessor, multiprocessors, and other processor-specific questions. Here is the first prompt:

```
Processor family (386, 486, 586/K5/5x86/6x86/6x86MX, Pentium-Classic, Pentium-MMX,
Pentium-Pro/Celeron/Pentium-II, Pentium-III/Celeron(Coppermine), Pentium-4,
K6/K6-II/K6-III, Athlon/Duron/K7, Crusoe, Winchip-C6, Winchip-2, Winchip-2A/
Winchip-3, CyrixIII/C3) [Pentium-III/Celeron(Coppermine)]
```

If the default processor architecture is incorrect, you should choose one of the listed ones. In my case, the default is wrong, so I enter **Pentium/ K6/TSC** as the processor family.

Next you're asked if you wish to configure your kernel to support Toshiba Laptops as shown below:

```
Toshiba Laptop support (CONFIG_TOSHIBA) [N/y/m/?]
```

If you are making this kernel for such a laptop, the default answer (N) is fine.

```
/dev/cpu/microcode - Intel IA32 CPU microcode support (CONFIG_MICROCODE)
[N/y/m/?]
```

If you wish to be able to update the microcode for your Intel IA32 (Pentium Pro, PII, PIII, Pentium 4, Celeron, Xeon, etc.) processors as they become available from Intel then say yes (y) here. To learn more about this visit **www.urbanmyth.org/microcode/**. Most Linux users will not require this.

```
/dev/cpu/*/msr - Model-specific register support (CONFIG_X86_MSR) [N/y/m/?]
```

If you wish to allow system programs to access the x86 Mode-Specific Register (MSRs), enter **y** or accept the default value.

```
/dev/cpu/*/cpuid - CPU information support (CONFIG_X86_CPUID) [N/y/m/?]
```

If you wish to allow programs to access CPU identification available in Intel CPUs then say yes (y) here. Enabling this will create a device called /dev/cpu/CPU_number/cpuid that shows CPU identification information. For example /dev/cpu/0/cpuid displays information on the first CPU of your system.

If you have two CPUs you will have /dev/cpu/0/cpuid and /dev/cpu/1/cpuid devices.

```
High Memory Support (off, 4GB, 64GB) [off]
```

If you have less then 4GB of RAM you can accept the default (off) value or else enter 4GB if you have 4GB of physical RAM, or if you have higher then 4GB you can enter 64GB here.

```
defined CONFIG_M686
```

```
Math emulation (CONFIG_MATH_EMULATION) [N/y/?]
```

Unless you have a (really old) processor that does not have a math coprocessor built in, you should choose the default by pressing Enter here.

```
MTRR (Memory Type Range Register) support (CONFIG_MTRR) [N/y/?]
```

This is probably the first question that does not quite make sense to you (unless you are an expert in *x*86 CPU design) and to most beginning kernel hackers. So what can you choose here? The default option is often the right one for most cases. Also, you can find what Memory Type Range Register (MTRR) support means by entering the **?** character at the prompt. You get the help screen as shown here:

```
CONFIG_MTRR:


On Intel Pentium Pro and Pentium II systems the Memory Type Range
Registers (MTRRs) may be used to control processor access to memory ranges. This
is most useful when you have a video (VGA) card on a PCI or AGP bus. Enabling
write-combining allows bus write transfers to be combined into a larger transfer
before bursting over the PCI/AGP bus. This can increase performance of image
write operations 2.5 times or more. This option creates a /proc/mtrr file which
may be used to manipulate your MTRRs. Typically the X server should use this.
This should have a reasonably generic interface so that similar control
registers on other processors can be easily
supported.


Saying Y here also fixes a problem with buggy SMP BIOSes which only set the
MTRRs for the boot CPU and not the secondary CPUs. This can lead to all sorts of
problems.


You can safely say Y even if your machine doesn't have MTRRs, you'll just add
about 3k to your kernel.


See Documentation/mtrr.txt for more information.
```

As you can see, this is quite helpful. Because I am configuring this kernel for a server, I do not care much about the video, so I choose "N" here.

```
Symmetric multi-processing support (CONFIG_SMP) [Y/n/?]
```

If you have multiple processors on your system and would like to turn on symmetric multiprocessing support, choose the default. In my case, I do not have a motherboard with multiple processors; therefore, I chose to decline SMB support.

General setup

In this section, you configure the general options.

```
Networking support (CONFIG_NET) [Y/n/?]
```

Perhaps there are a few out there who want to run Linux and not have networking support, but for most users, the default is a must.

```
SGI Visual Workstation support (CONFIG_VISWS) [N/y/?]
```

If you are not using an SGI system, choose the default.

```
PCI support (CONFIG_PCI) [Y/n/?]
```

Unless you are on a really old *x*86 system that has only an ISA bus, the default is fine.

 On Sparc systems you might not need PCI support if you have only sbus cards.

```
PCI access mode (BIOS, Direct, Any) [Any]
```

The default option allows the kernel to detect the PCI configuration by using the direct method; if that fails, it gets PCI configuration from the system BIOS, so the default is fine.

```
PCI device name database (CONFIG_PCI_NAMES) [Y/n/?]
```

By default, the kernel stores all known PCI device names until it has finished booting up and has finished building the /proc/pci and /proc/ioports entries. The default answer is acceptable.

```
EISA support (CONFIG_EISA) [N/y/?]
```

Unless you have Extended Industry Standard Architecture (EISA) bus device you can choose the default answer.

```
MCA support (CONFIG_MCA) [N/y/?]
```

Unless you have an IBM PS/2 Micro Channel Architecture (MCA)-based system, you do not need MCA support.

```
Support for hot-pluggable devices (CONFIG_HOTPLUG) [Y/n/?]
```

If you have devices that can be plugged in or unplugged while the system is running, you can accept the default answer.

```
PCMCIA/CardBus support (CONFIG_PCMCIA) [Y/m/n/?]
```

If you have PCMCIA or PC card devices in your system, choose the default answer or else choose no here. If you choose the default answer you will have to choose answers for the following:

```
CardBus support (CONFIG_CARDBUS) [Y/n/?]
i82365 compatible bridge support (CONFIG_I82365) [N/y/?]
Databook TCIC host bridge support (CONFIG_TCIC) [N/y/?]
```

The default values should be acceptable in most cases.

```
System V IPC (CONFIG_SYSVIPC) [Y/n/?]
```

Many programs need Inter Process Communication (IPC); therefore, the default is a must.

```
BSD Process Accounting (CONFIG_BSD_PROCESS_ACCT) [N/y/?]
```

This allows a program to ask the kernel to dump information about a process, such as a process owner's UID, creation time, and memory stats. This is not required; answer either way.

```
Sysctl support (CONFIG_SYSCTL) [Y/n/?]
```

This option allows dynamic changing of various kernel parameters in the /proc file system without a reboot or recompilation of the kernel. This is a must for all systems.

```
Kernel core (/proc/kcore) format (ELF, A.OUT) [ELF]
```

This option allows you to set the binary time for the kernel core. The default ELF is highly recommended over A.OUT, which is a depreciated format.

```
Kernel support for a.out binaries (CONFIG_BINFMT_AOUT) [Y/m/n/?]
```

Traditionally, the A.OUT format has been used to create executable and library programs; however, the new Executable and Linkable Format (ELF) has been in use for a while. You might want to keep support in a module instead of making it part of the kernel. Hence, choose the "m" option for module.

```
Kernel support for ELF binaries (CONFIG_BINFMT_ELF) [Y/m/n/?]
```

ELF support is a must; therefore, the default is fine.

```
Kernel support for MISC binaries (CONFIG_BINFMT_MISC) [Y/m/n/?]
```

If you plan on running Java or DOS executables using interpreters, you might want to have the miscellaneous binary support as a module.

```
Power Management support (CONFIG_PM) [Y/n/?]
```

Most modern motherboards have power management capability so the default answer should be okay.

```
ACPI support (CONFIG_ACPI) [N/y/?]
```

You should choose the default answer because ACPI support is experimental in the current kernel.

```
Advanced Power Management BIOS support (CONFIG_APM) [N/y/?]
```

If you are not concerned about saving power, the default is fine.

```
Memory Technology Device (MTD) support (CONFIG_MTD) [N/y/m/?]
```

If you have flash cards or other memory devices for your system, you can enable MTD support or choose the default answer (N).

```
Parallel port support (CONFIG_PARPORT) [N/y/m/?]
```

If you plan on connecting a printer or other parallel port devices to your Linux system, choose "y" for adding support to the kernel or "m" to have support available as a module.

Plug and Play support

In my personal experience, Plug and Play should really be called Plug and Pray (don't know who said it first). I urge you not to enable PNP in something so nice as Linux.

```
Plug and Play support (CONFIG_PNP) [N/y/?]
```

You should know the answer to this prompt. If you have a card that works only in PNP mode, you are likely to encounter problems. The best thing to do is buy hardware that has an option to turn off PNP.

Block devices

In this section, you are asked about disk drives.

```
Normal PC floppy disk support (CONFIG_BLK_DEV_FD) [Y/m/n/?]
```

Because most systems have floppy drives, this should be set to yes.

```
XT hard disk support (CONFIG_BLK_DEV_XD) [N/y/m/?]
```

Modern PCs don't use XT hard disks any more so you should choose the default answer unless you happen to have XT hard disks.

```
Compaq SMART2 support (CONFIG_BLK_CPQ_DA) [N/y/m/?] okcmpk
Compaq Smart Array 5xxx support (CONFIG_BLK_CPQ_CISS_DA) [N/y/m/?]
Mylex DAC960/DAC1100 PCI RAID Controller support
(CONFIG_BLK_DEV_DAC960) [N/y/m/?]
Loopback device support (CONFIG_BLK_DEV_LOOP) [N/y/m/?] y
Network block device support (CONFIG_BLK_DEV_NBD) [N/y/m/?]
Multiple devices driver support (RAID and LVM) (CONFIG_MD) [N/y/?]
```

Networking options

Networking is one of the most important sections. Here, you decide on various networking issues.

```
Packet socket (CONFIG_PACKET) [Y/m/n/?]
```

Applications such as tcpdump use the Packet protocol; therefore, you should accept the default answer.

```
Kernel/User netlink socket (CONFIG_NETLINK) [N/y/?]
```

If you want to use your system as a firewall, or you want to use the `arpd` daemon to maintain an internal ARP cache, say yes here.

```
Network firewalls (CONFIG_FIREWALL) [N/y/?]
```

If you would like to use your system as a packet-filtering firewall, choose yes.

```
Network aliasing (CONFIG_NET_ALIAS) [N/y/?] ?
```

If you have multiple network interfaces for your system, choose yes.

```
Socket Filtering (CONFIG_FILTER) [N/y/?] ?
```

This feature allows programs to attach filters to sockets and to control how data goes through the socket. Unless you use such programs, the default answer is fine.

```
Unix domain sockets (CONFIG_UNIX) [Y/m/n/?]
```

Sockets are standard Unix mechanisms for establishing and accessing network connections. Therefore, the default answer is fine.

```
TCP/IP networking (CONFIG_INET) [Y/n/?]
```

This is a no-brainer: yes.

```
IP: multicasting (CONFIG_IP_MULTICAST) [N/y/?]
```

Typically, you use IP multicasting for transferring large amounts of data such as real-time, broadcast-quality video that uses large bandwidth connections. Unless you have such needs, the default is fine.

```
IP: advanced router (CONFIG_IP_ADVANCED_ROUTER) [N/y/?]
```

If you intend to run your Linux system mostly as a router (as a computer that forwards and redistributes network packets), choose yes.

```
IP: kernel level autoconfiguration (CONFIG_IP_PNP) [N/y/?]
```

This enables automatic configuration of the IP addresses of devices, and of the routing table during kernel boot, based on either information supplied at the kernel command line or by BOOTP or RARP protocols.

```
IP: optimize as router not host (CONFIG_IP_ROUTER) [N/y/?] ?
```

Some Linux network drivers use a technique called copy and checksum to optimize host performance. However, if your machine acts as a router most of the time and is forwarding most packets to another host, this is a waste of space, and so you can therefore select the default answer.

IP: tunneling (CONFIG_NET_IPIP) [N/y/m/?]

Tunneling means encapsulating data of one protocol within another protocol and sending it over a channel that understands the encapsulating protocol. This particular tunneling driver implements encapsulation of IP within IP, which sounds kind of pointless but can be useful if you want to make your (or some other) machine appear on a different network than it is physically connected to or to use mobile-IP facilities (allowing laptops to seamlessly move between networks without changing their IP addresses).

IP: GRE tunnels over IP (CONFIG_NET_IPGRE) [N/y/m/?] ?

GRE (Generic Routing Encapsulation) allows encapsulating of IPv4 or IPv6 over the existing IPv4 infrastructure.

IP: multicast routing (CONFIG_IP_MROUTE) [N/y/?]

If you are setting up a multicast router enable this or else choose the default answer.

IP: TCP Explicit Congestion Notification support (CONFIG_INET_ECN) [N/y/?]

If you are setting up a Linux router and want to use Explicit Congestion Notification (ECN) to notify network clients about the status of the network congestion, enable this by entering y; otherwise, choose the default.

IP: aliasing support (CONFIG_IP_ALIAS) [N/y/?]

If you wish to attach multiple IP addresses to a single network interface, choose yes here.

IP: TCP syncookie support (disabled per default) (CONFIG_SYN_COOKIES) [N/y/?]

Normal TCP/IP networking is open to an attack known as *SYN flooding*. This Denial of Service (DoS) attack prevents legitimate remote users from connecting to your computer during an ongoing attack and requires very little work from the attacker, who can operate from anywhere on the Internet. SYN cookies provide protection against this type of attack. If you choose yes here, the TCP/IP stack uses a cryptographic challenge protocol known as *SYN cookies* to enable legitimate users to continue to connect even when your machine is under attack. There is no need for legitimate users to change their TCP/IP software, but SYN cookies may prevent correct error reporting on clients when the server is overloaded. If this happens frequently, you better turn them off. If you choose Y here, note that default does not enable SYN cookies; you can enable them by choosing yes to /proc filesystem support and Sysctl support below and executing the following command:

```
echo 1 >/proc/sys/net/ipv4/tcp_syncookies
```

at boot time after the /proc file system mounts.

```
The IPv6 protocol (EXPERIMENTAL) (CONFIG_IPV6) [N/y/m/?]
```

If you wish to have support of the next-generation IP protocol (Ipv6; current version is Ipv4) then enable this option or else choose the default answer.

```
Kernel httpd acceleration (EXPERIMENTAL) (CONFIG_KHTTPD) [N/y/m/?]
```

If you wish to use the kernel level HTTP daemon which serves only static pages and redirects all other requests to your Apache Web server (or any other Web server that you run) then enable this option.

When you enable this module you can start it from /etc/ rc.d/rc.local using the following line:

```
echo 1 > /proc/sys/net/khttpd/start
```

```
Asynchronous Transfer Mode (ATM) (EXPERIMENTAL) (CONFIG_ATM) [N/y/?]
```

If you plan on using ATM networking technology with your Linux system then choose yes; otherwise choose the default answer.

```
The IPX protocol (CONFIG_IPX) [N/y/m/?]
```

Unless you need support for Novell networking, the default answer is fine.

```
Appletalk DDP (CONFIG_ATALK) [N/y/m/?]
```

Unless you need AppleTalk networking support, the default answer is fine.

`DECnet Support (CONFIG_DECNET) [N/y/m/?]`

Unless you need DECnet networking support, the default answer is fine.

`802.1d Ethernet Bridging (CONFIG_BRIDGE) [N/y/m/?]`

If you wish to make your Linux system an Ethernet bridge, which connects to Ethernet network segments and makes them appear as a single Ethernet segment, then enable this option; otherwise, choose the default answer.

`CCITT X.25 Packet Layer (EXPERIMENTAL) (CONFIG_X25) [N/y/m/?]`

Most likely you do not need X.25 protocol support unless you want to use Linux system with frame relay hardware.

`LAPB Data Link Driver (EXPERIMENTAL) (CONFIG_LAPB) [N/y/m/?]`

Choose the default answer unless you want to use Link Access Procedure, Balanced (LAPB), which is part of X.25 protocol used for frame relays.

`802.2 LLC (EXPERIMENTAL) (CONFIG_LLC) [N/y/?]`

Again, if you do not use X.25 protocol then choose the default answer.

`Frame Diverter (EXPERIMENTAL) (CONFIG_NET_DIVERT) [N/y/?]`

If you wish to divert packets of data in promiscuous mode then you can enable this option. Most likely you do not need to do so.

`Acorn Econet/AUN protocols (EXPERIMENTAL) (CONFIG_ECONET) [N/y/m/?]`

Most likely you do not need to deal with this protocol. Choose the default answer.

`WAN router (CONFIG_WAN_ROUTER) [N/y/m/?]`

If you are not setting up your Linux system as a Wide Area Network (WAN) router you can choose the default answer.

`Fast switching (read help!) (CONFIG_NET_FASTROUTE) [N/y/?]`

If you wish to enable high-speed data transfer between network cards then enable this.

If you enable this you cannot perform network packet filtering.

```
Forwarding between high speed interfaces (CONFIG_NET_HW_FLOWCONTROL) [N/y/?]
```

Enable this if you wish to turn on network hardware-based bandwidth throttling in a fast network.

```
QoS and/or fair queueing (CONFIG_NET_SCHED) [N/y/?]
```

This option should be turned on if you wish to enable the fair queuing scheme to control Quality of Service (QoS) during peak network traffic. Enabling this will allow you to choose different algorithm for prioritizing packets of different types when there are too many to handle. I recommend enabling it. If you do enable it you will have to select schedulers options from the following selection:

```
CBQ packet scheduler (CONFIG_NET_SCH_CBQ) [N/y/m/?] (NEW)

CSZ packet scheduler (CONFIG_NET_SCH_CSZ) [N/y/m/?]

The simplest PRIO pseudoscheduler (CONFIG_NET_SCH_PRIO) [N/y/m/?] (NEW)

RED queue (CONFIG_NET_SCH_RED) [N/y/m/?] (NEW)

SFQ queue (CONFIG_NET_SCH_SFQ) [N/y/m/?] (NEW)

TEQL queue (CONFIG_NET_SCH_TEQL) [N/y/m/?] (NEW)

TBF queue (CONFIG_NET_SCH_TBF) [N/y/m/?] (NEW)

GRED queue (CONFIG_NET_SCH_GRED) [N/y/m/?] (NEW)

Diffserv field marker (CONFIG_NET_SCH_DSMARK) [N/y/m/?] (NEW)

Rate estimator (CONFIG_NET_ESTIMATOR) [N/y/?] (NEW)

Packet classifier API (CONFIG_NET_CLS) [N/y/?] (NEW)
```

Use the ? option to learn about the different schedulers and use the one that you feel is most appropriate for your network.

Telephony options

If you wish to enable telephony support, choose yes here. Most users will not need to enable support for telephony devices.

```
Linux telephony support (CONFIG_PHONE) [N/y/m/?]
```

Additional block devices

Next you will be asked if you wish to support ATA, IDE hard drives. If you are not using IDE hard drive then say no (n) to the following question and skip this section.

```
ATA/IDE/MFM/RLL support (CONFIG_IDE) [Y/m/n/?]
```

If you do say yes (default) then you will be asked if you want the EIDE support as shown below:

```
Enhanced IDE/MFM/RLL disk/cdrom/tape/floppy support (CONFIG_BLK_DEV_IDE) [Y/m/n/?]
```

Most likely if you use a non-SCSI hard drive it is EIDE type, so you should choose the default answer.

```
Use old disk-only driver on primary interface (CONFIG_BLK_DEV_HD_IDE) [N/y/?]
```

You should accept the default for this question unless you plan on using old disk-only driver.

```
Include IDE/ATA-2 DISK support (CONFIG_BLK_DEV_IDEDISK) [Y/m/n/?]
```

You should choose the default answer for the above question because most of the newer EIDE-type drives use ATA-2 technologies.

```
Use multi-mode by default (CONFIG_IDEDISK_MULTI_MODE) [Y/n/?]
```

The default answer is good for most newer hard drives. Choose the default answer.

```
PCMCIA IDE support (CONFIG_BLK_DEV_IDECS) [N/y/m/?]
```

If you are setting up a Linux system with PCMCIA IDE drives then enable this option; otherwise, choose the default answer.

```
Include IDE/ATAPI CDROM support (CONFIG_BLK_DEV_IDECD) [Y/m/n/?]
```

If you use a IDE/ATAPI CD-ROM, choose the default answer.

```
Include IDE/ATAPI TAPE support (CONFIG_BLK_DEV_IDETAPE) [N/y/m/?]
```

If you use an IDE/ATAPI tape drive, choose the default answer.

```
Include IDE/ATAPI FLOPPY support (CONFIG_BLK_DEV_IDEFLOPPY) [N/y/m/?]
```

If you use an IDE/ATAPI tape drive, choose the default answer.

```
SCSI emulation support (CONFIG_BLK_DEV_IDESCSI) [N/y/m/?]
```

This is not useful for most users; choose the default answer.

IDE CHIPSET support/bugfixes

You will be asked a series of questions about chipset support and bugfixes in this section. You should choose the appropriate chipset based on your motherboard. If you do not know the chipset in your motherboard you should accept default, which will work in most cases.

SCSI support

If you have SCSI disks, a CD-ROM, tape drives, or other SCSI devices, this section allows you to configure support for such devices. You should answer the following questions based on available SCSI hardware:

```
SCSI support (CONFIG_SCSI) [Y/m/n/?]
SCSI disk support (CONFIG_BLK_DEV_SD) [Y/m/n/?]
SCSI tape support (CONFIG_CHR_DEV_ST) [N/y/m/?]
SCSI CD-ROM support (CONFIG_BLK_DEV_SR) [N/y/m/?]
SCSI generic support (CONFIG_CHR_DEV_SG) [N/y/m/?]
```

```
Probe all LUNs on each SCSI device (CONFIG_SCSI_MULTI_LUN) [Y/n/?]
```

Unless you have a SCSI device with multiple Logical Unit Numbers (LUN), choose no here.

```
Verbose SCSI error reporting (kernel size +=12K)
(CONFIG_SCSI_CONSTANTS) [Y/n/?]
```

The error messages regarding your SCSI hardware are easier to understand if you choose yes here.

```
SCSI logging facility (CONFIG_SCSI_LOGGING) [N/y/?]
```

This turns on a logging facility you can use to debug a number of SCSI-related problems. If you choose yes, you have to enable logging by using the following command in /etc/rc.d/rc.local.

```
echo "scsi log token [level]" > /proc/scsi/scsi
```

Here, *token* can be error, scan, mlqueue, mlcomplete, llqueue, llcomplete, hlqueue, or hlcomplete. The *level* controls the verbosity of the log and can be any positive number, including 0.

The rest of the questions in the SCSI section are specific to SCSI host adapters. You should choose support for only the adapter(s) you have installed.

Firewire and I20 support

If you have Firewire or I20 devices you should select the support option for them.

> Both of these types of devices are supported using experimental drivers and therefore are not yet very reliable.

Network device support

In this section, you configure various network device features.

```
Network device support (CONFIG_NETDEVICES) [Y/n/?]
```

You must say yes to the preceding question if you want network devices

```
ARCnet support (CONFIG_ARCNET) [N/y/m/?]
```

Unless you have ARCnet network interface cards, the default is fine.

```
Dummy net driver support (CONFIG_DUMMY) [M/n/y/?] ?
```

This driver allows you a dummy network interface device that you can use to fool a network client program. Keeping this as a module might be handy; hence, the default is recommended.

```
EQL (serial line load balancing) support (CONFIG_EQUALIZER)
[N/y/m/?]
```

This feature is not useful for most system configurations. Thus, the default answer is recommended.

```
Ethernet (10 or 100Mbit) (CONFIG_NET_ETHERNET) [Y/n/?]
```

Because most networks use 10 Mbits/sec or 100 Mbits/sec Ethernets these days, you should choose the default answer.

Next you will be asked about your network card. Depending on your network card vendor you will have to select support for that card. If you do not find your card-related query, chances are that you have a generic card and that the default settings will work just fine. For example, if you have a no-brand name PCI NE2000 compatible card you can enable support for when you are asked the following question:

```
PCI NE2000 support (CONFIG_NE2K_PCI) [N/y/m/?]
```

Choose the above only when you are sure you have a PCI card but it is not a brand name card (which may have proprietary, unsupported modules).

```
Wireless LAN (non-hamradio) (CONFIG_NET_RADIO) [N/y/?]
```

If you have wireless LAN then choose yes here to enable support for it. Note that most Wireless Access Point (WAP) have a regular Ethernet interface that can be connected to your system and therefore you do not need wireless LAN support in such cases.

```
Token Ring driver support (CONFIG_TR) [N/y/?]
```

If you use a token ring network then enable support for it here; otherwise, choose the default answer.

```
Fibre Channel driver support (CONFIG_NET_FC) [N/y/?]
```

If you have fiber channel devices then you need to enable this support; otherwise, choose the default answer.

```
Red Creek Hardware VPN (EXPERIMENTAL) (CONFIG_RCPCI) [N/y/m/?]
```

If you do not have Red Creek hardware, choose the default answer.

```
Traffic Shaper (EXPERIMENTAL) (CONFIG_SHAPER) [N/y/m/?]
```

If you wish to control outgoing network traffic flow, enable this experimental support by choosing yes.

```
Wan interfaces support (CONFIG_WAN) [N/y/?]
```

If you have Wide Area Network cards, enable WAN support by choosing yes; otherwise, choose the default answer.

```
PCMCIA network device support (CONFIG_NET_PCMCIA) [Y/n/?]
```

If you have PCMCIA network cards, enable WAN support by choosing yes; otherwise, choose the default answer.

Amateur radio, IrDA ISDN, and old CD-ROM support

I assume that you're not going to use Amateur Radio, IrDA (Infrared), ISDN, or old CD-ROM support; hence, the default answers to the following questions are sufficient:

```
Amateur Radio support (CONFIG_HAMRADIO) [N/y/?]

IrDA subsystem support (CONFIG_IRDA) [N/y/m/?]

ISDN support (CONFIG_ISDN) [N/y/m/?]

Support non-SCSI/IDE/ATAPI CD-ROM drives (CONFIG_CD_NO_IDESCSI) [N/y/?]
```

If you are planning on using an ISDN card to provide Internet connectivity for your server, I highly recommend that you get an ISDN router instead of an internal card. I have tried a few name-brand ISDN cards that do not work very well. On top of the problems of dealing with yet another card (IRQ and I/O address resources are limited on a PC), the price difference between an internal card and an external ISDN router is not significant.

Input core support

If you have USB based Human Interface Device (HUD) then enable support for it by answering yes (y) below:

```
Input core support (CONFIG_INPUT) [N/y/m/?]
```

If you want to enable joystick support, enable the input core support here.

Character devices

In this section, you are asked about terminal configuration.

```
Virtual terminal (CONFIG_VT) [Y/n/?]
```

This feature allows you to have virtual terminals. The default answer is required unless you are installing the kernel in an embedded Linux system.

```
Support for console on virtual terminal (CONFIG_VT_CONSOLE) [Y/n/?]
```

This feature allows you to turn a virtual terminal into a system console. This is required for the same reason as the last answer.

```
Support for console on serial port (CONFIG_SERIAL_CONSOLE) [N/y/?]
```

If you would like to use your computer's serial port as the system console, choose yes here.

```
Extended dumb serial driver options (CONFIG_SERIAL_EXTENDED) [N/y/?]
```

Unless you enable the serial port as a system console in the last question, choose the default answer here.

```
Unix98 PTY support (CONFIG_UNIX98_PTYS) [Y/n/?]
```

This feature provides support for the UNIX 98 pseudo-terminal numbering convention, which is superior to the traditional Linux pseudo-terminal number convention. You should choose the default answer.

If you choose the default answer, you are asked the following question to set the maximum number of UNIX 98 PTYs the system can use:

```
Maximum number of Unix98 PTYs in use (0-2048) (CONFIG_UNIX98_PTY_COUNT) [256]
```

For most cases, the default value should be sufficient.

Mice support

If you have a mouse attached to your system then choosing the default answer is recommended in the below prompt:

```
Mouse Support (not serial mice) (CONFIG_MOUSE) [Y/n/?]
```

Joystick support

If you want to enable joystick support then enable the input core support.

Tape drive support

If you have QIC-02 tape, you can choose to add support for it here.

```
QIC-02 tape support (CONFIG_QIC02_TAPE) [N/y/m/?]
```

Watchdog card support

If you would like to create a watchdog timer so that it can reboot the system in case of a failure, answer yes here.

Watchdog Timer Support (CONFIG_WATCHDOG) [N/y/?]

If you enable this feature, you have to create a special device called /dev/watchdog (major,minor=130,10) by using the mknod program. Then, you can use a watchdog daemon program that writes to this special device every minute. If the kernel detects that the daemon has not written to the device for one minute, it reboots the system.

/dev/nvram support (CONFIG_NVRAM) [N/y/m/?]

This feature allows you to create the special device /dev/nvram to have read/write access to nonvolatile memory in the real-time clock. Unless you know what you are doing, choose the default answer.

Enhanced Real Time Clock Support (CONFIG_RTC) [N/y/?]

This feature allows you to create a special device, /dev/rtc, which you can use to access the real-time clock in your system. Unless you know what you are doing, choose the default answer.

Ftape, the floppy tape, video and misc. device support

If you have a floppy controller-based tape drive, you need to choose to add support for it here.

Ftape (QIC-80/Travan) support (CONFIG_FTAPE) [N/y/m/?]
/dev/agpgart (AGP Support) (CONFIG_AGP) [Y/m/n/?]

AGP (Accelerated Graphics Port) support will allow you to enable advanced AGP video card features. Choose the default answer if you have an AGP video card.

Direct Rendering Manager (XFree86 DRI support) (CONFIG_DRM) [Y/n/?]

If you use X Windows system (using Xfree86) then choose the default answer to enable the Direct Rendering Infrastructure (DRI) support which enhances your X experience by providing security, synchronization, and Direct Memory Access (DMA) transfers for your video cards. If you enable this you will have to select a module suitable for your video cards.

Currently the 3dfx Banshee/Voodoo3+, 3dlabs GMX 2000, ATI Rage 128, ATI Radeon, Intel I810, and Matrox G200/G400 cards are supported.

PCMCIA serial device support (CONFIG_PCMCIA_SERIAL_CS) [N/y/m/?]

If you do not have a PCMCIA serial device, choose the default answer.

Video For Linux (CONFIG_VIDEO_DEV) [N/y/m/?]

If you have video capture devices, enable this option by choosing yes; otherwise, choose the default answer.

File systems

In this section, you configure the kernel for various file system-specific features.

Quota support (CONFIG_QUOTA) [N/y/?]

If you would like to have disk quota support built into the kernel, choose yes here.

Kernel automounter support (CONFIG_AUTOFS_FS) [Y/m/n/?]

If you would like remote file systems (such as NFS file systems) automatically mounted and unmounted, choose to add direct or module-based support for the automounter here. Also, answer yes (y) to the following:

Kernel automounter version 4 support (also supports v3) (CONFIG_AUTOFS4_FS)
[Y/m/n/?]
Reiserfs support (CONFIG_REISERFS_FS) [N/y/m/?]

If you wish to enable journaling file system support, choose yes (y) here.

ADFS file system support (CONFIG_ADFS_FS) [N/y/m/?]

If you wish to support the Acorn Disc Filing System, enable this option.

Amiga FFS file system support (EXPERIMENTAL) (CONFIG_AFFS_FS)
[N/y/m/?]

If you wish to support the Amiga FFS filesystem, enable this option.

Apple Macintosh file system support (EXPERIMENTAL) (CONFIG_HFS_FS) [N/y/m/?]

If you wish to support the Apple Macintosh file system, enable this option.

```
BFS file system support (EXPERIMENTAL) (CONFIG_BFS_FS) [N/y/m/?]
```

If you wish to support the BFS file system, enable this option.

```
DOS FAT fs support (CONFIG_FAT_FS) [N/y/m/?]
```

If you wish to support the DOS file system, enable this option.

```
EFS file system support (read only) (EXPERIMENTAL) (CONFIG_EFS_FS) [N/y/m/?]
```

If you wish to support the EFS file system, enable this option.

```
Virtual memory file system support (former shm fs) (CONFIG_TMPFS) [Y/n/?]
```

If you wish to create Tmpfs file system that keeps all the files in virtual memory, enable this option by choosing the default answer. Unlike RAM disks, the Tmpfs file system is not fixed size.

```
Simple RAM-based file system support (CONFIG_RAMFS) [N/y/m/?]
```

If you wish to keep files in RAM, use Tmpfs instead of the simple RAM-based file system. The default choice is recommended.

```
ISO 9660 CD-ROM file system support (CONFIG_ISO9660_FS) [Y/m/n/?]
```

This enables standard CD-ROM file system support and should be enabled in most systems; the default answer is recommended.

```
Microsoft Joliet CD-ROM extensions (CONFIG_JOLIET) [N/y/?]
```

The Joliet file system is a Microsoft extension to ISO9660 that should be enabled only for those who plan on using CD-ROM media that are burned as Joliet file systems.

```
Minix fs support (CONFIG_MINIX_FS) [N/y/m/?]
```

Minix fs is a predecessor to Linux native file system (ext2); you most likely do not need this support.

```
FreeVxFS file system support (VERITAS VxFS(TM) compatible) (CONFIG_VXFS_FS)
[N/y/m/?]
```

Most systems will not need support for FreeVxFS file system and therefore the default answer is most likely appropriate.

```
NTFS file system support (read only) (CONFIG_NTFS_FS) [N/y/m/?]
```

If you plan to mount (in read-only mode) Windows NT/2000 file system (NTFS) on your Linux system, enable support for it or else choose the default answer.

```
OS/2 HPFS file system support (CONFIG_HPFS_FS) [N/y/m/?]
```

If you plan to mount IBM OS/2 HPFS file system on your Linux system then enable support for it or else choose the default answer.

```
/proc filesystem support (CONFIG_PROC_FS) [Y/n/?]
```

The /proc file system is a must have for any modern Linux system; therefore the default answer is highly recommended.

```
/dev file system support (EXPERIMENTAL) (CONFIG_DEVFS_FS) [N/y/?]
```

If you wish to use the devfs file system in place of the traditional /dev directory then you should enable this here. Because /dev is critical to Linux operations and devfs is not mature yet, I recommend that you choose the default answer until devfs is standard.

```
/dev/pts filesystem for Unix98 PTYs (CONFIG_DEVPTS_FS) [Y/n/?]
```

If you chose to add support for UNIX 98 pseudo-terminals, you need to add /dev/pts file system support here.

```
QNX4 file system support (read only) (EXPERIMENTAL) (CONFIG_QNX4FS_FS) [N/y/m/?]
```

If you plan to use QNX4 file system on your Linux system, enable support for it by choosing yes; otherwise, choose the default answer.

```
ROM filesystem support (CONFIG_ROMFS_FS) [N/y/m/?]
```

Most systems do not need file systems of this type.

```
Second extended fs support (CONFIG_EXT2_FS) [Y/m/n/?]
```

Extended fs is the primary file system for Linux; therefore, the default answer is a must.

```
System V and Coherent filesystem support (CONFIG_SYSV_FS) [N/y/m/?]
```

A default answer for this question should work for most systems:

```
UDF file system support (read only) (CONFIG_UDF_FS) [N/y/m/?]
```

If you plan to UDF file system on your Linux system then enable support for it; otherwise choose the default answer.

```
UFS filesystem support (CONFIG_UFS_FS) [N/y/m/?]
```

Note that the UFS file system support is required if you choose to mount disk partitions created by other operating systems such as Solaris *x*86 or BSD.

Network file systems

In this section you configure the kernel for advanced network file systems.

```
Coda filesystem support (advanced network fs) (CONFIG_CODA_FS)
[N/y/m/?]
```

The Coda file system is not yet popular enough, and I do not recommend adding it to the kernel; you might choose to add it as a module.

```
NFS filesystem support (CONFIG_NFS_FS) [Y/m/n/?]
```

If you plan to use NFS, choose the default answer. In such a case you will also have to choose whether you want to support NFS version 3 clients below:

```
Provide NFSv3 client support (CONFIG_NFS_V3) [N/y/?]
```

Because NFS version 3 is fairly new, you should enable it to experience the benefits.

```
NFS server support (CONFIG_NFSD) [Y/m/n/?]
```

If you wish to run an NFS server on your system, choose the default answer.

```
Provide NFSv3 server support (CONFIG_NFSD_V3) [N/y/?]
```

If you wish to run an NFS version 3 compliant NFS server on your system, enable this option.

```
SMB filesystem support (to mount WfW shares etc.) (CONFIG_SMB_FS) [N/y/m/?]
```

If you would like to mount Windows 9*x*/NT file systems on your Linux system as SMB file systems, you need to choose yes or set this feature to be a module.

```
NCP filesystem support (to mount NetWare volumes) (CONFIG_NCP_FS) [N/y/m/?]
```

Unless you are planning on mounting NetWare volumes on your Linux system, choose the default answer.

Partition types

If you would like to have support for disk partitions based on BSD, Macintosh, Solaris, and so on, answer the following questions accordingly:

```
BSD disklabel (BSD partition tables) support (CONFIG_BSD_DISKLABEL) [N/y/?]
Macintosh partition map support (CONFIG_MAC_PARTITION) [N/y/?]
SMD disklabel (Sun partition tables) support (CONFIG_SMD_DISKLABEL) [N/y/?]
Solaris (x86) partition table support (CONFIG_SOLARIS_X86_PARTITION) [N/y/?]
```

In most cases, the default answers are sufficient.

Console drivers

In this section, you are able to set the following:

```
VGA text console (CONFIG_VGA_CONSOLE) [Y/n/?]
```

If you would like to have a VGA text console, choose the default answer.

```
Video mode selection support (CONFIG_VIDEO_SELECT) [N/y/?] ?
```

If you would like to be able to specify text mode on kernel bootup, choose yes to enable this option, or choose the default answer.

```
MDA text console (dual-headed) (EXPERIMENTAL) (CONFIG_MDA_CONSOLE) [N/y/m/?]
```

Most likely you do not use MDA or Monochrome Hercules Graphics adapters, and therefore the default should be appropriate for most situations.

```
Support for frame buffer devices (EXPERIMENTAL) (CONFIG_FB)
[N/y/?]
```

The *frame buffer* is a programming interface that is available for many video devices to makes graphics development very portable. If your video hardware supports frame buffer, enable this option.

Sound

If you are setting up a workstation then most likely you have a sound card. In such case you should answer yes below:

```
Sound card support (CONFIG_SOUND) [N/y/m/?]
```

Choose the appropriate sound hardware support from the list of vendor-specific sound hardware questions that follow the above.

USB support

Most modern PCs have USB support, so you should choose the default answer to the following question:

```
Support for USB (CONFIG_USB) [Y/m/n/?]
```

You will be asked if you wish to enable verbose debug messages for your USB hardware. Choose the default answer.

```
USB verbose debug messages (CONFIG_USB_DEBUG) [N/y/?]
```

Kernel hacking

The only option available in this section is the support for the Magic SysRq key. If you enable support for this key by answering yes to the following question, you are able to press SysRq+Alt+PrintScreen to dump status information even when the system has crashed.

```
Magic SysRq key (CONFIG_MAGIC_SYSRQ) [N/y/?]?
```

This is only useful for kernel developers, and so you should choose no here if you're not one.

After you have answered all these questions, the configuration script creates a .config file in the /usr/src/linux directory. You might want to view the content of this file to ensure that all features are configured as you think they are.

If you are not interested in finding how else you can configure the kernel but are ready to compile the kernel, skip the next two sections, and proceed to "Compiling, installing, and booting the new kernel."

Configuring the kernel using make menuconfig

One major problem with the make config-based configuration script is that if you make a mistake, you can't fix it without starting over. Also, you can't review your choices unless you use a text editor to manually view the /usr/src/linux/.config file. To remedy these shortcomings (at least for beginning kernel hackers), use the make menuconfig utility. This runs a menu-driven configuration tool that is much more user-friendly than the make config script. The Main Menu screen is shown in Figure 11-1.

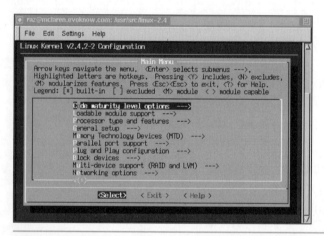

Figure 11-1 *The Main Menu for the make menuconfig script.*

As you can see, the user interface is quite simple and easy to navigate. However, the configuration questions are exactly the same as in the make config-based configuration that I discuss in the last section (see that section for help on how to answer these questions). make menuconfg also allows you to save and load configuration files. In other words, you can create multiple configuration files with different settings and use these configuration files to experiment with various features of the new kernel.

Although the make menuconfig is quite user-friendly, it imposes extra requirements on remote kernel configuration. For example, if you plan to configure and compile the kernel over a Telnet connection to a remote server, you have to make sure the Telnet client program on your side is capable of good terminal emulation, which is required for a full-screen menu application. Also, note that make menuconfig is not the fanciest way to configure a kernel. That title goes to the make xconfig script, which is described in the next section.

Configuring the kernel using make xconfig

As you may have guessed from the script name, make xconfig requires the X Window System. On systems with X installed, this is the preferred method of kernel configuration. Figure 11-2 shows the Linux Kernel Configuration window, which appears when the make xconfig script is run from a GUI that's running X.

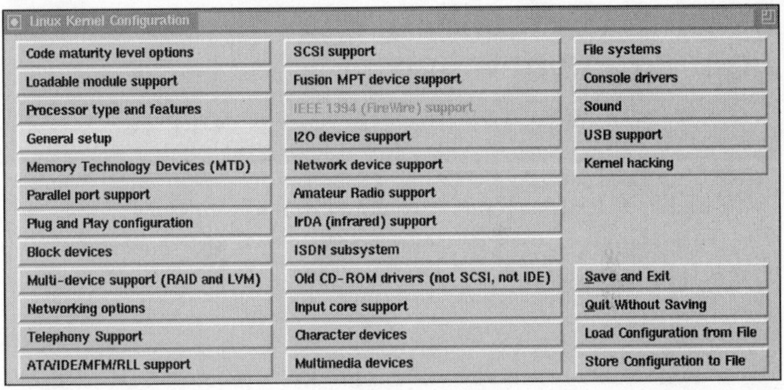

Linux Kernel Configuration		
Code maturity level options	SCSI support	File systems
Loadable module support	Fusion MPT device support	Console drivers
Processor type and features	IEEE 1394 (FireWire) support	Sound
General setup	I2O device support	USB support
Memory Technology Devices (MTD)	Network device support	Kernel hacking
Parallel port support	Amateur Radio support	
Plug and Play configuration	IrDA (infrared) support	
Block devices	ISDN subsystem	
Multi-device support (RAID and LVM)	Old CD-ROM drivers (not SCSI, not IDE)	Save and Exit
Networking options	Input core support	Quit Without Saving
Telephony Support	Character devices	Load Configuration from File
ATA/IDE/MFM/RLL support	Multimedia devices	Store Configuration to File

Figure 11-2 *The Linux Kernel Configuration window.*

You can click any button to open a dialog box where you can configure a particular section of the entire configuration. For example, Figure 11-3 shows the Processor type and features dialog box.

As you can see, this is quite a user-friendly interface. Another advantage of this interface is that you can open multiple sections by clicking the appropriate buttons. For example, if you are configuring the Partitions Type section and want to confirm that you have enabled UFS file system support in the Filesystems section, you can click the buttons for these two sections and verify your selections.

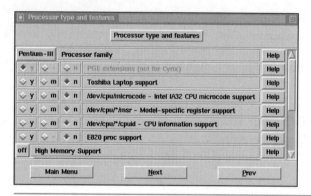

Figure 11-3 *The Processors type and features dialog box.*

Compiling, installing, and booting the new kernel

Now you need to compile, install, and boot the newly configured kernel. Here is how:

1. Before you can compile the kernel, you need to run the following command to ensure all dependencies within the source are set up correctly:

   ```
   make dep
   ```

   This should return without error unless a problem exists with the kernel source code itself.

2. To compile and create a compressed Linux kernel, run the following command:

   ```
   make bzImage
   ```

3. If you have configured any part of the kernel as a module during configuration, you have to run the following command to compile the modules:

   ```
   make modules
   ```

4. After you have compiled the modules, install them in the /lib/ modules/2.*x.x* directory by using the following command:

   ```
   make modules_install
   ```

5. Now you need to copy the new kernel to the /boot directory as follows:

   ```
   cp /usr/src/linux-2.x.x/arch/i386/boot/bzImage /boot/
   vmlinuz-2.x.x
   ```

6. Also copy and rename the new System.map file to the /boot directory as follows:

   ```
   cp /usr/src/linux-2.x.x/System.map /boot/System.
   map-2.x.x
   ```

7. Now remove the existing symbolic link for System.map as follows:

   ```
   rm -f /boot/System.map
   ```

8. Finally, create a new symbolic link called /boot/System.map as follows:

   ```
   ln -s /boot/System.map-2.x.x /boot/System.map
   ```

9. You also need to create a new initial ramdisk as follows:

   ```
   mkinitrd /boot/initrd-2.x.x.img 2.x.x
   ```

10. The final step before you boot the new kernel is to prepare LILO for the new kernel. See the "Configuring LILO" section earlier in this chapter for details on how you can create a new configuration segment in /etc/lilo.conf for the new kernel. After you have modified the /etc/lilo.conf file and have run /sbin/lilo, you can reboot the system and attempt to use the new kernel, as discussed in the "Booting with the new kernel" section earlier in this chapter.

If all things go well, you have a fresh, new, custom-configured kernel running all of your favorite Linux applications from now on.

 TIP

Do not forget to make a new boot floppy using the mkbootdisk --device /dev/fd0 2.x.x command.

Patching a Kernel

You are likely to encounter situations when the entire kernel code does not change, only the small pieces. In such a case you need to know how to patch your kernel source and create a new kernel. It is not uncommon to have a situation when you need to patch an existing kernel to get something working the way you want. You can patch the kernel source from the /usr/src directory by using the following command:

```
gzip -cd patchXX.gz | patch -p0
```

 If multiple patches are available for a kernel, apply the patches in order. In other words, apply patch01.gz before you apply pach02.gz, and so on.

As an alternative, you can use the patch-kernel script to automate this process. Store the patch file(s) in the /usr/src directory, and from the /usr/src directory, run the following command:

```
./linux/scripts/patch-kernel
```

After patching the kernel, follow the instructions for compiling and installing the new kernel as discussed earlier in this chapter.

Setting Up Kernel Parameters by Using kernelcfg

Because the modern Linux kernel supports modules you can load and unload automatically via the kerneld daemon, you might need to configure one or more parameters for these modules to work properly. You can use kernelcfg for just such a job. Figure 11-4 shows the main Kernel Configurator window.

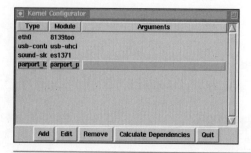

Figure 11-4 *Using the Kernel Configurator to configure modules.*

As you can see, you can add, delete, or modify module configuration information by using the Kernel Configurator. All module configuration information is stored in /etc/conf.modules. You can either modify this file manually or use the Kernel Configurator (kernelcfg) tool. To understand how to configure a module, take a look at the following sample /etc/conf.modules file, which is what the kernelcfg tool manages.

```
alias scsi_hostadapter ncr53c8xx
alias eth0 ne
options ne io=0x340 irq=5
```

To add a new module configuration, click the Add button, and select the module name from the drop-down menu, as in Figure 11-5.

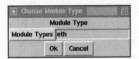

Figure 11-5 *Adding a new module configuration for* kerneld.

After you select the module name from the list of available modules, you can click OK to continue. If the module requires any arguments, you can add them in the next screen, as in Figure 11-6.

Figure 11-6 *Adding arguments for the new module configuration.*

After you add the arguments and click the OK button in the argument entry window, the new module configuration appears in the main window. You can also edit or delete an existing module configuration by using the appropriate buttons on the interface.

After you are done making changes, you should restart the kerneld daemon by clicking the Restart kerneld button.

Part III

Configuring Services

In this part I show you how to configure the most commonly used services in Linux, including Apache Web server, Sendmail SMTP mail server, POP mail server, Wu-FTPD FTP server, BIND DNS server, and Samba file server.

Chapter 12

The Apache Web Server

IN THIS CHAPTER

- Installing the Apache Web server
- Setting up Apache
- Controlling Apache
- Creating virtual Web sites
- Authenticating Web users
- Monitoring Apache and logging access

Apache Web server is more popular than any other Web server software in the world. In fact, Apache is used in approximately 60 percent of all the Web sites in the world. Apache Web server supports many platforms, including Linux. In this chapter I will discuss how you can install, configure, and manage Apache Web Server on Red Hat Linux.

System Requirements for Apache

If you are planning on building Apache from source, which is what I highly recommend since compiling your own will give you a leaner, meaner server, then you need to make sure that your system meets the requirements stated in Table 12-1.

Table 12-1 *Requirements for Building Apache from Source*

Resource	Required?	Requirements
Disk Space	Mandatory	Approximately 12MB of disk space is needed to compile and install Apache from source distribution. However, if you add many modules that are not part of the standard source distribution, your space requirements will increase.
		After it is installed, Apache only needs approximately 5MB of disk space. However, I highly recommend that you do not delete the source distribution until you have finished reading this chapter.
ANSI C Compiler	Mandatory	ANSI C compiler is required. For most systems, the GNU C compiler (GCC) from the Free Software Foundation is highly recommended. The version you should have is 2.7.2 or above. GCC can be found at **www.gnu.org**.
Perl 5 Interpreter	Recommended	You do not need Perl to compile Apache, but some of the support scripts, such as **apxs**, **split-logfile**, **log_server_status**, and **dbmmanage**, which are found in the support subdirectory of your source distribution, are Perl scripts. You need Perl only if you plan to use those scripts. I highly recommend that you install Perl on your system. Perl version 5.003 or above will work fine.
Dynamic Shared Object (DSO) support	Optional	Instead of compiling modules in the Apache binary itself you can create dynamic modules called DSO that can be loaded via the **httpd.conf** file at startup. DSO modules enable you to experiment with modules and configurations more freely than compiling everything in **httpd**. Currently, DSO support is available for Linux.

Note that an Apache server using a DSO module may be approximately 20 percent slower at startup and approximately 5 percent slower during run-time. On top of that, DSO is not always available in all platforms. Therefore, I do not recommend DSO for a production environment. DSO is great, however, for experimenting with modules in a development or staging environment.

Before displaying the Powered by Apache logo on your Web server, you want to make sure your Web server has enough "power" to run it. Fortunately,

Apache does not require massive computing resources to run: it runs fine on a Linux system with 5 to 12MB of hard disk space and 8MB of RAM. However, if you want to run Apache to serve Web pages, launch CGI processes, and take advantage of all the wonderful stuff that the Web has to offer, you'll want enough disk space and RAM to reflect your load requirements. You can go about this in two ways: you can ask someone who runs a similar site with Apache and find out what type of system resources they're using, or you can try to figure out your realistic needs after you've installed Apache on your system.

In the latter case, you can use system utilities such as ps, top, and so on to display memory usage by an Apache process. You can then determine the total memory needed by multiplying a single process's memory usage by the number of Apache processes that you want to run, which should give you a reasonable estimate of your site's RAM requirements for Apache. If you plan to run several CGI programs on your Apache server, you have to determine memory usage for these programs as well, and take this additional need into account. One of the ways you can determine your CGI program memory requirements is to run the CGI program and use the top utility to see how much memory it takes, and then multiply the amount by the number of CGI requests you want to serve simultaneously.

The disk requirements for Apache source or binary files shouldn't be a concern with most systems because Apache binaries take no more than 1MB of space and the source file is about 5MB. You should really pay attention, however, to the log files that Apache creates, because each log entry takes up approximately 80 bytes of disk space. If you expect to get about 100,000 hits in a day, for example, your Apache access log file may be 8,000,000 bytes.

Finally, consider whether you have appropriate bandwidth for running a Web server. Estimating your bandwidth requirement is not an easy task, but you can come up with ballpark figures by doing a bit of math. Here is what you will need:

- The average Web page size for your Web site. You can run the following command in your document root directory to find out the average size of your Web pages.

```
find path_to_doc_root  -type f -name "*.html" -ls |
\
```

```
awk 'BEGIN{ FILECNT = 0; T_SIZE = 0;} \
         { T_SIZE += $7; FILECNT++} \
     END{print "Total Files:", FILECNT, \
                "Total Size:", T_SIZE, \
                "Average Size:", T_SIZE  /
FILECNT;}'
```

Don't forget to replace *path_to_doc_root* with the actual document root directory of your Web site. For example, for a Web site with document root /www/mysite/htdocs, the above script returns the following output:

```
Total Files: 332 Total Size: 5409725 Average Size:
16294.4
```

- Now determine how many average-sized pages you can serve assuming that Apache had no bottleneck of its own and totally ignoring the bandwidth utilization by the incoming requests. For example, say you have an ISDN (128Kbps) connection to the Internet and your average file size is 16KB. Because 128 Kbps = 128/8 Kbps = 16 Kbps, you can send one average-sized file per second. If you include the other overhead, such as bandwidth needed for the inbound request traffic, you probably cannot service one request per second. In this case your network is a big bottleneck if you wanted to allow N (where $N > 1$) simultaneous users to connect to your Web site. For example, if you have an ISDN connection and want to service 12 simultaneous users per second when the average file size is 16K, you need 12 × ISDN (128 Kbps) connections, which is a T-1 (1.53 Mbps).

Downloading the Software

Before you download the Apache software for the first time, you should note a few things. There's a good chance that you will find two versions of Apache available: one is an official release version, and one is a beta release version that has the latest code and features. For example, if you see an Apache version 2.0.2 and a version called 2.3b3, then the first version is an official release and the second is a beta version. A third beta such as 2.3b3 is likely to be stable because 2.3b1 and 2.3b2 came before it, but using a beta version is not recommended for a production Web server. To download the version you want, go to `www.apache.org/dist/httpd/`.

TIP

To find the Apache mirror server that's geographically closest to you, run the mirror Apache finder script at `www.apache.org/dyn/closer.cgi`.

This is the distribution directory of the Apache software. Here, you will find both the release and the beta versions of the software in multiple compression packages. Following are a few examples of the various types of compression formats that are used to distribute source code:

```
httpd_2.0.4.tar.Z
httpd_2.0.4.tar.gz
httpd_2.0.4.zip


httpd_2.3b3.tar.gz
httpd_2.3b3_win32.exe
```

Typically with Red Hat Linux, all you need are the `tar`, `gnuzip`, or `gzip` utilities to decompress the files. For example, to decompress the `httpd_version.tar.gz` file (where version is whatever version you have downloaded such as 2.0.4) on a Red Hat Linux system, you use the `tar xvzf httpd_version.tar.gz` command. You could also use the `gzip -d httpd_version.tar.gz ; tar xvf httpd_version.tar` command, which will decompress and extract all the files in a subdirectory while keeping the relative path for each file intact.

The binaries are usually kept in a different directory, where each operating system has a subdirectory of its own.

XREF

If you decide to download a prebuilt binary version of Apache, you can skip to the "Installing Apache from binary packages" section later in this chapter.

Installing Apache

You have two options for installing Apache, including from binaries or by configuring the Apache source yourself. The binary installation is faster and easier, but installing from the source code allows you more freedom to customize Apache to suit your needs. The following sections discuss both options.

Installing Apache from source code

Installing Apache from source distribution is preferred method because it allows you to configure the server per your needs. Any binary installation that you download will come with someone else's configuration, which you might not be able to alter yourself even with Apache's highly configurable status. For example, if you download and install a binary that comes configured with CGI support, you have to live with the CGI support even if you will never run CGI programs. Of course, had the CGI module been configured as a dynamically shared module, you could disable it very easily, but not if the module is statically built into a binary. So, to compile a lean and mean Apache server, you should install Apache from the source distribution, which you must download from the official Apache Web site or a designated mirror site.

Configuring the Apache source before installing

The Apache source distribution comes with the `configure` script, which allows you to configure the source tree before you compile and install the binaries. From the Apache source distribution directory, you can run this script as follows:

```
./configure --prefix=apache_installation_dir
```

The `--prefix` option tells Apache to install the binaries and other necessary configuration and support files in *apache_installation_dir*. For example, the following command configures the Apache source so that all the binaries and supporting files will be installed in the `/usr/local/apache` directory:

```
./configure --prefix=/usr/local/apache
```

There are many options that you can use with the `configure` script. Table 12-2 shows the common configuration options available.

Table 12-2 *Common Options for the Configure Script*

Option	Meaning
--help	Print this message
--version	Print the version of **autoconf** that created configure Directory and filenames.
--prefix=*prefix*	Install architecture-independent files in *prefix* [/usr/local/apache2]
--disable-*feature*	Do not include FEATURE (same as –enable-FEATURE=no)
--enable- feature[=*arg*]	Include feature[arg=yes]
--with-*package*[=*arg*]	Use package [arg=yes]
--without-*package*	Do not use package (same as –with-package=no)
--enable-modules=*module-list*	Enable one or more named modules
--enable-mods-shared=*module-list*	Enable one or more named modules as shared modules
--disable-access	Host-based access control
--disable-auth	User-based access control
--disable-include	Server-Side Includes (SSI)
--disable-http	HTTP protocol handling
--disable-mime	Mapping of file-extension to MIME
--disable-log-config	Logging configuration
--enable-vhost-alias	Mass -hosting module
--disable-negotiation	Content negotiation
--disable-dir	Directory request handling
--disable-imap	Internal imagemaps
--disable-actions	Action triggering on requests
--enable-speling	Correct common URL misspellings
--disable-userdir	Mapping of user requests
--disable-alias	Translation of requests
--enable-rewrite	Enable URL rewriting rules
--disable-so	DSO capability
--enable-so	DSO capability

Continued

Table 12-2 *Continued*

Option	Meaning
--disable-env	Clearing/setting of ENV vars
--enable-mime-magic	Automatically determine MIME type
--enable-cern-meta	CERN-type meta files
--enable-expires	Expires header control
--enable-headers	HTTP header control
--enable-usertrack	User-session tracking
--enable-unique-id	Per-request unique IDs
--disable-setenvif	Base ENV vars on headers
--enable-tls	TLS/SSL support
--with-ssl	Use a specific SSL library installation
--with-mpm=MPM	Choose the process model for Apache to use: MPM={beos threaded prefork spmt_os2 perchild}
--disable-status	Process/thread monitoring
--disable-autoindex	Directory listing
--disable-asis	As-is filetypes
--enable-info	Server information
--enable-suexec	Set UID and GID for spawned processes
--disable-cgid	CGI scripts
--enable-cgi	CGI scripts
--disable-cgi	CGI scripts
--enable-cgid	CGI scripts

Most of these options are not required for most sites. Typically, all you need is to specify the --prefix option and any options to enable or disable one or more modules. For example, say you do not want to install the CGI module on your system. You can run the configure script using the --disable-cgi --disable-cgid options to disable CGI support. Similarly, to disable the Server-Side Include (SSI) support you can use the --disable-include option.

Configuring Apache source after the initial configuration

After you have configured Apache using the `configure` script, you can use the `config.status` script instead of `configure` for any subsequent configuration needs. By using the `config.status` script, you can reuse your previous configuration and add or subtract new options.

For example, say you configured Apache with the following command:

`./configure --prefix=/usr/local/apache --disable-cgi --disable-cgid`

Then, a few days later you decide to disable SSI. You can now use the following command:

`./config.status --disable-include`

When you recompile Apache, the CGI modules will not be included because `./config.status` stores the options that you specified using the `configure` script earlier.

Compiling and installing Apache

After you have configured the Apache source using the `configure` script, follow these steps to compile and install Apache:

1. Run the `make` command to compile the source.

2. Run the `make install` command to install the `httpd` and support files in the directory you specified using the `--prefix` option. You can see the directory structure that Apache set up in the "The Apache directory structure" section a bit later in this chapter.

Installing Apache from binary packages

You can download the Apache binaries appropriate for your system from `www.apache.org/dist/httpd/binaries` directory. Download the latest version and extract the compressed file into a temporary directory. To determine how to install the binaries in your specific platform, you must read the `INSTALL.bindist` file, which is included in each binary distribution.

If you wish to install the Apache RPM (which stands for *Red Hat Package Manager*) package for your Linux system, do the following:

1. Go to http://rpmfind.net and search for the string Apache to locate the Apache RPM packages. From the search result, locate the latest version of the binary Apache RPM distribution and download it.

2. As root, run the rpm -ivh *apache_rpm_package.rpm* command to install the package. For example, to install the apache-2.0.4-i386.rpm for a Red Hat Linux (Intel) system, run the rpm -ivh apache-2.0.4-i386.rpm command.

See the next section to check out Apache's basic directory structure.

The Apache Directory Structure

After installing Apache, you can change to the directory where you installed Apache and browse the new directory to get a feel for how Apache is set up. For example, if you use --prefix=/usr/local/apache with the configure script during source tree configuration, make install creates the following directory structure:

```
/usr/local/apache
|
+---include
+---lib
+---bin
+---conf
+---htdocs
|   |
|   +--manual
|       |
|       +--developer
|       +--howto
|       +--images
|       +--misc
|       +--mod
|       +--platform
|       +--programs
|       +--search
```

```
|     +--vhosts
|
+---icons
|  |
|  +---small
|
+---logs
+---cgi-bin
```

The following list gives a brief description of each of the directories in the Apache directory structure:

- /include — Contains all the C header (include) files that are needed only if you develop Web applications that integrate with Apache, or if you want to use third-party software with Apache that require the header files. On a production server you can remove this directory after installation.

- /lib – Houses the Apache Portable Run-Time (APR) library files. These files are required for running Apache, as well as other support utilities such as **ab**.

- /bin — Contains the programs shown in Table 12-3.

- /conf — Houses the configuration files for Apache, which are listed in Table 12-4.

- /htdocs — The default document root directory for the main Apache server. The httpd.conf file sets the DocumentRoot directive to this directory. By default the htdocs directory also has the entire Apache manual installed in a subdirectory.

- /icons — Used to store various Apache icons that are needed for displaying the directory listing.

- /logs — Used to store the Apache server logs, the CGI daemon socket (cgisock), and the PID file (httpd.pid).

- /cgi-bin — The default CGI script directory, which is set by using theScriptAlias directive in httpd.conf. By default, Apache comes with two simple CGI scripts — printenv and test-cgi. Each of these scripts prints out CGI environment variables when requested via the http://server_name/cgi-bin/script_name URL.

Table 12-3 *Apache Programs in the bin Directory*

Apache Programs	Purpose
Ab	ab is short for ApacheBench. This program enables you to benchmark Apache server.
Apachectl	A handy script that enables you to start, restart, and stop Apache server. See Chapter 3 for more information on this script.
Apxs	A tool for building and installing extension modules for Apache. This program allows you to build DSO modules that can be used in Apache by using the **mod_so** module. For more information on this program, see http://*your_server_name*/manual/programs/apxs.htm.
Htdigest	Creates and updates user authentication information when message digest (MD5) authentication is being used. For more information on this program, see http://*your_server_name*/manual/programs/htdigest.html.
Htpasswd	Creates and updates user authentication information that is used in basic HTTP authentication.
Httpd	The Apache Web server program.
Logresolve	Converts (resolves) IP addresses from a log file to host names.
Rotatelogs	Rotates Apache log files when they reach a certain size.

Table 12-4 *Apache config Directory Contents*

Configuration File	Purpose
httpd.conf	The Apache configuration file.
httpd-std.conf	The sample copy of the httpd.conf file, which is not required by Apache. For new Apache users, this file can act as a means for recovering the default httpd.conf.
highperformance.conf	A sample configuration file that gives some pointers for configuring Apache for high performance.
highperformance-std.conf	A sample copy of the highperformance.conf file, which is not required by Apache.
Magic	This file stores the data for **mod_mime_magic** Apache module, which is used to guess a MIME type for a file
mime.types	This file decides which MIME-type headers are sent to the Web client for a given file.

For more information about MIME types, please read RFC (Request for Comments; a standard document describing a technology or protocol) 2045, 2046, 2047, 2048, and 2077. The Internet media-type registry is at ftp://ftp.iana.org/in-notes/iana/assignments/media-types.

These scripts are good for testing whether CGI configuration is working for you. However, I highly recommend that you remove these scripts after you have CGI configuration working. It is not a good idea to have a script lying around that displays your system environment information to anyone in the world. The less you tell the world about how your system works or about what is available on your system, the more secure your system will be.

Configuring the Server

By default, Apache reads a single configuration called `httpd.conf`. Every Apache source distribution comes with a set of sample configuration files. In the standard Apache source distribution, the `conf` directory contains sample configuration files with the `-dist` extension.

Before you modify this file, create a backup copy of the original. You never know when you may want to start from square one again.

The `httpd.conf` file has two types of information: comments and server directives. Lines starting with a leading # character are treated as comments for developers, which are ignored when the server parses the file.

Except for the comments and blank lines, the server treats all other lines as either complete or partial directives. A directive is like a command for the server; it tells the server to perform a certain task in a particular fashion. While editing the `httpd.conf` file, you need to make certain decisions regarding how you want the server to behave. In the following sections, I show you what these directives mean and how you can use them to customize you server.

Configuring the global environment for Apache

The directives discussed in this section create the global environment for the Apache Server. The following sections discuss directives in the same order that they appear in the `httpd.conf` file.

ServerRoot

The very first directive merely sets the directory for ServerRoot, which is the top-level directory of the Web server.

This is the parent directory for all server-related files. The default value for ServerRoot is set to whatever you chose for the `--prefix` option during source configuration using the `configure` script. By default, the `make install` command that is executed during server installation copies all the server binaries in `ServerRoot/bin`, server configuration files in `ServerRoot/conf`, and so on.

You should only change the value of this directive if you have manually moved the entire directory from the location it resided in when it was installed to another location. For example, if you run `cp -r /usr/local/apache /home/apache` and want to configure Apache to work from the new location, change this directive to `ServerRoot /home/apache`. Remember to change other direct references to reflect the new location. Also note that whenever you see a relative directory name in the configuration file, Apache will prefix the directory specified by ServerRoot to the path to construct the actual path. You will see an example of this in the PidFile directive.

PidFile

The PidFile directive sets the PID (process ID) file path. By default, PidFile is set to `logs/httpd.pid`, which translates to `ServerRoot/logs/httpd.pid` (i.e., `/usr/local/apache/logs/httpd.pid`, assuming your server root is `/usr/local/apache`). Whenever you want to find the PID of the main Apache process that runs as root and spawns child processes, you can run the following command (replacing *ServerRoot* with an appropriate directory value):

```
cat ServerRoot/logs/httpd.pid
```

If you change PidFile to point to a different location, make sure the directory in which the httpd.pid file resides is not writable by anyone but the root user.

ScoreBoardFile

This directive is used to point to a file that is used to exchange run-time status information between Apache processes. The ScoreBoardFile directive is encapsulated within an if condition using the <IfModule> container as shown below:

```
<IfModule !perchild.c>
    ScoreBoardFile logs/apache_runtime_status
</IfModule>
```

This tells Apache to set the ScoreBoardFile directive to the *ServerRoot*/logs/apache_runtime_status file only if you have chosen a Multi-processing Module (MPM) other than perchild. Because the default MPM for Linux is threaded instead of perchild, the if condition will be true and Apache will set the ScoreBoardFile directive. If you have a RAM disk, you may consider putting this file in the RAM disk to increase performance a bit. In most cases you should leave this alone.

Timeout

Timeout sets the server timeout in seconds. The default should be left alone.

KeepAlive, MaxKeepAliveRequests, and KeepAliveTimeout

These directives are used to control the keep-alive behavior of the server. You do not need to change them.

<IfModule> containers

Depending on what Multi-processing Module (MPM) you have chosen, one of the next three <IfModule> containers will be used by Apache. For example, if you configured Apache on a Linux system using the default MPM mode (threaded), than the following <IfModule> container will be used:

```
<IfModule threaded.c>
```

```
    StartServers           3
    MaxClients             8
    MinSpareThreads        5
    MaxSpareThreads        10
    ThreadsPerChild        25
    MaxRequestsPerChild    0
</IfModule>
```

On the other hand, if you used --with-mpm=prefork during source configuration then the following <IfModule> container will be used:

```
<IfModule prefork.c>
    StartServers           5
    MinSpareServers        5
    MaxSpareServers        10
    MaxClients             20
    MaxRequestsPerChild    0
</IfModule>
```

Similarly, the --with-mpm=perchild option forces Apache to use the last <IfModule> container as shown below:

```
<IfModule perchild.c>
    NumServers             5
    StartThreads           5
    MinSpareThreads        5
    MaxSpareThreads        10
    MaxThreadsPerChild     20
    MaxRequestsPerChild    0
</IfModule>
```

Because the default threaded MPM is most suitable for Red Hat Linux you need to focus on StartServers, MaxClients, MinSpareThreads, MaxSpareThreads, ThreadsPerChild, MaxRequestsPerChild. These directives are discussed in the following sections.

StartServers

StartServers is set to 3 by default, which tells Apache to start three child servers as it starts. You can start more servers if you want, but Apache is pretty good at increasing the number of child processes as needed based on load. So, changing this is not required.

MaxClients

In the default-threaded MPM mode, the total number of simultaneous requests that Apache can process is MaxClients x ThreadsPerChild. So, the default maximum for simultaneous requests is 8 x 25 = 200 (you can see the default settings for these directives in the "<IfModule> containers" section earlier in the chapter). If you use the preforking MPM mode, the maximum request is limited to MaxClients. The default maximum of 200 simultaneous requests should work well for most sites, so you can leave the defaults alone.

MinSpareThreads

The MinSpareThreads directive specifies the minimum number of idle threads; leave the default (5) as is.

MaxSpareThreads

The MaxSpareThreads directive specifies the maximum number of idle threads; leave the default as is. In the default-threaded mode, Apache kills child processes to control minimum and maximum thread count.

ThreadsPerChild

This directive defines how many threads (25 by default) are created per child process.

Because on Windows there is only one child process and it owns all the threads, if you are running Apache on a Windows system you should set ThreadsPerChild to the maximum number of simultaneous requests you want to handle.

MaxRequestsPerChild

This directive sets the number of requests a child process can serve before getting killed. The default value of 0 makes the child process serve requests forever. I do not like the default value because it allows Apache processes to slowly consume large amounts of memory when a faulty mod_perl script or even a faulty third-party Apache module leaks memory. If you do not plan to run any third-party Apache modules or `mod_perl` scripts, you can keep the default setting or else set it to a reasonable number. A setting of 30 ensures that the child process is killed after processing 30 requests. Of course, new child processes are created as needed.

Configuring the main server

The main server configuration applies to the default Web site that Apache serves. This is the site that will come up when you run Apache and use the server's IP address or host name on a Web browser.

Port

The very first directive in this section of the `httpd.conf` file is the Port directive, which sets the TCP port that Apache listens to for connections. The default value of 80 is the standard HTTP port. If you change this to another number such as 8080, you can only access the server using a URL such as `http://hostname:8080/`. You must specify the port number in the URL if the server runs on a non-standard port.

There are many reasons for running Apache on non-standard ports, but the only good one I can think of is that you do not have permission to run Apache on the standard HTTP port. As a non-root user you can only run Apache on ports higher than 1024.

After you have decided to run Apache on a port, you need to set the User and Group directives to tell Apache the user and group names to use. These two directives are very important for security reasons. When the primary Web server process launches a child server process to fulfill a request, it changes the child's UID and GID according to the values set for these directives. If the child processes are run as root user processes, this can lay your server open for attack by hackers. I highly recommend that you run the child server processes as a very low privileged user belonging to a very low privileged group. In Red Hat Linux, the user named `nobody` (usually UID = -1) and the group named `nogroup` (usually GID = -1) are low privileged, and are ready made for this purpose. You should consult your `/etc/group` and `/etc/passwd` files to verify these settings.

By taking the precaution of running the primary Web server as a non-root (regular) user, the server will not be able to change the UID and GID of child processes because only root user processes can change the UID or GID of other processes. Therefore, if you run your primary server as the user named `ironsheik` in a group named `sheiks`, all child processes will have the same privileges of `ironsheik` and the `sheiks` group.

If you plan on using the numeric format for the user and/or group IDs, you need to insert a # symbol before the numeric value. You can find numeric IDs in the /etc/passwd and in /etc/group files.

ServerAdmin

ServerAdmin defines the e-mail address that is shown when the server generates an error page. Set this to your e-mail address or that of the administrator you want to specify.

ServerName

Now you need to set the host name for the Server using the ServerName directive. This directive is commented out by default since Apache install cannot guess what host name to use for your system. So, if your host name is called www.domain.com, set the ServerName directive accordingly. Be sure, however, that the host name you enter here has proper domain name server (DNS) records that point it to your server machine.

DocumentRoot

Like all other Web servers, Apache needs to know the path of the top-level directory where Web pages will be kept. This directory is typically called the *document root directory.* The DocumentRoot directive instructs the server to treat the supplied directory as the root directory for all documents.

Be careful what directory you specify; this is a very important decision. For example, if the directive is set to the / (root) directory, every file on the system becomes accessible by the Web server. Of course, you can protect files by providing proper file permission settings, but setting the document root to the physical root directory of your system is definitely a major security risk.

The best place to point the DocumentRoot directive to is a specific sub-directory of your file system. If you have used the `--prefix=/usr/local/apache` option in configuring the Apache source, this directive will be set as follows:

```
DocumentRoot "/usr/local/apache/htdocs"
```

Just because your document root points to a particular directory, this does not mean the Web server cannot access directories outside your document tree. You can easily enable it to do so using symbolic links (with proper file permission) or using aliases. From an organizational and security-conscious perspective, I don't recommend using a lot of symbolic links or aliases to access files and directories outside your document tree. Still, it's sometimes necessary to keep a certain type of information outside the document tree, even if you need to keep the contents of such a directory accessible to the server on a regular basis – just be careful that you don't inadvertently open a back door to your system. If you have to add symbolic links to other directory locations outside the document tree, make sure that when you back up your files, your backup program can back up symbolic links properly.

Option and AllowOverride

The Option and AllowOverride directives are enclosed in a <Directory> container as follows:

```
<Directory />
    Options FollowSymLinks
    AllowOverride None
</Directory>
```

The scope of the enclosed directives is limited to the named directory (with any subdirectories.); however, you may only use directives that are allowed in a directory context.

In this directive, the Options and the AllowOverride directives apply to DocumentRoot, which is the top-level directory of the main Web site. Because directives enclosed within a directory container apply to all the subdirectories of the named directory, the directives apply to all directories within DocumentRoot and all of its subdirectories.

The Options directive is set to FollowSymLinks, which tells Apache to allow itself to traverse any symbolic link within DocumentRoot. Because the Options directive is only set to follow symbolic links, no other options are available to any of the directories within DocumentRoot. So implicitly, the Options directive is as follows:

```
Options FollowSymLinks  -ExecCGI -Includes -Indexes -MultiViews
```

However, be assured that the main idea behind such a restrictive default value for the Options directive is to create a very closed (i.e., secure) server. Because only symbolic link traversal is allowed, you must explicitly enable other options as needed on a per directory basis. This is a very good thing from a security prospective. The next directory container opens up the DocumentRoot directory as shown below:

```
<Directory "/usr/local/apache/htdocs">
    Options Indexes FollowSymLinks MultiViews
    AllowOverride None
    Order allow,deny
    Allow from all
</Directory>
```

If your DocumentRoot is different, change the named directory path. Here is what the above configuration means to Apache:

- The named directory and its subdirectories can be indexed. If there is an index file, it will be displayed; in the absence of one, the server creates a dynamic index for the directory. The Options directive specifies this.

- The named directory and all its subdirectories can have symbolic links that the server can follow (that is, use as a path) to access information. The Options directive also specifies this.

- The named directory and all its subdirectories can be part of content negotiations. The MultiViews option for the Options directive sets this. For example, when the given Options directive is enabled within the DocumentRoot directory as shown above, a request for www.domain.com/ratecard.html can be answered by a file called ratecard.html.bak, or ratecard.bak, ratecard.old, etc., if ratecard.html is missing. This may or may not be desirable, depending on your needs.

- No options specified here can be overridden by a local access control file (specified by the AccessFileName directive in httpd.conf; the default is .htaccess). This is specified using the AllowOverride directive.

- The Allow directives are evaluated before the Deny directives. Access is denied by default. Any client that does not match an Allow directive or *does* match a Deny directive will be denied access to the server.

- Access is permitted for all.

The default settings for these directives should be sufficient.

If your server is going to be on the Internet, you may want to remove the FollowSymLinks option from the Options directive line. Leaving this option creates a potential security risk. For example, if a directory in your Web site does not have an index page, the server displays an automated index that shows any symbolic links you may have in that directory. This could result in sensitive information being inadvertently displayed to Web surfers, or allow anyone to run an executable that resides in a carelessly linked directory.

UserDir

The UserDir directive tells Apache to consider UserDir as document root (~username/UserDir) of each user of the Web site. This only makes sense if you have multiple users on the system and want to allow each one to have his very own Web directory. The default setting is

```
UserDir public_html
```

which means that if you set up your Web server's name to be www. company.com, and you have two users (say joe and bob) their personal Web site URLs would be as shown:

```
http://www.company.com/~joe Physical directory: ~joe/public_html
http://www.company.com/~bob Physical directory: ~bob/public_html
```

Note that on Red Hat Linux systems, ~ (tilde) expands to a user's home directory. The directory specified by the UserDir directive resides in each user's home directory, and Apache must have read and execute permissions to read files and directories within the public_html directory. This can be accomplished using the following commands on a Red Hat Linux system:

```
chown -R user.Apache_server_group  ~user/dir_assigned_in_UserDir
chmod -R 770 ~user/dir_assigned_in_UserDir
```

For example, if the user name is joe and Apache's group is called httpd, and public_html is assigned in the UserDir directive, the preceding commands will look like this:

```
chown -R joe.httpd ~joe/public_html
chmod -R 2770 ~joe/public_html
```

The first command, chown, gives user joe and the group httpd full ownership of all the files and directories in the public_html directory. The next command, chmod, sets the access rights to 2770 (that is, only the user joe and the group httpd have full read, write, and execute privileges in public_html and all files and subdirectories under it. This also ensures that when a new file or subdirectory is created in the public_html directory, the newly created file has the group ID set, which enables the Web server to access the new file without the user's intervention.

If you create user accounts on your system by using a script (such as /usr/sbin/adduser script on Linux systems), you may want to incorporate the Web site creation process in this script. Just add a mkdir command to create a default public_html directory (if that's what you assign to the UserDir directive) to create the Web directory. Add the chmod and chown commands to give the Web server user permission to read and execute files and directories under this public directory.

DirectoryIndex

Next, you need to configure the DirectoryIndex directive, which has the following syntax:

```
DirectoryIndex [filename1, filename2, filename3, ... ]
```

This directive specifies which file the Apache server should consider as the index for the directory being requested. For example, when a URL such as www.yourcompany.com/ is requested, the Apache server determines that this is a request to access the / (document root) directory of the Web site. If the DocumentRoot directive is set as follows

```
DocumentRoot "/www/www.yourcompany.com/public/htdocs"
```

then the Apache server looks for a file named /www/www.yourcompany. com/public/htdocs/index.html; if it finds the file, Apache services the request by returning the content of the file to the requesting Web browser. If the DirectoryIndex is assigned welcome.html instead of the default index. html, however, the Web server will look for the following site instead:

```
/www/www.yourcompany.com/public/htdocs/welcome.html
```

If the file is absent, Apache returns the directory listing by creating a dynamic HTML page.

You can specify multiple index filenames in the DirectoryIndex directive. For example:

```
DirectoryIndex index.html index.htm welcome.htm
```

tells the Web server that it should check for the existence of any of the three files, and that if any one is found, it should be returned to the requesting Web client.

AccessFileName

The AccessFileName directive defines the name of the per-directory access control configuration file. The default name, .htaccess, has a leading period to hide the file from normal directory listing. The only reason to change the name to something else is to increase security by using an obscure name, which is not much of a security benefit. However, if you do change the filename to something else make sure you change the regular expression ^\.ht to ^\.whatever where .whatever is the first view character of what you set AccessFileName to.

The following <Files ...> container tells Apache to disallow access to any file that starts with a .ht (e.g. .htaccess or .htpasswd). This corresponds to the default AccessFileName.

```
<Files ~ "^\.ht">
    Order allow,deny
    Deny from all
</Files>
```

UseCanonicalName

UseCanonicalName, which is typically set to On, tells Apache to create all self-referencing URLs using *ServerName:Port* format. Leaving it on is a good idea.

TypesConfig

The TypesConfig directive points to the MIME configuration file `mime.types` that resides in the default `conf` directory. You do not need to change this directive unless you have relocated this file somewhere else.

DefaultType

The DefaultType directive sets the Content-Type header for any file whose MIME type cannot be determined from the file extension. For example if you have a file *DocumentRoot*/myfile, Apache uses the DefaultType setting, which is `text/plain`, as the content type for the file. This means that when the Web browser requests and receives such a file in response, it displays the contents in the same way that it displays a plain-text file. But, for example, if you think that most of your unknown file contents should be treated as HTML you can use `text/html` in place of `text/plain`.

The next `<IfModule ...>` container tells Apache to enable the MIME magic module (mod_mime_magic) if it exists and to use the MIMEMagicFile as the magic information (bytes patterns) needed to identify MIME type of files. The default should be left alone unless you want to change the path of the magic file.

```
<IfModule mod_mime_magic.c>
    MIMEMagicFile conf/magic
</IfModule>
```

@Heading 3:HostnameLookups

The HostnameLookups directive tells Apache to enable DNS lookup per request if this directive is set to On. However, the default setting is `Off` and therefore no DNS lookup is performed to process a request, which speeds up response time. Performing a DNS lookup to resolve IP address to hostname is a time-consuming step for a busy server and should only be done using the `logresolve` utility. Leave the default as is.

ErrorLog

The ErrorLog directive is very important; it points to the log file that is dedicated to recording server errors. The default value of `logs/errors` translates to *ServerRoot*/`logs/error_log`, which should work unless you want to write a log in a different place. Generally it's a good idea to create a log partition where you can keep your logs; it's also preferable that your log partition is on one or more dedicated log disks. If you have such a hardware configuration you might want to change the directive to point to a new log path.

LogLevel

The LogLevel directive sets the level of logging that will be done. The default value of `warn` is sufficient for getting started. The LogFormat directives dictate what is logged and in what format. The CustomLog directive sets the path for the access log, which stores your server hits. By default it uses the common (CLF) format that is defined in a LogFormat directive, which is discussed in the "Creating log files" section below. Consider the advice about keeping logs on their own disk and partition and then make changes to the path if necessary.

> Some common advice for all logs: Whatever directory you keep logs in, make sure that only the primary server process has write access in that directory. This is a major security issue, because allowing other users or processes to write to the log directory can allow someone unauthorized to take over your primary Web server process UID, which is normally the root account.

ServerSignature

The ServerSignature directive displays the server name and the server's version number in a server-generated page such as dynamic directory index pages, error pages, etc. If you feel uncomfortable about displaying your server information so readily to everyone, set it to `Off`. I do.

Alias

The Alias directive defines a new directory alias called `/icons/` to point to `/usr/local/apache/icons/` (i.e., *ServerRoot*/`icons/`). The icon

images stored in this directory are used to display dynamic directory listings when no DirectoryIndex-specified files are found in that directory.
You should leave the alias alone unless you changed the path of the icons
directory. The directory container that follows the alias definition sets the
permission for this icon directory. I do not like the idea that it allows directory browsing (i.e., dynamic directory indexing) by setting Options to
Indexes, and so I suggest you change Options Indexes to Options
−Indexes.

ScriptAlias

The ScriptAlias directive is used to set a widely used CGI script alias
directory /cgi-bin/ to point to /usr/local/apache/cgi-bin/ (i.e.,
ServerRoot/cgi-bin/). If you plan on using CGI scripts from the main
server, keep it or else remove this directive. Or, if you want to move the
CGI script directory to another location, change the physical path given in
the directive to match yours.

Never set the CGI script path to a directory within your document root (i.e., *DocumentRoot*/somepath) because keeping CGI scripts under the document root directory opens it
up for various potential security issues. Set your CGI script
path and DocumentRoot at the same level. For example, if
you set DocumentRoot to /a/b/c/htdocs then set Script-
Alias to point to /a/b/c/cgi-bin not /a/b/c/htdocs/
cgi-bin or /a/b/c/htdocs/d/cgi-bin, etc.

Next a <Directory ...> container places restrictions on the ScriptAlias
directory to ensure that no directory-level options are allowed. Here, the
Options directive is set to None (which means the contents of ScriptAlias
is not browsable), symbolic links within the ScriptAlias directory are not
followed, and so on.

Other directives

The rest of the directives are not important to get up and running so I will
ignore them for now. They include IndexOptions, AddIconByEncoding,
AddIconByType, AddIcon, DefaultIcon, ReadmeName, HeaderName,
IndexIgnore, AddEncoding, AddLanguage, AddCharset, BrowserMatch,
AddType.

However, two of these other directives that you might want to consider changing if needed are LanguagePriority and AddDefaultCharset.

By default, the LanguagePriority directive sets the default language to en (English), which may not work for everyone in the world. So, you might want to change the default language to be your native language if it is supported (many languages are supported, but not all). The AddDefaultCharset should also be set to the character set that best suits your locale needs. If you do not know what character set you should use, you can leave the defaults alone and find out what character set you need and change it later.

Now save your configuration changes in `httpd.conf`.

Starting and Stopping the Server

After you've customized `httpd.conf`, you're ready to run the server. I will assume that you've installed Apache in `/usr/local/apache` directory. If you have not installed Apache in this directory, make sure that you replace all references of `/usr/local/apache` to whatever directory is appropriate in the following discussion.

Starting Apache

Run the `/usr/local/apache/bin/apachectl start` command to start the Apache Web server. If `apachectl` complains about one or more syntax errors, you should fix the error in the `httpd.conf` file and retry.

Also check the ErrorLog log file (i.e., `/usr/local/apache/logs/ error_log`) for error messages (if any). If you see errors in the log file you need to fix them first. Some of the most common errors are:

- **Not running the server as the root user.** You must start Apache as the root user. Once Apache is started, it will spawn child processes that will use the UID and GID that are specified in the User and Group directives. Most people get confused about this issue and try to start the server using the user account specified in the User directive.

- **Incorrect port settings.** If Apache complains about being unable to "bind" to an address, then either another process is already using the port you have configured Apache to use, or you are running `httpd` as a normal user but are trying to use a port below 1024 (such as the default port 80).

- **Missing log file paths.** Make sure that both ErrorLog and Custom-Log paths exist and are made not writable by anyone but the Apache server.

- **Configuration typos.** Any time you change the `httpd.conf` configuration file, you can run `/usr/local/apache/apachectl configtest` to verify that you don't have a syntax error in the configuration file.

The quickest way to check and see whether or not the server is running is to try the following command:

```
ps auxw | grep httpd
```

This command uses the `ps` utility to list all the processes that are in the process queue and then pipes this output to the `grep` program, which searches the output for lines that match the keyword `httpd` and then displays each matching line. If you see one line with the word root in it, that's your primary Apache server process. Note that when the server starts, it creates a number of child processes to handle the requests. If you started Apache as the root user, the parent process continues to run as root, while the children change to the user specified in the `httpd.conf` file.

You can create the script shown in Listing 12-1 and keep it in `/etc/rc.d/init.d/` directory.

Listing 12-1 *The httpd script*

```
#!/bin/sh
#
# httpd    This shell script starts and stops the Apache server
# It takes an argument 'start' or 'stop'
# to receptively start and stop the
# server process.
#
# Notes: You might have to change the
# path information used
# in the script to reflect your
# system's configuration.
#
```

Continued

Listing 12-1 *Continued*

```
APACHECTL=/usr/local/apache/bin/apachectl

[ -f $APACHECTL ] || exit 0

# See how the script was called.
case "$1" in
  start)
        # Start daemons.
        echo -n "Starting httpd: "
        $APACHECTL start
        touch /var/lock/subsys/httpd
        echo
        ;;
  stop)
        # Stop daemons.
        echo -n "Shutting down httpd: "
        $APACHECTL stop

        echo "done"
        rm -f /var/lock/subsys/httpd
        ;;
  *)
        echo "Usage: httpd {start|stop}"
        exit 1
esac
exit 0
```

To start Apache automatically after a reboot, simply run the following command once:

```
ln -s /etc/rc.d/init.d/httpd /etc/rc.d/rc3.d/S99httpd
```

This command creates a special link called S99httpd in the /etc/rc.d/ rc3.d (run level 3) directory that links to /etc/rc.d/init.d/httpd script. When your system boots up, this script is executed with the start argument and Apache starts automatically.

To terminate Apache automatically when the system is being rebooted, run the following command once:

```
ln -s /etc/rc.d/init.d/httpd /etc/rc.d/rc3.d/K99httpd
```

This ensures that the httpd script is run with the stop argument when the system is shutting down.

Stopping a standalone Apache server

To stop the Apache server, run /usr/local/apache/bin/apachectl stop command. Apache also makes it convenient for you to find the PID (process ID) of the root Web server process. The PID is written into a file assigned to the PidFile directive. This PID is for the primary httpd process. Do not attempt to kill the child processes manually—the parent process will recreate them as needed.

Another way to stop the Apache server is to run the following command:

```
kill -TERM 'cat /usr/local/apache/logs/httpd.pid'
```

This command runs the kill command with the -TERM signal (i.e. -9) for the process ID returned by cat /usr/local/apache/logs/httpd. pid (i.e., cat *PidFile*) command.

Restarting a standalone Apache server

To stop the Apache server, run the /usr/local/apache/bin/apachectl restart command.

You can use the kill command, as follows:

```
kill -HUP 'cat /usr/local/apache/logs/httpd.pid'
```

When restarted with apachectl restart or by using the HUP signal with kill, the parent Apache process (run as the root user) kills all its children, reads the configuration file, and restarts a new generation of children as needed. This type of restart is sudden to the Web clients that were promised to be served by the then-alive child processes, so you may want to consider using graceful with apachectl instead of restart option and WINCH instead of the HUP signal with the kill command.

This could take some time on a busy site.

Testing Apache

After you have started the Apache server, access it via a Web browser by using the appropriate host name. For example, if you are running the Web browser on the server itself, than use `http://localhost/` to access the server. However, if you want to access the server from a remote host, use the fully qualified host name of the server. For example to access a server called `apache.pcnltd.com`, use `http://apache.pcnltd.com`.

If you have set the Port directive to a non-standard port (i.e., not 80), don't forget to include the `:port` in the URL. For example, `http://localhost:8080` will access Apache server on port 8080.

If you have not made any changes to the default `htdocs` directory, you'll see the default page that is shipped with the Apache distribution; this needs to be replaced with your own content.

Finally, you want to make sure the log files are updated properly. To check your log files, enter the log directory and run the following command:

```
tail -f  /path/to/access_log
```

With the -f option specified, the `tail` utility lets you view a growing file. Now, use a Web browser to access the site, or if you are already there, simply reload the page you currently have on the browser. You should see an entry added to the listing on the screen. Press the Reload button a few more times to ensure the access file is updated accordingly. If you see the updated records, your access log file is working. Press Control+C to exit from the `tail` command session. If you don't see any new records in the file, you should check the permission settings for the log files and the directory in which they are kept.

Another log to check is the error log file. Use the following command to view the error log entries as they come in:

```
tail -f  /path/to/error_log
```

Simply request nonexistent resources (such as a file you don't have) on your Web browser, and you will see entries being added. If you observe this, the error log file is properly configured.

If all of these tests were successful, then you have successfully configured your Apache server. Congratulations!

Hosting Virtual Web Sites

Apache's httpd.conf configuration file separates virtual host configuration from the main server configuration using the <VirtualHost> container. For example, look at the following httpd.conf file:

```
# httpd.conf file


ServerName main.server.com
Port 80
ServerAdmin mainguy@server.com
DocumentRoot "/www/main/htdocs"


ScriptAlias /cgi-bin/ "/www/main/cgi-bin/"
Alias /images/  "/www/main/htdocs/images/"


<VirtualHost 192.168.1.100>
ServerName vhost1.server.com
ServerAdmin vhost1_guy@vhost1.server.com
DocumentRoot "/www/vhost1/htdocs"
ScriptAlias /cgi-bin/ "/www/vhost1/cgi-bin/"
</VirtualHost>


<VirtualHost 192.168.1.110>
ServerName vhost2.server.com
ServerAdmin vhost2_guy@vhost2.server.com
DocumentRoot "/www/vhost2/htdocs"
ScriptAlias /cgi-bin/ "/www/vhost2/cgi-bin/"
Alias /images/ "/www/vhost2/htdocs/images/"
</VirtualHost>
```

In the preceding file, two virtual Web sites called vhost1.server.com and vhost2.server.com are defined in their own <VirtualHost> containers. All the directives included in each of the <VirtualHost> containers apply only to the virtual host it serves. So, when a Web browser requests http://vhost1.server.com/index.html the Apache Web server looks for the index.html page in /www/vhost1/htdocs directory. Similarly, when a Web browser requests `http://vhost2.server.com/cgi-bin/` `hello.pl`, the script is run from the `/www/vhost2/cgi-bin` directory.

However, many directives in the main server configuration (i.e., any directive outside of <VirtualHost> container) still apply to virtual hosts that do not override them. For example, notice that the `vhost1.server.` `com` in the above example does not have an Alias directive for the `/images/` directory alias. So, when a Web browser requests the `http://vhost1.` `server.com/images/pretty_pic.gif` file, the picture is served from `/www/main/htdocs/images` directory. Because the `vhost2.server.com` does override the `/images/` alias with its own, a similar request will be served from `/www/vhost2/htdocs/images` directory instead.

As you can see, you can allow virtual hosts to inherit configuration from the main server, which makes the virtual host configuration quite manageable in large installations where some contents can be shared. If, for example, you decided only to have a central CGI repository and allow virtual hosts to use the scripts stored there, you do not need to create a ScriptAlias directive in each virtual host container. Simply use one ScriptAlias directive in the main server configuration and you are done. Each virtual host can use the alias as if it were part of its own configuration.

How to use name-based virtual hosts

This method of creating virtual hosts is the most recommended because it requires only a single IP address for hosting hundreds or more virtual Web sites. The only tiny issue with name-based virtual hosting is that it does not work for Web browsers that do not support HTTP/1.1 protocol. However, only the very early Web browsers such as Microsoft IE 1.*x* or Netscape Navigator 1.*x*, don't support HTTP/1.1, and so this is really not a big issue any more. Most people are using 3.*x* or later versions of the major Web browsers, which are compatible with name-based virtual hosting technique.

Now, lets look at an example. Say you have an IP address 192.168.1.100 and want to host `vhost1.domain.com` and vhost2.domain.com on the same server. Here is how you can do that:

1. Create the appropriate DNS records on your DNS server to point `vhost1.domain.com` and `vhost2.domain.com` to 192.168.1.100.

2. Create the following configuration segment in the `httpd.conf` file:

```
NameVirtualHost 192.168.1.100

<VirtualHost 192.168.1.100>
    ServerName vhost1.domain.com
    ServerAdmin someone@vhost1.domain.com
    DocumentRoot "/www/vhost1/htdocs"

    #
    # Any other directives you need
    # can go here
    #

</VirtualHost>

<VirtualHost 192.168.1.100>
    ServerName vhost2.domain.com
    ServerAdmin someone@vhost2.domain.com
    DocumentRoot "/www/vhost2/htdocs"

    #
    # Any other directives you
    # need can go here
    #

</VirtualHost>
```

Don't forget to create the document root directories if you don't have them already. Also, if you need to add more directives in each of the virtual host configuration you can do so.

3. Restart Apache using `/usr/local/apache/apachectl restart` command and access each of the virtual hosts using `http://vhost1.domain.com` and `http://vhost2.domain.com`.

As you can see from the above example configuration, both virtual host containers use the same IP address (192.168.1.100). So how does Apache know which virtual site is being requested when a request comes via the 192.168.1.100 IP address? Well, it turns out that HTTP/1.1 requires that a new header called Host be present in each request that the Web browser makes to a Web server. For example, the following is a header dump of an HTTP request from a Web browser to a server running on `rhat.domain.com`:

```
GET / HTTP/1.1
Host: rhat.domain.com
Accept: text/html, text/plain
Accept: postscript-file, default, text/sgml, */*;q=0.01
Accept-Encoding: gzip, compress
Accept-Language: en
User-Agent: Lynx/3.0.0dev.9 libwww-FM/2.14
```

When Apache sees the `Host: rhat.domain.com` header, it can immediately service the request by using the appropriate virtual host with a matching ServerName.

How to use IP-based virtual hosts

An IP-based virtual host is one of the two types of virtual hosts that Apache supports. In such a setup, each virtual host is given a unique IP address. For example:

```
<VirtualHost 192.168.1.1>
    ServerName vhost1.server.com
    # Other directives go here
</VirtualHost>

<VirtualHost 192.168.1.2>
    ServerName vhost2.server.com
    # Other directives go here
</VirtualHost>
```

```
<VirtualHost 192.168.1.3>

   ServerName vhost3.server.com

   # Other directives go here

</VirtualHost>
```

Each of these IP addresses must be bound to the appropriate Ethernet interface on the server. For example, the above configuration requires that a system hosting the above sites must have the following DNS records in its DNS server configuration file:

```
; Address Records
vhost1.server.com.   IN   A 192.168.1.1
vhost2.server.com.   IN   A 192.168.1.2
vhost3.server.com.   IN   A 192.168.1.3


; Reverse DNS records
1            IN PTR   vhost1.server.com.
2            IN PTR   vhost2.server.com.
3            IN PTR   vhost3.server.com.
```

Each of these addresses must be bound to one or more Ethernet interfaces on the server. Typically, on a Linux system multiple IP addresses can be bound using IP aliasing technique. For example:

```
/sbin/ifconfig eth0    192.168.1.1 up
/sbin/ifconfig eth0:0 192.168.1.2 up
/sbin/ifconfig eth0:1 192.168.1.3 up
```

Here, all of three IP addresses are bound to Ethernet interface eth0 and its two aliases eth0:0 and eth0:0. Now the system will respond to each of these IP addresses.

How to use multiple main servers as virtual hosts

Using multiple main servers as virtual hosts is only recommended when you are required (typically due to non-technical reasons) to maintain different httpd.conf files.

Before you actually go ahead with this method, consider carefully whether you can avoid creating multiple main server instances and simply go with <VirtualHost> containers instead.

For example, say you have 16 IP addresses and want to provide 16 different clients (or departments) with their own httpd.conf files so that each entity can manage everything on its own; they can even create virtual hosts of their own by using <VirtualHost> containers within their own httpd.conf files.

Listing 12-2 shows a simplified version of httpd.conf (called httpd-100.conf) that uses the Listen directive to tell Apache to only service the 192.168.1.100 IP address associated with the system it is running.

Listing 12-2 *The httpd-100.conf file*

```
ServerType standalone
ServerRoot "/usr/local/apache"
PidFile /usr/local/apache/logs/httpd-192.168.1.100.pid
ScoreBoardFile /usr/local/apache/logs/httpd-192.168.
1.100.scoreboard
Timeout 300
KeepAlive On
MaxKeepAliveRequests 100
KeepAliveTimeout 15
MinSpareServers 60
MaxSpareServers 100
StartServers 50
MaxClients 200
MaxRequestsPerChild 0
Port 80
Listen 192.168.1.100:80
User prod
Group prod
ServerName prod.domain.com
ServerAdmin kabir@prod.domain.com
DocumentRoot "/www/prod/htdocs"
```

Notice that the Listen directive also takes a port number as a parameter. In the above example, Apache is told to listen to the given IP address on port 80. The Port directive is still necessary because its value is used in Apache-generated, self-referencing URLs.

Listing 12-3 shows another simplified httpd.conf file called httpd-101.conf that tells Apache to listen to only the 192.168.1.101 address.

Listing 12-3 *The httpd-101.conf file*

```
ServerType standalone
ServerRoot "/usr/local/apache"
PidFile /usr/local/apache/logs/httpd-192.168.1.101.pid
ScoreBoardFile /usr/local/apache/logs/httpd-192.168.1.
101.scoreboard
Timeout 300
KeepAlive On
MaxKeepAliveRequests 100
KeepAliveTimeout 15
MinSpareServers 5
MaxSpareServers 10
StartServers 5
MaxClients 10
MaxRequestsPerChild 0
Port 80
Listen 192.168.1.101:80
User stage
Group stage
ServerAdmin lance@stage.domain.com
DocumentRoot "/www/stage/htdocs"
```

A system that wants to run two main Apache servers using the above configuration files must have the following:

- One or more Ethernet interfaces responding to the named IP addresses. For example, on a Linux system you can bind Ethernet interface eth0 to both 192.168.1.100 and 192.168.1.101 using the following IP-aliasing command:

  ```
  /sbin/ifconfig eth0 192.168.1.100 up
  /sbin/ifconfig eth0:0 192.168.1.101 up
  ```

Of course, if a system has multiple Ethernet interfaces and you want to use a main server for each interface, you don't need to use IP aliases.

■ The IP addresses must have host names associated with them. For the above configuration files, 192.168.1.100 is associated with prod.domain.com and 192.168.101 is associated with stage. domain.com.

A system that has such IP addresses bound to its interface(s) can now run two main Apache daemons by using the following commands:

```
/usr/local/apache/bin/httpd -f conf/httpd-100.conf
/usr/local/apache/bin/httpd -f conf/httpd-101.conf
```

If you run the ps auxww | grep httpd | grep root | grep conf command you will see two main Apache servers running as the root user.

Authenticating and Authorizing Users

The mod_auth module is Apache's default authentication module. This module allows you to authenticate users whose credentials are stored in text files, typically with a text field containing a username and encrypted password. You can also use a text file to create user groups, which can be used to create authorization rules.

I recommend that you use mod_auth-based authentication for small numbers of users only, say for a few hundred users or so. My personal experience shows that when a text file reaches even a low few thousands (1K3K) usernames, lookup performance goes down dramatically. Therefore, if you have a very large user base, I do not recommend this module.

This module is compiled into Apache by default. You can use /usr/local/apache/bin/httpd -l to verify if this module is already compiled into your Apache binary. If not, you have to use the --enable-module=auth option with the configure script and recompile and install your Apache distribution. I assume that you have mod_auth compiled by default.

Understanding the mod_auth directives

The mod_auth module offers the Apache directives AuthUserFile, Auth-GroupFile, and AuthAuthoritative. The following sections give you a closer look at these directives and some examples that use this module.

AuthUserFile

This directive sets the name of the text file that contains the user names and passwords that are used in the basic HTTP authentication. You must provide a fully qualified path to the file to be used.

> **Syntax:** AuthUserFile *filename*
>
> **Context:** Directory, per-directory access control file
>
> **Override:** AuthConfig

For example, the following file is usually created using a utility called htpasswd, which is available as a support program in the standard Apache distribution:

```
AuthUserFile /www/mobidac/secrets/.htpasswd
```

The format of this file is very simple. Each line contains a single user name and an encrypted password. The password is encrypted using the standard crypt() function.

It is important that the AuthUserFile-specified file resides outside the document tree of the Web site. Putting it inside a Web-accessible directory can allow someone to download it.

AuthGroupFile

This directive specifies a text file to be used as the list of user groups for basic HTTP authentication. The file name is the absolute path to the group file.

Syntax: `AuthGroupFile` *filename*

Context: Directory, per-directory access control file

Override: AuthConfig

You can create this file using any text editor. The format of this file is as follows:

`groupname:` *username username username* `...`

For example, the following command creates a group called `startrek`, which has four users: `kirk`, `spock`, `picard`, and `data`:

`startrek: kirk spock picard data`

The Caution icon in the AuthUserFile section also applies to this directive.

AuthAuthoritative

If you are using more than one authentication scheme for the same directory, you can set this directive to `Off` so that when a user name/password pair fails with the first scheme, it is passed on to the next (lower) level.

Syntax: `AuthAuthoritative On | Off`

Default setting: `AuthAuthoritative On`

Context: Directory, per-directory access control file

Override: AuthConfig

For example, if you are using mod_auth_mysql and the standard mod_auth module to provide authentication services, and a user name/password pair fails for one of them, the next module is used to authenticate the user, if possible. When a user name/password pair fails all modules, the server reissues a 401 status header and sends the WWW-Authenticate response header for re-authentication. However, if a particular module successfully authenticates a user name/password pair, the lower-level modules never receive the user name/password pair.

I recommended that you leave the default because you should not design a trickle-down authentication scheme where a user may fail one and pass another.

Creating a member-only section in your Web site

Using the mod_auth directives you can create a member-only section on your Web site that requires username/password-based authentication. For example, say that you want to create a member-only section called http://your_server_name/memberonly. Here's how:

1. Determine which physical directory you want to restrict access to. Most people use a directory within the DocumentRoot-specified directory, but you can use whatever directory you want as long as the Apache user (set by User directive) is allowed to read the contents of the directory. Here I assume that your DocumentRoot is set to /www/mysite/htdocs and that you want to restrict access to a directory named /www/mysite/htdocs/memberonly. Make changes accordingly, based on your own DocumentRoot settings and filenames.

2. Modify the httpd.conf file to create a new alias called /memberonly/, as shown below:

   ```
   Alias /memberonly/ "/www/mysite/htdocs/memberonly/"
   ```

3. Add the following directives in httpd.conf file to set up /memberonly/ as a restricted section that requires user authentication.

   ```
   <Location /memberonly/>

       AuthName "Member-Only Access"

       AuthType  Basic

       AuthUserFile /www/secrets/.members

       require valid-user

   </Location>
   ```

In the preceding, the AuthName directive simply creates a label that is displayed by the Web browsers to the users. This label should be something meaningful so the user knows what is being requested. Make sure you use double-quotes as shown above. The AuthType is always set to Basic since HTTP only supports Basic authentication by default. The AuthUserFile points to a password file called .members. The require directive states that only valid users are allowed access.

4. Use the `htpasswd` utility to create a password file. Assuming you have installed Apache in `/usr/local/apache`, the `htpasswd` command should be run as follows only for the first time:

`/usr/local/apache/bin/htpasswd -c path_to_password_ file username`

The -c option is only needed to create the file and should be used just once. For example, to create the first user called `mrbert` for the above `/memberonly/` configuration, run the following command:

`/usr/local/apache/bin/htpasswd -c /www/secrets/. members mrbert`

5. To ensure that the user is created in the password file, view its contents using a text editor. Also make sure that only the Apache user (set using the User directive) can access this file. For example, if you run Apache as httpd user, you can run `chown httpd:httpd /www/ secrets/.members && chmod 750 /www/secrets/.members` commands to ensure that only `httpd` user (and group) can read this file.

6. Restart the Apache server by using the `/usr/local/apache/bin/ apachectl` restart command.

Now access the member-only section using `http://your_server_ name/memberonly/` and you should be prompted for a username and password. You should see the value of the AuthName ("Member-Only Access") in the displayed dialog box. Enter an invalid username and password and you should see a rejection message. Finally, enter a valid username and password (created with the `htpasswd` utility). You should have access to the restricted section.

 If you're using the default common log format to log access, you'll be able to see logged in usernames in your log files.

Creating a member-only section using .htaccess file

In the last section I discussed how you could create a member-only section using configuration in `httpd.conf` file. Such configuration is not suitable

for organizations such as Internet Service Providers (ISP) or other large
companies with many departments running virtual Web sites on the same
Web server. In these cases, adding a member-only configuration in `httpd.`
`conf` might not be very manageable because you will have to add or remove
configurations as various users (in case of an ISP setup) request such
changes. The best approach in such an environment is to use `.htaccess`-
based authentication.

When using `.htaccess`-based authentication, you can allow a user or
department to create as many member-only sections as they want without
your involvement — a blessing for a busy system administrator. If you wish
to use .htaccess file for member-only authentication, follow these steps:

1. Add the following directive to your `httpd.conf` file:

```
AccessFileName .htaccess
```

 If you wish to enable the `.htaccess`-based authentication
for only a virtual host then add this directive within the appropriate `<VirtualHost>` container.

2. Change the following default configuration:

```
<Directory />

    Options FollowSymLinks

    AllowOverride None

</Directory>
```

to

```
<Directory />

    Options FollowSymLinks

    AllowOverride AuthConfig

</Directory>
```

This allows use of the authorization directives (AuthDBMGroup-
File, AuthDBMUserFile, AuthGroupFile, AuthName, AuthType,
AuthUserFile, Require, etc.) in an `.htaccess` file.

3. Restart the Apache server using `/usr/local/apache/bin/`
`apachectl restart` command.

4. Now you can create an `.htaccess` file in any Web-accessible directory and control access to it. You need to have the following directives
in the `.htaccess` file:

```
AuthName "Enter Label Here"

AuthType Basic

AuthUserFile user_password_file

Require valid-user
```

For example, if you have a directory called `/www/mysite/htdocs/`
`asb` and want to restrict access to this directory to users listed in
`/www/mysite/secrets/users.pwd` then you would use the following configuration:

```
AuthName "ASB Member Only Access"

AuthType Basic

AuthUserFile /www/mysite/secrets/users

Require valid-users.pwd
```

5. Make sure that the `.htaccess` file is readable only by the Apache user
(set using User directive). For example, if you run Apache as `httpd`
then run the `chown httpd:httpd .htaccess && chmod 750`
`.htaccess` command from the directory where you keep the file.

Creation or modification of an `.htaccess` file does not
require restarting Apache server, so you can try out the
restricted section of your Web site and see if the authentication process is working properly.

Grouping users for restricted access to different Web sections

If you need to allow different users to access different parts of your Web
site, you have several choices. Instead of using require valid-user, which
opens up the restricted section for all valid users, you can use specific user
names. For example, in the following directives only `cgodsave` and
`jolson` have access to the `/financial` section and `esmith` and `jkirk`
have access to the `/sales` section:

```
<Location /financial>
   AuthName "Members Only"
   AuthType Basic
   AuthUserFile /www/mysite/secrets/.users.pwd
   Require cgodsave jolson
</Location>

<Location /sales>
   AuthName "Members Only"
   AuthType Basic
   AuthUserFile /www/mysite/secrets/.users.pwd
   Require esmith jkirk
 </Location>
```

However, naming all users in the configuration is a cumbersome and often unmanageable undertaking. An alternative approach is to create separate password files so that the above configuration segments look as follows:

```
<Location /financial>
   AuthName "Members Only"
   AuthType Basic
   AuthUserFile /www/mysite/secrets/.financial-team.pwd
   Require valid-user
</Location>

<Location /sales>
   AuthName "Members Only"
   AuthType Basic
   AuthUserFile /www/mysite/secrets/.sales-team.pwd
   Require valid-user
 </Location>
```

Now add only the users (in this case cgodsave and jolson) who should be added to /www/mysite/secrets/.financial-team.pwd and do the same for those users (esmith and jkirk) that should be added to /www/mysite/secrets/.sales-team.pwd.

However, if maintaining multiple password files is not appealing to you, you can use another approach. For example, take a look at the following configuration segments:

```
<Location /financial>
    AuthName "Members Only"
    AuthType Basic
    AuthUserFile /www/mysite/secrets/.members.pwd
    AuthGroupFile /www/mysite/secrets/.groups
    Require group financial
  </Location>

<Location /sales>
    AuthName "Members Only"
    AuthType Basic
    AuthUserFile /www/mysite/secrets/.members.pwd
    AuthGroupFile /www/mysite/secrets/.groups
    Require group sales
  </Location>
```

Here the same `.members.pwd` password file is being used for both locations, but each location uses a different group. The group file is common because a group file can contain multiple groups. The group file `/www/mysite/secrets/.groups` is a simple text file which for the above example looks like the following:

```
financial: cgodsave jolson
sales: esmith jkirk
```

Now adding new users to any of the groups does not require that you change the `httpd.conf` file (or if you are using `.htaccess` files, in which case you do not need the `<Location>` containers). You can simply add the user to the appropriate group in the group file after you have created the user account by using the `htpasswd` command as shown earlier in this chapter.

Authorizing access via hostname or IP addresses

In this authorization scheme, access is controlled by the host name or the host's IP address. When a request is made for a certain resource, the Web server checks to see if the requesting host is allowed access to the resource and then takes appropriate action based upon its findings.

The standard Apache distribution includes a module called mod_ access, which enables access control that is based on the Internet host name of a Web client. The host name can be either a fully qualified domain name (FQDN), such as blackhole.mobidac.com, or an IP address, such as 192.168.1.100. The module provides this access control support using the following Apache directives: Allow, Deny, Order, Allow from env= variable, and Deny from env=variable.

Allow directive

This directive enables you to define a list of hosts (containing one or more hosts or IP addresses) that are allowed access to a certain directory.

Syntax: Allow from host1 host2 host3 ...

Context: <Directory>, <Location>, per-directory access control file

Override: Limit

When more than one host or IP address is specified, they should be separated with space characters. Table 12-5 shows the possible values for the directive.

Table 12-5 *Possible Values for the allow Directive*

Value	Example	Description
All	Allow from all	This reserved word allows access for all hosts. The example shows how to use this option
A fully qualified domain name (FQDN) of a host	Allow from wormhole.mobidac. com	Only the host that has the specified domain name FQDN is allowed access. The allow directive in the example only allows access to wormhole.mobidac.com. Note that this compares whole components; toys.com would not match etoys.com.

Continued

Table 12-5 *Continued*

Value	Example	Description
A partial domain name of a host	`Allow from .mainoffice. mobidac.com`	Only all the hosts that match the partial host name are allowed access. The example permits all the hosts in the `.mainoffice.mobidac.com` network to access the site. For example, `developer1.mainoffice.mobidac.com` and `developer2.mainoffice.mobidac.com` have access to the site. However, `developer3.baoffice.mobidac.com` is not allowed access.
A full IP address of a host	`Allow from 192.168.1.100`	Only the specified IP address is allowed access. The example shows a full IP address (all four octets of IP are present), 192.168.1.100, that is allowed access.
A partial IP address	`Example 1: Allow from 192.168.1` `Example 2: Allow from 130.86`	When not all four octets of an IP address are present in the allow directive, the partial IP address is matched from left to right, and hosts that have the matching IP address pattern (that is, it is part of the same subnet) are allowed access. In the first example, all hosts with IP addresses in the range of 192.168.1.1 to 192.168.1.255 have access. In the second example, all hosts from the network are allowed access.
A network/netmask pair	`Allow from 192.168.1.0/255.255.255.0`	This enables you to specify a range of IP addresses using the network and the netmask address. The example allows only the hosts with IP addresses in the range of 192.168.1.1 to 192.168.1.255 to have access.
A network/nnn CIDR specification	`Allow 206.171.50.0/24`	Similar to the previous entry, except the netmask consists of nnn high-order 1 bits. The example is equivalent to allowing from 206.171.50.0 to 255.255.255.0.

Deny

This directive is the exact opposite of the allow directive: it enables you to define a list of hosts that are denied access to a specified directory.

Syntax: `Deny from host1 host2 host3 ...`

Context: <Directory>, <Location>, per-directory access control file

Override: Limit

Like the Allow directive, Deny can accept all the values shown in Table 12-5.

Order

This directive controls how Apache evaluates both allow and deny directives.

Syntax: `order deny, allow | allow, deny | mutual-failure`

Default setting: `order deny, allow`

Context: <Directory>, <Location>, per-directory access control file

Override: Limit

For example, the following example denies the host `myboss.mycompany.com` access and allows all other hosts to access the directory:

```
<Directory /mysite/myboss/rants>
    Order Deny, Allow
    Deny from myboss.mycompany.com
    Allow from all
</Directory>
```

The value for the order directive is a comma-separated list that indicates which directive takes precedence. Typically, the directive that affects all hosts is given lowest priority. In the preceding example, because the allow directive affects all hosts, it is given the lower priority.

Although Allow, Deny, and Deny, Allow are the most widely used values for the order directive, you can use another value, mutual-failure, to indicate that only those hosts appearing on the allow list but not on the deny list are granted access. Note that in all cases, every Allow and Deny directive is evaluated.

Allow from env=variable

This directive, a variation of the allow directive, allows access when the named environment variable is set.

Syntax: `Allow from env=variable`

Context: <Directory>, <Location>, per-directory access control file

Override: Limit

This is only useful if you are using other directives such as Browser-Match to set an environment variable. For example, say you want to allow Microsoft Internet Explorer 6.01, the latest version of Internet Explorer, to access a directory where you stored some HTML files with embedded VBScript. Because the other leading Web browser, Netscape Navigator, does not support VBScript directly, you'd rather not have Navigator users go into the directory. In such a case, you can use the BrowserMatch directive to set an environment variable when Internet Explorer 6.01 is detected. The directive would be as follows:

```
BrowserMatch "MSIE 6.01" ms_browser
```

Now you can use a <Directory> container to specify the Allow directive as follows:

```
<Directory /path/to/Vbscript_directory >
    Order Deny,Allow
    Deny from all
    Allow from env=ms_browser
</Directory>
```

Here the Apache server sets the `ms_browser` environment variable for all browsers that provide the "MSIE 6.01" string as part of the user-agent identifier. The Allow directive will only allow browsers for which the `ms_browser` variable is set.

Deny from env=variable

This directive, a variation of the deny directive, denies access capability for all hosts for which the specified environment is set.

Syntax: `Deny from env=variable`

Context: <Directory>, <location>, per-directory access control file

Override: Limit

For example, if you want to deny access to all the hosts using the Microsoft Internet Explorer browser, you can use the BrowserMatch directive to set a variable called `ms_browser` whenever a browser identifies itself to the server with the string "MSIE."

```
BrowserMatch "MSIE" ms_browser
```

Now you can use a <Directory> container to specify the Deny directive, as follows:

```
<Directory /path/to/vbscript_directory >
   Order Deny,Allow
   Allow from all
   Deny from env=ms_browser
</Directory>
```

If you are interested in blocking access to a specific HTTP request method, such as GET, POST, and PUT, you can use the <Limit> container to do so. For example, the following allows POST requests to the cgi-bin directory only if hosts in the `yourdomain.com` domain make them:

```
<Location /cgi-bin>
   <Limit POST>
      Order Deny,Allow
      Deny from all
      Allow from yourdomain.com
   </Limit>
</Location>
```

In other words, if `yourdomain.com` has some HTML forms that send user input data via the HTTP POST method, only the users in `yourdomain.com` will be able to use these forms effectively. Typically, CGI applications are stored in the `cgi-bin` directory, and many sites feature HTML forms that use the POST method to dump data to CGI applications. Using the preceding host-based access control configuration, a site can allow anyone to run a CGI script but only allow a certain site (in this case, `yourdomain.com`) to actually post data to one or more CGI scripts.

This gives the CGI access in such a site a bit of a read-only character. That is, everyone can run applications that generate output without taking any user input, but only users of a certain domain can provide input.

Combining authentication and authorization

The basic HTTP user authentication support in mod_auth and access authorization support in mod_access can be combined to implement practical access control problems. For example, say that you want to allow a group of users access to the /aolbuddies/ sections of your Web site only if they are browsing the Web site via an AOL connection. Here is the configuration that you can add to httpd.conf after replacing the path and filenames as appropriate:

```
Alias /aolbuddies/ "/path/to/aolbuddies/"


<Location /aolbuddies/>
    Deny from all
    Allow from .aol.com
    AuthName "AOL Buddies Only"
    AuthType Basic
    AuthUserFile /path/to/.myusers.pwd
    AuthGroupFile /path/to/.mygroups
    Require group aolbuddies
    Satisfy all
</Location>
```

You must add all your AOL buddies as users in /path/to/.myusers. pwd and also create a group called aolbuddies in /path/to/.mygroupsm, which lists all the AOL buddies (users in /path/to/.aol that you added earlier) in it. When an AOL user connects to http://your_server/ aolbuddies/ via AOL, she will be prompted for a username and password. If she enters a username that belongs to the aolbuddies group and her password is correct, she will be allowed access. The Satisfy all directive tells Apache to only allow access to those who pass both authentication and authorization tests.

Monitoring and Logging Apache

Apache enables you to monitor these two types of information via the Web:

- Server configuration information
- Server status (uptime, total requests served, total data transfer, resource usage)

Server configuration information is static. Being able to quickly access a running server's configuration information can be very useful, however. Server status information, on the other hand, is dynamic. Using Apache's Web-based server status monitoring capabilities, you can monitor status information such as the server's uptime, total requests served, total data transfer, status of child processes, and system resource usage. Both types of information are quite valuable, so I discuss them both in the following sections, starting with how to monitor configuration information.

Accessing configuration information

You can access configuration information by using the mod_info module. This module provides a comprehensive overview of the server configuration, including all installed modules and directives in the configuration files. This module is contained in the mod_info.c file. It is not compiled into the server by default. You have to compile it using the `--enable-info` option with the `configure` script. For example:

```
./configure --prefix=/usr/local/apache \
            --with-mpm=prefork \
            --enable-info
```

This command configures Apache to be installed on the `/usr/local/apache` directory, configures the source to run as a pre-forking server, and enables the mod_info module.

After you've compiled this module in the server, you can view server configuration information via the Web by adding the following configuration to the `httpd.conf` file:

```
<Location /server-info>
    SetHandler server-info
    Order deny,allow
```

```
     Deny from all
     Allow from 127.0.0.1 .domain.com
</Location>
```

This allows the localhost (127.0.0.1) and every host on your domain to access the server information. Do not forget to replace `.domain.com` with your top-level domain name. For example, if your Web site is `www.evoknow.com`, you need to add:

```
Allow from 127.0.0.1 .nitec.comevoknow.com
```

The dot in front of the domain name allows any host in the domain to access the server information. However if you wish to limit this to a single host called `sysadmin.domain.com` than change the Allow from line to be:

```
Allow from 127.0.0.1 sysadmin.domain.com
```

After the server is configured and restarted, the server information is obtained from the localhost (i.e., by running a Web browser such as `lynx` on the server itself) by accessing `http://localhost/server-info`.

This returns a full configuration page for the server and all its modules. If you wish to access it from a different location, use the fully qualified server name in place of localhost. For example, if your Web server is called `www.evoknow.com`, you can access the server information using `http://www.evoknow.com/server-info`.

The mod_info module also provides a directive called `AddModuleInfo`, which has the following syntax:

```
AddModuleInfo module_name descriptive_text
```

This directive enables you to add descriptive text in the module listing provided by the mod_info module. The descriptive text could be anything including HTML text. For example:

```
AddModuleInfo mod_info.c
'See <a href="http://localhost/manual/mod/mod_info.html">man mod_info</a>'
```

This shows an HTML link next to the listing of mod_info.c as shown below.

```
Module Name: mod_info.c
Content handlers: (code broken)
```

```
Configuration Phase Participation: Create Server Config, Merge Server Configs
Module Directives:
AddModuleInfo - a module name and additional information on that module
Current Configuration:
AddModuleInfo mod_info.c 'man mod_info'


Additional Information:
Man mod_info
```

This "man mod_info" link provides a quick way to get more information on the module from the Apache online manual.

You can also limit the information displayed on the screen. To view server configuration only, for example, use: `http://server/server-info?server`, which shows the following information:

```
Server Version: Apache/2.0.14 (Unix)
Server Built: Dec 14 2001 12:12:28
API Version: 20010224:1
Hostname/port: rhat.evoknow.com:80
Timeouts: connection: 300    keep-alive: 15
MPM Information: Max Daemons: 20 Threaded: no Forked: yes
Server Root: /usr/local/apache
Config File: conf/httpd.conf
```

To view the configuration for a single module, use `http://server/server-info?module_name.c`. For example, to view information on only the mod_cgi module, run `http://server/server-info?mod_cgi.c`, which shows the following information:

```
Module Name: mod_cgi.c
Content handlers: (code broken)
Configuration Phase Participation: Create Server Config, Merge Server Configs
Module Directives:
ScriptLog - the name of a log for script debugging info
ScriptLogLength - the maximum length (in bytes) of the script debug log
ScriptLogBuffer - the maximum size (in bytes) to record of a POST request
Current Configuration:
```

To view a list of currently compiled modules, use: `http://server/server-info?list`, which shows the modules compiled in Apache.

Enabling status pages

The mod_status module enables Apache administrators to monitor the server via the Web. An HTML page is created with server statistics. This module also produces another page that is machine-readable. The information displayed on both pages includes:

- Current time on the server system
- Time when the server was last restarted
- Time elapsed since the server was up and running
- Total number of accesses served so far
- Total bytes transferred so far
- The number of children serving requests
- The number of idle children
- The status of each child, the number of requests that child has performed, and the total number of bytes served by the child
- Averages giving the number of requests per second, the number of bytes served per second, and the average number of bytes per request
- The current percentage CPU used by each child and used in total by Apache
- The current hosts and requests being processed

Some of the above information is only available when you enable them by using the ExtendedStatus directive, which is discussed later in this section.

Like the mod_info module, this module is also not compiled by default in the standard Apache distribution, so you need to use the --enable-status option with the `configure` script and then compile and install Apache.

Viewing status pages

After you have the mod_status module compiled and built into your Apache server, you need to define a URL location for Apache to use to display the information. In other words, you need to tell Apache which URL will bring up the server statistics on your Web browser.

Say for example that your domain name is `domain.com` and you want to use the following URL:

```
http://www.domain.com/server-status
```

Using the `<Location ...>` container, you can tell the server that you want it to handle this URL by using the server-status handler found in the mod_status module. The following will do the job:

```
<Location /server-status>
    SetHandler server-status
    Order deny,allow
    Deny from all
    Allow from 127.0.0.1 .domain.com
</Location>
```

Here, the SetHandler directive sets the handler (server-status) for the previously mentioned URL. After you've added the configuration in `httpd.conf`, restart the server and access the URL from a browser. The above-mentioned `<Location>` container enables you to access the status information from any host in your domain or from the server itself. Don't forget to change the `.domain.com` with your real domain name and also don't forget to leave the leading dot alone.

To view extended status information, add the ExtendedStatus On directive in the server configuration context. For example, your entire server status-related configuration in `httpd.conf` could look as follows:

```
ExtendedStatus On
<Location /server-status>
    SetHandler server-status
    Order Deny, Allow
    Deny from all
    Allow from 127.0.0.1 .domain.com
</Location>
```

You can also have the status page update itself automatically using the `http://server/server-status?refresh=n` URL to refresh the page every *n* seconds.

Simplifying the status display

The status page displayed by the module provides extra information that makes it unsuitable for using as a data file for any data analysis program. For example, if you wanted to create a graph from your server status data using a spreadsheet program, you would need to clean up the data manually; however, the module provides a way for you to create machine-readable output from the same URL by modifying it by using ?auto, as in http://server/server-status?auto.

Storing server status information

Apache comes with a Perl script (found in the support directory of the source distribution) called log_server_status, which can be used to periodically store server status information (using the auto option) in a plain text file.

You can run this script as a cron job to grab the status information on a desired time frequency. Before you can use the script, however, you may have to edit the script source to modify the value of the $wherelog, $port, $server, and $request variables. The default values are:

```
$wherelog = "/var/log/graph/"; # Logs path
$server = "localhost";          # Name of server
$port = "80";                   # Port on server
$request = "/status/?auto";     # Request to send
```

For most sites the following should work:

```
$wherelog = "/var/log/apache";
$server   = "localhost";
$port     = "80";
$request  = "/server-status?auto"
```

Change the value of $wherelog to a path where you would like to store the file created by the script. Make sure the path already exists or else create it using mkdir -p pathname. For example, mkdir -p /var/log/apache ensures that all the directories (/var, /var/log, /var/log/apache) are created as needed. The $port variable value should be the port number of the server you want to monitor. The default value of 80 is fine if your server is running on this standard HTTP port. The $server variable should be assigned the host name of your server. The default value localhost is fine if the script and the server run on the same system. If the server is on another machine, however, specify the fully qualified host name (for example, www.mydomain.com) as the value. The $request variable should be set to whatever you used in the <Location> directive plus the ?auto query string.

If you do not like the record format the script uses, you can modify the following line to fit your needs:

```
print OUT "$time:$requests:$idle:$number:$cpu\n";
```

The script uses a socket connection to the Apache server to send the URL request; therefore, you need to make sure you have socket support for Perl. For example, on a Linux system the Perl socket code is found in socket.ph. You can use the locate socket.ph command to make sure that this file exists in your system.

Creating log files

Knowing the status and the configuration information of your server is helpful in managing the server, but knowing who or what is accessing your Web site(s) is also very important, as well as exciting. You can learn this information by using the logging features of Apache server. In this sections, I discuss the details of how logging works and how to get the best out of Apache logging modules.

As Web server software started appearing in the market, many Web server log analysis programs started appearing as well. These programs became part of the everyday work life of many Web administrators. Along with all these came the era of log file incompatibilities, which made log analysis difficult and cumbersome; a single analysis program didn't work on all log files. Then came the Common Log Format (CLF) specification, which enabled all Web servers to write logs in a reasonably similar manner and thus makes log analysis easier from one server to another.

By default, the standard Apache distribution includes a module called mod_log_config, which is responsible for the basic logging, and it writes CLF log files by default. You can alter this behavior using the LogFormat directive. However, CLF covers logging requirements in most environments. The contents of each line in a CLF log file are explained as follows.

The CLF log file contains a separate line for each request. A line is composed of several tokens separated by spaces:

host ident authuser date request status bytes

If a token does not have a value, then it is represented by a hyphen (-). Tokens have the following meanings:

- *host* — The fully qualified domain name of the client, or its IP address.

- *ident* — If the IdentityCheck directive is enabled and the client machine runs `identd`, then this is the identity information reported by the client.

- *authuser* — If the requested URL required a successful Basic HTTP authentication, then the user name is the value of this token.

- *date* — The date and time of the request.

- *request* — The request line from the client, enclosed in double quotes (").

- *status* — The three-digit HTTP status code returned to the client.

- *bytes* — The number of bytes in the object returned to the client, excluding all HTTP headers.

See Appendix B for a list of all HTTP/1.1 status codes.

The date field can have the following format:

```
date = [day/month/year:hour:minute:second zone]
```

For example:

```
[03/Jul/2001:00:22:01 -0800]
```

The field sizes are given in Table 12-6.

Table 12-6 *Date Field Sizes*

Fields	Value
day	2 digits
month	3 letters
year	4 digits
hour	2 digits

Fields	Value
minute	2 digits
second	2 digits
zone	(`+` | `-`) 4*digit

Now take a look at the directives that can be used with mod_log_ config. There are four directives available in this module, as discussed in the following sections.

TransferLog directive

This directive sets the name of the log file or program where the log information is to be sent. By default, the log information is in the Common Log File (CLF) format.

Syntax: TransferLog *filename* | *"| path_to_external_program"*

Default setting: None

Context: Server config, virtual host

This format can be customized using the LogFormat directive. Note that when the TransferLog directive is found within a virtual host container, the log information is formatted using the last LogFormat directive found within the context. If a LogFormat directive is not found in the same context, however, the server's log format is used.

The TransferLog directive takes either a log file path or a pipe to an external program as the argument. The log filename is assumed to be relative to the ServerRoot setting if no leading / character is found. For example, if the ServerRoot is set to /etc/httpd, then the following tells Apache to send log information to the /etc/httpd/logs/access.log file:

```
TransferLog logs/access.log
```

When the argument is a pipe to an external program, the log information is sent to the external program's standard input (STDIN).

A new program is not started for a VirtualHost if it inherits the TransferLog from the main server. If a program is used, then it is run under the user who started httpd. This will be the root account if the server was started by root. Be sure that the program is secure.

LogFormat directive

This directive sets the format of the default log file named by the Transfer-Log directive. If you include a nickname for the format on the directive line, you can use it in other LogFormat and CustomLog directives rather than repeating the entire format string.

Syntax: `LogFormat format [nickname]`

Default setting: `LogFormat "%h %l %u %t \"%r\" %>s %b"`

Context: Server config, virtual host

A LogFormat directive that defines a nickname does nothing else; that is, it only defines the nickname, and it doesn't actually apply the format.

CustomLog directive

Like the TransferLog directive, this directive enables you to send logging information to a log file or an external program. Unlike the TransferLog directive, however, it enables you to use a custom log format that can be specified as an argument.

Syntax: `CustomLog file | pipe [format | nickname]` `[env=[!]environment_variable]`

Context: server config, virtual host

For example:

```
CustomLog logs/access.log "%h %l %u %t \"%r\" %>s %b"
```

Each line in the `access.log` file will be written using the given format specifiers. The format specifies a format for each line of the log file. The options available for the format are exactly the same as for the argument of the LogFormat directive. If the format includes any spaces (which it will do in almost all cases), it should be enclosed in double quotes. Instead of an actual format string, you can use a format nickname defined with the Log-Format directive. For example:

```
LogFormat "%h %t \"%r\" %>s" myrecfmt
CustomLog logs/access.log myrecfmt
```

Here the access.log will have lines in the myrecfmt format.

Also, note that the TransferLog and CustomLog directives can be used multiple times in each server to cause each request to be logged to multiple files. For example:

```
CustomLog logs/access1.log common
CustomLog logs/access2.log common
```

Here the server creates two log entries per request and stores each one in access1.log and access2.log. This is really not useful unless you use a different format per log and need each format for a different reason.

Finally, if you use the mod_setenvif (installed by default) or the URL rewrite module (mod_rewrite, which is *not* installed by default) to set environment variables based on a requesting URL, you can create conditional logging using the env=[!]*environment_variable* option with the CustomLog directive. For example, say that you allow people to download a PDF white paper and want to log all downloads in a log file called whitepaper.log in your usual log directory. Here is the necessary configuration:

```
SetEnvIf Request_URI \.pdf$ whitepaper
CustomLog logs/whitepaper.log common env=whitepaper
CustomLog logs/access.log common env=!whitepaper
```

In the preceding, the first line sets the environment variable whitepaper whenever a requesting URL ends in .pdf extension. Then when the entry is to be logged, Apache uses the env=whitepaper settings for the first CommonLog directive to determine if it is set. If it is set, a log entry using the common format is made to the logs/whitepaper.log file. When the whitepaper environment is not set, the log entry is made to the logs/access.log file as usual.

Customizing your log files

Although the default common log format meets most log requirements, sometimes it is useful to be able to customize logging data. For example, you may want to log the type of browsers that are accessing your site so that your Web design team can determine what type of browser-specific HTML to use. Or, perhaps you want to know which Web sites are sending (that is, referring) visitors to your sites. All this is accomplished quite easily in Apache. The default logging module, mod_log_config, supports custom logging.

Custom formats are set with the LogFormat and CustomLog directives of the module. The format argument to LogFormat and CustomLog is a string. This format string can have both literal characters and special % format specifiers. When literal values are used in this string, they are copied into the log file for each request. The % specifiers, however, are replaced with corresponding values. The special % specifiers are shown in Table 12-7.

Table 12-7 *Special % Specifiers for Log Entries*

% Specifier	Description
%a	The client's IP address.
%A	The server's IP address.
%B	Bytes sent, excluding HTTP headers, 0 for no byte sent.
%b	Bytes sent, excluding HTTP headers, - for no byte sent.
%c	Connection status when response is done. The 'X' character is written if the connection was aborted by the client before a response could be completed. If the client uses the keep-alive protocol, a '+' will be written to show that connection was kept alive after the response until timeout. A '-' is written to signify that connection was closed after the response.
%{mycookie}C	The contents of a cookie called mycookie.
%D	The amount of time (in microseconds) taken to complete the response.
%{myenv}e	The contents of an environment variable called myenv.
%f	The filename of the request.
%h	The remote host that made the request.
%H	The request protocol (e.g., HTTP 1/1).
%{ IncomingHeader }i	The contents of IncomingHeader; that is, the header line(s) in the request sent to the server. The i character at the end denotes that this is a client (incoming) header.
%l	If the IdentityCheck directive is enabled and the client machine runs identd, then this is the identity information reported by the client.
%m	The request method (GET, POST, PUT, and so on).
%{ ModuleNote }n	The contents of the note ModuleNote from another module.

% Specifier	Description
`%{ OutgoingHeader }o`	The contents of OutgoingHeader; that is, the header line(s) in the reply. The `o` character at the end denotes that this is a server (outgoing) header.
`%p`	The port to which the request was served.
`%P`	The process ID of the child that serviced the request.
`%q`	The query string.
`%r`	The first line of the request.
`%s`	Status returned by the server in response to the request. Note that when the request gets redirected, the value of this format specifier is still the original request status. If you want to store the redirected request status, use `%..>s` instead.
`%t`	Time of the request. The format of time is the same as in CLF format.
`%{format}t`	The time, in the form given by format. You can also look at the man page for the **strftime** function.
`%T`	The time taken to serve the request, in seconds.
`%u`	If the requested URL required a successful Basic HTTP authentication, then the user name is the value of this format specifier. The value may be bogus if the server returned a 401 status (Authentication Required) after the authentication attempt.
`%U`	The URL path requested.
`%v`	The name of the server or the virtual host to which the request came.
`%V`	The server name per the UseCanonicalName directive.

It is possible to include conditional information in each of the preceding specifiers. The conditions can be the presence (or absence) of certain HTTP status code(s). For example, say that you want to log all referring URLs that pointed a user to a nonexistent page. In such a case, the server produces a 404 status (Not Found) header. So, to log the referring URLs, you can use the format specifier:

```
'%404{Referer}i'
```

Similarly, to log referring URLs that resulted in an unusual status, you can use the following specifier:

```
'%!200,304,302{Referer}i'
```

Notice the use of the ! character to denote the absence of the server status list.

Similarly, to include additional information at the end of the CLF format specifier, you can extend the CLF format, which is defined by the format string:

```
"%h %l %u %t \"%r\" %s %b"
```

For example:

```
"%h %l %u %t \"%r\" %s %b \"%{Referer}i\" \"%{User-agent}i\"".
```

This format specification logs CLF format data and adds the Referer and User-agent information found in client-provided headers in each log entry.

This section shows you about adding custom fields in the log file, but what if you need to store this data in more than one log file? In the next section, I discuss how to use multiple log files.

Using error logs

Without logging errors, you will be unable to determine what's wrong with CGI scripts or directory or file permissions and where the error occurs. Because error logging is a must, it is supported in the core Apache server and not in a module such as mod_log_config.

The ErrorLog directive enables you to log all types of errors that Apache encounters. In this section, we look at how you can incorporate your Apache error logs into the widely used syslog facility. syslog is the traditional way of logging messages sent out by daemon (server) processes. You may ask, "Apache is a daemon, so why can't it write to syslog?" It can, actually. All you need to do is replace your existing ErrorLog directive in the httpd.conf configuration file with

```
ErrorLog syslog
```

and then restart Apache. Using a Web browser, access a nonexistent page on your Web server and watch the syslog log file to see if it shows an httpd entry. You should take a look at your /etc/syslog.conf file for clues about where the httpd messages will appear.

For example, Listing 12-4 shows /etc/syslog.conf.

Listing 12-4 *The /etc/syslog.conf file*

```
/etc/syslog.conf
# Log all kernel messages to the console.
# Logging much else clutters up the screen.
#kern.*                         /dev/console


# Log anything (except mail) of level
# info or higher.
# Don't log private authentication messages!
*.info;mail.none;authpriv.none    /var/log/messages


# The authpriv file has restricted access.
authpriv.*                      /var/log/secure


# Log all the mail messages in one place.
mail.*                          /var/log/maillog


# Everybody gets emergency messages,
# plus log them on another machine.
*.emerg                               *


# Save mail and news errors of level
# err and higher in a special file.
uucp,news.crit                  /var/log/spooler


# Save boot messages also to boot.log
local7.*                        /var/log/boot.log
```

There are two important lines (as far as Apache is concerned) in this listing. They are:

```
*.info;mail.none;authpriv.none    /var/log/messages
*.emerg                               *
```

The first line tells `syslog` to write all messages of the info type (except for mail and private authentication) to the `/var/log/messages` file, and the second line states that all emergency messages should be written to all log files. Using the LogLevel directive, you can specify what type of messages Apache should send to `syslog`. For example:

```
ErrorLog syslog
LogLevel debug
```

Here, Apache is instructed to send debug messages to `syslog`. If you want to store debug messages in a different file via `syslog`, then you need to modify `/etc/syslog.conf`. For example:

```
*.debug            /var/log/debug
```

Adding this line in `/etc/syslog.conf` and restarting `syslogd` (kill -HUP *syslogd_PID*) and Apache enables you to store all Apache debug messages to the `/var/log/debug` file. There are several log level settings:

- Emerg — Emergency messages
- Alert — Alert messages
- Crit — Critical messages
- Error — Error messages
- Warn — Warnings
- Notice — Notification messages
- Info — Information messages
- Debug — Messages logged at debug level will also include the source file and line number where the message is generated, to help debugging and code development.

If you want to see updates to your `syslog` or any other log files as they happen, you can use the `tail` utility. For example, if you want to see updates for a log called `/var/log/messages` as they occur, use the following command:

```
tail -f /var/log/messages
```

Log maintenance

By enabling logging, you may be able to save a lot of work. However, the logs themselves do add some extra work for you: they need to be maintained. On Apache sites with high hit rates or many virtual domains, log files can become huge in a very short time, which could easily cause a disk-space crisis. When log files become very large, you should rotate them.

You have two options for rotating your logs: you can use a utility that comes with Apache called `rotatelog`; or you can use `logrotate`, a facility that is available on most Linux systems.

Rotating log files with rotatelog

Apache comes with a support utility called `rotatelog` that allows you to rotate your log files. You can use this program as follows:

```
TransferLog "| path_to_rotatelogs logfile rotation_time_in_seconds"
```

For example, if you want to rotate the access log every 86,400 seconds (that is, 24 hours), use the following line:

```
TransferLog "| /path/to/rotatelogs /var/logs/httpd 86400"
```

You will have each day's access log information stored in a file called `/var/logs/httpd.`*nnnn*, where *nnnn* represents a long number.

Rotating log files with logrotate

The `logrotate` utility rotates, compresses, and mails log files. It is designed to ease the system administration of log files and enables the automatic rotation, compression, removal, and mailing of log files on a daily, weekly, or monthly basis, or on a size basis. Normally, `logrotate` is run as a daily `cron` job. Read the man pages for `logrotate` to learn more about it.

You should create a script called `/etc/logrotate.d/apache` as shown in Listing 12-5 to automatically rotate Apache logs.

Listing 12-5 *The /etc/logrotate.d/apache file*

```
# Note that this script assumes the following:
#
# a. You have installed Apache in /usr/local/apache
# b. Your log path is /usr/local/apache/logs
# c. Your access log is called access_log (default in Apache)
# d. Your error log is called error_log (default in Apache)
```

Continued

Listing 12-5 *Continued*

```
# e. The PID file, httpd.pid, for Apache is stored in the log
#    directory (default in Apache)
#
# If any of the above assumptions are wrong, please change
# the path or filename accordingly.
#
/usr/local/apache/logs/access_log {
    missingok

    compress
    rotate 5
    mail webmaster@yourdomain.com
    errors webmaster@yourdomain.com
    size=10240K

    postrotate
        /bin/kill -HUP \
        `cat /usr/local/apache/logs/httpd.pid 2>/dev/null` \
        2> /dev/null || true
    endscript
}


/usr/local/apache/logs/error_log {
    missingok

    compress
    rotate 5
    mail webmaster@yourdomain.com
    errors webmaster@yourdomain.com
    size=10240K
```

```
postrotate
    /bin/kill -HUP \
    `cat /usr/local/apache/logs/httpd.pid 2>/dev/null` \
    2> /dev/null || true
endscript
}
```

This configuration specifies that both the Apache access and error log files will be rotated whenever each grows over 10MB (10240K) in size, and that the old log files be compressed and mailed to webmaster@ yourdomain.com after going through five rotations, rather than being removed. Any errors that occur while processing the log file are mailed to root@yourdomain.com.

Resolving IP addresses to host names using logresolve

For performance reasons you should have disabled host name lookups by setting the HostNameLookups directive to Off. This means that your log entries show IP addresses instead of host names for remote clients. When analyzing the logs, it helps to have the host names so that you can determine who came from where more easily. For example, here are a few sample log entries from my /usr/local/apache/logs/access_log file:

```
207.183.233.19 - - [15/Mar/2001:13:05:01 -0800] "GET /book/images/back.gif
HTTP/1.1" 304 0
207.183.233.20 - - [15/Mar/2001:14:45:02 -0800] "GET /book/images/forward.gif
HTTP/1.1" 304 0
207.183.233.21 - - [15/Mar/2001:15:30:03 -0800] "GET /book/images/top.gif
HTTP/1.1" 304 0
```

If you had HostNameLookups turned on, Apache will resolve the client IP addresses 207.183.233.19, 207.183.233.20, and 207.183.233.21 into appropriate host names. When HostNameLookups is set to On and default LogFormat directive is set as shown below

```
LogFormat "%h %l %u %t \"%r\" %>s %b" common
```

and you used the common format in logging using CustomLog logs/access_log common, these sample log entries will look as follows:

```
nano.evoknow.com - - [15/Mar/2001:13:05:01 -0800] "GET /book/images/back.
gif HTTP/1.1" 304 0
rhat.evoknow.com - - [15/Mar/2001:14:45:02 -0800] "GET /book/images/forward.gif
HTTP/1.1" 304 0
r2d2.evoknow.com - - [15/Mar/2001:15:30:03 -0800] "GET /book/images/top.
gif HTTP/1.1" 304 0
```

Because turning on DNS lookups causes the Apache server to take more time in completing a response, it is widely recommended that host name lookups should be performed separately by using a utility called logresolve, which can be found in your Apache bin directory (/usr/local/apache/bin). The log_resolver.sh script, shown in Listing 12-6 uses the logresolve utility to perform host name lookups.

Listing 12-6 *An example log_resolver.sh file*

```
#!/bin/sh


#
# Make sure you change the pathnames according to
# your Apache installation
#


# Fully qualified path name (FQPN) of the
# log resolver utility
LOGRESOLVER=/usr/local/apache/bin/logresolve


# Statistic file generated by the utility
STATFILE=/tmp/log_stats.txt


# Your Apache Log file
LOGFILE=/usr/local/apache/logs/access_log


# New log file that has IP addressed resolved
OUTFILE=/usr/local/apache/logs/access_log.resolved
```

```
# Run the command
$LOGRESOLVER -s $STATFILE < $LOGFILE > $OUTFILE


exit 0;
```

When this script is run from the command line or as a cron job, it creates a file called /usr/local/apache/logs/access_log.resolved, which will contain all the IP addresses resolved to their respective host names. Also, the script generates a statistics file called /tmp/log_stats.txt that shows you cache usage information, total resolved IP addresses, as well as other info that resolver utility reports. An example of such a statistics file follows:

```
logresolve Statistics:
Entries: 3
     With name    : 0
     Resolves     : 3
Cache hits        : 0
Cache size        : 3
Cache buckets     :      IP number * hostname
   130    207.183.233.19 - nano.evoknow.com
   131    207.183.233.20 - rhat.evoknow.com
   132    207.183.233.21 - r2d2.evoknow.com
```

Notice that the utility could not utilize the cache because all three IP addresses that it resolved (for the sample log entries shown above) are unique. However, if your log file has IP addresses from the same host, the cache will be used to resolve them instead of blindly making DNS requests.

If you think you can use this script, I recommend that you run it as a cron job. For example, on my Apache Web server running on Linux, I simply add the script to /etc/cron.daily to create a resolved version of the log every day.

Chapter 13

Configuring E-mail Services

E-mail is the prerequisite of modern day communication. Millions of e-mails are sent among millions of people every day. In this chapter I discuss how you can set up e-mail service by using SMTP and POP mail servers.

Setting Up DNS for Mail Service

Before you can get your own SMTP server running on your Red Hat Linux server, you need to create an appropriate DNS configuration for e-mail delivery. Here is how. You can use Mail Exchange (MX) records to identify SMTP mail server resources in a DNS configuration for a domain.

See Chapter 15 for details on MX records.

Say that you want to designate a host called `mail.yourdomain.com` as your SMTP mail server for the domain `yourdomain.com`. The Start of Authority (SOA) record for `yourdomain.com` must include a line such as:

```
IN  MX  preference_value mail_server_hostname.
```

In the preceding, `preference_value` is a positive (integer) number and useful only when you have multiple SMTP mail servers. If you have just a single SMTP mail server, this number can have any value. For example:

```
IN  MX  5  mail.yourdomain.com.
```

Here the single SMTP mail server `mail.yourdomain.com` has been set to preference level 5. Here is an example of the multiserver scenario:

```
IN  MX  10  fast-mail-server.ad-engine.com.
IN  MX  20  slow-mail-server.ad-engine.com.
```

In this example, the preference number plays a vital role. When an SMTP mail server from anyone on the Internet wishes to send mail to `someone@ad-engine.com`, it first performs a DNS query to locate the MX record for `ad-engine.com`. The MX record returned to the SMTP mail server will be similar to that shown in the preceding code. The SMTP mail server then selects `fast-mail-server.ad-engine.com` as the preferred mail server for the delivery because it has the higher priority (that is, the lower preference number) of the two available servers. The SMTP mail server then tries to initiate an SMTP connection (using port 25) with the `fast-mail-server.ad-engine.com` computer. If the `fast-mail-server.ad-engine.com` server is not available for any reason, the `slow-mail-server.ad-engine.com` server is selected for delivery. Having multiple MX records provides you with redundancy in your mail delivery system, which is very important if e-mail is a critical part of your organization.

 Always use a host name in an MX record that has its own A record. In other words, do not use host aliases in MX records. See RFC 1123 for details.

After you have set up DNS with appropriate MX records, test the configuration via `nslookup –q=mxyourdomain` command. If you have configured DNS properly, you see the MX records you just created. After this is taken care of, you are ready to set up the SMTP mail service.

Setting Up SMTP Mail Service

The very first step in setting up an SMTP service is to decide which SMTP mail server you would like to use for your Red Hat Linux system. Many SMTP mail server products are available. However, sendmail stands out among the rest because of its long history of worldwide deployment. sendmail is also the default SMTP mail server for Red Hat Linux, and so I use sendmail as the SMTP server for this chapter.

You can run telnet localhost 25 command from your Linux system to see if you already have sendmail server installed on port 25. If you can connect to the mail server using the last command, you can disconnect by pressing Ctrl+C and then skip the installation section discussed in the following sections.

Installing sendmail

Like any other server software you install on your Red Hat system, sendmail also comes in RPM packages. However, you do need to install multiple RPM packages; they are:

- sendmail-*version.architecture*.rpm — The main distribution

- sendmail-cf-*version.architecture*.rpm — The mail sendmail configuration file distribution

- sendmail-config-*version.architecture*.rpm — The auxiliary configuration files distribution

- sendmail-doc-*version.architecture*.rpm — The documentation distribution

The first three RPM packages can be found on official Red Hat CD-ROM 1 and 2. The last documentation package can be downloaded from www.rpmfind.net.

Installing these packages is quite simple; just run rpm -ivh *package_name* to install each package.

If you have installed a previous version of `sendmail` during Red Hat Linux installation, remove the `sendmail` packages before you install a new version; they might not be exactly compatible. To uninstall an RPM package, use the `rpm -e package_name` command. You can also locate the exact package name of an RPM package using the `rpm -q partial_package_name` command.

After you install the packages, you are ready to configure `sendmail`. The primary configuration file for `sendmail` is `/etc/sendmail.cf`.

Configuring sendmail to listen to network interface

By default `sendmail` only listens to the 127.0.0.1 interface, the loopback interface, which means that you cannot send or receive mail beyond your local mail server system. This is not ideal for most scenarios because you want to send and receive mail to and from other machines — that's the whole point in e-mail. In such cases, follow these steps to enable `sendmail` to accept connections from all hosts:

1. As root, remove the following line from the `/etc/mail/sendmail.mc` file:

   ```
   DAEMON_OPTIONS(`Port=smtp,Addr=127.0.0.1, Name=MTA')
   ```

If you wish to keep the line as a comment instead, simply add `dnl` in front of the line such that the line reads as follows:

   ```
   dnl DAEMONOPTIONS(`Port=smtp,Addr=127.0.0.1,
   Name=MTA')
   ```

2. Back up your `/etc/sendmail.cf` file to `/etc/sendmail.cf.good`.

3. Run `m4 /etc/mail/sendmail.mc > /etc/sendmail.cf` to create a new `/etc/sendmail.cf` file that has the network interface restriction either removed or commented out.

4. Restart sendmail using the `/etc/rc.d/init.d/sendmail`
`restart` command.

Now sendmail will listen to your non-loopback network interface
as well as the loopback interface.

Starting and stopping sendmail

Although you have not yet configured the sendmail server, you can still
run it. To start sendmail manually, you can run the following command:

```
/usr/sbin/sendmail -qqueue_processing_interval
```

You have to replace the *queue_processing_interval* with a time. Typically,
the time is specified in minutes or hours. For example, to have sendmail
process the mail queue every 15 minutes, you can use –q15m; or, as another
example, to process the queue every hour you could use –q1h. You can also
specify seconds (s), days (d), or weeks (w). For example, you can specify
–q1h30m so that sendmail processes the query every hour and a half.

> If you do not have a full-time Internet connection, you may
> use /usr/sbin/sendmail –bd –o DeliveryMode=d to
> start sendmail in deferred mode, which avoids the use of
> DNS until it is run again via /usr/sbin/sendmail –q. If you
> connect periodically, you can put /usr/sbin/sendmail –q
> in a cron job so that when your connection is up, the queue
> is processed automatically.

If you want sendmail to start automatically after each boot, make sure
you create a symbolic link (starting with S*xx* where *xx* is a number) from
your default run level directory to the `/etc/rc.d/init.d/sendmail`
script. For example, to run sendmail after each boot for a multiuser system (run level 3), I can create the following symbolic link:

```
ln -s /etc/rc.d/init.d/sendmail /etc/rc.d/rc3.d/S85sendmail
```

This symbolic link ensures that sendmail starts automatically after
each boot. If you take a look at this script, you will see that sendmail is
started with the –bd option, which starts it as a daemon, a background
process. You may wish to modify the `/etc/rc.d/init.d/sendmail`
script to reflect the queue interval requirements for your site. You might

also want to add the following code just before the line (daemon /usr/ sbin/sendmail —bd) in the script to automatically run `newaliases` and `makemap` on the configuration files at boot:

```
newaliases
for i in virtusertable access domaintable mailertable
do
  if [ -f /etc/mail/$i ] ; then
     echo "Making $i database for sendmail..."
     makemap hash /etc/mail/$i < /etc/mail/$i
     sleep 1
  fi
done
sleep 1
```

This ensures that all the configuration databases are rebuilt each time you start the server process.

You can use the `/etc/rc.d/init.d/sendmail` script to start, stop, and restart `sendmail` quite easily as well. To stop `sendmail`, run the following command:

```
/etc/rc.d/init.d/sendmail stop
```

To restart `sendmail`, run the following command:

```
/etc/rc.d/init.d/sendmail restart
```

You can also force `sendmail` to process its queue immediately by using the —q option. For example:

```
/usr/sbin/sendmail -q
```

This command forces the immediate processing of the entire queue. If you prefer to process the queue partially, you can use the —qSstring option to process queues for only those messages that have the named string as part of the sender address. For example, the following command forces `sendmail` to process all the queued mail for sender `kabir`:

```
/usr/sbin/sendmail -qSkabir
```

This feature can be handy when you have lots of mail waiting in a queue. You can also use —qRstring to force `sendmail` to process messages that have the named string as part of the recipient address.

TIP   You can run the mqueue command to identify the messages currently in the queue.

Understanding and configuring /etc/sendmail.cf

The /etc/sendmail.cf file is really not meant for humans. It is meant for the sendmail daemon, and therefore the syntax is optimized for the daemon as well. If you are new to sendmail, the configuration file may scare you as it has many administrators over many years. The /etc/sendmail. cf configuration file is considered the most complex configuration file a Unix administrator has to deal with in his or her professional career. I agree.

A complete book can be (and has been) written about the configuration that goes in /etc/sendmail.cf. However, not every administrator needs to know all the sordid details about /etc/sendmail.cf configuration; in fact, in most cases you do not even need to modify this configuration file, as it comes equipped with commonly required configurations.

In this section I provide a brief overview of the /etc/sendmail.cf configuration file to help you understand how things are set up in the file and also enable you to follow instructions found at the sendmail Web site (www.sendmail.org) to implement certain features as needed. The information you find in this chapter is enough to get you up and running with sendmail and also provides you with enough know-how to follow clearly written instructions in implementing configuration changes. What you will not learn here is how to create your own configuration rules; this process requires extensive understanding of the inner workings of the sendmail configuration.

The sendmail.cf file contains the following types of configuration information:

- Blank lines are ignored.

- Comment lines, designated by a leading "#" sign, are also ignored.

- Lines starting with C, D, F, H, O, P, V, K, M, S, or R are configuration lines.

- Lines starting with a leading whitespace character are continuation lines.

In the following sections I discuss various configurations in brief so that you have an idea about which one does what.

S and R: Address rewrite rules

An "S" line is used to mark the start of a new rewrite rule. The syntax for such a line is S*rule*, where *rule* is the rule name or number. For example, S3 marks the start of rule set 3.

An "R" line defines an address rewrite rule. A rewrite rule can be simply thought of as a statement such as the one that follows:

```
If (current e-mail address matches rule's left-hand-side
pattern) then
    Replace current address
            with the rule's right-hand-side pattern
end
```

It has the following syntax:

```
RLHS    RHS   optional_comments
```

Here, *LHS* is the left-hand-side pattern, and *RHS* is the right-hand-side pattern of the rule. For example:

```
R$* < $* > $* <@>       $: $1 < $2 > $3
```

Here, the left-hand-side pattern is $* < $* > $* <@>, and the right-hand-side pattern is $: $1 < $2 > $3. Both left- and right-hand-side patterns are composed of various metasymbols such as $*, $+, $-, $=x, and $~x.

Rewrite rules are quite complex and in most cases will not require any changes on your part. However, if you are planning on writing your own rewrite rules, you should read the Sendmail Installation and Operation Guide bundled with the sendmail documentation which can be read using info sendmail command.

D: Define macro

The "D" lines define a macro. The syntax is as follows:

```
Dmacro_name string
```

For example:

```
DP someword
```

This is same as $P = someword, and whenever $P is referenced elsewhere, it is expanded to someword.

Typically, you do not need to add, delete, or remove any "D" macro definitions.

C and F: Define classes

The "C" lines are similar to "D" lines. The syntax for such a line is as follows:

```
Cclass_name string1 string2 . . .
```

For example:

```
CA str1 str2 str3
```

Here the A class is a list of str1, str2, and str3 strings.

The "F" lines are the same as "C" lines, except for the fact that an "F" line is used to specify a class that is read from a file. For example:

```
Fw/etc/mail/sendmail.cw
```

Here, the w class is a list of all the domain names in the /etc/mail/sendmail.cw file. This file must contain a single entry per line. The only other "F" line you will notice in your sendmail.cf file is:

```
FR-o /etc/mail/relay-domains
```

Here the class R is a list of all domain names in /etc/mail/relay-domains. Notice the –o option, which makes the line optional. In other words, sendmail won't complain if this file is empty. Typically, you do not need to make any changes here. However, if you want sendmail to complain if no relay domains are defined, you can remove the –o option from the preceding FR line.

M: Define mailer

An "M" line is used to create a mailer definition. The syntax for such a line is as follows:

```
Mmailer name field = value, field = value, . . .
```

For example, in the following example mailer SMTP is being defined:

```
Msmtp,  P=[IPC], F=mDFMuX, S=11/31, R=21/31, E=\r\n, L=990,
        T=DNS/RFC822/SMTP
```

Typically, you do not need to make any changes in standard mailer definitions.

H: Define header

An "H" line is used to create a header definition. The syntax for such a line is as follows:

```
H[?flags?]<header name>: <header template>
```

For example, each of the following "H" lines defines a mail header:

```
H?P?Return-Path: <$g>
HReceived: $?sfrom $s $.$?_($?s$|from $.$_)
        $.by $j ($v/$Z)$?r with $r$. id $i$?u
        for $u; $|;
        $.$b
H?D?Resent-Date: $a
H?D?Date: $a
H?F?Resent-From: $?x$x <$g>$|$g$.
H?F?From: $?x$x <$g>$|$g$.
H?x?Full-Name: $x
H?M?Resent-Message-Id: <$t.$i@$j>
H?M?Message-Id: <$t.$i@$j>
```

You should not make any changes in header definitions.

O: Set option

The "O" lines are used to set global options for sendmail. The syntax for such a line is as follows:

```
O option name = value
```

Table 13-1 shows all the options available in the latest version (8.9.*x*) of sendmail.

Table 13-1 *sendmail Options*

Option	Explanation
AliasFile=/etc/mail/aliases	Sets the name of the alias database file. Change this only if you keep the alias database someplace other than /etc/mail/aliases.
AliasWait=30m	Sets the default timeout (in minutes) for aliases to load at startup. Do not change.
AutoRebuildAliases=True	If set to True, sendmail tries to rebuild the aliases database if necessary and possible. Do not change.
BlankSub=.	Sets the blank substitution character. Do not change.
CheckAliases=False	If set to True, checks the right-hand side of an alias in the aliases database for validity. Default is set to False. No change recommended.
ClassFactor=1800	Used to compute priority of a message. Do not change.
ConnectionCacheSize=2	The maximum number of open connections that will be cached at any time.
ConnectionCacheTimeout=5m	The maximum time (in minutes) that a cached connection will be kept open during idle period.
ConnectionRateThrottle=20	Allows no more than the specified number of daemon processes for incoming connections per second. Setting this to 0 will allow unlimited (i.e., as many as are permitted by your system resources) number of daemon processes per second.
DefaultUser=8:12	Default user and group for mailers. The UID 8 is default for user mail in /etc/passwd and GID 12 is default for group mail in the /etc/group file. Changes not recommended.
DeliveryMode=background	Runs sendmail in the background. No change required.
EightBitMode=pass8	Sets how 8-bit data is handled. Keep the default.
ForkEachJob=FALSE	When set to TRUE, a separate process if forked to service each message in the queue. No change required.
ForwardPath=$z/.forward.$w+$h: $z/.forward+$h:$z/.forward.$w: $z/.forward	Sets the path for searching for the .forward file for each user. No changes required.
HelpFile=/usr/lib/sendmail.hf	Sets the location of the help file.

Continued

Table 13-1 *Continued*

Option	Explanation
HoldExpensive=False	When set to **True**, expensive mailers (marked using the **F=e** flag in the "M" line for the mailer) are not allowed to connect immediately. Keep the default.
HostStatusDirectory= .hoststat	Sets the directory name for the host status information. The default value sets the directory to be **/var/spool/mqueue/.hoststat**. No change required.
HostsFile=/etc/hosts	Sets the name of the hosts file. No change required.
LogLevel=8	Sets the default log level. No change required.
MatchGECOS=False	When this is set to **True**, **sendmail** will perform a fuzzy search in the **/etc/passwd** file to locate a similar username in the GECOS field of each password entry. Default is recommended.
MaxDaemonChildren=40	Maximum number of forked child processes at any time.
MaxHopCount=30	Maximum number of times a message can be processed before it is rejected.
MaxMessageSize=5000000	Maximum size of a message in bytes. Messages larger then this size will not be accepted.
MeToo=False	When an alias contains the sender herself, **sendmail** automatically removes the sender from the expansion. If this option is set to **True**, the sender will receive the mail in such a case. You might want to set this to **True** because it could reduce some tech-support calls from users who wish to receive mail even if it originated from themselves.
MinFreeBlocks=100	The minimum number of free blocks that must be present before **sendmail** will accept a message. This ensures that someone cannot wipe out your disk space by mail bombing (i.e., sending multiple copies of large mail messages) your server. You might want to increase this number to a higher number than the default.
MinQueueAge=10m	A message must be in the queue for at least the specified number of minutes before it is processed.
NoRecipientAction= add-to-undisclosed	When a message does not contain an appropriate recipient header, the specified action is taken. The default value creates a **To: undisclosed-recipients** header.

Option	Explanation
OldStyleHeaders=True	Toggle old/new header format. No change required.
OperatorChars=.:%@!^/[]+	List of token delimiter characters. No change required.
PrivacyOptions=needvrfyhelo, restrictmailq, restrictqrun,goaway	See the "Securing **sendmail**" section on ensuring privacy later in this chapter for details.
QueueDirectory=/var/ spool/mqueue	The fully qualified pathname of the queue directory.
QueueLA=8	When the system's load average exceeds the specified number, do not send messages but instead queue them.
QueueSortOrder=Host	Sets the queue sort order. The default value allows **sendmail** to sort the queue using the host names of the recipients. You can change this to **Priority** to sort mail using **priority** header, or you can set this to **Time** to sort by submission time.
RecipientFactor=30000	This value is used to penalize the priority of a message that has a large number of recipients.
RefuseLA=12	When the system's load average exceeds the specified value, refuse incoming connections.
RetryFactor=90000	This value is used to lower message retry priority. No change recommended.
RunAsUser=mail	This value sets the username **sendmail** uses for all its child processes. In other words, **sendmail** child processes that are forked to service the actual requests do not run as the superuser; this therefore enhances security. No change recommended.
SendMimeErrors=True	When set to **True**, error messages are set using MIME formats. No change required.
SevenBitInput=False	When set to **True**, a message is converted into 7-bit data. Do not change the default value.
O SmtpGreetingMessage=$j Sendmail $v/$Z; $b	Sets the greeting message that **sendmail** issues when a connection is made. If you do not like to tell the world about the version of **sendmail** you use, remove the **$v/$Z** variables from this line. This might provide fewer clues for someone who is trying to exploit any security holes.
StatusFile=/var/log/ sendmail.st	The fully qualified pathname of the status file.

Continued

Table 13-1 *Continued*

Option	Explanation
SuperSafe=True	Toggle super safe mode. Default setting is recommended.
TempFileMode=0600	Sets the default mode for the temporary files in the queue.
Timeout.command=30m	Default timeout value for SMTP commands.
Timeout.connect=3m	Default timeout value for connection.
Timeout.datablock=1h	Default timeout value for data blocks.
Timeout.datafinal=1h	Default timeout value for final "." in the data.
Timeout.datainit=5m	Default timeout value for the DATA command.
Timeout.fileopen=60s	Default timeout value for **opening .forward** and **:include:** files.
Timeout.helo=5m	Default timeout value for the HELO command.
Timeout.hoststatus=10m	After the specified timeout period host becomes stale.
Timeout.initial=5m	Default timeout value for the initial greeting message.
Timeout.mail=10m	Default timeout value for the MAIL command.
Timeout.misc=2m	Default timeout value for the NOOP or VERB commands.
Timeout.queuereturn. non-urgent=7d	Value specifies time to elapse before nonurgent message is returned to sender.
Timeout.queuereturn. normal=5d	Value specifies time to elapse before normal message is returned to sender.
Timeout.queuereturn. urgent=2d	Value specifies time to elapse before urgent message is returned to sender.
Timeout.queuereturn=5d	Value specifies time to elapse before a message is returned to sender.
Timeout.queuewarn. non-urgent=12h	Value specifies time to elapse before a warning is sent to the sender about yet-undelivered nonurgent message.
Timeout.queuewarn.normal=6h	Value specifies time to elapse until a warning is sent to the sender about yet-undelivered normal message.
Timeout.queuewarn.urgent=2h	Value specifies time to elapse until a warning is sent to the sender about yet-undelivered urgent message.
Timeout.queuewarn=6h	Value specifies time to elapse until a warning is sent to the sender about yet-undelivered message.
Timeout.quit=2m	Default timeout value for the QUIT command.
Timeout.rcpt=30m	Default timeout value for the RCPT command.

Option	Explanation
Timeout.rset=5m	Default timeout value for the **RSET** command.
UnixFromLine=From $g $d	Defines the format used for Unix-style **From** line. Do not change the default.
UnsafeGroupWrites=True	When set to **True**, files such as **.forward** and **:include:** are considered unsafe when they are writable by a group. Do not change the default.
UseErrorsTo=False	When set to True and an error occurs, **sendmail** will use the **ErrorsTo** header (if available) to report the error. Do not change the default.

P: Precedence definitions

A "P" line is used to set values for the Precedence: header field. The syntax for such a line is as follows:

```
Pfield name = value
```

For example:

```
Pfirst-class=0
```

V: Configuration version level

A "V" line is used for compatibility with older versions of a configuration. You do not need to make any changes to such a line.

K: Key file declaration

A "K" line is used to define a map. The syntax for such a line is as follows:

```
Kmap name mapclass arguments
```

For example:

```
Kaccess hash -o /etc/mail/access.db
```

Configuring /etc/mail/* files

I discuss the sendmail configuration files found in the /etc/mail directory in this section.

Restricting access to your sendmail server using /etc/mail/access

This configuration file can be used to create an access restriction database for your sendmail server. You can control access to your sendmail server on a per-domain, subdomain, IP address, or network basis. The configuration lines in this file have the following format:

```
host_or_user  access_control_option
```

Here, a host or user can be a fully or partly qualified host name, domain name, IP address, network address, or e-mail address such as wormhole. evoknow.com, .com, 192.168.1.10, 192.168.1.0, spammer@somewhere. com, or whatever. The available configuration options are shown in Table 13-2.

Table 13-2 *Configuration Options for the /etc/mail/access Database*

Option	Description
OK	Accept mail even if other configuration rules would want to reject mail from the specified host or the user.
RELAY	Acts as an SMTP mail relay for the specified host. In other words, accept mail intended for users on the specified domain and also allow users on the specified domain to send mail via the server. Do not reject mail from the specified domain even if other rules would like you to do so.
REJECT	Reject all (incoming/outgoing) mail for the specified domain.
DISCARD	Discard the message completely using the $#discard mailer. Discarded messages are accepted but silently kept undelivered so that the sender thinks they have been delivered.
501 <message>	Do not accept mail if sender address partially or fully matches the specified user@host.
553 <message>	Do not accept mail if sender address does not contain host name.
550 <message>	Do not accept mail for specified domain name.

Here is an example /etc/mail/access configuration:

```
Any-spam-maker.com      REJECT
client-domain.com       RELAY
annoying-company.com    DISCARD
dumbguy@dumb-net.com    501 You can't use this mail server.
```

Here all mail from `any-spam-maker.com` will be rejected; all incoming and outgoing mail to and from `client-domain.com` will be relayed; all mail from `annoying-company.com` will be accepted but silently discarded, and any mail from `dumbguy@dumb-net.com` will be rejected with the "You can't use this mail server" message.

Note that `sendmail` does not directly use the `/etc/mail/access` configuration file. It uses a DBM database version of the file. To create the necessary DBM file for your `/etc/mail/access` file, run the following command:

```
makemap hash /etc/mail/access < /etc/mail/access
```

This command creates the necessary DBM database file (such as `/etc/mail/access.db`) in the same directory. You do not need to restart the `sendmail` daemon any time you modify this file.

Creating aliases for users with/etc/mail/aliases

This configuration file enables you to create an alias database for users. For example, say that you would like to create an alias called `carol.godsave` for a user called `carol`. You can do that using this configuration file, which has the following format:

```
alias_name: comma-separated_list_of_users
```

To create the `carol.godsave` alias, you can add a line in this configuration file as follows:

```
carol.godsave: carol
```

When `sendmail` receives mail for `carol.godsave@yourdomain.com`, it will be delivered to the `carol` account on your mail server. One of the commonly used functions of aliases is to create local groups. For example:

```
web-developers: keith, cynthea, jason
```

The preceding line defines an alias, `web-developers`, which can be used to send e-mail messages to the specified users.

The default `/etc/mail/aliases` file already contains a set of default aliases. Make sure you change them as needed. Also note that if you have a user with the same name as an alias, the e-mail will be sent to the user(s) specified in the alias. For example:

```
root: kabir
```

When mail is sent to root@evoknow.com, even though there is a user account called root on the mail server, the mail will still be sent to user kabir. You can also chain aliases. For example:

```
root: kabir
kabir: mohammed
```

Here the alias called root resolves to the alias called kabir, which resolves to a username called mohammed. So, mail sent to root@localhost on the system (with the above alias configuration) can go to the mailbox of a user called mohammed.

Note that sendmail does not directly use the /etc/mail/aliases configuration file. It uses a DBM database version of the file. To create the necessary DBM file for your /etc/mail/aliases file, run the following command:

```
newaliases
```

This command creates the necessary DBM database file (such as /etc/mail/aliases.db) in the same directory. You do not need to restart the sendmail daemon any time you modify this file.

 Running newaliases is equivalent to running the sendmail —bi command.

Mapping domains using /etc/mail/domaintable

This configuration file can be used to create a domain name-mapping database such as:

```
Yet-another-domain.com yourdomain.com
```

Here, yet-another-domain.com has been mapped to yourdomain. com. So when mail is received for user@yet-another-domain.com, it is translated to user@yourdomain.com. Note that the destination domain (yourdomain.com) must be a fully qualified domain name. Also note that the domain mapping in the domain table is reflected into headers; that is, this is done in rule set 3.

Note that `sendmail` does not directly use the `/etc/mail/domaintable` configuration file. It uses a DBM database version of the file. To create the necessary DBM file for your `/etc/mail/domaintable` file, run the following command:

```
makemap hash /etc/mail/domaintable < /etc/mail/domaintable
```

This command creates the necessary DBM database file (such as `/etc/mail/domaintable.db`) in the same directory. You do not need to restart the `sendmail` daemon any time you modify this file.

Rerouting mail for domains using /etc/mail/mailertable

This configuration file can be used to create a database to override default mail routing for certain domains. The format of this file is as follows:

```
source_domain mailer:replacement_domain or user@host
```

For example:

```
visitor-01.mydomain.com local:visitor1
```

When mail for `visitor-01.mydomain.com` arrives, it is rerouted to the local user visitor1. Note that you can use only the mailers that are specified in the `/etc/sendmail.cf` file using an "M" line. A quick look in the `/etc/sendmail.cf` file shows `qsmtp`, `procmail`, `smtp`, `esmtp`, `smtp8`, `relay`, `usenet`, `uucp`, `uucp-ol`, `suucp`, `uucp-new`, `uucp-om`, `uucp-uuom`, `local`, and `prog` to be defined as mailers.

Note that you can also specify partial domain names as the source domain name. For example:

```
.mydomain.com  smtp:mail-hub.mydomain.com
```

Here, mail for `*.mydomain.com` hosts will be relayed to the `mail-hub.mydomain.com` server via the SMTP mailer.

You must have appropriate MX record for source domain or mail will never be delivered. See Chapter 15 for details.

Consider another example:

```
ad-engine.com smtp:kabir@integrationlogic.com
```

Here all mail for `ad-engine.com` will be delivered to user `kabir@
integrationlogic.com` via the SMTP mailer as long as `ad-engine.
com` is listed in the `/etc/mail/sendmail.cw` file.

Note that `sendmail` does not directly use the `/etc/mail/
mailertable` configuration file. It uses a DBM database version of the
file. To create the necessary DBM file for your `/etc/mail/mailertable`
file, run the following command:

```
makemap hash /etc/mail/mailertable < /etc/mail/mailertable
```

This command creates the necessary DBM database file (for example,
`/etc/mail/mailertable.db`) in the same directory. You do not need to
restart the `sendmail` daemon any time you modify this file.

Setting up mail relays using /etc/mail/relay-domains

The latest version of `sendmail` (v 8.9.*x*) denies unauthorized relaying of
mail by default. In other words, if `sendmail` is not explicitly told to accept
mail destined for another domain, it will refuse to do so. For example, say
that you run the latest version of `sendmail` on a host called `mail.
mydomain.com`. If someone from anywhere tries to use `mail.
mydomain.com` to deliver mail to another SMTP server, your `sendmail`
server will refuse such requests by default. This is done to eliminate mail
relay abuse by people who send unsolicited e-mail messages.

To allow legitimate domains to use your `sendmail` server as a relay, you
need to specify them in this file. You should add your own domain and any
other friendly domains for which you want to allow relay operation. For
example:

```
evoknow.com
```

```
integrationlogic.com
```

```
ad-engine.com
```

You can also use IP addresses in the form of a network address or a full IP.
To test the relay configuration, run:

```
echo '$=R' | sendmail -bt
```

This command should display all the allowed domains.

Setting up local delivery destinations: /etc/mail/sendmail.cw

You can use this file to specify the names of hosts and domains for which the sendmail server will receive e-mail. An example of this file is shown here:

```
evoknow.com
ad-engine.com
classifiedworks.com
```

Here, each line specifies a domain name that the sendmail server services.

Creating virtual mail servers using /etc/mail/virtualtable

If you would like to provide mail support for multiple domains, you can set up virtual mail service using sendmail. For example, say that you would like to provide virtual mail service for a domain called yourclient.com. Here's how:

1. Add the domain (yourclient.com) in the /etc/mail/sendmail. cw file so that sendmail will accept mail for this host.

2. Add the domain (yourclient.com) in the /etc/mail/relay-domains file so that sendmail will relay messages for this domain.

To map the virtual domain users to one or more local accounts, use the /etc/mail/virtusertable file as follows:

```
virtual_e-mail address   real_e-mail_address
```

Here are some examples:

```
webmaster@yourclient.com   mike
mike@yourclient.com        mike
info@yourclient.com        jason
jason@yourclient.com       jason
```

In the preceding, e-mail for virtual e-mail addresses such as webmaster@ yourclient.com and mike@yourclient.com goes to local user mike, and similarly, mail for info@yourclient.com and jason@yourclient.

com goes to another local user, jason. This provides yourclient.com
with a mail server they didn't have. To the rest of the world, it appears that
yourclient.com has a mail server. If you also do the yourclient.com
domain's DNS service for this domain, you can make the entire process
look very professional by doing the following things:

- Add an A record in the yourclient.com domain's DNS that
  points to your sendmail server. For example, if your sendmail
  server host's IP address is 192.168.1.10, you can add the following
  line in the DNS configuration file for the yourclient.com
  domain.

```
mail.yourclient.com.   IN   A   192.168.1.10
```

- Add an MX record in the yourclient.com domain's SOA record
  that points to mail.yourclient.com. For example:

```
IN  MX 5 mail.yourclient.com.
```

This makes the rest of the (unsuspecting) world think that yourclient.
com has a real mail server, as long as you have sendmail set up with the
virtual configuration discussed previously.

Web site clients of ISPs often request virtual mail service. In other
words, people or companies that pay an ISP to do Web site hosting
(www.client-domain.com) also often request to have virtual mail service.
In such a case, creating a single /etc/mail/virtusertable is often
unmanageable. For example, if you are hosting hundreds of domains,
/etc/mail/virtusertable will be a point of human error every time
you or your assistant administrator modify the file. In such a case, you can
create a more manageable solution. For example, say you need two virtual
mail services for two clients called client-a.com and client-b.com.
Here is what you do:

- Create a separate virtual e-mail map file for each domain. Use a naming convention such as domain.ftr (.ftr is short for *fake-to-real*).

- Create an /etc/mail/client-a.ftr file, which contains the content of what will normally go in /etc/mail/virtusertable for
  this domain. For example, this file could look like the following:

```
user1@client-1.com client1
webmaster@client-1.com unix@home-town-isp.com
@client-1.com client1
```

In this sample file, the `user1@client-1.com` address has been mapped to the local account client1, the `webmaster@client-1.com` has been mapped to a remote ISP account, and all other possible e-mail addresses for the domain have been mapped to the local account. The last entry is quite useful and often requested. It allows the `client-1.com` domain to use whatever e-mail address they want on their Web site or other business publications and advertising and still get the mail in the right place. For example, if `www.client-1.com` publishes an e-mail address called `info@client-1.com`, anyone sending mail to that account is happily serviced by the client1 user.

- Now create the `/etc/mail/client-b.ftr` file for the second client. This file is likely to be similar to the previous example, but suppose that the `client-b.com` owner wants all e-mail addresses to be automatically mapped to her existing accounts in your hometown ISP mail server. In such a case this map file will look as follows:

  `@client-b.com %1@home-town-isp.com`

- Now that you have two virtual user map files, you can create the final `/etc/mail/virtusertable` file using the following commands:

  `touch /etc/mail/virtusertable`

  `cat *.ftr > /etc/mail/virtusertable`

  Here, the first command creates the `/etc/mail/virtusertable` file if it does not already exist. The second command concatenates all the `.ftr` files to `/etc/mail/virtusertable`. This effectively creates the final `/etc/mail/virtusertable`.

- Now you can run the `makemap` program to create the database version of the file as follows:

  `makemap hash /etc/mail/virtusertable < /etc/mail/virtusertable`

As you can see in the preceding example, creating multiple virtual user map files can help you to keep track of individual domains quite easily. Any time you want to change a domain specific map, just modify the domain's `ftr` file and create the final `/etc/mail/virtusertable` file using the technique discussed here.

Because most mail client programs enable users to set outgoing From: lines to whatever they wish, you may not need to do anything to map outgoing traffic for virtual sites. However, if you wish to make sure outgoing mail from users of virtual mail sites translates to their virtual domains, you can use the /etc/mail/genericstable file.

Take, for example, a virtual mail site called classifiedworks.com, for which you have an .ftr file such as /etc/mail/classifiedworks.ftr, which has the following line:

```
sales@classifiedworks.com  sheila
```

Here, the sales@classifiedworks.com address is mapped to a local user called sheila. Now when sheila sends mail using the sendmail server, you want her mail to appear as sheila@classifiedworks.com and not sheila@yourdomain.com. In such a case, create a /etc/mail/genericstable file with the following line:

```
sheila  sales@classifiedworks.com
```

As you can see here we are reversing the content of virtusertable file. In the spirit of keeping domain-specific information separate, you may wish to create a separate reverse map file per domain. Let's say this file will have an extension called .rtf. After you have created such a file for each domain you do virtual mail service for, you can create a combined /etc/mail/genericstable file as follows:

```
touch /etc/mail/genericstable
cat *.rtf > /etc/mail/genericstable
```

Now run the makemap program to create the database version of this file:

```
makemap hash /etc/mail/virtusertable < /etc/mail/virtusertable
```

In summary, for each virtual mail domain, create an .ftr file that maps fake e-mail addresses to real ones and make another file to map real addresses to fake e-mail addresses. After these files are made, you combine them to create a /etc/mail/virtusertable (for *.ftr) and /etc/mail/genericstable file (for *.rtf). Then run makemap as just shown to create the database versions of these files. This completes the process as long as you have each of the virtual domains listed in /etc/mail/sendmail.cw and /etc/mail/relay-domains files.

Testing Your sendmail Configuration

As you can see, you have quite a few configuration files to deal with to get `sendmail` working the way you want. Because there is a lot to configure, chances are high that something won't work exactly the way you want. Therefore I recommend that you do the following:

- Always back up your configuration before making any changes.
- Every time you make a change to your `sendmail` configuration, test it before proceeding too far.

In the following sections I show you a few examples of how you can test typical configuration issues.

Testing sendmail address rewrite rules

You can test how the `sendmail` rules behave. To perform such testing, run `sendmail` as follows:

```
sendmail -bt
```

This command runs `sendmail` in address mode and provides you with a prompt to interact with it. At the prompt you can enter a test command such as:

```
rewrite_rule_#s  test_address
```

For example, to see what `sendmail`'s rewrite rule 0 will do with kabir@evoknow.com, run the following command:

```
0 kabir@evoknow.com
```

The output on my `sendmail` system is shown here:

```
ADDRESS TEST MODE (ruleset 3 NOT automatically invoked)
Enter <ruleset> <address>
> 0 kabir@evoknow.com
rewrite: ruleset   0   input: kabir @ evoknow . com
rewrite: ruleset 199   input: kabir @ evoknow . com
rewrite: ruleset 199 returns: kabir @ evoknow . com
```

```
rewrite: ruleset  98   input: kabir @ evoknow . com
rewrite: ruleset  98 returns: kabir @ evoknow . com
rewrite: ruleset 198   input: kabir @ evoknow . com
rewrite: ruleset 198 returns: $# local $: kabir @ evoknow . com
rewrite: ruleset   0 returns: $# local $: kabir @ evoknow . com
```

As you can see, the kabir@evoknow.com address is delivered using the local mailer. Consider another example. Say that you have the following /etc/mail/domaintable map:

```
ad-engine.com evoknow.com
```

Any mail destined for ad-engine.com should be rerouted to nitec.com. Here is a test:

```
ADDRESS TEST MODE (ruleset 3 NOT automatically invoked)
Enter <ruleset> <address>
> 3,0 kabir@nitec.com
rewrite: ruleset   3   input: kabir @ evoknow . com
rewrite: ruleset  96   input: kabir < @ evoknow . com >
rewrite: ruleset  96 returns: kabir < @ ad-engine . com . >
rewrite: ruleset   3 returns: kabir < @ ad-engine . com . >
rewrite: ruleset   0   input: kabir < @ ad-engine . com . >
rewrite: ruleset 199   input: kabir < @ ad-engine . com . >
rewrite: ruleset 199 returns: kabir < @ ad-engine . com . >
rewrite: ruleset  98   input: kabir < @ ad-engine . com . >
rewrite: ruleset  98 returns: kabir < @ ad-engine . com . >
rewrite: ruleset 198   input: kabir < @ ad-engine . com . >
rewrite: ruleset  90   input: < ad-engine . com > kabir < @ ad-engine . com . >
rewrite: ruleset  90   input: ad-engine . < com > kabir < @ ad-engine . com . >
rewrite: ruleset  90 returns: kabir < @ ad-engine . com . >
rewrite: ruleset  90 returns: kabir < @ ad-engine . com . >
rewrite: ruleset  95   input: < > kabir < @ ad-engine . com . >
rewrite: ruleset  95 returns: kabir < @ ad-engine . com . >
rewrite: ruleset 198 returns: $# esmtp $@ ad-engine . com . $: kabir < @ ad-
engine . com . >
rewrite: ruleset   0 returns: $# esmtp $@ ad-engine . com . $: kabir < @ ad-
engine . com . >
```

Here the address kabir@nitec.com is rewritten as kabir@
ad-engine.com, and sendmail shows that it will deliver it via ESMTP
(expensive SMTP) mailer because ad-engine.com is not listed in
/etc/mail/sendmail.cw. If it were, the preceding test would show the
following output:

```
ADDRESS TEST MODE (ruleset 3 NOT automatically invoked)
Enter <ruleset> <address>
> 3,0 kabir@ad-engine.com
rewrite: ruleset   3   input: kabir @ ad-engine . com
rewrite: ruleset  96   input: kabir < @ ad-engine . com >
rewrite: ruleset  96 returns: kabir < @ ad-engine . com . >
rewrite: ruleset   3 returns: kabir < @ ad-engine . com . >
rewrite: ruleset   0   input: kabir < @ ad-engine . com . >
rewrite: ruleset 199   input: kabir < @ ad-engine . com . >
rewrite: ruleset 199 returns: kabir < @ ad-engine . com . >
rewrite: ruleset  98   input: kabir < @ ad-engine . com . >
rewrite: ruleset  98 returns: kabir < @ ad-engine . com . >
rewrite: ruleset 198   input: kabir < @ ad-engine . com . >
rewrite: ruleset 198 returns: $# local $: kabir
rewrite: ruleset   0 returns: $# local $: kabir
```

Notice that I used 3,0 as the rule set because rule set 3 is involved in the
domaintable translation and the ruleset 0 is involved in parsing the
address.

Testing /etc/mail/* database files

Any time you modify your files /etc/mail/access, /etc/mail/
aliases, /etc/mail/domaintable, /etc/mail/mailertable, /etc/
mail/virtusertable, and so on, you should make sure sendmail can
perform lookups properly. For example, say that you just created the following alias in the /etc/mail/alias file:

```
root: kabir
```

After running the `newaliases` command, you want to find out if sendmail can do appropriate alias lookups. To test a database lookup, run sendmail —bt and at the address test mode prompt, enter the following:

```
/map database name key
```

For example, to test the `/etc/mail/aliases` database for the alias root, I can run the following command

```
/map aliases root
```

which shows the following output:

```
map_lookup: aliases (root) returns kabir
```

Using sendmail to see the SMTP transaction verbosely

You can also use `sendmail` to see how it delivers a message to the destination. For example:

```
sendmail -vt
```

Here the —vt option tells `sendmail` to be verbose and scan for `To:`, `From:`, `Cc:`, and `Bcc:` headers in the input. After the preceding command is run, it waits for user input. At this point you can enter something like this:

```
To: kabir@integrationlogic.com
From: someone@somewhere.com
Subject: Testing sendmail

This is a test.

.
```

After entering a short message as shown here, press Ctrl+D to exit message entry mode. `sendmail` will then display an SMTP transaction similar to the one shown here:

```
kabir@integrationlogic.com... Connecting to mail.integrationlogic.com. via
esmtp...
220 wormhole.integrationlogic.com ESMTP Sendmail 8.10.1/8.10.1; Sun, 21 Feb 1999
19:57:00 -0500
>> EHLO picaso.nitec.com
250-wormhole.integrationlogic.com Hello picaso.evoknow.com [206.171.50.50],
pleased to meet you
250-EXPN
250-VERB
250-8BITMIME
250-SIZE
250-DSN
250-ONEX
250-ETRN
250-XUSR
250 HELP
>> MAIL From:<kabir@picaso.evoknow.com> SIZE=77
250 <kabir@picaso.evoknow.com>... Sender ok
>> RCPT To:<kabir@integrationlogic.com>
250 <kabir@integrationlogic.com>... Recipient ok
>> DATA
354 Enter mail, end with "." on a line by itself
>> .
250 TAA16439 Message accepted for delivery
kabir@integrationlogic.com... Sent
(TAA16439 Message accepted for delivery)
Closing connection to mail.integrationlogic.com.
>> QUIT
221 wormhole.integrationlogic.com closing connection
```

The lines that start with **>>** are sent by the local **sendmail** server (picaso.nitec.com) to the remote **sendmail** server (mail. integrationlogic.com).

Using the sendmail debug flag

You can use the -d*X* option (where *X* is a debug level) along with -bv to see what action sendmail takes for a particular address. For example:

```
sendmail -bv -d0 kabir@evoknow.com
```

This produces the following output on my sendmail server:

```
Version 8.10.1
 Compiled with: MAP_REGEX LOG MATCHGECOS MIME7TO8 MIME8TO7 NAMED_
BIND NETINET NETUNIX NEWDB NIS QUEUE SCANF SMTP USERDB XDEBUG


============ SYSTEM IDENTITY (after readcf) ============
     (short domain name) $w = picaso
 (canonical domain name) $j = picaso.evoknow.com
       (subdomain name) $m = evoknow.com
          (node name) $k = picaso.evoknow.com

========================================================


kabir@evoknow.com... deliverable: mailer local, user kabir
```

As you can see, the –d0 option causes sendmail to display various items of information about sendmail itself. The last line in the preceding output shows how sendmail will handle the given address. If you specify –d without any debug level number, you will see all the debugging information you ever wanted.

Using a test configuration file

When you are playing around with sendmail.cf, it is a good idea to create a test version of the /etc/sendmail.cf file and modify only the test copy. This way, you do not lose any working configuration. Here is how you can test a new configuration.

- Create a copy of /etc/sendmail.cf with a new name. Here I assume you call the test configuration /etc/sendmail-test.cf.
- To run sendmail with your new test configuration file, use the –C option. For example, /usr/sbin/sendmail –Csendmail-test. cf uses /etc/sendmail-test.cf.

- If you would like to use a different queue (that is, other than
  `/var/spool/mqueue`) for the test configuration, use the `–oQ`
  option. For example, `/usr/sbin/sendmail –Csendmail-test.`
  `cf –oQ/var/spool/test-mqueue` uses the `/var/spool/test-`
  `mqueue` directory for the test configuration.

At this point, you should have `sendmail` configured as required. The
following section discusses a few security issues concerning your `sendmail`
configuration.

Securing sendmail

Being one of the oldest mail servers, `sendmail` has had its share of security
holes and blame. The most recent version of `sendmail` has been released
with strict security in mind.

Securing your configuration files

Beginning with version 8.9.*x*, `sendmail` has tightened the restrictions on
configuration file permissions. For example, if I run `chmod –R 664 /etc/`
`mail/*` to change the file permissions for the configuration files and then
try to restart `sendmail`, I get the following error messages:

```
Starting sendmail: /etc/sendmail.cf: line 93: fileclass: cannot
open /etc/mail/sendmail.cw: Group writable directory

WARNING: Group writable directory /etc/mail
/etc/mail/virtusertable.db: could not create: Permission denied

WARNING: Group writable directory /etc/mail
/etc/mail/access.db: could not create: Permission denied

WARNING: Group writable directory /etc/mail
/etc/mail/domaintable.db: could not create: Permission denied

WARNING: Group writable directory /etc/mail
/etc/mail/mailertable.db: could not create: Permission denied
```

In general, you should do the following to make sure `sendmail` is safe to run in your system:

- Ensure that the `/etc/sendmail.cf` and `/etc/mail/*` files and directories are readable by only the root user or the username you specified in the `RunAsUser` line in the `/etc/sendmail.cf` file. All these files and directories should be writable by root (or another superuser) only.

- Do not enable group write permission for any of the configuration files, directories, or any other file that `sendmail` needs to read.

Under no circumstances should you enable group write access for any of the configuration files. Although `sendmail` allows you to disable the file permission and ownership-related security features using the `DontBlameSendmail` option, I highly recommend that you fix the `permission/ownership` problem rather than disable the checks in `sendmail`. If you want to keep the security checks as they are, ensure that user home directories where `.forward` files are kept are not writable by any group. The `.forward` file itself should have a 644 (rw-r—r—) permissions setting. You should also make sure that any directory in the path of a file that `sendmail` reads has the group write access disabled. If you must use the `DontBlameSendmail` option to introduce security holes, read the documentation supplied with `sendmail` to know how to use this feature.

After you have made sure that file/directory-level permissions are set properly and `sendmail` does not spit out any warning or error message because of permission/ownership of files and directories, you should also make sure that logging is properly enabled. By default, `sendmail` will write logs via `syslogd`, and therefore you should write the following line in your `/etc/syslog.conf` file.

```
mail.*          /var/log/maillog
```

You can change the log filename to your liking; typically this file is named `maillog` or `mail.log`. Also make sure you that you have an entry such as the following in `/etc/logrotate.d/syslog` file.

```
/var/log/maillog {
    postrotate
        /usr/bin/killall -HUP syslogd
    endscript
}
```

This command restarts `syslogd` after `logrotate` processes the `/var/log/maillog` file.

Ensuring a stricter mode of operating and privacy

You can force `sendmail` to enforce stricter adherence to the SMTP protocol when clients connect to your server, and you can also control how users interact with `sendmail`. This is done using an option line such as the following:

```
O PrivacyOptions=needvrfyhelo,restrictmailq,restrictqrun,goaway
```

The values for `PrivacyOptions` are shown in Table 13-3.

Table 13-3 *PrivacyOptions for sendmail*

Option	Explanation
public	Allows open access.
needmailhelo	Client must use HELO or EHELO before issuing a MAIL command.
needexpnhelo	Client must use HELO or EHELO before issuing an EXPN command.
noexpn	Client cannot use EXPN command.
needvrfyhelo	Client must use HELO or EHELO before issuing a VRFY command.
novrfy	Client cannot use VRFY command.
notrn	Client cannot use ETRN command.
noverb	Client cannot use VERB command.
restrictmailq	Restrict use of mailq command. When this option is set only the root user and the owner and group users of the queue directory can run the mailq command.
restrictqrun	Restricts the –q option. When this option is set, only the root user and the owner of the queue directory can use this option.
noreceipts	Do not return success code upon success.

Continued

Table 13-3 *Continued*

Option	Explanation
goaway	Do not allow SMTP status queries.
authwarnings	Insert X-Authentication-Warning: headers in messages.

Setting Up POP Mail Service

The Post Office Protocol (POP) is widely used to retrieve mail stored by an SMTP server. Like SMTP, this protocol is also very simple.

How does it work?

Consider how a POP client retrieves mail from a POP server. I will use a Telnet client to demonstrate this as I did for SMTP, as shown in the following list:

1. Because POP server listens to TCP port 110, I can Telnet to my POP server, blackhole.evoknow.com, as follows:

   ```
   telnet blackhole.evoknow.com 110
   ```

   I am greeted with the following message from the POP server:

   ```
   +OK POP3 blackhole.evoknow.com v4.47 server ready
   ```

2. Then I type the following POP command to tell the server which user's mailbox I want to open:

   ```
   USER kabir
   ```

   It responds with the following message:

   ```
   +OK User name accepted, password please
   ```

3. Then I enter the password for the user kabir using the following POP command:

   ```
   PASS mypwd1
   ```

The POP server responds with the following message:

```
+OK Mailbox open, 3 messages
```

As you can see, I have three messages on the server.

4. Next, I produce a listing of the messages using the following POP command:

```
LIST
```

The POP server replies as follows:

```
+OK Mailbox scan listing follows
1 1387
2 588
3 590
```

5. To retrieve one of these messages (#3), I enter the following POP command:

```
RETR 3
```

The server returns the message with the following response code:

```
+OK 590 octets
Return-Path: <kabir@evoknow.com>
Received: from evoknow.com (picaso.evoknow.com [206.171.50.51])
        by blackhole.evoknow.com (8.8.7/8.8.7) with ESMTP id
KAA01647
        for <sales@evoknow.com>; Wed, 08 Aug 2001 10:05:39 -0800
Message-ID: <36D19B4D.969597E6@evoknow.com>
Date: Mon, 22 Feb 1999 10:00:45 -0800
From: Mohammed Kabir <kabir@evoknow.com>
X-Mailer: Mozilla 4.5 [en] (WinNT; I)
X-Accept-Language: en
MIME-Version: 1.0
To: sales@evoknow.com
Subject: TEST 2
```

```
Content-Type: text/plain; charset=us-ascii
Content-Transfer-Encoding: 7bit
Status:

THIS IS TEST 2
.
```

As you can see, the entire POP transaction is quite simple. In the next section I show you how you can set up your system with POP support.

 Read the Request for Comments (RFC) 1939 document to learn more about POP3. You can access RFC documents at http://rfc.net/rfc1939.html.

Installing a POP3 server

The latest version of the POP protocol is 3, and so you want to install a POP3 server. The IMAP package included in your Red Hat CD-ROM includes a POP3 server. To install POP3, just install the IMAP package using the usual rpm -ivh *package_name* command.

Configuring POP3 service

After you have installed the server, you need to modify the /etc/inetd. conf file so that you have a line such as the following:

```
pop-3   stream tcp    nowait root   /usr/sbin/tcpd ipop3d
```

If you have a pop-2 line, you can comment it out, as POP2 is not widely used and most recent POP clients support POP3. After you have set up the preceding line in /etc/inetd.conf, you need to check the /etc/services file to make sure you have the following lines:

```
pop-3   110/tcp  # PostOffice V.3
pop     110/tcp  # PostOffice V.3
```

After you have checked these two files, you can restart the inetd daemon using killall -HUP inetd to allow it to listen for POP3 requests on TCP port 110. When requests for POP3 connections come to the system, the `inetd` daemon will launch the `ipop3d` daemon to handle the requests. Your POP3 server is now ready to service requests.

Configuring SMTP/POP Mail Clients

After you have both SMTP and POP3 servers configured, you need to set up mail client software for your users. If your users access their mail by Telneting in to the mail server, you need to install one or more mail client packages such as `mail`, `pine`, and `procmail`. People who use Telnet to access their mail can use the mail-forwarding feature quite easily.

For example, if a user wants to send her mail to a different account or to another mail server, she can add a `.forward` file in her home directory to make `sendmail` deliver mail to the requested address. The format of the `.forward` file is quite simple. To forward all mail for a user called `mrfrog` to `mrfrog@freemail-domain.net`, you edit `~mrfrog/.forward` such that the `mrfrog@freemail-domain.net` address is in a line by itself. Also make sure that the file permissions for `.forward` allow only the owner to read and write the file; everyone else should have read-only access to it.

In most cases, however, users access mail via a Windows machine running a POP3 client. To enable users to configure a typical Windows POP3/SMTP mail client, all you need to supply each user is the following information:

- Username
- Password
- Incoming POP3 mail server IP or host name
- Outgoing SMTP mail server IP or host name

Note that you will have to permit such clients to use your `sendmail` server as a relay, or else the client will not be able to send mail out. For example, if your mail server is accessed via America Online, you will have to add `aol.com` to your `/etc/mail/relay-domains` file.

Chapter 14

Configuring FTP Services

IN THIS CHAPTER

- Setting up FTP service
- Setting up an anonymous FTP site
- Configuring a guest FTP account
- Setting up virtual FTP sites
- Becoming an efficient FTP user

Red Hat Linux ships with the `Wuarchive-ftpd`, which is the default `FTP server`. More affectionately known as `wu-ftpd`, it is an FTP server daemon developed at Washington University. The most popular FTP server on the Internet, `wu-ftpd` is used on thousands of FTP sites all around the world.

If you choose to install FTP service during the Red Hat Linux installation, the `wu-ftpd` server is installed by default. However, if you are not sure whether or not you have already installed the `wu-ftpd` server, you can just query the RPM database of installed packages as follows:

```
rpm -qa | grep wu-ftpd
```

The `rpm -qa` command lists all the installed RPM packages, and the piped `grep wu` command matches the `wu-ftpd` pattern in the package names that are output by the `rpm` command, thus enabling you to see if any package has the `wu-ftpd` string pattern in its name. For example, the preceding command shows `wu-ftpd-2.6.1-16` on my Red Hat Linux machine. The version number on your system will vary, as a new version of `wu-ftpd` is likely to be shipped with later versions of Red Hat Linux.

If you do not get any output for the preceding command, you currently do not have the wu-ftpd server installed and need to proceed with the installation as described in the following sections. On the other hand, if you see a version of wu-ftpd already installed, you can skip the installation section and go right to the "Configuring FTP service" section.

Installing wu-ftpd Server

When it comes to installing wu-ftpd server, you have two options: install the precompiled RPM package version of wu-ftpd or get the source from the URL ftp://ftp.academ.com/pub/wu--ftpd/private/ and compile it yourself. Because the Red Hat–provided wu-ftpd RPM package is quite suitable for most people, I do not describe the second process, which requires compiling it on your own.

I highly recommend that you use the wu-ftpd RPM package unless you have a very special reason for compiling and installing from the source. In the latter case, make sure you read the bundled documentation with great care.

Installing from your Red Hat CD-ROM

To install wu-ftpd from your Red Hat CD-ROM, follow these steps:

1. As root, mount your Red Hat CD-ROM and change directory to RedHat/RPMS.

2. Run the following command to locate the RPM package for wu-ftpd server:

   ```
   ls | grep wu-ftpd
   ```

3. After you have located the filename of the RPM package for wu-ftpd, you can run the following command to install the package:

   ```
   rpm —ivh name of the wu-ftpd package
   ```

   For example, the following command installs the 2.6.1-16 version of wu-ftpd for Intel 80x86 computers (your version number and system architecture may vary):

   ```
   rpm —ivh wu-ftpd-2.6.1-16.i386.rpm
   ```

Installing from a Red Hat FTP Server

If you do not have the Red Hat CD-ROM or you want to install the latest version over the Internet, you can run the following command:

```
rpm -ivh URL
```

For example, to install the wu-ftpd-version.i386.rpm package from an anonymous FTP server called ftp://ftp.cdrom.com/ that mirrors the Red Hat distribution, I run the following command:

```
rpm -ivh ftp://ftp.cdrom.com/pub/linux/redhat/redhat-\ 7.1/i386/RedHat/RPMS/
wu-ftpd-version.i386.rpm
```

If you want to install from such a server, always make sure that you first determine the right URL by browsing the site via a Web browser. The URL will vary with your system architecture (i386, Alpha, Sparc, or what have you), as well as with the versions of Red Hat Linux and the wu-ftpd software.

Also note that if you are trying to install a newer version of wu-ftpd while keeping an older version, you have to supply the --force option in the rpm command line.

Configuring FTP Service

After you have installed wu-ftpd or confirmed that you have it installed as part of the Red Hat installation, you are ready to configure your new FTP server. Your FTP server configuration consists of the following files:

- /etc/services
- /etc/xinetd.d/wu-ftpd
- /etc/ftpaccess
- /etc/ftpconversions
- /etc/ftpgroups
- /etc/ftphosts
- /etc/ftpusers

The wu-ftpd server, like many other TCP/IP-based servers, runs via the Internet super-server called xinetd, which listens for an FTP connection on port 21. When such a connection request is detected, it launches the `wu-ftpd` server. At startup, `xinetd` looks at two files to determine which service (port) is associated with a server. These two files are `/etc/services` and the `/etc/xinetd.d/wu-ftpd`.

/etc/services

As you may already know, the `/etc/services` file describes the TCP/IP services available on your Linux server. The lines that matter for the FTP server configuration are as follows:

```
ftp-data        20/tcp
ftp             21/tcp
```

These two lines tell `xinetd` which ports to use for the data and command functions of the FTP service respectively. The default port declarations are standard and should not be changed.

The FTP specification (RFC 765) specifies the FTP data port (20) as one less than the command port (21). The data port value is really not derived from the declaration in `/etc/services`. However, including the data port declaration in the `/etc/services` file prevents it from being accidentally used for something else.

The preceding lines tell `xinetd` which ports belong to the FTP service, but it still needs to know which server software is responsible for the service. This is defined in files kept in the `/etc/xinetd.d` directory. The FTP service is defined in `/etc/xinetd.d/wu-ftpd file`.

/etc/xinetd.d/wu-ftpd

The default version of this file looks as follows:

```
# default: on
# description: The wu-ftpd FTP server
# serves FTP connections.
# It uses normal, unencrypted usernames and passwords
# for authentication.
```

```
service ftp
{
        socket_type            = stream
        wait                   = no
        user                   = root
        server                 = /usr/sbin/in.ftpd
        server_args            = -l -a
        log_on_success         += DURATION USERID
        log_on_failure         += USERID
        nice                   = 10
        disable                = yes
}
```

Here, the service ftp is tied with the server software called in.ftpd, which is the name of the wu-ftpd executable.

The –l and –a server arguments are specified by default. The –l option specifies that each FTP session be logged via the syslog facility, and the –a option specifies that the access control configuration specified in /etc/ftpaccess be enabled. These two arguments are very useful and should not be removed. To enable FTP service you must change disable = yes to disable = no in this file. For other options, see the ftpd man page.

If you make any changes to /etc/xinetd.d/wu-ftpd or /etc/services, make sure you tell xinetd to reload the configuration by sending a SIGUSR1 signal as follows:

```
kill -USR1 PID_of_xinetd
```

or

```
killall —USR1 xinetd
```

/etc/ftpaccess

This file is the main configuration file for the FTP server and contains configuration information in the following format:

```
keyword  one_or_more_options
```

The default /etc/ftpaccess file is shown in Listing 14-1.

Listing 14-1 *The default /etc/ftpaccess file*

```
class    all    real,guest,anonymous   *

email root@localhost

loginfails 5

readme   README*     login
readme   README*     cwd=*

message /welcome.msg            login
message .message                cwd=*

compress         yes            all
tar              yes            all
chmod      no    guest,anonymous
delete     no    guest,anonymous
overwrite  no    guest,anonymous
rename     no    guest,anonymous

log transfers anonymous,real inbound,outbound

shutdown /etc/shutmsg

passwd--check rfc822 warn
```

This file is the most important configuration file for the server, and I discuss it in great detail in the following sections. You can specify five types of configuration information in this file, which are access configuration, informational configuration, logging configuration, permission configuration, and miscellaneous configuration. These configuration options are discussed in the sections below.

Access configuration

You can specify access configuration using the `class`, `deny`, `limit`, `nore-trieve`, `loginfails`, `private`, `autogroup`, and `guestgroup` keywords.

`class`

```
Syntax: class  classname  typelist  addrglob
Default: class  all  real,guest,anonymous  *
```

The `class` keyword is used to define a class name and specify the type of users that belong to the class. It also specifies the IP addresses or the domain names from which the class members can access the FTP server. The arguments are as follows:

- *classname* is an arbitrary name for the class.

- *typelist* is a comma-separated list of user types. Three types of users are available: `real`, `anonymous`, and `guest`. A real user is someone who has a valid username and password in the `/etc/passwd` or `/etc/shadow` file. The anonymous and guest accounts are discussed in detail later in this chapter.

- *adrglob* can be an IP address of a host, a partial IP address with wildcards (such as `206.171.50.*`), a host name such as `blackhole.evoknow.com`, or a partial domain name with wildcards (such as `*.evoknow.com`).

The default `/etc/ftpaccess` file contains a class definition called `all` that specifies that users of types `real`, `guest`, and `anonymous` can access the FTP server from anywhere. The wildcard character `*` is used to denote "anywhere." Now consider the following example:

```
class   all   real 206.171.50.*
```

Here, FTP access is granted only to real users who access the server from the 206.171.50.0 network. Note that you can also use domain names instead of IP addresses. For example:

```
class   all   real *.evoknow.com *.ad--engine.com
```

The preceding class definition allows real users to log on from any machine in the evoknow.com and ad--engine.com domains.

If you are not planning on allowing anonymous or guest accounts on your FTP server, you can remove the "guest" and "anonymous" keywords from the default typelist for the all class.

deny This keyword is used to deny FTP service to hosts that match the IP addresses or domain names specified.

Syntax: deny   *addrglob   message_file*

For example, the following instruction tells the FTP server to deny access to anyone trying to access the server from a U.S. university:

deny *.edu

Here is another example:

deny *.com /etc/goaway.msg

This configuration denies FTP access to anyone in a .com domain and also displays the /etc/goaway.msg file.

limit This keyword limits the number of simultaneous user logins for the named class.

Syntax: limit *class n times message_file*

The arguments for limit are as follows:

- *n* is the number of users allowed access.
- *times* is when the limit should apply. The time can be specified in a 24-hour clock format. For example, 0700–1700 is a range that covers 7 a.m. to 5 p.m. The time format can also include days, as shown in Table 14-1.

Table 14-1 *The Time Format for limit*

Keyword	What It Means
Any	Any time
Wk	Any weekday
Sa	Saturday
Su	Sunday
Mo	Monday
Tu	Tuesday
We	Wednesday
Th	Thursday
Fr	Friday

You can combine the days as well. For example, SaSu07–17 covers the weekend from 7 a.m. to 5 p.m. Here is an example configuration that sets limits on access:

```
class   local   real          *.evoknow.com
class   remote  anonymous      *

limit local  200  Any /etc/msgs/msg.toomany
limit remote 100  Any /etc/msgs/msg.toomany
```

The preceding configuration allows up to 200 users from the evoknow. com domain to log on at any time. At the same time it allows only 100 anonymous users to access the system at any time.

noretrieve This keyword denies FTP users the ability to retrieve named files.

Syntax: noretrieve *filename filename* . . .

For example, the following line denies anyone the ability to retrieve the /etc/passwd file:

```
noretrieve /etc/passwd
```

A message such as /etc/passwd is marked unretrievable is displayed. Note that if the filename does not include a fully qualified path name, all files with such names are marked unretrievable. For example, the following line prevents anyone from retrieving any file named passwd or core from any directory:

```
noretrieve passwd core
```

Note that you cannot use wildcards in the filename.

loginfails This keyword defines the number of times a user can attempt to log on before getting disconnected. When a user fails to enter a valid username/password pair for a login for the specified number of times, an error message is logged and the user is disconnected.

Syntax: loginfails *number*

Default: loginfails 5

private The wu-ftpd server provides an extended set of FTP commands that are nonstandard. One of these commands is called SITE. This command is considered a security risk, and therefore use of the private keyword is also not recommended. In fact, the SITE command is disabled in the default version of wu-ftpd that ships with Red Hat Linux. You have to compile wu-ftpd yourself to enable SITE, which is not recommended.

Syntax: private *yes_or_no*

guestgroup This keyword specifies the user groups that are to be considered as guest user accounts. See the section "Creating a guest FTP account" in this chapter for more details.

Syntax: guestgroup *groupname groupname* . . .

autogroup This keyword enables you to change the effective group ID for an anonymous user if she belongs to one or more classes specified.

Syntax: autogroup *groupname class* [*class* . . .]

Informational configuration

You can specify an informational configuration using the banner, email, message, and readme keywords.

banner You can use this keyword to display the contents of the specified file. Typically, many systems use banners to identify the systems and also to provide user policy and contact information.

Syntax: banner *filename*

If you use the banner keyword to display a file before login, some nonstandard FTP clients may fail to log on, because they are unable to handle multiline responses from the server.

email This directive sets the e-mail address of the FTP site administrator.

Syntax: email *user@host*

Default: email root@localhost

message Use this keyword to set the name of a file to display when the user logs into the system or uses the **change directory** command to change directories.

Syntax: message path {when {class . . .}}

Default: message /welcome.msg   login

message .message cwd=*

For example, the first default setting in the preceding code displays the contents of the /welcome.msg file at successful user login. The second default setting shows the contents of the .message file whenever the user changes a directory. Nothing displays when the file to be displayed is missing.

The file to be displayed can contain one or more of the magic cookie strings shown in Table 14-2.

Table 14-2 *Magic Cookie Strings for Message Files*

Cookies	Replacement Text
%C	The current working directory
%E	The maintainer's e-mail address, as defined in `ftpaccess`
%F	Free space in partition of CWD (kilobytes)
%L	The local hostname
%M	The maximum number of users allowed in this class
%N	The current number of users in this class
%R	The remote hostname
%T	The local time (in the form "Thu Nov 15 17:12:42 2000")
%u	The username as determined via RFC 931 authentication
%U	The username given at login time

Listing 14-2 shows the `/welcome.msg` file I use for my Red Hat Linux system.

Listing 14-2 *An example /welcome.msg file*

```
Hello %U

Welcome to %L.  You are user %N of possible %M users.
You are logging in from %R.

Local time is %T

Feel free to email (%E) if you have
any questions or comments.

Your current directory is %C (Free %F KB)
```

 The message file is displayed only once per directory. Also, if you plan to display message files for anonymous access, use relative paths to the base of the anonymous FTP directory tree.

readme This keyword is similar to the message keyword discussed previously. However, instead of displaying the contents of the named file, it makes the FTP server notify the user about the existence of the file and also tells the user about the modification date and time of the file.

Syntax: `readme  path  {when  {class . . .}  }`

Default: `readme README*  login`

        `readme README*  cwd=*`

Logging configuration

You can specify a logging configuration using the `log  commands` and `log transfers` keywords.

log commands This keyword enables you to log FTP commands for one or more types of users.

Syntax: `log commands typelist`

For example, the following directive logs all the FTP commands performed by all anonymous users:

`log commands anonymous`

log transfers This keyword enables you to log file transfers to and from the system. The default setting makes the server log both inbound and outbound file transfers for anonymous and real users.

Syntax: `log transfers typelist directions`

Default: `log transfers anonymous,real inbound,outbound`

Permission configuration

The following keywords enable you to control file/directory permission settings for users.

chmod This keyword enables or disables the `chmod` command (`site chmod`) for user types specified in the list. For example, the default setting disables this command for both guest and anonymous users.

Syntax: chmod *yes|no typelist*

Default: chmod no   guest,anonymous

 The chmod command is not available by default.

delete This keyword enables or disables the delete (del) command for users specified in the type list. For example, the default setting disables the delete command for both guest and anonymous users.

Syntax: delete *yes|no typelist*

Default: delete no   guest,anonymous

overwrite This keyword enables or disables the overwriting of files by the users specified in the typelist. For example, the default setting disables file overwriting for both guests and anonymous users.

Syntax: overwrite *yes|no typelist*

Default: overwrite no   guest,anonymous

rename This keyword enables or disables the rename command for specified users in the typelist. For example, the default setting disables the rename command for both guest and anonymous users.

Syntax: rename *yes|no typelist*

Default: rename no guest,anonymous

umask This keyword enables or disables the umask command (site umask) for specified users in the typelist.

Syntax: umask *yes|no typelist*

 The umask command is not available by default.

passwd-check This keyword defines the type of passwords required for anonymous users. The default setting requires the password for an anonymous access to be an e-mail address but does not enforce this rule if the user fails to enter a valid e-mail address. The server just warns the user about the invalid password.

Syntax: passwd-check *none|trivial|rfc822* (*enforce|warn*)

Default: passwd-check rfc822 warn

When you don't want password checking, set the passwd-check keyword as follows:

```
passwd-check none
```

If you set the checking to be trivial, the server checks only for the existence of an @ character in the password.

path-filter This keyword enables you to restrict certain filenames, specifically those used in file uploads by users specified in typelist.

Syntax: path-filter   *typelist   mesg   allowed_charset {disallowed regexp . . .}*

upload This keyword allows you to enable or disable an upload directory.

Syntax: upload *root_dir dirglob yes|no owner group*

For example, the following directive enables the /dropbox directory as an upload directory where files are owned by root and the group ownership is set to ftp:

```
upload  /home/ftp /dropbox  yes root ftp 0600
```

The uploaded files have a permission setting of 0600. Note that /home/ftp must be the home directory of the user ftp. If the uploader should not be allowed to create new subdirectories under the /dropbox directory, then the preceding upload line needs to be changed to:

```
upload /home/ftp /dropbox  yes root ftp 0600 nodirs
```

On the other hand, if the uploader should be allowed to create subdirectories, then nodirs can be replaced with dirs.

Miscellaneous configuration

The following keywords allow you to control miscellaneous settings.

alias This keyword enables you to create an alias for a directory.

Syntax: `alias string dir`

For example, the following allows a user to type the `cd redhat` command to change to `/pub/linux/distributions/redhat` directory:

```
alias redhat  /pub/linux/distributions/redhat
```

cdpath This keyword adds the specified directory to the search path of the change directory (`cd`) command.

Syntax: `cdpath dir`

For example:

```
cdpath /pub/linux/redhat
```

Now if a user enters the command `cd RPMS`, the server first looks for a directory called RPMS in the user's current directory. If it fails to find one, it looks for an alias called RPMS, and if it fails to find an alias RPMS, then it tries to change directory to `/pub/linux/redhat/RPMS`.

compress This keyword enables or disables the compression feature for specified classes.

Syntax: `compress yes|no class [classg . . .]`

Default: `compress yes all`

The default setting allows the compression feature for the class called `all`, which by default covers all real, anonymous, and guest users. When the default is left alone and the `ftpconversions` file is not modified, all the users who use the FTP service are able to compress files on the fly. For example, a user who wants to get the entire contents of a directory as a compressed file can enter the `get directoryname.tar.gz` command, and a compressed tar file is downloaded.

tar This keyword enables or disables the `tar` (tape archive file) feature for specified classes. The default setting allows the compression feature for the class called `all`, which by default covers all the real, anonymous, and guest users. When the default is left alone and the `ftpconversions` file is not modified, all the users who use the FTP service are able to `tar` files on the fly.

Syntax: `tar yes|no classg [class . . .]`

Default: `tar yes all`

For example, a user who wants to get the entire contents of a directory as a compressed file can enter the `get directoryname.tar` command to download a `tar` file.

shutdown This keyword specifies the file that the FTP server monitors from time to time to detect a shutdown event. You can create this file using the `ftpshut` command.

Syntax: `shutdown path`

Default: `shutdown /etc/shutmsg`

For example, to shut down the server immediately, you run the following command:

```
ftpshut now
```

However, you can schedule a shutdown in such a way that the logged-in users have some time before the shutdown begins. For example, say the current date is Monday, December 13, 1999, and the time is 1600 (in 24-hour format). To shut down the system in an hour, you can use the following command:

```
ftpshut -d 30 1700
```

This creates the `/etc/shutmsg` file as follows:

```
1999 11 13 17 00 0010 0030
System shutdown at %s
```

The format of the first line is as follows:

```
YYYY MM DD HH MM   HHMM HHMM
```

The *YYYY* is the year, *MM* is the month (0–11), *DD* is the day (1–31), *HH* is the hour (0–23), and *MM* is the minute (0–59). The first *HHMM* pair is the offset in time for denying new connections, and the second *HHMM* pair is the offset in time for disconnecting current connections. As you can see, the –d 30 option set the last *HHMM* pair to 0030 in the example file just shown. The deny offset for new connections by default is 10 minutes, but you can change that with –1 option. Also note that you can supply a more customized warning message then the default System shutdown at %s using one or more of the magic cookies shown in Table 14-3.

Table 14-3 *Magic Cookies for FTPSHUT Warning Message*

Magic Cookie	Replacement Text
%s	The time the system is going to shut down
%r	The time new connections will be denied
%d	The time current connections will be disconnected

In addition to these cookies, you can use all the cookies shown in Table 18-2. To create such a message, run the ftpshut command as follows:

ftpshut -d *MM* -1 *MM HHMM* "Shutdown at %s. Be done by %d."

Don't forget to replace the *MM, HHMM,* and so on with appropriate values. Also note that when you are ready to restart the FTP service, you have to remove the /etc/shutmsg file.

virtual If you have multiple IP addresses for your Linux system and would like to offer virtual FTP services, you can use this keyword. See the "Creating virtual FTP sites" section later in this chapter for details.

Syntax: virtual *address root|banner|logfile path*

/etc/ftpconversions

The /etc/ftpconversions file stores the FTP server's conversion database. The default configuration for this file is sufficient for almost all install-ations. If you need more information, see the man page for ftpconversions.

/etc/ftpgroups

The file /etc/ftpgroups is important only if you allow the nonstandard SITE commands. The wu-ftpd package that ships with Red Hat Linux comes with the SITE commands disabled. This is done to enhance security, as SITE commands have been known to create security holes in earlier versions of the server. For the sake of completeness, I describe the purpose of this file, but I strongly discourage its use.

When a not-so-security-savvy FTP administrator enables the SITE commands, she needs to set up the /etc/ftpgroups file as follows:

```
groupname:encrypted password:realgroup
```

Typically, the SITE GROUP and SITE GPASS commands are used to allow an already-logged-in FTP user to upgrade her group privileges. The /etc/ftpgroups file provides the necessary mapping for a user of *group-name* to be upgraded to the *realgroup* when a valid password is entered by using the SITE GPASS command. Also note that the *realgroup* must be a group in the /etc/group file.

/etc/ftphosts

The file /etc/ftphosts is used to control FTP access to specific accounts from various hosts. To allow a user to log on from one or more hosts, use a line such as the following:

```
allow  username  addrglob [addrglob. . .]
```

This command allows the specified user to log on from the specified hosts. For example:

```
allow  joegunchy *.evoknow.com
```

Here the user joegunchy is allowed to log on from any machine in the evoknow.com domain. To deny a user the ability to log onto the server from one or more hosts, you can use the following line:

```
deny username  addrglob [addrglob. . .]
```

For example, to prevent joegunchy from logging into the server from the 206.171.50.0 network, you can use the following command:

```
deny joegunchy  206.171.50.*
```

/etc/ftpusers

The file /etc/ftpusers specifies the list of users who are not allowed to access the FTP server. The default /etc/ftpusers file contains the following users:

- root
- bin
- daemon
- adm
- lp
- sync
- shutdown
- halt
- mail
- news
- uucp
- operator
- games
- nobody

These accounts are not allowed to log on because they are not real user accounts. If you need to stop a real user from being able to FTP to the server, you can put the username in this file.

At this point you have learned about all the configuration files necessary to run the FTP server. In the following sections I discuss some common FTP server configuration issues.

Because a lot of configuration is needed for proper FTP service, you might want to have a way to verify your configuration files from time to time. You can do this with a utility called ftpck, which you can download from the following FTP site: ftp://ftp.landfield.com/wu--ftpd/ftpck/.

Creating an Anonymous FTP Site

Having an anonymous FTP site could be a mixed blessing. It can be a great medium for distributing files that need to be widely distributed. In fact, all the free software packages (including the Red Hat Linux distribution) that you can download from the Internet are stored in many anonymous FTP sites all around the world. Just think what a nightmare it would be if you needed accounts on each of the FTP servers on the Internet to get access to free software. It is simply not practical. This problem has been solved with anonymous FTP service.

 Anonymous FTP service is also a common gateway for hackers to get into a system, so think twice before you decide to create an anonymous FTP server.

In the following sections I show you how to install and configure an anonymous FTP server.

Installing an anonymous FTP server

Assuming that you have decided to create an anonymous FTP server because you really need it, this section gives you a look at what it takes to make one. Fortunately, Red Hat makes it very easy to create an anonymous FTP server. All you need is the `anonftp` RPM package. First, query your RPM database to find out if you've already installed the `anonftp` package. Run the following command:

```
rpm -qa | grep anonftp
```

This command shows you the package name, such as `anonftp-4.0-4`, if you've already installed the `anonftp` package as part of your Red Hat Linux installation. If you haven't, however, there is no output from the preceding command. In such a case, get the latest `anonftp` package from your Red Hat CD-ROM and run the following command:

```
rpm -ivh anonftp-version.i386.rpm
```

If you do not know the version number, run `ls -l anonftp*.`
`rpm` command from the RPMS directory of your official Red
Hat CD-ROM. This will show you the RPM package name.

If you want to install the latest version from a Red Hat mirror site, run
the following command:

```
rpm —ivh ftp://ftp.cdrom.com/pub/linux/redhat/redhat-\
7.0/i386/RedHat/RPMS/anonftp-version.i386.rpm
```

Note that your `anonftp` package name varies with your system architecture and `anonftp` version. Also note that the `anonftp` package does
not install if you do not already have an FTP server such as the `wu-ftpd`.

After you have installed the `anonftp` package, you have an anonymous
FTP server ready to run.

Make sure that you have the user account called `ftp` without
any password in the `/etc/passwd` file before you can use
anonymous FTP service. The FTP user account line in your
`/etc/passwd` should look similar to this: `ftp:*:14:50:`
`FTP User:/home/ftp:/bin/true.`

Checking out the installation contents

If you're curious to see the installation contents, run the following command to see the files the package installed:

```
rpm -qlp anonftp-3.0-6.i386.rpm
```

Note that all files have been installed under the `~ftp` directory (that is,
the home directory of the `ftp` account — see the `/etc/passwd` file). Now
consider these files in detail.

Change directory to `~ftp` and enter `ls -l`. You see the following
directories:

```
[kabir@picaso ~ftp]# ls -l
total 4
```

```
d-x-x-x        2 root  root  1024 Nov  5 19:29 bin
d-x-x-x        2 root  root  1024 Nov  5 19:29 etc
drwxr--xr--x  2 root  root  1024 Nov  5 19:29 lib
dr--xr--sr--x 2 root  ftp   1024 Sep 10 17:21 pub
```

Now change directory to the bin subdirectory and run ls -l as before; you see something like the following:

```
[kabir@picaso ~ftp/bin]# ls -l
total 313
---x-x-x 1 root  root   15236 Nov  5 20:02 compress
---x-x-x 1 root  root   46356 Nov  5 20:02 cpio
---x-x-x 1 root  root   45436 Nov  5 20:02 gzip
---x-x-x 1 root  root   29980 Nov  5 20:02 ls
---x-x-x 1 root  root   62660 Nov  5 20:02 sh
---x-x-x 1 root  root  110668 Nov  5 20:02 tar
lrwxrwxrwx 1 root  root       4 Nov  5 20:02 zcat - gzip
```

These are the utilities that you need to provide an anonymous FTP service. The ls utility is used to provide the directory listings, and the compression utilities are used to provide on-the-fly compression/decompression capabilities.

If you're wondering why these files are here, the answer is that when someone accesses the anonymous FTP server, the server performs a chroot to the ~ftp directory. The chroot program is a utility that allows the server to treat the ~ftp directory as the root directory of the system. In other words, when an anonymous FTP user logs into the server, the server does a chroot to ~ftp and thus hides the real file system, showing only what is under the ~ftp directory. This is why you need a copy of the etc, bin, and lib directories with an absolutely minimal number of files. The lib directory contains the system library files needed for the programs in the bin directory. The ~ftp/pub directory is where you should keep the publicly distributable files.

Adding an incoming or dropbox directory

If you need an incoming or dropbox directory where anonymous users can upload files, follow these steps:

1. Create a subdirectory in the ~ftp directory for uploads. This directory is typically called incoming, and so I use this name here.

2. Add the following line in your /etc/ftpaccess file:

   ```
   upload   /home/ftp   /incoming yes root ftp 0600 nodirs
   ```

3. Make sure that you change /home/ftp to the appropriate directory. For example, if your ~ftp is really /data/ftp, then change /home/ ftp to /data/ftp in the preceding line. Also, if you want to allow anonymous users to be able to create subdirectories under ~ftp/ incoming, remove the nodirs option in the preceding line.

4. Run the following commands:

   ```
   chown -R root.ftp ~ftp/incoming

   chmod -R 1733 ~ftp/incoming
   ```

   The chown command sets root as the owner and ftp as the group for the incoming directory. The chmod command changes the incoming directory permissions such that root has read, write, and execute (rwx) permissions and the group and the world have write and execute (wx) permissions. It also sets the sticky bit for the directory and all its files. See the nearby sidebar for more info on the sticky bit.

5. Finally, make sure that you have the anonymous user type listed in at least one of the class definitions in your /etc/ftpaccess file. By default real, guest, and anonymous are all included in the default "all" class, so you do not need to do anything unless you have altered the default class definitions.

"Hand me one of them sticky bits . . ."

The *sticky bit* protects the files from being deleted by regular users. Normally when a directory has write and execute permissions set for everyone, any user of that system can delete a file in that directory. The sticky bit stops that by allowing only the creator of the file to delete the file. Because the FTP server writes the file setting root being the owner, no one but root is allowed to delete the uploaded files.

After you have taken these steps, you should FTP to the server as an anonymous user and make sure you can upload files in the specified directory only. Because you do not have read access to the ~ftp/incoming directory, you should not be able to see the files you upload using the ls command. However, you are still able to download the uploaded files if you supply the proper filenames.

Security and anonymous FTP

Creating an anonymous FTP site is already a security risk, and having an uploadable directory is adding more risk. However, many organizations have successfully run anonymous FTP servers for years, so do not be extremely discouraged: just be cautious. Here are some guidelines for enhancing anonymous FTP server security:

- Ensure that the ftp account in /etc/passwd is using an invalid password. For example, your ftp account entry in the passwd file should look like the following:

  ```
  ftp:*:14:50:FTP User:/home/ftp:/bin/true
  ```

- The ~ftp/bin directory should be owned by root and not by the ftp account. The binaries such as ls, compress, and tar that you have in the ~ftp/bin directory also must be owned by the root user. The ~ftp/bin directory and its contents should be executable and no more. You can run the following command to ensure that all files in the ~ftp/bin directory are just executable:

  ```
  chown -R root.root ~ftp/bin; chmod -R 111 ~ftp/bin
  ```

- The ~ftp/etc directory should be owned by the root user, and it must be only executable. You can make it so using the following commands:

  ```
  chown -R root.root ~ftp/etc; chmod 111 ~ftp/etc
  ```

- Contents of the ~ftp/etc directory must be only readable and owned by root. Run the following command to make sure the permissions are set up correctly:

  ```
  chown -R root.root ~ftp/etc; cd ~ftp/etc; chmod 444 *
  ```

- Do not ever copy your /etc/passwd or /etc/group files into
  ~ftp/etc directory. The ~ftp/etc/passwd and ~ftp/etc/group
  files are dummy files needed to satisfy programs that look for them
  when running under ~ftp as the root directory due to the server's
  chroot to ~ftp.

- Finally, as a general security rule, make sure that no files or directories in ~ftp are owned by the ftp user.

Creating a Guest FTP Account

A guest FTP account is a real account with a real username and password.
However, the only difference between the guest and the real FTP is that
when a guest user accesses an FTP server she does not see anything other
than her own home directory. When a guest user logs into an FTP server,
the server does a chroot operation to the guest user's home directory, thus
making the home directory of the guest user appear as the entire file system. The great advantage is that the user is unable to see anything else,
such as system files and other user directories. This security feature is
worth spending the time in configuring guest user accounts. Apart from
the extra work required to configure guest accounts, the other sacrifice is
the redundant use of the disk space. Like an anonymous FTP user, each
guest user has to have her own set of binaries for simple things like ls,
gzip, and tar. However, considering how the cost of disk space gets lower
and lower every day, perhaps disk space is not really an issue for most people.

The easiest way to set up a guest account is to use the anonftp package,
even if you do not want to provide anonymous FTP service. Just install the
package temporarily for the purpose of creating a single guest account. The
following sections show you the steps to creating a guest account.

Step 1: Creating the guest user account

Become root and create the guest user account as you create a real user
account. I assume this guest user account is called mrfrog and that it was
created using the usual useradd command as follows:

```
useradd mrfrog
```

Now set a desired password for mrfrog using the following command:

```
passwd mrfrog
```

Step 2: Stop Telnet access

Now change mrfrog's default shell to /bin/true using the following command:

```
chsh mrfrog
```

When prompted for the new shell path, enter /bin/true. This command disallows mrfrog from Telneting to the system and browsing other user files or system files. After all, we disallow all that when this user accesses the system via the FTP server.

Now edit the /etc/passwd file and append /./ to the existing home directory path. For example, if the /etc/passwd file has a line similar to the following:

```
mrfrog:1dev33vylewv.:516:519::/home/mrfrog:/bin/true
```

then change it to

```
mrfrog:1dev33vylewv.:516:519::/home/mrfrog/./:/bin/true
```

The /./ sequence determines where the chroot() function is performed.

Now edit the /etc/shells file and add /bin/true at the end of the file. This change makes the /bin/true program a valid shell option. Note that the /bin/true program does nothing and exits immediately after it is run. This feature makes it a good candidate for a shell that needs to be validated but denies the user anything and then exits. Because an exit from the shell logs out the user, the user never gets a chance to do anything when attempting a Telnet connection.

Step 3: Install the anonftp package

If you already have the anonftp package installed on your system, skip this step and go to the next one. If you don't have it installed, get the latest anonftp package and install it by running the rpm command:

```
rpm -ivh anonftp-3.0-6.i386.rpm
```

Your `anonftp` package name varies based on your system architecture and `anonftp` version. Also note that the `anonftp` package does not install if you don't already have an FTP server such as `wu-ftpd`.

Step 4: Copy the anonftp package files to the guest user's home directory

Change directory to `~ftp` and use the following command to copy all the files and directories to, for example, `~mrfrog`:

```
tar cvf - * | ( cd ~mrfrog ;  tar xvf  -)
```

All `mrfrog` really needs are the `~ftp/bin`, `~ftp/etc`, and `~ftp/lib` directories. You can delete the `~ftp/pub` directory or any other directory from your `~ftp` directory.

Step 5: Update the ~mrfrog/etc/passwd and ~mrfrog/etc/group files

Now edit the `~mrfrog/etc/passwd` file and remove the line for the `ftp` user. Append the exact password line for `mrfrog` from the `/etc/passwd` file. However, remove `mrfrog`'s password and replace it with a * to make it invalid. For example:

```
mrfrog:1dev33vylewv.:516:519::/home/mrfrog/./:/bin/true
```

Copy this line to `~mrfrog/etc/passwd` and replace the password so that the line looks like the following:

```
mrfrog:*:516:519::/home/mrfrog/./:/bin/true
```

Now, modify the `~mrfrog/etc/group` file and add the `mrfrog` line found in `/etc/group`.

 I assume that you have not somehow disabled Red Hat's default feature for automatic creation of a private group by the same name as the new user. In other words, when you create a user with the `useradd` program, it automatically creates a private group for that user with the same name. So when you created `mrfrog`, you should have also automatically created a group called `mrfrog` in the `/etc/passwd`. If you have changed the default behavior of the `useradd` program or manually created the user, make sure you create a group for this user and add it to the `~mrfrog/etc/group` file. Also, remove the `ftp` group from the `~ftp/etc/group` file.

Step 6: Set directory and file permissions

Change the directory/file permissions as follows:

```
chown mrfrog.mrfrog ~mrfrog
chmod 750 ~mrfrog
```

The `chown` command sets the user and group ownership to `mrfrog`'s user and group. The second command makes the `~mrfrog` directory accessible only to the `mrfrog` user and group.

```
chown --R root.root ~mrfrog/etc  ~mrfrog/bin ~mrfrog/lib
```

This command changes the ownership of the `etc`, `bin`, and `lib` subdirectories under `~mrfrog` to the root user and group.

```
cd ~mrfrog
chmod --R 111 *
```

The first command changes directory to `~mrfrog`, and the second one makes all the files and directories executable only for everyone.

```
cd etc; chmod  444 *
```

These commands change directory to the `~mrfrog/etc` directory and change the file permissions to read-only for everyone.

Step 7: Set the guestgroup in /etc/ftpaccess

Because we want the real user `mrfrog` to be a guest user, we need to add `mrfrog`'s group (which is also called `mrfrog`) to the `guestgroup` group list. For example, the following line in /etc/ftpaccess file allows any member of the mrfrog group (found in /etc/group) to be a guest user:

```
guestgroup mrfrog
```

In other words, the FTP server performs the chroot operation. For the mrfrog user, the FTP server changes root directory to /home/mrfrog.

Step 8: Test the account

Now FTP to the server and log on as mrfrog. If everything is set up correctly, you see nothing other than the home directory of this user. Try to upload a file or create a directory. You should be allowed to do these operations. However, whether or not mrfrog is allowed to delete, overwrite, or rename files depends on the settings for these operations in /etc/ftpaccess. For example, the default /etc/ftpaccess file includes the following lines:

```
chmod      no   guest,anonymous
delete     no   guest,anonymous
overwrite  no   guest,anonymous
rename     no   guest,anonymous
```

These lines prohibit the guest accounts from performing chmod, delete, overwrite, or rename operations. If you wish to allow these for the guest accounts, you have to remove the guest from the default typelist in these lines and turn them into the following lines:

```
chmod      no   anonymous
delete     no   anonymous
overwrite  no   anonymous
rename     no   anonymous
```

Finally, if you don't wish to keep the anonftp package around or do not want to have anonftp capabilities on your FTP server, you can remove the package files from the appropriate (~ftp) directory, or just run the following command:

```
rpm --e anonftp---3.0-6.i386.rpm
```

Don't forget to use the appropriate filename, because your version or architecture might be different from the description in this line.

Creating Virtual FTP Sites

If you have multiple domains and need to support separate FTP servers (ftp.domain--1.com, ftp.domain--2.com, and so on), you can use virtual FTP service. Virtual FTP service enables you to share a single-server system for multiple domains. You can configure the wu-ftpd server at least two different ways to support virtual FTP service. I discuss both methods here. Because both methods require that you have IP address aliases set up on your system, I discuss the IP-aliasing method first.

Creating IP aliases

In order to have virtual FTP servers, first you need to have appropriate DNS records for each FTP host. You need multiple IP addresses (one per FTP server host) to be routed to your FTP server machine. Using the IP aliasing technique, you have to create virtual Ethernet interfaces for all the IP addresses. For example, say that I have to create two virtual FTP servers (ftp.client--01.com and ftp.client--02.com) on an FTP server called ftp.evoknow.com. Also assume that I have already set up DNS records for each domain such that the following lines are true:

```
; In client--01.com DNS database
ftp.client--01.com.  IN  A   206.171.50.51


; In client--02.com DNS database
ftp.client--02.com.  IN  A   206.171.50.52


; In evoknow.com DNS database
ftp.evoknow.com.  IN  A   206.171.50.50
```

After setting up IP aliases and routes on the ftp.evoknow.com machine (per instructions found in Chapter 6), if I run the following command

```
cat /proc/net/aliases
```

I see the following IP aliases:

```
Device  family  address
eth0:0  2       206.171.50.51
eth0:1  2       206.171.50.52
```

Now take a look at the simplest way of creating virtual hosts.

Creating a limited virtual FTP service

This method is simpler than the other but is also quite limited. Although you will have virtual FTP service, you won't be able to customize it as much. If you want a completely customizable service (like the primary FTP server), then skip to the section "Creating a complete virtual FTP service."

To create this limited version of virtual FTP service, you need to make multiple copies of the anon-ftp package–created file/directory structure. Simply install the anonftp package and make copies of it for each virtual host. For the preceding example, I create two virtual FTP site directories (/home/client1/ftp and /home/client2/ftp) and copy all the contents of the /home/ftp files and directories. One of the easiest ways to make an exact copy of /home/ftp is to run the following commands:

```
cd /home/client1/ ; cp --a /home/ftp .
cd /home/client2/ ; cp --a /home/ftp .
```

These commands copy the /home/ftp file/directory structure in the virtual site directories. Now edit the /etc/ftpaccess file to add virtual keywords as follows:

```
virtual 206.171.50.51 root    /home/client1/ftp
virtual 206.171.50.51 banner  /home/client1/ftp/banner.msg
virtual 206.171.50.51 logfile /home/client1/ftp/xferlog

virtual 206.171.50.52 root    /home/client2/ftp
virtual 206.171.50.52 banner  /home/client2/ftp/banner.msg
virtual 206.171.50.52 logfile /home/client2/ftp/xferlog
```

Don't forget to replace IP addresses and directory paths with those you chose earlier. You should now modify the `banner.msg` file for each host to reflect any site-specific information you want to display. Also, you do not need the `pub` subdirectory for your virtual FTP sites, so you can remove it from each site.

After you create the preceding configuration, your virtual FTP servers are ready for testing. FTP to each of the virtual IP addresses and notice how the banner files are different for each host. Although quite easy to create, this virtual setup lacks the capability to fully customize the look and feel of the server. For example, you cannot use the `email` keyword in `/etc/ftpaccess` to point to different e-mail addresses that are appropriate for the virtual sites.

Note that the `ftpshut` command supplied with standard `wu-ftpd` does not support shutdown of virtual sites, because it writes the shutdown message file in only a single location specified by the `shutdown` keyword in the `/etc/ftpaccess` file. Also, when the time comes to restart the server, you need to remove the shutdown message file manually. To overcome this nuisance, you might want to get the replacement `ftpshut/ftprestart` utilities from the following Web site:

www.landfield.com/wu--ftpd/restart

You need to compile and build these utilities yourself.

Creating a complete virtual FTP service

Creating a complete virtual FTP service is the more complete method of hosting virtual FTP servers. This method requires you to patch the `wu-ftpd` source and compile it on your own.

Follow these steps to create a virtual FTP service:

1. Download the wu-ftpd source code. You can download it from www.wu-ftpd.org/.

   You also need the patch file from the following FTP site:

   ftp://ftp.meme.com/pub/software/wu-ftpd-*version*/

2. Read the README file that comes with the patch tar-ball file and apply the patch to the `wu-ftpd` source that you downloaded earlier.

3. Compile and install the patched wu-ftpd per the instructions provided in the wu-ftpd source package. Install the new FTP server to the default location /usr/sbin/in.ftpd.

   The newly patched wu-ftpd program (in.ftpd) now accepts an argument for the -a option. Normally, -a tells the server that you want it to read the /etc/ftpaccess file. Now the patched version allows the server to specify a different path for the ftpaccess file. So this option allows the new server to look at different ftpaccess configuration files that are needed to create virtual FTP sites.

4. Now modify the /etc/xinetd.d/wu-ftpdfile so that the FTP service is defined as follows:

```
service ftp
{
    flags             = REUSE NAMEINARGS
    socket_type       = stream
    wait              = no
    user              = root
    server            = /usr/sbin/tcpd
    server_args       = /usr/sbin/in.ftpd
    log_on_success   += DURATION USERID
    log_on_failure   += USERID
    nice              = 10
    disable           = no


}
```

This file invokes the FTP server via the TCP wrapper (tcpd). Now modify the /etc/hosts.allow file for each FTP server (that is, the primary server and all the virtual FTP servers) so that the lines are similar to the ones that follow:

```
# For the primary server
ftpd@206.171.50.50 : ALL : twist exec \
/usr/sbin/in.ftpd -l -a /etc/ftp/ftpaccess


# For the virtual FTP server
ftpd@206.171.50.51 : ALL : twist exec \
/usr/sbin/in.ftpd -l -a /etc/ftp/client1.ftpaccess


# For the second virtual FTP server
ftpd@206.171.50.52 : ALL : twist exec \
/usr/sbin/in.ftpd -l -a /etc/ftp/client2.ftpaccess
```

5. Now create the `/etc/ftp` directory and move the `/etc/ftpaccess` file into that directory.

6. Make two copies of the `/etc/ftp/ftpaccess` file such that you have `/etc/ftp/client1.ftpaccess` and `/etc/ftp/client2.ftpaccess` files.

7. Remove any virtual keywords from the `/etc/ftp/ftpaccess` file used for the mail FTP server.

8. Modify the `client1.ftpaccess` file so that it has a line such as the following:

   ```
   virtual 206.171.50.51 root /home/client1/ftp
   ```

9. Similarly, modify the `client2.ftpaccess` file to have a line such as:

   ```
   virtual 206.171.50.52 root /home/client2/ftp
   ```

   Don't forget to replace the IP addresses and the directory path with your own.

10. Now copy the anonftp files in the `/home/client1/ftp` and `/home/client2/ftp` directories.

11. Restart the xinetd server using the following command:

    ```
    killall -USR1 xinetd
    ```

    That's all there is to it! Now you have two virtual FTP sites that can be accessed via their respective host names or IP addresses.

Monitoring transfer log

Logging is very important for FTP service because you want to know who is doing what with your files. The `wu-ftpd` server logs transfers in the `xferlog` file, which typically resides in the `/var/log` directory. You can customize logging using the `log commands` and `log transfers` keywords discussed earlier.

If you are interested in monitoring `xferlog` on a regular basis, you can try `Dumpxfer`. You can download this package from the following FTP address:

```
ftp://ftp.microimages.com/tools/dumpxfer.1.2.tar.gz.
```

Becoming an Efficient FTP User

In this section I show you how to use FTP service effectively to download or upload files to and from FTP servers.

Using command-line FTP client

Virtually all modern operating systems have a command-line FTP client available by default. Yes, even the newer Windows (98 or more recent) have a built-in command-line FTP client. Interestingly, almost all the FTP clients on various popular operating systems behave pretty much in the same fashion. So, if you know how to use the Linux FTP client, you should be able to use it under Windows or even Mac OS X (which is based on FreeBSD).

Connecting to a FTP server

To FTP to a site called `ftp.domain.com` from any machine with a command-line FTP client run `ftp ftp.domain.com` command from the Linux shell or xterm window under the X Window System, or the equivalent. For example, run this command from the DOS shell window under Windows.

After you've run this command from a shell window, the FTP client attempts to connect to the FTP site. Once you're connected you'll be presented with username and password prompts. Enter the appropriate username and password. If you want to access the remote FTP site as an anonymous user, you can enter **anonymous** or **ftp** as the username and then enter your e-mail address as the password.

Navigating the FTP site

After you are logged in, you can navigate directories using the cd command and view directory listing using dir or ls command. Any time you wish to know what directory you are currently browsing you can enter the pwd command to view the directory path.

Setting the transfer mode

By default, most FTP clients set the transfer mode to binary, which should work for all situations. If you do not see a message during your session about the transfer mode, you can set it to binary by entering bin or binary as the command. If for some reason you need to switch to text mode transfer, you can enter text to change to text mode.

Downloading files and directories

To download a file from the site you can enter get *filename* command. The file will be downloaded to the current directory of your local system. To get multiple files from a directory you can use the mget *filename1 filename2 filename3 [filenameN]* command.

You can also use wild cards such as mget *.file_extension to download files with a specific extension. For example, mget *.gif *.jpeg allows you to download all GIF and JPEG files in the current directory of the local system from the current directory of the remote FTP site.

When using the mget command you will notice that the FTP client will prompt you before each file is downloaded. If you wish to have it download these files without asking you for each one, simply use the prompt command to toggle the prompt mode and than run the mget command. Also, if you wish to see a visual indication of files being downloaded you can enter hash command to toggle displaying of # character as download progresses.

For very large downloads displaying # is useless because you will have many screens full of them.

If you are downloading files from a Linux FTP server to a Linux FTP client system you can take advantage of a special feature that is often also found in other Unix-based FTP servers that allows you to download an entire directory by specifying the get *directory_name* command. You can even compress the transfer, which speeds up the download. For example to download a directory called pub in compress mode you can enter `get pub.gz` command. Note that such commands only work if the FTP server permits this operation.

Restarting a failed download

If your download session fails due to a system or network problem you can restart the download by issuing a `reget filename` command after you have logged on to the FTP server again. This is a great technique for recovering failed download transfers of large files. For example, if you have downloaded 10MB of a 30MB file and got interrupted due to a network problem or system error, you can connect back to the FTP server again and issue the `reget` command for the same filename. This will save you time and reduce bandwidth waste.

Uploading files

The precondition for uploading a file is to have the appropriate permissions to upload into a FTP server. Never upload files to someone else's FTP server without permission; this can be considered as a serious criminal activity.

Assuming that you have permission to upload files on to the FTP server you are connected to, run the `put filename` command to upload the named file from your local system's current directory. If the file is in a different directory you can change your local system's current directory using the `lcd` command. For example, if you started the FTP client from the `/tmp` directory and want to upload a file from the `/root/myfiles` directory after you are at the FTP client prompt, you can run `lcd /root/myfiles` to set the local system's current directory to `/root/myfiles`. Then you can run the `put` command to upload a file.

If you wish to upload multiple files you can run `mput filename1 filename2 ... [filenameN]` command, or you can use wildcards such as `mput *.file_extension` to upload files of certain extension.

If you have permission to create/delete directories in the FTP site, you can use `mkdir directory` and `rmdir directory` commands to do so respectively. Also, if you wish to rename a file on the server use the `rename filename` command.

Escaping to your current shell

When you are connected to a FTP site you can still escape temporarily to your current shell window by entering ! at the FTP command prompt. You can return to your FTP session by entering exit command at the shell prompt.

Aborting file transfer

After you have started upload or download transfer you can abort it by pressing the Ctrl+C key sequence for a few seconds. Upload transfer is aborted immediately; download transfers might take a few seconds or more.

Closing FTP connection

After you have completed your upload or download tasks, you can simply terminate the FTP connection by entering quit the command.

Using .netrc to automate FTP sessions

If you perform routine download or upload tasks from one or more FTP sites you can save yourself some typing by creating a .netrc file in your home directory. The Linux FTP client automatically reads this file for a matching record for the host name it is currently connecting to. For example, Listing 14-3 shows a sample .netrc file for a host name called ftp.domain.com.

Listing 14-3 *An example .netrc file*

```
machine ftp.domain.com
login your_username
password your_password
macdef init
bin
prompt
cd /some/path
get filename
quit
```

Whenever you connect to ftp.domain.com this sample .netrc file will be read from your home directory (i.e., ~/.netrc) and the FTP client will use the *your_username* and *your_password* as the password to log you in. The macdef init line defines an initialization macro, which is simply a list of commands that you want the client program to perform automatically. Here the first command is bin, which sets the binary transfer mode; the next command toggles the prompt mode; the cd /some/ *path* command changes the path on the FTP server and then uses the get *filename* command to download a file and finally uses the quit command to terminate the connection.

 Notice that there are two blank lines after the last command (quit); these indicate that this macro ends there.

You can add multiple machine records to automate FTP upload or download for commonly used FTP servers.

 You must set the .netrc file permission to be 600 so that only the file owner can read or write the file. You can run chmod 600 ~/.netrc command to set this permission.

Although the above-mentioned permission setting ensures that no one but the owner can read the .netrc file, you may wish to remove the password line if you do not wish to save your password in a text file only protected via a permission setting. This way you can still use the automation that .netrc provides, with the exception that you will be prompted for the password once.

When the FTP client can't find a matching machine record for the FTP server you are trying to connect, it looks for a default setting to be used. For example, you can add the following line as the very last line in your .netrc file:

```
default login anonymous password your@email_address
```

Now whenever you try to connect to an FTP site that does not have a machine record in .netrc, it will use the default login (anonymous).

 This may not be desirable if you connect to many non-anonymous FTP sites and do not wish to add them in your .netrc file.

Chapter 15

Configuring DNS

Domain Name Service (DNS) makes the Internet more user-friendly. The basic idea behind DNS is to allow host names to be translated into IP addresses. In this chapter I show you how to configure your Red Hat Linux system as a DNS client, and how to set up a DNS server on your system using the most widely used DNS server software called BIND. I also show you how to verify your DNS configuration and enhance its security.

Configuring a DNS Client

If you plan on accessing other Internet host computers from your Red Hat Linux system, you need to configure it as a DNS client system. The client part of DNS is called the *resolver*. The resolver is a set of routines in the C library that allows any program to perform DNS queries. The resolver comes standard with Red Hat Linux. In this section, you will learn to configure the resolver.

Typically, the Red Hat installation program asks you about your DNS server and automatically configures the necessary resolver configuration file. However, it is often necessary to change the resolver configuration to reflect any changes to the DNS server you use. For example, if you configure your resolver during Red Hat installation and later change your ISP, you need to configure it again manually. This section shows you how.

If you are planning on using your ISP's DNS server for resolving names and IP addresses, ask your ISP to give you the hostname and the IP address of its DNS servers. After you have the required information, you can configure the resolver.

First you need to modify the resolver configuration file called `/etc/resolv.conf`. Listing 15-1 shows a typical `/etc/resolv.conf` file for a domain called `evoknow.com`.

Listing 15-1 *An example /etc/resolv.conf file*

```
# Default Domain
domain evoknow.com


# Default search list
search evoknow.com


# First name server
nameserver 206.171.50.50


# Second name server
nameserver 206.171.50.55
```

Like many other common Linux configuration files, this file has a very simple format. Any blank line or lines starting with # are ignored. The only meaningful lines are the ones with a domain, search, or name server directive.

The domain directive enables you to specify the default domain name for the system. If you do not have this line set to the domain name of your system, the default domain name is automatically extracted from the host name of your system.

The search directive is used to influence how the resolver searches for host names that are not fully qualified. For example, if I want to enter a `ping www` command in a shell on the system with the preceding resolver configuration file, the `ping` program asks the resolver to resolve www. Because www is a partial host name, the resolver creates a full host name using the search list (for example, `www.evoknow.com`) and tries to resolve an IP for that host. For example, if I set the search directive to `integrationlogic.com` in the preceding listing and make the same `ping` request, the resolver returns the IP address for `www.integrationlogic.com`. If you do not provide a search directive, the default domain name is automatically applied when partial host names need to be resolved.

The `name server` directive specifies the domain name server that the resolver should use to query. You can (and should) specify multiple name server directives in the configuration file. Each domain name server is queried in order of appearance in the configuration file. For example, if a program requests the resolver to resolve a host name called `www.ad-engine.com`, the resolver first tries to resolve the name to an IP using the 206.171.50.50 domain name server. If the 206.171.50.50 domain name server fails to return a response (that is, if the query times out), then the second domain name server, 206.171.50.55, is contacted. Currently, you are allowed to list only three name server directives in the configuration file. It is generally a good idea to have at least two name server directives set to two different name servers.

You can set the `name server` directive to any domain name server's IP address on the Internet. However, you should use only the closest name server IP addresses in order to reduce delay in domain name resolution. Also, never use someone's domain name server IP address in your resolver configuration file without permission. It is considered rude and might have legal consequences if your resolver places a heavy load on someone's name server.

So far you have learned how to configure the DNS resolver on your system to use remote DNS servers. It is also possible to hard-code one or more IP addresses to their respective host names in the `/etc/hosts` file. This file has a very simple format as follows:

```
IP address  hostname  short_cut  hostname
```

Here is an example of an `/etc/hosts` file:

```
206.171.50.50 picaso.evoknow.com  picaso
127.0.0.1    localhost        localhost
```

The resolver can use this file to resolve an address when the remote DNS servers are not available. Also, if you have a small network and do not want to run a local DNS server, you may use this file to resolve local host names. However, when both the remote DNS server and the `/etc/hosts` file are available, the resolver needs to know in which order to process DNS queries. You can set the order in the `/etc/host.conf` file using the `order` directive. For example:

```
order hosts,bind
```

If your `/etc/host.conf` file has this order directive, then the resolver first attempts to use the `/etc/hosts` file to service the query. If the file does not contain an entry that can be used, the DNS servers specified in the `/etc/resolv.conf` file are used.

TIP

If you have a large user base, you can improve DNS-related performance by using a local DNS server over an `/etc/hosts` file, because reading the file for each new DNS request can be quite slow.

After you've set up the files just described, your DNS resolver configuration is complete. The easiest way to test your DNS configuration is to try to `ping` a computer on the Internet. If the `ping` program fails because of an unknown host name, double-check your DNS resolver configuration for typos.

Running your own DNS server has quite a few administrative benefits. For example, if you own one or more Internet domains, you can add, delete, or modify DNS records as you please. In the following section you learn how to set up a DNS server on your Red Hat Linux system.

Installing the BIND DNS Server

Red Hat Linux comes with the Berkeley Internet Name Domain (BIND) server software. If you have not installed it during the operating system installation phase, you can install the RPM version of the software. For example, to install the 9.1.0-10 version of BIND software for the Intel x86 platform, I located the `bind-9.1.0-10.i386.rpm` package in the Red Hat Linux CD-ROM's RPMS directory and ran the following command:

```
rpm -ivh bind-9.1.0-10.i386.rpm
```

The RPM package of the BIND software just described comes with three programs: `/usr/sbin/named` (the name server itself), `/usr/sbin/named-xfer` (the accessory program for the name server), `/usr/sbin/ndc` (a program to control the name server), and `/usr/doc/bind-8.2.2/named-bootconf.pl` (an accessory Perl script to convert older configuration files to the new format). After you've installed the BIND software, you're ready to configure DNS.

Understanding the Basics of DNS Configuration

The primary configuration file for the BIND domain name server daemon, named, is `/etc/named.conf`. At startup, the named server reads this configuration file to determine how it should function.

The /etc/named.conf file

This file consists of comments, statements, and blank lines, as described in the following sections.

Comments

A comment line can be a single line that starts with two forward slash characters. For example:

```
// This is a comment line in named.conf
```

Or it can be a line that starts with a # character as follows:

```
# This is a comment line in named.conf
```

Or it can be a multiline comment that starts with /* and ends with */. For example:

```
/*
    This is a multiline comment in named.conf

*/
```

Apart from the comments and blank lines, which are ignored by named, the real configuration lines are called statements, which have the following syntax:

```
keyword {
        // details of the statement
};
```

named can make use of many types of statements. I will discuss only the most commonly used here.

Options statement

The options statement enables you to set up global options for the name server. You should use only a single options statement in the named.conf file. If no options statement is specified, a default options statement with each option set to its default is used. Many options can go inside the options statement block, enclosed by the {}. The commonly used options are as follows:

```
options {
    directory path_name;
    statistics-interval number;
    forwarders { [ in_addr ; [ in_addr ; ... ] ] };
    forward ( only | first );
};
```

The directory option enables you to specify the working directory path of the name server. If a directory is not specified, the working directory defaults to ".", the directory from which the server was started. The directory specified should be an absolute path. Also note that when you specify a relative directory as part of another statement block, the relative directory is assumed to be relative to the working directory.

The statistics-interval option allows you to control the frequency of statistics produced by the name server. By default, the name server writes statistics to the default log (using `syslogd` in `/var/messages`) every hour. If you want to change this default behavior, add this option and specify the desired interval between statistics logging in number of minutes. If you find the statistics to be not useful enough to warrant regular reporting and would like to reduce your log file size a bit, set the number to zero to disable this feature.

If you would like your name server to forward DNS queries to other name servers, you can set a list of IP addresses of the remote name servers using the `forwarders` option. For example:

```
forwarders { 206.171.50.10; 206.177.175.10; };
```

Here two IP addresses of two different name servers are listed. Each pair of IP addresses needs to be separated by a semicolon. The default forwarder list is empty, and therefore no forwarding is performed; all queries are answered by the name server itself.

The `forward` option is useful only if the `forwarders` list is not empty. This option controls how the name server behaves. If you set this option to `first` (the default), then the name server sends all the queries to the forwarders. If the forwarders time out or cannot answer the query, the name server then tries to do the lookup by itself.

If you set the forward option to only, then the name server queries only the forwarders and does not try to look up the answer itself.

For most sites, the options statement will look something like the following:

```
options {
  directory "/var/named"
};
```

In other words, the most common use of the `options` statement is just to specify the working directory of the server. (The *working directory* is where you keep all the domain- or zone-specific files.)

Zone statement

Apart from the `options` statement, the `zone` statement is the only other type of statement that you find in virtually any site's `named.conf` configuration. To set up a name service for an Internet domain, you need to create a zone statement in the `/etc/named.conf` file. Three commonly used zone statements look as follows:

```
zone domain_name {
  type master;
  file path_name;
};


zone domain_name {
  type slave;
  masters { ip_addr; [ ip_addr; ... ] };
  file path_name;
};


zone "." {
  type hint;
  file path_name;
};
```

The first `zone` statement is used for a *master* (primary) *zone*. For example, if you want your name server to be the authoritative name server for a particular domain, you should set up a *master zone*. For example:

```
zone "ad-engine.com" {
  type master;
  file "ad-engine.db";
};
```

Here, the name server is configured as the primary name server for the `ad-engine.com` domain. Notice that the file option is used to specify the filename of the zone- or domain-specific configuration. If the filename you specify here is relative to the working directory of the server, it must reside inside the working directory.

If you're setting up multiple name servers for a particular domain, you can set only one to be the master or authoritative name server using the `type master` option. The rest of the name servers (as many as you wish) must be set up as the slave name servers. For example:

```
zone "ad-engine.com" {
    type slave;
    masters { 206.171.50.10; };
    file "ad-engine.db";
};
```

Here, the current name server is being set up as a slave name server for the `ad-engine.com` domain. The `masters` list specifies one or more IP addresses that the slave contacts to update its copy of the zone. If the file option is specified, then the replica of the zone's configuration is written to the file.

TIP   Use of `file` is recommended, because it often speeds server startup.

You can specify as many zone statements as you need in the `/etc/named.conf` file. However, you should never specify multiple zone configurations for each zone or domain. For example, you should not set up a name server to be the master and the slave name server for the same zone.

Finally, the other commonly used zone statement is the third kind: the `special` zone statement. The domain name is . and the type of name server is `hint` or cache. This special zone is used to specify a set of root name servers. When the name server starts up, it uses this list (`hints`) to find a root name server and get the most recent list of root name servers.

Now take a look at the zone- or domain-specific configuration, as discussed in the next section.

Domain- or zone-specific configurations

For each Internet domain or zone, you need two configuration files. One configuration file is for setting up the forward DNS (host name-to-IP) translation, and another one is for setting up the reverse DNS (IP-to-host name) translation. For example:

```
zone "ad-engine.com" {
  type master;
  file "ad-engine.db";
};

zone "50.171.206.in-addr.arpa" {
  type master;
  file "db.206.171.50";
};
```

I have the preceding two zone statements in `/etc/named.conf`. These two zone statements set up my name server as the authoritative master (primary) name server for the `ad-engine.com` domain. In other words, all host name-to-IP translations (also known as forward DNS) for the `ad-engine.com` are handled by this name server. The second zone statement sets up the name server as the master (primary) name server for the 206.171.50.0 network. In other words, all IP-to-host name translations (also known as reverse DNS) for this network are also handled by this name server. The first zone statement states that the `ad-engine.com` domain's forward zone configuration information is kept in the `ad-engine.db` file, and the second zone statements states that the reverse DNS configuration for the 206.171.50.0 network is stored in the file named `db.206.171.50`.

Both of these files consist of DNS resource record (RR) and optional comment lines. A DNS resource record has the following syntax:

```
{name}    {TTL}    addr-class    record-type    record-specific-data
```

The *name* field is always the name of the domain record, and it must always start in column 1. Traditionally, only the first DNS resource record sets the *name* field. For all the other resource records in a zone file, the *name* may be left blank; in that case, it takes on the name of the previous resource record. The second field, *TTL*, is an optional *Time to Live* field. This specifies how long this data is stored in the database. Leaving this field blank means that the default time to live is specified in the Start of Authority resource record (see the next section). The third field, *addr-class*, is the address class. The only widely used address class is IN for Internet addresses and other information. The fourth field, *record-type*, states the type of the resource record. The fifth field, *record-specific-data*, is the data for the record type in the fourth field. The commonly used resource records are discussed in the text that follows.

SOA: Start of Authority

The SOA or Start of Authority record is used to indicate the start of a zone. The syntax for the SOA record is as follows:

```
@   IN   SOA  nameserver.  contact_e-mail_address (
                serial_number     ; Serial
                refresh_number    ; Refresh
                retry_number      ; Retry
                expire_number     ; Expire
                minimum_number )  ; Minimum
```

The first field is the *name* field (discussed in the last section). This field is always set to @ and need not be repeated in any other resource record in the same file. The other fields and their descriptions are as follows:

- *nameserver* — This field specifies the host name of the current name server.

- *contact_e-mail_address* — This field specifies the e-mail address of the system administrator for the domain. The rest of the SOA record-specific data is used to set a serial number and various other default values.

- *serial_number* — This field specifies the version number of this zone file. Although you can use any positive number as your serial number, the common practice is to use a *YYYYMMDDNNN*-formatted number. Here, *YYYY* is the four-digit year, *MM* is the two-digit month, *DD* is the two-digit day of the month, and *NNN* is a three-digit number. So a serial number such as 20010215001 tells you that the last time the zone file was modified was 02/15/2001 and that there were two revisions on that date (000–001). Every time you update a zone file, you must increment the serial number or else the change does not take effect.

■ *refresh_number* — Indicates how often, in seconds, a secondary name server is to check with the primary name server to see if an update is needed. Note that if you update your master (or primary) zone file on the master name server and fail to update the serial number, the secondary name server will not update its copy of the zone information.

■ *retry_number* — This field indicates how long in seconds a secondary server should wait before retrying a failed zone transfer due to an external problem.

■ *expire_number* — The upper limit in seconds that a secondary name server is to use the zone data before it expires.

■ *minimum_number* — This field specifies the limit (in seconds) to be used for the Time to Live (*TTL*) field on resource records that do not specify one in the zone file. It is also an enforced minimum on *TTL* if it is specified some resource record (RR) in the zone. There must be exactly one SOA record per zone. Here is a sample SOA record for a domain called ad-engine.com:

```
@    IN    SOA   ns.ad-engine.com. kabir.ad-engine.com.
(
                 20010201000   ; Serial
                 7200          ; Refresh -  2 hours
                 3600          ; Retry   -  1 hour
                 43200         ; Expire  - 12 hours
                 3600 )        ; Minimum -  1 hour
```

Here's what's going on in the preceding example:

● The name server host name for ad-engine.com is ns. ad-engine.com, and the contact e-mail address is kabir@ ad-engine.com. Notice that the @ part of the e-mail address is replaced with a period in the SOA record.

- The first number is the serial number field. It specifies the version number of this zone file. In this example, the serial number tells us that the records were last updated on February 1, 2001.

- The refresh rate is set to 7,200 seconds (two hours). So, a secondary name server for ad-engine.com will poll the primary server to see if the serial number for the zone has increased or not. The commonly used values range from 2 to 12 hours, depending on how frequently you change a zone's configuration.

- The retry rate is set to 3,600 seconds (one hour). This means that if network trouble stops a secondary name server from contacting the primary server at the end of the refresh cycle (after every two hours in this case), the secondary server should wait another hour before retrying to communicate with the primary server.

- The expire rate is set to 43,200 seconds (12 hours). This allows the secondary server to treat its copy of the zone data as valid for 12 hours if it can't contact the primary server. This value is particularly important if you have set up a secondary DNS on a different network. You should set it high enough so that in case the primary name server or its network fails, the secondary server can provide DNS service for the longest outage period. In this example, the secondary name server will provide DNS service for 12 hours after it has failed to communicate with the primary server and will stop DNS service for that zone after the specified time. However, it will still try to communicate with the primary name server on a regular basis.

- The minimum elapsed time is the default *TTL* value for resource records. This specifies how long a resource record stays valid in a name server's cache. For example, when a name server queries the ad-engine.com name server for a certain DNS record, it keeps the answer for the query in its cache for 3,600 seconds (1 hour). If you change your DNS information frequently, you should set this to a low number; otherwise, set it to a high number.

NS: Name Server

The Name Server record is used to specify the name server responsible for a domain. The syntax is as follows:

```
IN NS name_server_hostname.
```

Notice that the *name* and *TTL* fields (of the resource record) are not specified, because the name needs to be specified only in SOA records using the @ character, and the *TTL* value is also specified in SOA records using the minimum number. For example:

```
IN NS ns.ad-engine.com.
```

This resource record specifies that `ns.ad-engine.com` is the name server for the current zone file. You can specify multiple NS records. In fact, you should have at least two NS records (one for the master and one for the slave name server). Also notice the period after the end of the name server host name. You must insert a period after all full host names in a zone file.

A: Address

The Address record specifies an IP address for a specific host name. An A record (short for Address record) translates a host name to an IP address. The syntax is as follows:

```
hostname IN A IP-address
```

For example:

```
www.ad-engine.com. IN A 206.171.50.51
```

You should have at least one A record per host. You can also use a short-cut for the host name. For example,

```
www IN A 206.171.50.51
```

is the same as the previous A record if the zone is `ad-engine.com`. In other words, if you do not specify a full host name, the domain name is appended to the short name. Thus `www` becomes `www.ad-engine.com`.

PTR: Domain Name Pointer

The Domain Name Pointer record is used to translate an IP address to a host name. This is also called the reverse Domain Name Service. The syntax for PTR record is as follows:

```
IP-address IN PTR hostname.
```

For example:

```
206.171.50.51 IN PTR www.ad-engine.com.
```

Here the IP address 206.171.50.51 is associated with the host www. ad-engine.com. You can use a shortened version as follows:

```
51 IN PTR www
```

Typically, an ISP does the primary reverse DNS for a network.

CNAME: Canonical Name

The Canonical Name record, CNAME, specifies an alias (host name) for the canonical (official) host name. The syntax is as follows:

```
alias IN CNAME canonical_hostname.
```

For example:

```
webserver.ad-engine.com. IN CNAME www.ad-engine.com.
```

Here, webserver.ad-engine.com is an alias for www.ad-engine.com. The shortened version is as follows:

```
webserver IN CNAME www
```

Note that when the webserver.ad-engine.com needs to be resolved to an IP address, the IP address of the www.ad-engine.com is returned. Therefore, you must make sure that at least one A record exists for the canonical host name.

MX: Mail Exchange

The Mail Exchange record is used to specify a host name that is set up as the SMTP mail server for a domain. The syntax is as follows:

```
IN MX preference_value mail_server_hostname.
```

For example:

```
IN MX 0 mail.ad-engine.com.
```

The preference number is useful only if you have more than one mail server. For example:

```
IN  MX 10 fast-mail-server.ad-engine.com.
IN  MX 20 slow-mail-server.ad-engine.com.
```

Here, the lower preference number indicates a higher precedence.

Now that you have learned the basics of DNS resource records, you are ready to create primary, secondary, and cache-only DNS servers.

Configuring a DNS Server Using bindconf

Normally it is not advisable to have X Window system on a server because it is not necessary to have such a GUI environment to manage the server and also because X can open your system to more hacker attacks because many X programs are constantly found to be buggy. However, if you must have the X Window system on your DNS server you can also take advantage of the Bind Configuration Tool (`bindconf`) to configure the DNS server (BIND). If you do not have X installed on your server, which is my recommendation, than you can skip to the next section.

If you do decide to use `bindconf`, you must never manually modify the `/etc/named.conf` file because `bindconf` will recreate the file every time you use `bindconf`. That is, if you manually modify this file your changes will be lost the next time you use `bindconf`!

When you run `bindconf` from an xterm window, a window similar to Figure 15-1 appears.

By default, `bindconf` creates a master zone called `localhost` with the appropriate reverse DNS configuration. This is shown in the main menu window. This configuration is used for the loopback address only.

Figure 15-1 *The bindconf main screen.*

Creating a forward master DNS zone for a domain

Say you want to create a forward master zone for a new domain called `evoknow.com`. Do the following:

1. Click the Add button in the main `bindconf` window and you will see a screen as shown in Figure 15-2. Select Forward Master Zone option and enter the appropriate domain name in the name entry area and click OK to continue.

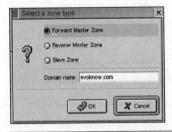

Figure 15-2 *Selecting a zone type.*

2. You will see a screen as shown in Figure 15-3. You can change the contact address to a more appropriate address than `root@ localhost`.

Figure 15-3 *The Name to IP Translation window.*

If you wish to set the zone life cycle information, click the Time Settings button, which brings up the screen shown in Figure 15-4. Set the refresh rate, retry rate, expiration rate, minimum time, etc., to any desired settings. In most cases the default values are fine.

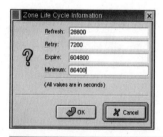

Figure 15-4 *The Zone Life Cycle Information window.*

3. Now you must add a name server (NS) record for this domain. Before you can add a NS record, make sure you have defined an A (Address) record for the name server host. Clicking the Add button under Records in the window shown in Figure 15-3 brings up the screen shown in Figure 15-5. Select Host as the resource record type and enter a host name and IP address for this A record.

Figure 15-5 *Adding an A (Address) record.*

Add as many hosts as you want for this domain in the same manner. In this example I have added ns1.evoknow.com and mail. evoknow.com.

4. From the window shown in Figure 15-3, select the domain name (evoknow.com) and click the Edit button to bring up the Settings for *domain* window, as shown in Figure 15-6. Under the Name Servers section, click the Add button and enter the name of the name server host, which in this example is ns1.evoknow.com. Similarly, if you have set up a host for your mail server you can add it under the Mail Exchangers section, as shown in this example. Mail exchanger priority is an arbitrary number. If you set up multiple mail servers, the lowest numbered mail server will be considered the highest-priority mail server. Click OK to return to the main menu.

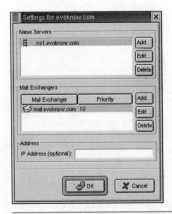

Figure 15-6 *Adding name servers and mail servers for the new domain.*

5. After you have added at least one name server to the new domain configuration, you can choose File ➪ Apply in the main menu screen and a new `/etc/named.conf` is be created with appropriate master configuration for the chosen domain (`evoknow.com` in this case). Also, a new zone file will be created in the `/var/named` directory called `evoknow.com.zone`, which includes the zone's master configuration data.

Creating a reverse master zone configuration for a domain

Say you want to create a reverse master zone for a new domain called `evoknow.com`. Do the following:

1. Make sure you have already created the forward master zone as discussed in the previous section.

2. Click the Add button in the main `bindconf` window and you will see a screen like that shown in Figure 15-7. Select Reverse Master Zone option and enter the first three octets of the IP address of the network in the IP address entry area. Click OK to continue.

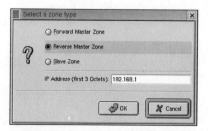

Figure 15-7 *Adding a reverse zone.*

3. In the IP to Name translation screen (shown in Figure 15-8), you should add the name server and any other hosts that you would like to provide reverse DNS for.

4. After you have added all the hosts, you should click OK and return to the main menu, which should display your forward and reverse

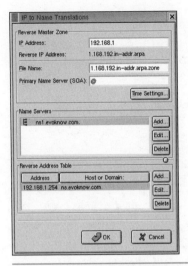

Figure 15-8 *Adding name server(s) and other host(s) in reverse DNS configuration.*

zone configuration names. Choose File ⇨ Apply to apply your configuration, create the necessary reverse zone file, update /etc/named.conf.

Manually Configuring a DNS Server

If you are not using the X Window System-based bindconf tool, you must manually configure the DNS server by editing and creating the configuration files using a text editor such as vi.

Configuring the master (primary) DNS server

This instructions in this section assume that I have a DNS server (named) running on the ns.evoknow.com host and that I just registered a domain called classifiedworks.com with Internic. Now I want to set up DNS on ns.evoknow.com to provide primary name service for the new domain. Here's how.

1. First, I need to create the following zone statement in the `/etc/named.conf` file:

```
zone "classifiedworks.com" {

   type master;

   file "classifiedworks.db";

   };
```

This statement specifies that my name server is the master name server for the `classifiedworks.com` domain.

2. Now I need to create a zone file called `classifiedworks.db` in the name server's working directory (specified by the `options {` `directory_ path };` statement). Listing 15-2 is an example of such a zone file for the `classifiedworks.com` domain.

Listing 15-2 *A example zone file*

```
@    IN   SOA  ns.evoknow.com. kabir.evoknow.com. (
                 1999020100   ; Serial
                 7200         ; Refresh -  2 hours
                 3600         ; Retry   -  1 hour
                 43200        ; Expire  - 12 hours
                 3600 )       ; Minimum -  1 hour

     IN NS ns.evoknow.com.
     IN MX 10 mail.evoknow.com.

www IN CNAME www.evoknow.com.
ftp IN A 206.171.50.55
```

Here I have set up SOA and NS records to state that ns. evoknow.com is the name server for the `classifiedworks.com` domain.

3. Because I want to receive mail for this domain on the `mail.` `evoknow.com` host, I set up an MX record that does just that.

4. I set up an alias called www.classifiedworks.com for www.
evoknow.com.

5. Finally, I set up an A record for ftp.classifiedworks.com to
point to 206.171.55.

Using the various resource records, you can configure the zone file as
you need. After the zone file is configured and stored in the working directory of the DNS server, the primary name server configuration for the
domain is complete.

Configuring the slave (secondary) DNS server

Configuring a slave or secondary DNS server is quite simple. The only file
you need to update by hand is the /etc/named.conf file. For example, say
that I want to use a DNS server called ns2.evoknow.com as the secondary
name server for the classifiedworks.com domain. The very first thing I
need to do is create a zone statement such as the following in the
/etc/named.conf file of the ns2.evoknow.com named server:

```
zone "classifiedworks.com" {
   type slave;
   file "classifiedworks.db";
};
```

Because this is a slave or secondary server, I do not need to create the
classifiedworks.db file by hand. I can just grab the file from the primary name server for the classifiedworks.com domain using a
program called named-xfer, which comes with the named distribution. Because I know the name of the primary name server for the
classifiedworks.com domain to be ns.evoknow.com, I can run the
named-xfer command as follows:

```
named-xfer -z classifiedworks.com -f classifiedworks.db \
-s 0 ns.evoknow.com
```

Here the −z option specifies the zone name, the −f option specifies the
zone file name, and the −s option specifies the name server where the
information currently resides.

After running this program, a file called `classifiedworks.db` is created in the current directory. After I move the file to the working directory of the named server on the `ns2.evoknow.com` machine, the secondary DNS configuration for the `classifiedworks.com` domain is complete.

Configuring the reverse DNS server

If you own your network IP addresses, you will have to do reverse DNS for them. For example, if you own an IP network called 206.171.50.0 and use it in your forward DNS configuration for a domain called `evoknow.com`, you will have to set up a reverse DNS zone for this network. Here is how.

1. First, modify the `/etc/named.conf` file to include a new zone as follows:

```
zone "50.171.206.in-addr.arpa" {

    type master;

    file "db.206.171.50";

};
```

Notice the special zone name (`50.171.206.in-addr.arpa`) used in the preceding zone configuration. To create a reverse DNS zone name, you must reverse your network number and append `in-addr.arpa` at the end of the name.

2. Now you need to create db.206.171.50 in the working directory of the named server. Note that the filename for the reverse DNS zone can be anything, but it is customary to use the db.*network-address* names. This file is similar to the other zone files I have shown so far; the only difference is that it will have PTR records instead of A, CNAME, and so on. Listing 15-3 shows an example of the db.206.171.50 file.

Listing 15-3 *An example reverse DNS zone file (db.206.171.50)*

```
@    IN   SOA  ns.evoknow.com. kabir.evoknow.com. (
              1999020100   ; Serial
              7200         ; Refresh - 2 hours
```

```
3600          ; Retry   - 1 hour
43200         ; Expire  - 12 hours
3600 )        ; Minimum - 1 hour
```

```
IN   NS   ns.evoknow.com.
```

```
51.50.171.206.in-addr.arpa.   IN   PTR ns.evoknow.com.
52.50.171.206.in-addr.arpa.   IN   PTR mail.evoknow.com.
53.50.171.206.in-addr.arpa.   IN   PTR www.evoknow.com.
```

Here, the PTR records are provided to map three different IP addresses to three different hostnames. You can also specify the preceding PTR records in shortened form as follows:

```
51   IN   PTR ns.evoknow.com
```

```
52   IN   PTR mail.evoknow.com
```

```
53   IN   PTR www.evoknow.com
```

In most cases, your ISP will own the IP addresses for your network and should be prepared to provide master reverse DNS service. However, there is one special network for which you must provide reverse name service: 127.0.0, which is used for the local loopback interface IP (127.0.0.1). Because no one has authority over this loopback network, everyone must provide reverse DNS service themselves. This is why you will always need to have a special zone statement in your /etc/named.conf file that looks like the following:

```
zone "0.0.127.in-addr.arpa" {

    type master;

    file "named.local";

};
```

3. You will also have to have the named.local zone file in the working directory of your name server. This file is shown in Listing 15-4.

Listing 15-4 *The named.local file*

```
@    IN  SOA   localhost. root.localhost. (
                1999020100  ; Serial
                7200        ; Refresh -  2 hours
                3600        ; Retry   -  1 hour
                43200       ; Expire  - 12 hours
                3600 )      ; Minimum -  1 hour


     IN  NS   localhost.


1    IN  PTR localhost.
```

Configuring a cache-only slave DNS server

Technically, all DNS servers are cache-enabled; that is, DNS servers use cache by default. However, if you do not want to provide DNS service for any Internet domains and desire only to improve DNS query performance for your network, you can run a cache-only DNS server. Such a server will have an /etc/named.conf file as shown in Listing 15-5.

Listing 15-5 *An example /etc/named.conf file*

```
zone "." {
  type hint;
  file "named.ca";
};


zone "0.0.127.in-addr.arpa" {
  type master;
  file "named.local";
};
```

The first zone statement specifies that the name server use the named.ca file to determine root name server names at startup. And the second zone statement provides the reverse name service for the local loop-back network. That's all you need to create a cache-only name server.

Controlling the DNS server

The named distribution comes with a nifty program called ndc that provides a simple command-line interface for controlling the name server. Using this tool you can start and stop the name server; reload DNS configuration files, and also view statistics.

Starting the name server

Your name server should start automatically at boot. If it does not start automatically, you need to take the following steps:

1. Log into your name server system as root and change directory to /etc/rc.d/init.d. Make sure that you have a script called named in this directory. If you are missing this script, you should reinstall the BIND distribution RPM from your Red Hat CD-ROM.

2. After you have confirmed that you have the /etc/rc.d/init.d/ named script, change to your default system run level's (see /etc/ inittab) rc directory. For most systems the default run level is 3; if yours is also the same, change directory to /etc/rc.d/rc3.d/.

3. Make a symbolic link called S*XX*named that points to the /etc/rc.d/init.d/named script. Replace *XX* in S*XX*named with a high number such as 55 or 85 to ensure that the system does not try to start the name server before network interfaces are set up properly. For example, to make a symbolic link called S55named to point to the named script, you can run the following command:

   ```
   ln -s /etc/rc.d/init.d/named S55named
   ```

   After you have created this link, your system will start the name server every time you boot your system. If, however, you prefer to run the name server manually, you can use the ndc program as follows:

   ```
   ndc start
   ```

Reloading new name server configuration

After you modify any of the zone files or the /etc/boot.conf file, you must restart the name server to make the changes effective. You can force the name server to reload the new configuration as follows:

```
ndc reload
```

Don't forget to modify the serial number in the SOA record for any zone file you modify, or else the name server will not load the new configuration. To restart the name server by killing it first, you can use restart instead of reload in the preceding line.

Stopping the name server

If for any reason you need to stop the name server, just run the ndc command as follows:

```
ndc stop
```

Viewing name server statistics

You can use the ndc program to generate various name server statistics in the working directory of the name server. Run the following command:

```
ndc stats
```

This command will create a file called named.stats in the name server's working directory. This statistics file will show various items of information, including the number of queries per resource record.

Testing Your DNS Server

Every time you modify your DNS information, do not forget to test the configuration using a name server query tool. In this section I discuss how you can test your name server configurations by using the dig utility.

Many tools are available for manually querying name servers, including `dig`. If you would like to have a few commonly used query tools, install the `bind-utils` RPM distribution from your Red Hat CD-ROM. The `bind-utils` distribution comes with `dig`, `dnsquery`, `host`, `nslookup`, and more.

Say that you just registered a new domain with Internic and have already set up the necessary DNS configuration on your name server. After restarting the name server, you want to test the configuration via `dig`. You can run `dig` using the following syntax:

```
dig @nameserver domain [query_type]
```

The *nameserver* can be a DNS server's host name or IP address. If you're running `dig` on the same machine as the DNS server you wish to test, you don't need to specify the DNS server using `@nameserver` as long as your `/etc/resolv.conf` has a line that makes the target DNS server the default name server for that machine. The *domain* in the above syntax is the domain name or the host name for which you want to find a DNS record of type *query_type*. By default *query_type* is set to A (Address) record. For example:

```
dig @ns.aminews.com evoknow.com ns
```

Here the DNS server `ns.aminews.com` is asked to locate NS record for `evoknow.com` domain. Lets look at another example:

```
dig www.evoknow.com A
```

Here the default DNS server (i.e., the one set in `/etc/resolv.conf`) is being asked to locate the A (Address) record for a host name called `www.evoknow.com`.

As you can see, you can use `dig` to dig up your DNS configuration quite easily by pointing it to the right name server and asking for the query types that you wish to check.

Managing DNS for Virtual Domains

A single name server can provide name service for many domains. This feature allows a single system to host a large number of Internet domains. In fact, that's how most Internet service provider (ISP) companies provide Web sites for their customers. Because such a domain is hosted on another domain (for example, the ISP's own domain), they are called *virtual domains*. Virtual domains are quite common these days. It almost seems as if everyone I know has a domain of their own.

Automating virtual domains with the makesite script

If you need to create a lot of virtual domains for your customers on a daily basis, you might want to automate the process as much as you can. Listing 15-6 shows a Perl script called makesite that I often use to create a virtual domain.

Listing 15-6 *The makesite script*

```
#!/usr/local/bin/perl -w

use strict;

#
# Purpose: makesite creates virtual sites.
# It uses a set of templates to create DNS, and HTTPD
# configurations files.
#
# Note: this is a very *simple* script.
#
###################################################

use Time::localtime;
```

```perl
my $site              = $ARGV[0] or &syntax;

my $MAKESITE_DIR      = '/scratch/dns/makesite';

my $USER              = 'httpd';

my $GROUP             = 'httpd';

my $PERMISSION        = '2770';

my $BASE_DIR          = '/tmp';

my $HTDOCS            = 'htdocs';

my $CGIBIN            = 'cgi-bin';

my $NAMED_PATH        = '/var/named';

my $NAMED_FILE_EXT    = '.db';

my $NAMED_TEMPLATE    = "$MAKESITE_DIR/named.template";

my $NAMED_CONF        = '/etc/named.conf';

my $HTTPD_CONF        = '/usr/local/apache/etc/httpd.conf';

my $VHOST_TEMPLATE    = "$MAKESITE_DIR/httpd.template";

my $LOG_FILE          = "$BASE_DIR/makesite.log";


my $dir = $site;

my @domain_types = qw(com net org edu);

my ($domain_ext, $thesite_dir, $public_dir,

    $htdocs_dir, $cgibin_dir, $named_file,

    $dir_len, $temp_len);


my $tm = localtime(time);

my $date = sprintf("%s-%02s-%02s-%02d-%02d", $tm->year+1900,

                                             $tm->mon+1,

                                             $tm->mday,

                                             $tm->hour,

                                             $tm->min);


my $serial = sprintf("%s%02d%02d000",        $tm->year+1900,

                                             $tm->mon+1,

                                             $tm->mday);


$site =~ y/[A-Z]/[a-z]/;
```

Continued

Listing 15-6 *Continued*

```
# Get the length with the EXT
$dir_len = length($dir);

foreach $domain_ext (@domain_types){ $dir =~ s/\.$domain_ext//g; }

# Get the new length without the EXT
$temp_len = length($dir);

# If the user has not entered an extension then show syntax.
&syntax if($temp_len == $dir_len);

$named_file = $NAMED_PATH . '/' . $dir . $NAMED_FILE_EXT ;
$thesite_dir = $BASE_DIR . '/' . $dir;
$htdocs_dir = $BASE_DIR . '/' . $dir . '/' . $HTDOCS;
$cgibin_dir = $BASE_DIR . '/' . $dir . '/' . $CGIBIN;

die "$thesite_dir already exist! Aborted!\n" if(-e $thesite_dir);

system("mkdir $thesite_dir");
system("mkdir $htdocs_dir");
system("mkdir $cgibin_dir");

&createNamedFile($named_file,$site,"$dir$NAMED_FILE_EXT");
&createIndexFile($htdocs_dir,$site);
&createVirtualHostConf( domain=>$site,
                        website=>"www.$site",
                        cgibin=>$cgibin_dir,
                        htdocs=>$htdocs_dir);

system("chown -R $USER.$GROUP $thesite_dir");
system("chmod -R $PERMISSION $thesite_dir");

open(FP,">$LOG_FILE") || die "Can't write to log file.\n";
print FP "$date created www.$site [$htdocs_dir] site.\n";
close(FP);
```

```
exit 0;

sub createNamedFile{
   my $file = shift;
   my $domain = shift;
   my $database = shift;
   my $line;

   open(OUT,">$file") || die "Can't write $file\n";
   open(FP,$NAMED_TEMPLATE) || die "Can't open $NAMED_TEMPLATE\n";
   while($line=<FP>){
      $line =~ s/<DOMAIN>/$domain/g;
      $line =~ s/<SERIAL>/$serial/g;
      print OUT $line;
      }
   close(FP);
   close(OUT);

   open(FP,">$NAMED_CONF") || die "Can't open $NAMED_CONF\n";
   print FP <<ZONE;

// $domain was created on $date
zone "$domain" {
        type master;
        file "$database";
};

ZONE
   close(FP);
   }

sub createIndexFile{
   my $htdocs = shift;
   my $domain = shift;
```

Continued

Listing 15-6 *Continued*

```
open(FP,">$htdocs/index.html") || die "Can't write index.html \n";

print FP <<INDEX_PAGE;

<HTML>

<HEAD> <TITLE> $domain </TITLE> </HEAD>

<BODY BGCOLOR="white">

<CENTER>

 This is $domain Web site

 <p> It was created on $date </p>

</CENTER>

</BODY>

</HTML>
INDEX_PAGE


close(FP);

}


sub createVirtualHostConf{

 my %params = @_;
 my $line;
 open(OUT,">$HTTPD_CONF") || die "Can't open $HTTPD_CONF $!\n";

 open(FP,$VHOST_TEMPLATE) || die "Can't open $VHOST_TEMPLATE $!\n";
 while($line=<FP>){
   $line =~ s/<DOMAIN>/$params{domain}/g;
   $line =~ s/<CGI-BIN-DIR>/$params{cgibin}/g;
   $line =~ s/<HTDOCS-DIR>/$params{htdocs}/g;
   $line =~ s/<WWW-SITE>/$params{website}/g;
   print OUT $line;


 }
 close(FP);
 close(OUT);

 }
```

```
sub syntax{
    print <<SYNTAX;


    makesite <virtual Internet domain>
    Example: makesite evoknow.com


SYNTAX
    exit 0;
    }
```

How makesite works

The purpose of this Perl script is to enable me to create a virtual Web site with proper DNS and Apache Web server configuration without doing many file editing tasks. For example, say that I want to create a new Web site called www.newdomain.com. If I were to do everything manually, I would have to do the following:

1. Add a new zone statement in the /etc/named.conf file for newdomain.com.

2. Add a new zone file for newdomain.com in the working directory of the name server. I would have to create this from scratch or copy and modify an existing domain file.

3. Create a Web site document root and CGI script directory for the domain in the appropriate Web space on the server.

4. Modify the Apache server configuration file so that Apache treats www.newdomain.com as a new Web site.

Because manually configuring these important files can be error prone, I decided to write the makesite script that does all of these steps. For example, to create the www.newdomain.com site with proper DNS and Apache configuration, I can run the following command:

```
makesite newdomain.com
```

This command adds a zone statement such as the following in the /etc/named.conf file:

```
// newdomain.com was created on 1999-02-03-13-30

zone "newdomain.com" {
  type master;
  file "newdomain.db";
  };
```

This statement creates a newdomain.db file in /var/named (the working directory for my name server), which is shown in Listing 15-7.

Listing 15-7 *The /var/named/newdomain.db file*

```
@  IN  SOA  newdomain.com. hostmaster.newdomain.com. (
                19990206000  ; serial YYYYMMDDXXX
                7200         ; refresh
                3600         ; (1 hour) retry
                1728000      ; (20 days) expire
                3600)        ; (1 hour) minimal TTL


; Name Servers
   IN  NS  ns.evoknow.com.
   IN  MX  10 mail.evoknow.com.


; CNAME records
www  IN  CNAME  www.evoknow.com.
```

The script then appends the following lines to the end of the Apache server configuration (httpd.conf) file, as follows:

```
#
# Domain Configuration for www.newdomain.com
#

<VirtualHost www.newdomain.com>
  ServerName www.newdomain.com
  ServerAdmin webmaster@newdomain.com

  DocumentRoot /tmp/newdomain/htdocs
  ScriptAlias /cgi-bin/ /tmp/newdomain/cgi-bin/
```

```
ErrorLog logs/www.newdomain.com.error.log
TransferLog logs/www.newdomain.com.access.log
```

```
</VirtualHost>
```

```
#
# End of Domain Configuration for www.newdomain.com
#
```

Finally, the script creates the following directory structure and the index.html page for the Web site:

```
/www/newdomain
/www/newdomain/htdocs—the document root for the Web site
/www/newdomain/cgi-bin—the cgi-bin directory
```

The index.html page is stored in the /www/newdomain/htdocs/ directory. The script also sets up the permissions for the Web site directories so that only a specified user and group have read/write permissions.

Because the script does all the dirty work, I can create many virtual sites without constantly worrying about configuration problems. Finally, when I'm done making sites, I can restart the name server and the Web server to bring all the sites online. This is really a simple yet useful tool. The makesite script takes the domain name as the argument and uses two text template files to create the name server and the Web server configuration information. Listing 15-8 shows the named.template file that's used to create the name server configuration.

Listing 15-8 *The named.template file*

```
@    IN SOA <DOMAIN>.  hostmaster.<DOMAIN>. (
                       <SERIAL>    ; serial YYYYMMDDXXX
                       7200        ; refresh
                       3600        ; (1 hour) retry
                       1728000     ; (20 days) expire
                       3600)        ; (1 hour) minimal TTL

; Name Servers
```

Continued

Listing 15-8 *Continued*

```
IN  NS  ns.evoknow.com.
IN  MX  10 mail.evoknow.com.


; CNAME records
www  IN  CNAME  www.evoknow.com.
```

If you look carefully, you will see the two special tags (<DOMAIN> and <SERIAL>) in this template file. The makesite script reads this template and replaces these tags with appropriate information. Because the idea is to create a virtual Web site with a proper DNS configuration, you do not need to create any A records. For example, the preceding configuration states that the www.<DOMAIN> (for example, www.newdomain.com) is an alias of www.evoknow.com. Using A records makes maintenance of many virtual Web sites time-consuming if IP changes are required. I use the CNAME record so that if www.evoknow.com host's IP needs to be changed, I do not need to modify the virtual domain's configuration files at all.

Listing 15-9 shows the httpd.template file used to create the Apache server configuration.

Listing 15-9 *The httpd.template file*

```
#
# Domain Configuration for <WWW-SITE>
#


<VirtualHost <WWW-SITE>
  ServerName <WWW-SITE>
  ServerAdmin webmaster@<DOMAIN>

  DocumentRoot <HTDOCS-DIR>
  ScriptAlias /cgi-bin/ <CGI-BIN-DIR>/

  ErrorLog logs/<WWW-SITE>.error.log
  TransferLog logs/<WWW-SITE>.access.log

</VirtualHost>
```

```
#
# End of Domain Configuration for <WWW-SITE>
#
```

As with the previous template, you may notice that a few custom tags are used in this file. These tags get replaced with appropriate information as well.

Modifying makesite to your own uses

To use this Perl script in your own environment, follow these steps:

1. Modify the following lines in the beginning of the script:

```
my $MAKESITE_DIR = '/usr/local/src/makesite';
```

by changing the directory path to the location of the makesite files.

2. Change the username if you run your Apache Web server using another user ID, such as nobody.

```
my $USER = 'httpd';
```

3. Change the group name if you run your Apache Web server using another group like 'nobody' or something else:

```
my $GROUP = 'httpd';
```

4. Change the permission value as you see fit (this value allows only the $USER and $GROUP to have full access in the Web site directory):

```
my $PERMISSION = '2770';
```

5. Change the value of the $BASE_DIR variable to the base directory of all of your Web sites:

```
my $BASE_DIR = '/www';
```

6. Change the value of the $HTDOCS variable to the relative name of the document root directory name for httpd.conf file. The current setting creates $BASE_DIR/<sitename>$HTDOCS (default: /www/<sitename>/htdocs) as the document root for the Web site:

```
my $HTDOCS = 'htdocs';
```

7. Change the value of the $CGIBIN variable to the relative directory name if you do not want the Apache ScriptAlias directive to be set to $BASE_DIR/<sitename>/$CGIBIN (default: /www/<sitename>/cgi-bin):

```
my $CGIBIN = 'cgi-bin';
```

8. Change the value of the $NAMED_PATH variable to the directory to the working directory of your name server:

```
my $NAMED_PATH = '/var/named';
```

9. Change the value of the $LOG_FILE variable to point to somewhere else if you do not want to write the makesite log file in the base directory (for example, you can set this to "/tmp/makesite.log" to write to the /tmp directory):

```
my $LOG_FILE = "$BASE_DIR/makesite.log";
```

10. Change the value of the $HTTPD_CONF variable to point to the httpd.conf file of your Web server:

```
my $HTTPD_CONF = '/usr/local/apache/etc/httpd.conf';
```

11. After you have made the preceding changes, you should modify the named.template and httpd.template files as you see fit and store both of these files in the directory where you keep the makesite script.

12. Finally, make sure that the script is executable and that the Perl interpreter line (the #! bang line) is set up correctly.

Hopefully, this will save you some work. If you know Perl programming, you can always fine-tune the script to your environment as much as you want.

Balancing Server Load Using the DNS Server

Organizations that manage multiple virtual domains often have multiple servers. In this section I show you how to use a DNS trick to balance load over many servers. The main idea is to share load among multiple servers of a kind, a practice typically used for balancing Web load over multiple Web servers. This trick is called *round robin DNS*.

Say that you have two Web servers, www1.yourdomain.com (192. 168.1.10) and www2.yourdomain.com (192.168.1.20), and you would like to balance the load for the www.yourdomain.com on these two servers by using *round robin DNS*. In your yourdomain.com zone file add the following lines:

```
www1 IN A 192.168.1.10
www2 IN A 192.168.1.20


www IN CNAME   www1
www IN CNAME   www2
```

Restart your name server and ping the www.yourdomain.com host. You will see the 192.168.1.10 address in the ping output. Stop and restart pinging the same host, and now you'll see the second IP address being pinged. This is due to the fact that the preceding configuration tells the name server to cycle through the CNAME records for www. In other words, the www.yourdomain.com host is both www1.yourdomain.com and www2.yourdomain.com.

Now when someone enters www.yourdomain.com, the name server will give out the first address once, and then for the next request it will give out the second address and keep on cycling between these addresses.

One of the disadvantages of the round robin DNS trick is that there is no way for the name server to know which system is heavily loaded and which is not; it just blindly cycles. If one of the servers crashes or becomes unavailable for some reason, the round robin DNS will still return the broken server's IP on a regular basis. This can be quite chaotic because some people will be able to get to the sites and some won't.

If your load demands better management and it is important to check your server's health, your best choice is to get a hardware solution by using the new hardware products such as the Web Director (www. radware.com/), Ace Director (www.alteon.com/), or Local Director (www.cisco.com/).

Understanding DNS Spoofing

When a DNS server is tricked into accepting and later using incorrect, non-authoritative information from a malicious DNS server, the first DNS server has been *spoofed.* Spoofing attacks can cause serious security problems for DNS servers that are vulnerable to such attacks, causing users to be directed to wrong Internet sites, for example, or e-mail to be routed to nonauthorized mail servers.

There are many methods of spoofing a DNS server. One method is called cache poisoning, which means that a malicious hacker manipulates DNS queries to insert data in an unprotected DNS server's cache. This poisoned data is later given out in response to client queries. Such data can direct clients to hosts that are running Trojan Web servers or mail servers to retrieve valuable information from users.

Another type of spoofing attack uses DNS ID prediction scheme. Each DNS packet has a 16-bit ID number associated with it, which a DNS server uses to determine what the original query was. A malicious hacker attacks DNS server called FOO by placing a recursive query, which in turn makes FOO perform queries on a remote DNS server bar whose information is going to be spoofed. By performing a Denial of Service (DoS) attack on FOO to make it less responsive and predicting the DNS ID sequence the hacker can place query responses to FOO before BAR can actually respond. This type of attack is harder to do but not impossible because the ID space is only 16 bit and DoS attack tools are common hacker-ware these days.

How can you protect your DNS server from spoofing attacks? Well, the first fix is to ensure that you run the latest release version of DNS server software and also to keep your DNS configuration secure and correct.

Running the latest stable version of the DNS server is as simple as getting the source or binary distribution of the software from the server vendor and installing it. Most people run the Berkeley Internet Name Domain (BIND) server. The latest version of BIND can be found at www.isc.org/products/BIND. Keeping your DNS configuration correct and secure is the challenge.

The next section gives you a look at a tool that will help you in keeping your DNS configuration correct.

Checking DNS Configuring Using Dlint

Poorly configured DNS servers can be great security risks because they can be exploited easily. You can use a free tool called Dlint to analyze any DNS zone and produce reports on many common configuration problems listed below:

- Hostnames that have A records must also have PTR records. DNS configurations that have A records but no corresponding PTR records cannot be verified by servers that wish to perform reverse DNS lookup on a host. Dlint will check for missing PTR record for any A record found in your in configuration.

- For each PTR record in the in-addr.arpa zone there should an equivalent A record. Missing A records for PTR records are reported.

- Dlint will recursively traverse subdomains (subzones) and look for configuration problems in them as well.

- Common typos or misplaced comments can create incorrect configuration; Dlint tries to catch such errors.

Now let's look at how you can install Dlint on your system.

Getting Dlint

You can download Dlint from www.domtools.com/dns/dlint.shtml. As of this writing the latest version of Dlint is 1.3.2. You can also use an online version of Dlint at www.domtools.com/cgi-bin/dlint/ nph-dlint.cgi. However, the online version has time restrictions so it is only recommended for trying out the tool. I highly recommend that you try it online and download the source code to install it on your system.

Installing Dlint

Dlint requires dig and Perl 5. dig is a DNS query utility found in the BIND distribution. Most likely you already have it installed. Run the dig localhost any command to see if you have dig on your system. If not, you can get dig from www.isc.org/bind.html. I will assume that you have both dig and Perl 5 installed on your Linux system.

To install Dlint, do the following:

1. As root, extract the Dlint source package using in a suitable directory. I extracted the `dlint1.4.0.tar` package using the `tar xvf`
   `dlint1.4.0.tar` command in the `/usr/src/redhat/SOURCES`
   directory. A new subdirectory is created when you extract the source
   distribution. Change to the new directory, which in my case is
   `dlint1.4.0`. Make sure that you substitute the appropriate Dlint
   version number (of the source distribution you downloaded) in all
   the instructions given here.

2. Run the `which perl` command to see where Perl interpreter is
   installed.

3. Run the `head -1 digparse` command to see the very first line of
   the `digparse` Perl script used by Dlint. If the path shown after the
   `#!` characters match the path shown by the `which perl` command,
   then you do not need to change it. If they mismatch, modify this file
   using a text editor and replace the path after `#!` with the path of
   your Perl interpreter.

4. Run the `make install` command to install Dlint, which will
   install the `dlint` and `digparse` scripts in `/usr/local/bin`.

Running Dlint

The main script in the Dlint package is called `dlint`. You can run this
script using the following command:

```
/usr/local/bin/dlint domain | in-addr.arpa-domain
```

For example, to run `dlint` for a domain called `evoknow.net`, you can
execute `/usr/local/bin/dlint    evoknow.net`. Listing 15-10 shows
an example output.

Listing 15-10 *Sample output from dlint*

```
;; run starting: Sat Dec 29 13:34:07 EST 2001
;; =============================================================
```

```
;; Now linting domain.com
;; Checking serial numbers per nameserver
;;      2001122901  ns2.domain.com.
;;      2001122901  ns1.domain.com.
;; All nameservers agree on the serial number.
;; Now caching whole zone (this could take a minute)
;; trying nameserver ns1.domain.com.
;; 3 A records found.
```

ERROR: "ns1.domain.com. A 172.20.15.1", but the PTR record for
          1.15.20.172.in-addr.arpa. is "k2.domain.com."

>   One of the above two records are wrong unless the host is a name server
>   or mail server.
>   To have 2 names for 1 address on any other hosts, replace the A record
>   with a CNAME record:
>   ns1.domain.com. IN   CNAME   k2.domain.com.

ERROR: "ns2.domain.com. A 172.20.15.1", but the PTR record for
          1.15.20.172.in-addr.arpa. is "k2.domain.com."

> One of the above two records are wrong unless the host is a name server
> or mail server.
>   To have 2 names for 1 address on any other hosts, replace the A record
>   with a CNAME record:
>   ns2.domain.com. IN   CNAME   k2.domain.com.

```
;; ============================================================
;; Now linting domain.com.
;; Checking serial numbers per nameserver
;;      2001122901  ns1.domain.com.
;;      2001122901  ns2.domain.com.
;; All nameservers agree on the serial number.
;; Now caching whole zone (this could take a minute)
```

Continued

Listing 15-10 *Continued*

```
;; trying nameserver ns1.domain.com.
;; 3 A records found.
ERROR: "ns1.domain.com. A 172.20.15.1", but the PTR record for
       1.15.20.172.in-addr.arpa. is "k2.domain.com."
       One of the above two records are wrong unless the host is a name
       server or mail server.
       To have 2 names for 1 address on any other hosts, replace the A record
       with a CNAME record:
       ns1.domain.com. IN      CNAME   k2.domain.com.


ERROR: "ns2.domain.com. A 172.20.15.1", but the PTR record for
       1.15.20.172.in-addr.arpa. is "k2.domain.com."
       One of the above two records are wrong unless the host is a name
       server or mail server.
       To have 2 names for 1 address on any other hosts, replace the A record
       with a CNAME record:
       ns2.domain.com. IN      CNAME   k2.domain.com.


;; no subzones found below domain.com., so no recursion will take place.
;; ===========================================================
;; dlint of domain.com. run ending with errors.
;; run ending: Sat  Dec 29 13:34:09 EST 2001
;; ===========================================================
;; dlint of domain.com run ending with errors.
;; run ending: Sat  Dec 29 13:34:09 EST 2001
```

As you can see, dlint is very verbose. The lines that start with a semi-colon are considered comments. All other lines are warnings or errors. Here, domain.com has a set of problems. The ns1.domain.com has an A record but the PTR record points to k2.domain.com instead of ns1. domain.com. Similarly, the ns2.domain.com host has the same problem. In other words, the domain.com configuration has the following lines:

```
ns1         IN      A       172.20.15.1
ns2         IN      A       172.20.15.1
k2          IN      A       172.20.15.1
```

It also has the following PTR record:

```
1       IN      PTR      k2.evoknow.net.
```

The `dlint` program suggests that CNAME records be used to resolve this problem. In other words, the configuration should be:

```
ns1             IN      A       172.20.15.1
ns2             IN      CNAME   ns1
k2              IN      CNAME   ns1
```

The PTR record should be:

```
1       IN      PTR      ns1.evoknow.net.
```

After fixing the errors in the appropriate configuration DNS files for domain.com, the following output is produced by the `/usr/local/bin/ dlint domain.com` command.

```
;; run starting: Fri Dec 29 13:38:00 EST 2000
;; ===========================================================
;; Now linting domain.com
;; Checking serial numbers per nameserver
;;      2001122901  ns2.domain.com.
;;      2001122901  ns1.domain.com.
;; All nameservers agree on the serial number.
;; Now caching whole zone (this could take a minute)
;; trying nameserver ns1.domain.com.
;; 1 A records found.
;; ===========================================================
;; Now linting domain.com.
;; Checking serial numbers per nameserver
;;      2001122901  ns1.domain.com.
;;      2001122901  ns2.domain.com.
;; All nameservers agree on the serial number.
;; Now caching whole zone (this could take a minute)
;; trying nameserver ns1.domain.com.
;; 1 A records found.
;; no subzones found below domain.com., so no recursion will take place.
;; ===========================================================
```

```
;; dlint of domain.com. run ending normally.
;; run ending: Fri Dec 29 13:38:01 EST 2000
;; ===========================================================
;; dlint of domain.com run ending normally.
;; run ending: Fri Dec 29 13:38:01 EST 2000
```

As you can see in the preceding, no error messages were reported. Of course, dlint can't catch all errors in your configuration, but it is a great tool to perform a level of quality control when you create, update, or remove DNS configuration information.

Securing BIND

BIND 9.*x* has been written by a large team of professional software developers to support the next generation of DNS protocol evolution. The new BIND supports back-end databases, authorization and transactional security features, SNMP-based management, IPv6 capability, etc. The code base of the new BIND has been audited and written in a manner that supports frequent audits by anyone who is interested.

The new BIND now supports the DNSSEC and TSIG security standards.

Using Transaction Signatures (TSIG) for zone transfers

Transaction Signature (TSIG) can be used to authenticate and verify the DNS data exchange. This means you can use TSIG to control zone transfer for domains you manage.

Typically, zone transfers happen from primary to secondary name servers. In the following named.conf segment of a primary name server, the IP addresses listed in the access control list (ACL) called dns-ip-list are only allowed to transfer the zone information for the yourdomain. com domain.

```
acl "dns-ip-list" {
    172.20.15.100;
    172.20.15.123;
        };
```

```
zone "yourdomain.com" {
  type master;
  file "mydomain.dns";
  allow-query    { any; };
  allow-update   { none; };
  allow-transfer { dns-ip-list; };
};
```

Unfortunately, malicious hackers can use IP spoofing tricks to trick a DNS server into performing a zone transfer. This potential calamity can now be avoided by using transaction signatures. Say that you want to limit the zone transfer for a domain called yourdomain.com to two secondary name servers with IP address 172.20.15.100 (ns1.yourdomain.com) and 172.20.15.123 (ns2.yourdomain.com).

You must make sure that the DNS servers involved in TSIG-based zone transfer authentication are kept time synchronized. You can create a cron job entry to synchronize each machine with a remote time server using rdate or ntp tools

The following steps show you how to use TSIG to ensure that IP spoofing tricks can't force a zone transfer between your DNS server and a hacker's DNS server.

1. Generate a shared secret key, which will be used to authenticate the zone transfer. Change directory to /var/named. Use the /usr/local/sbin/dnssec-keygen command to generate a set of public and private keys as follows:

   dnssec-keygen -a hmac-md5 -b 128 -n HOST zone-xfr-key

   The public key file is called Kzone-xfr-key.+157+08825.key and the private key file is Kzone-xfr-key.+157+08825.private. If you view the contents of the private key file you will see something similar to the following:

   Private-key-format: v1.2

   Algorithm: 157 (HMAC_MD5)

   Key: YH8Onz5x0/twQnvYPyh1qg==

The key here is the YH8Onz5x0/twQnvYPyh1qg== string. Using this string creates the following statement in the named.conf file of both ns1.yourdomain.com and ns2.yourdomain.com systems.

```
key zone-xfr-key {

    algorithm hmac-md5;

    secret "YH8Onz5x0/twQnvYPyh1qg==";

};
```

Don't forget to use the key string found in the file you generated. In other words, don't use the key from this example.

2. Now add the following statement in the /etc/named.conf file of the ns1.yourdomain.com server

```
server 172.20.15.123 {

    keys { zone-xfr-key; };

};
```

3. Similarly, add the following statement in the /etc/named.conf file of the ns2.yourdomain.com server.

```
server 172.20.15.100 {

    keys { zone-xfr-key; };

};
```

The full /etc/named.conf configuration segment of the yourdomain.com zone for the primary DNS server ns1.yourdomain.com is shown in Listing 15-11.

Listing 15-11 *An example configuration for a primary DNS server*

```
acl "dns-ip-list" {
    172.20.15.100;
    172.20.15.123;
        };
```

```
key zone-xfr-key {
  algorithm hmac-md5;
  secret "YH8Onz5x0/twQnvYPyh1qg==";
};


server 172.20.15.123 {
   keys { zone-xfr-key; };
};


zone "yourdomain.com" {
  type master;
  file "mydomain.dns";
  allow-query    { any; };
  allow-update   { none; };
  allow-transfer { dns-ip-list; };
};
```

The full /etc/named.conf configuration segment of the yourdomain.com zone for the secondary DNS server ns1. yourdomain.com is shown in Listing 15-12.

Listing 15-12 *An example configuration for a secondary DNS server*

```
acl "dns-ip-list" {
   172.20.15.100;
   172.20.15.123;
        };


key zone-xfr-key {
  algorithm hmac-md5;
  secret "YH8Onz5x0/twQnvYPyh1qg==";
};


server 172.20.15.100 {
   keys { zone-xfr-key; };
};
```

Continued

Listing 15-12 *Continued*

```
zone "yourdomain.com" {
  type master;
  file "mydomain.dns";
  allow-query    { any; };
  allow-update   { none; };
  allow-transfer { dns-ip-list; };
};
```

4. Restart named on both systems.

That's all there is to ensuring that zone transfers between the given hosts will now be taking place in a secure manner. To test that shared TSIG key is being used for zone transfer authentication, you can do the following:

1. Delete the yourdomain.com domain's zone file on the secondary DNS server (ns2.yourdomain.com).

2. Restart the secondary name server.

   The secondary DNS server should transfer the missing zone file from the primary DNS server. You should see the zone file created in the appropriate directory. If for some reason this file is not created, look at the /var/log/messages for errors; fix the errors and redo this verification process.

Note that if you change the shared TSIG key in any of the two hosts by a single character, the zone transfer will not be possible. You will get an error message in /var/log/messages that states that TSIG verification failed due to a bad key. Also note that because the named.conf file on both machines now has a secret key, you should ensure that the file is not readable by ordinary users.

TIP

If you wish to allow dynamic updates of DNS configuration if the request is signed using a TSIG key, then you can use the allow-update { key *keyname*; }; statement. For example, allow-update { key zone-xfr-key; }; statement in this example will allow dynamic updates between the hosts discussed here. For example, assuming that the public and the private key files for key named `zone-xfr-key` is in `/var/named/keys` directory, you can run `/usr/local/bin/nsupdate -k /var/named/keys:zone-xfr-key` to update DNS zone information for the `yourdomain.com` domain.

Running BIND as a non-root user

On a Linux kernel greater than 2.3.99, you can run BIND as a non-root user using the -u option. For example, the `/usr/local/sbin/named -u` nobody command starts BIND as the nobody user.

Hiding BIND version number

Because software bugs are associated with a certain version of the software, the version information becomes a valuable piece of information for malicious hackers. By finding out what version of BIND you run, he can figure out what exploits (if any) are out there for it and try to break in. For example:

```
dig @nameserver  bind.version TXT chaos
```

This command tries to reveal the BIND version number for the named DNS server. It is a good idea to not give version number willingly. You can simply override the version information given out by BIND by adding the `version` statement in the `options` section. For example, the following configuration segment tells `named` to display "Unsupported on this platform" when version information is requested:

```
options {
    # other global options go here
    version "Unsupported on this platform";
};
```

TIP Like the version number, you should not want to give out your host's information either. In the spirit of making a potential attacker's job harder, I recommend that you do not use HINFO or TXT resource records in your DNS configuration files.

Limiting queries

Most DNS servers on the Internet can be used by anyone to perform a query. This is absolutely not acceptable for a secure environment. A DNS spoof attack usually relies on this fact: that an attacker can ask your DNS server to resolve a query for which it (your server) cannot produce an authoritative answer. In other words, a typical spoofing technique is to ask your server to resolve a query for which your server might end up getting data from the hacker's own DNS server. For example, say that a hacker runs a DNS server for the `id10t.com` domain and your DNS server is authoritative for the `yourdomain.com` domain. Now, if you allow anyone to query your server for anything, the hacker can ask your server to resolve `gotcha.id10t.com`. Your DNS server ends up getting data from the hacker's machine, which is when the hacker plays his spoofing tricks to poison your DNS cache.

Now say that your network address is 168.192.1.0. To make sure that no one outside your network is allowed to query your DNS server for anything but the domains it manages, you need the following statement:

```
options {
  allow-query { 168.192.1.0/24; };
};
```

The `allow-query` directive ensures that all the hosts in 168.192.1.0 network can query the DNS server. Now if your DNS server is authoritative for the `yourdomain.com` zone, you can have the following /etc/named.conf segment:

```
options {
  allow-query { 168.192.1.0/24; };
};

zone "yourdomain.com" {
        type master;
        file "yourdomain.com";
        allow-query { any; };
};
```

```
zone "1.168.192.in-addr.arpa" {
        type master;
        file "db.192.168.1";
        allow-query { any; };
};
```

This ensures that anyone from anywhere can query the DNS server for yourdomain.com, but only the users in the 168.192.1.0 network can query the DNS server for anything.

Also, you should not allow anyone outside your network to perform recursive queries at all. To disable recursive queries for everyone but your network add the following in your global options section:

```
allow-recursion { 192.168.1.0/24; };
```

You can also disable recursion completely for everyone using the following option in the global options section.

```
recursion no;
```

 You can't disable recursion on a name server if other name servers use it as a forwarder.

Ideally, you should set up your authoritative name server(s) to perform no recursion. Only the name server(s) responsible for resolving DNS queries for your internal network should perform recursion. This type of setup is known as a *split DNS configuration*.

For example, say that you have two name servers—ns1.yourdomain. com (primary) and ns2.yourdomain.com (secondary)—that are responsible for a single domain called yourdomain.com. At the same time you have a DNS server called ns3.yourdomain.com, which is responsible for resolving DNS queries for your 192.168.1.0 network. In a split DNS configuration, you can set up both ns1 and ns2 servers to use no recursion for any domain other than the yourdomain.com and allow recursion on ns3 by using the allow-recursion statement discussed earlier.

Turning off glue fetching

When a DNS server returns a name server record (NS) for a domain and does not have an A record for the NS record, it attempts to retrieve one. This is called *glue fetching*, which can be abused by spoofing attackers. Turning off glue fetching is as simple as adding the following statement in the global options section of /etc/named.conf.

```
options no-fetch-glue
```

Chrooting the DNS server

The 9.*x* versions of BIND make it very easy to create a chroot jail for the DNS server. Here is how you can create a chroot jail for BIND.

1. As root, create a new user called dns by running the useradd dns -d /home/dns command.

2. Run the mkdir -p /home/dns/var/log /home/dns/var/run /home/dns/var/named /home/dns/etc command to create all the necessary directories.

3. Copy the /etc/named.conf file by running the cp /etc/named. conf /home/dns/etc/ command.

4. Copy everything from /var/named to /home/dns/var/named using the cp -r /var/named/* /home/dns/var/named/ command.

5. Run the chown -R dns:dns /home/dns command to make sure all the files and directories needed by named are owned by the dns user and its private group called dns. Note that if you plan on running named as root, use root:root instead of dns:dns as the username:groupname in this command.

6. Now run the name server by executing the /usr/local/sbin/ named -t /home/dns -u dns command.

If you plan on running named as root, do not specify the -u dns option.

Using DNSSEC (signed zones)

The DNSSEC (short for DNS Security Extension) is a public key cryptography-based authentication model, which introduced two new resource record types — KEY and SIG — to allow resolves and name servers to cryptographically authenticate the source of any DNS data. In other words, a DNS client can now prove that the response it received from a DNS server is authentic. Unfortunately, until DNSSEC use becomes widespread, its benefit cannot be realized. Here I will show you how you can create the necessary DNSSEC configuration for a domain called domain.com.

1. First, you must create a pair of public and private keys for the domain.com domain. From the /var/named directory, run the /usr/local/sbin/dnssec-keygen -a DSA -b 768 -n ZONE domain.com command. This command creates a 768-bit DSA-based private and public key pair: a public key file called Kdomain.com.+003+29462.key and a private key file called Kdomain.com.+003+29462.private. Note that the 29462 number is called a *key tag* and will vary. You should insert the public key in the zone file (domain.com.db) by inserting a line in the beginning of the file:

   $INCLUDE /var/named/Kdomain.com.+003+29462.key

2. The next step is to create a key set using the /usr/local/sbin/dnssec-makekeyset -t 3600 -e now+30 Kdomain.com.+003+29462 command. This command creates a key set whose Time To Live (*TTL*) value is 3600 seconds (i.e., 1 hour) and the set expires 30 days from now. This command creates a file called domain.com.keyset.

3. Next, sign the keyset using the /usr/local/sbin/dnssec-signkey domain.com.keyset Kdomain.com.+003+29462 command. This command creates a signed key file called domain.com.signedkey.

4. After the keyset is signed, you need to sign the zone file using the /usr/local/sbin/dnssec-signzone -o domain.com domain.db command, where domain.db is the name of the zone file in /var/named directory. This command creates a signed zone file called domain.db.signed.

5. Finally, you need to replace the zone file name for domain.com in the /etc/named.conf file. For example, the /etc/named.conf configuration segment below shows the zone declaration for domain.com:

```
zone "domain.com" IN {
        type master;
        file "domain.db.signed";
        allow-update { none; };
};
```

Chapter 16

Sharing Files and Printers with Windows

IN THIS CHAPTER

- Installing Samba from an RPM package
- Configuring Samba
- Managing Samba with a Web-based tool
- Serving files to your Windows users
- Accessing Windows files on Linux
- Securing your Samba server

A Samba server allows you to make your Linux disk space and printer available to Windows system over your network. Similarly, it allows you to access Windows disks and printers from Linux. The typical use of Samba is to make Linux disk space available to Windows users or other SMB-compliant (SMB is the protocol that Samba uses) systems. In this chapter you will learn how to install, configure, and secure Samba server on your Red Hat Linux system.

Installing Samba

If you choose the MS-DOS/Windows-compatibility option during Red Hat Linux installation, the Samba RPM packages were automatically installed. However, if you did not install Samba packages during installation, you can always install them by using the rpm command. For example, to install the Samba client/server package for an *x*86 Red Hat Linux system, I ran the following command from the `/RedHat/RPMS` directory of the official Red Hat CD-ROM:

```
rpm -ivh samba*.i386.rpm
```

When using this command to install the Samba package, do not forget to replace `samba-version.i386.rpm` with a real package filename.

Configuring Samba

When you install the Samba RPM package, it installs a configuration file called `smb.conf` in your `/etc/samba` directory. Listing 16-1 shows the default `/etc/samba/smb.conf` with some minor formatting changes.

Listing 16-1 *The default /etc/samba/smb.conf file*

```
/etc/samba/smb.conf

# This is the main Samba configuration file.

# You should read the smb.conf(5) manual page in

# order to understand the options listed

# here. Samba has a huge number of configurable

# options (perhaps too

# many!) most of which are not shown in this example

#

# Any line which starts with a ; (semi-colon) or a

# (hash) is a comment and is ignored. In this example

# we will use a for commentary and a;

# for parts of the config file that you

# may wish to enable

#

# NOTE: Whenever you modify this file you should

# run the command "testparm" to check that you

# have not many basic syntactic errors.

#

#======Global Settings ========================

[global]
```

```
# workgroup = NT-Domain-Name or Workgroup-Name
  workgroup = MYGROUP


# server string is the equivalent of the NT
# Description field
  server string = Samba Server


# This option is important for security.
# It allows you to restrict connections to machines
# which are on your local network. The following
# example restricts access to two C class networks and
# the "loopback" interface. For more examples of
# the syntax see
# the smb.conf man page
;   hosts allow = 192.168.1. 192.168.2. 127.


# if you want to automatically load your printer list rather
# than setting them up individually then you'll need this
  printcap name = /etc/printcap
  load printers = yes


# It should not be necessary to spell out the print system type unless
# yours is non-standard. Currently supported print systems include:
# bsd, sysv, plp, lprng, aix, hpux, qnx
  printing = lprng


# Uncomment this if you want a guest account, you must add this to /etc/passwd
# otherwise the user "nobody" is used
;   guest account = pcguest


# this tells Samba to use a separate log file for each machine
# that connects
  log file = /var/log/samba/%m.log
```

Continued

Listing 16-1 *Continued*

```
# Put a capping on the size of the log files (in Kb).
  max log size = 0


# Security mode. Most people will want user level security. See
# security_level.txt for details.
  security = user
# Use password server option only with security = server or
# security = domain
;   password server = <NT-Server-Name>


# Password Level allows matching of _n_ characters of the password for
# all combinations of upper and lower case.
;   password level = 8
;   username level = 8


# The following is needed to keep smbclient from
# spouting spurious errors when Samba is built with
# support for SSL.
ssl CA certFile = /usr/share/ssl/certs/ca-bundle.crt


# You may wish to use password encryption. Please read
# ENCRYPTION.txt, Win95.txt and WinNT.txt in the Samba documentation.
# Do not enable this option unless you have read those documents
;   encrypt passwords = yes
;   smb passwd file = /etc/samba/smbpasswd


# The following are needed to allow password changing from Windows to
# update the Linux system password also.
# NOTE: Use these with 'encrypt passwords' and 'smb passwd file' above.
# NOTE2: You do NOT need these to allow workstations to change only
#        the encrypted SMB passwords. They allow the Unix password
#        to be kept in sync with the SMB password.
;   unix password sync = Yes
;   passwd program = /usr/bin/passwd %u
```

```
;  passwd chat = *New*UNIX*password* %n\n *ReType*new*UNIX*password* %n\n
*passwd:*all*authentication*tokens*updated*successfully*


# Unix users can map to different SMB User names
;  username map = /etc/samba/smbusers


# Using the following line enables you to customize your configuration
# on a per machine basis. The %m gets replaced with the netbios name
# of the machine that is connecting
;   include = /etc/samba/smb.conf.%m


# Most people will find that this option gives better performance.
# See speed.txt and the manual pages for details
    socket options = TCP_NODELAY SO_RCVBUF=8192 SO_SNDBUF=8192


# Configure Samba to use multiple interfaces
# If you have multiple network interfaces then you must list them
# here. See the man page for details.
;   interfaces = 192.168.12.2/24 192.168.13.2/24


# Configure remote browse list synchronization here
# request announcement to, or browse list sync from:
# a specific host or from / to a whole subnet (see below)
;   remote browse sync = 192.168.3.25 192.168.5.255
# Cause this host to announce itself to local subnets here
;   remote announce = 192.168.1.255 192.168.2.44


# Browser Control Options:
# set local master to no if you don't want Samba to become a master
# browser on your network. Otherwise the normal election rules apply
;   local master = no


# OS Level determines the precedence of this server in master browser
# elections. The default value should be reasonable
;   os level = 33
```

Continued

Listing 16-1 *Continued*

```
# Domain Master specifies Samba to be the Domain Master Browser. This
# allows Samba to collate browse lists between subnets. Don't use this
# if you already have a Windows NT domain controller doing this job
;   domain master = yes


# Preferred Master causes Samba to force a local browser election on startup
# and gives it a slightly higher chance of winning the election
;   preferred master = yes


# Enable this if you want Samba to be a domain logon server for
# Windows95 workstations.
;   domain logons = yes


# if you enable domain logons then you may want a per-machine or
# per user logon script
# run a specific logon batch file per workstation (machine)
;   logon script = %m.bat
# run a specific logon batch file per username
;   logon script = %U.bat


# All NetBIOS names must be resolved to IP Addresses
# 'Name Resolve Order' allows the named resolution mechanism to be specified
# the default order is "host lmhosts wins bcast". "host" means use the unix
# system gethostbyname() function call that will use either /etc/hosts OR
# DNS or NIS depending on the settings of /etc/host.config, /etc/nsswitch.conf
# and the /etc/resolv.conf file. "host" therefore is system configuration
# dependent. This parameter is most often used to prevent DNS lookups
# in order to resolve NetBIOS names to IP Addresses. Use with care!
# The example below excludes use of name resolution for machines that are NOT
# on the local network segment
# - OR - are not deliberately to be known via lmhosts or via WINS.
; name resolve order = wins lmhosts bcast


# Windows Internet Name Serving Support Section:
# WINS Support - Tells the NMBD component of Samba to enable its WINS Server
```

```
;   wins support = yes


# WINS Server - Tells the NMBD components of Samba to be a WINS Client
#          Note: Samba can be either a WINS Server, or a WINS Client, but NOT
both
;   wins server = w.x.y.z


# WINS Proxy - Tells Samba to answer name resolution queries on
# behalf of a non WINS capable client, for this to work there must be
# at least one     WINS Server on the network. The default is NO.
;   wins proxy = yes


# DNS Proxy - tells Samba whether or not to try to resolve NetBIOS names
# via DNS nslookups. The built-in default for versions 1.9.17 is yes,
# this has been changed in version 1.9.18 to no.
   dns proxy = no


# Case Preservation can be handy - system default is _no_
# NOTE: These can be set on a per share basis
;   preserve case = no
;   short preserve case = no
# Default case is normally upper case for all DOS files
;   default case = lower
# Be very careful with case sensitivity - it can break things!
;   case sensitive = no


#=========================== Share Definitions ===========================
[homes]
   comment = Home Directories
   browseable = no
   writable = yes


# Un-comment the following and create the netlogon directory for Domain Logons
; [netlogon]
;    comment = Network Logon Service
```

Continued

Listing 16-1 *Continued*

```
;    path = /home/netlogon
;    guest ok = yes
;    writable = no
;    share modes = no


# Un-comment the following to provide a specific profile share
# the default is to use the user's home directory
;[Profiles]
;    path = /home/profiles
;    browseable = no
;    guest ok = yes


# NOTE: If you have a BSD-style print system there is no need to
# specifically define each individual printer
[printers]
   comment = All Printers
   path = /var/spool/samba
   browseable = no
# Set public = yes to allow user 'guest account' to print
   guest ok = no
   printable = yes


# This one is useful for people to share files
;[tmp]
;    comment = Temporary file space
;    path = /tmp
;    read only = no
;    public = yes


# A publicly accessible directory, but read only, except for people in
# the "staff" group
;[public]
;    comment = Public Stuff
;    path = /home/samba
```

```
;    public = yes
;    writable = yes
;    printable = no
;    write list = @staff

# Other examples.
#
# A private printer, usable only by fred. Spool data will be placed in fred's
# home directory. Note that fred must have write access to the spool directory,
# wherever it is.
;[fredsprn]
;    comment = Fred's Printer
;    valid users = fred
;    path = /homes/fred
;    printer = freds_printer
;    public = no
;    printable = yes

# A private directory, usable only by fred. Note that fred requires write
# access to the directory.
;[fredsdir]
;    comment = Fred's Service
;    path = /usr/somewhere/private
;    valid users = fred
;    public = no
;    writable = yes
;    printable = no

# a service which has a different directory for each machine that connects
# this allows you to tailor configurations to incoming machines. You could
# also use the %u option to tailor it by user name.
# The %m gets replaced with the machine name that is connecting.
;[pchome]
;    comment = PC Directories
;    path = /usr/pc/%m
```

Continued

Listing 16-1 *Continued*

```
;  public = no

;  writable = yes


# A publicly accessible directory, read/write to all users. Note that all files
# created in the directory by users will be owned by the default user, so
# any user with access can delete any other user's files. Obviously this
# directory must be writable by the default user. Another user could of course
# be specified, in which case all files would be owned by that user instead.
;[public]
;    path = /usr/somewhere/else/public
;    public = yes
;    only guest = yes
;    writable = yes
;    printable = no


# The following two entries demonstrate how to share a directory so that two
# users can place files there that will be owned by the specific users. In this
# setup, the directory should be writable by both users and should have the
# sticky bit set on it to prevent abuse. Obviously this could be extended to
# as many users as required.
;[myshare]
;    comment = Mary's and Fred's stuff
;    path = /usr/somewhere/shared
;    valid users = mary fred
;    public = no
;    writable = yes
;    printable = no
;    create mask = 0765
```

If you remove all the comment lines from the default /etc/samba/ smb.conf file, only three special configuration sections are defined in the file. They are discussed next.

Setting the [global] parameters

The [global] section defines Samba parameters that apply to all other configuration sections (that is, services that they define). The default [global] configuration is as follows:

```
[global]
   workgroup = MYGROUP
   server string = Samba Server
   printcap name = /etc/printcap
   load printers = yes
   printing = lprng
   log file = /var/log/samba/%m.log
   max log size = 0
   security = user
   socket options = TCP_NODELAY  \
                    SO_RCVBUF=8192 \
                    SO_SNDBUF=8192
   dns proxy = no
```

The following sections show you how to configure each of these parameters.

workgroup

Set this parameter to the Windows workgroup or Windows NT/2000 domain name that you want Samba to participate in as a node. For example, I use EVOKNOW as the Windows NT/2000 domain name so that I can set workgroup to EVOKNOW. When a Windows 9x or Windows NT/2000 system on my network browses the Network Neighborhood, it sees the Samba server under the EVOKNOW Windows NT/2000 domain. Set this to whatever workgroup or domain name is appropriate for your LAN.

server string

Set this parameter to provide a description for your Samba server. This description will be visible to Samba clients (such as a Windows 9x machine).

printcap name

Use this parameter to set the `printcap` file path. The default value of `/etc/printcap` should work for you. The `/etc/printcap` file is used to describe your printer's capabilities. If you have one or more printers attached to your Linux server and you want to make all of your printers available to the Windows systems on your LAN, set this parameter along with the load printers parameter.

load printers

Use this parameter to tell Samba to automatically make local printers available to any SMB client computer on the network. Set this to `yes` if you want to enable this feature; set it to no if you prefer to specify printer configurations in individual configuration sections.

printing

The `printing` parameter is used to set the `print` command. The default value of `lprng` tells Samba to use the `lpr` command.

log file

Use this parameter to set the filename of the Samba log file. The default setting writes a log file per client. This is done using the `%m` macro, which expands to the client name. For example, if you keep the log file setting as is and access the Samba server from a Windows machine called `r2d2`, a log file called `/var/log/samba/ r2d2.log` is created.

max log size

Use this parameter to control the maximum log file size, in kilobytes.

security

The `security` parameter is the most important of all the global parameters. Use it to tell Samba how to perform client authentication. The following are the four possible values for security, along with a description of what the Samba server does when security is set to each:

- **user.** The Samba server tells the client to supply a username/ password pair for authentication. If you use the same username/ password pairs on your Windows systems and Linux systems, set the security parameter to user. For example, if you have a user called joe on a Windows NT/2000 Server and have the same user on the Samba server with the same password, set this parameter to user.

- **share.** The Samba server expects a password with each request for a service. No usernames are required. Use this setting if your Windows systems and the Linux Samba server do not have the same set of username/password pairs.

- **server.** The Samba server tells the client to supply a username/ password pair, just like when you set this parameter to user, but the Samba server does not verify the username/password pair itself. It uses another SMB server to authenticate the user. For this reason, when you set security to server, you must also set the password server parameter, which is used to name a SMB server that will be responsible for authentication. If you want to centralize your usernames/ passwords for SMB activity on a Windows NT/2000 server, set the password server parameter to point to the Windows NT/2000 server.

If you use a Windows NT/2000 as your password server to do all the authentication for Samba, make sure that you do not have the guest account on the Windows NT/2000 system enabled. If the guest account is enabled, any time that a username/password pair fails because of an incorrect password, Windows NT/2000 will still provide a valid response to the Samba server, because Windows NT/2000 will simply assign guest privileges to the failed authentication attempt and return a success response to the Samba server.

- **Domain.** The Samba server uses the domain controller to authenticate users. Passwords must be transmitted in encrypted format and therefore encrypted passwords option needs to be set to **yes**.

The default setting for `security` is `user`, which means that a client has to supply a plain-text password along with a username. The Samba server verifies this username/password pair by using the `/etc/password` file. However, the later versions of Windows 9x and Windows NT/2000 don't use plain-text (also known as clear-text) passwords, by default. Microsoft decided to use encrypted passwords as part of upgrades to its OS service packs. Because these Windows clients do not supply plain-text passwords, they can't be verified; therefore, the Samba server refuses to service them. To remedy this problem, you have two options:

- Enable plain-text passwords on Windows systems. This option is acceptable if any of the following conditions are true:

  - You already allow plain-text-based services, such as FTP and Telnet, between your Windows machine and a Red Hat Linux server.

  - Your network is not connected to the Internet, so use of plain-text passwords does not pose a great threat to your organization.

  - You just want to get Samba working first and then either deal with encrypted passwords or plan on delegating all authentication tasks to a Windows NT/2000 system in the long run.

- Use encrypted passwords for authentication.

You probably will choose the first option, so it is described next. The details of using encrypted passwords for authentication are provided in the last section of this chapter.

If you are using Windows 98, Windows 95 with Service Pack 3 or later, or Windows NT with Service Pack 3 or later, follow these steps to enable plain-text passwords:

1. Run the Windows Registry editor program called RegEdit by clicking the Start button, choosing Run, entering **regedit** in the command field, and clicking OK.

2. For Windows 9x, locate the following Registry key:

```
/HKEY_LOCAL_MACHINE
    /System
        /CurrentControlSet
```

```
/Services
    /VxD
        /VNETSUP
```

For Windows NT/2000 with Service Pack 3 or later, locate the following Registry key:

```
/HKEY_LOCAL_MACHINE
    /SYSTEM
        /CurrentControlSet
            /Services
                /Rdr
                    /Parameters
```

3. After you locate the VNETSUP branch (for Windows 9x) or the Parameters branch (for Windows NT/2000) in the Registry tree, select Edit ⇨ New and choose to create a new DWORD value.

4. RegEdit will insert a new DWORD value called New Value #1 in the Registry. Rename this new value EnablePlainTextPassword and double-click this new name.

5. A dialog box pops up, enabling you to set a value for the EnablePlainTextPassword you just created. Enter 1 as the value and close RegEdit as usual.

6. Reboot your Windows system.

This ensures that your Windows system is able to use plain-text passwords for SMB authentication.

socket options

By default, the socket options parameter in the global configuration section is set to TCP_NODELAY SO_RCVBUF=8192 SO_SNDBUF=8192, which enhances Samba performance on certain platforms. Leave this parameter as is.

dns proxy

This parameter affects how the Samba suite's built-in Windows Internet Name Server (nmbd) behaves when a Windows system name (NetBIOS name) cannot be resolved to an IP address. If you set this parameter to yes, the nmbd server treats the NetBIOS name as an Internet domain name and tries to resolve it by using the DNS protocol. Keep the default setting.

Setting the [homes] parameters

The [homes] section is a special configuration section that allows you to set up home directory access from Windows systems. In other words, a user with a valid username/password on the Red Hat system can access her home directory on the Linux system from a Windows system. The default [homes] configuration is as follows:

```
[homes]
    comment = Home Directories
    browseable = no
    writable = yes
```

Here is how you can change these parameters:

- **comment.** Exactly what its name suggests. Set this to whatever you wish.

- **browseable.** Controls whether or not home directories are visible in a browser list (such as the Network Neighborhood) or when the NET VIEW command is used from the Windows command prompt. Set this to yes or no depending on your needs.

- **writable.** Controls whether or not a user can write to his or her own home directory. For most practical purposes, this should be set to yes. If you set this to no, a user will have only read-only access to her own home directory.

Setting the [printers] parameters

The [printers] section is of interest only if you have one or more printers attached to your Red Hat Linux system. The default [printers] configuration is as follows:

```
[printers]
    comment = All Printers
    path = /var/spool/samba
```

```
browseable = no
guest ok = no
printable = yes
```

Here is how you can change these parameters:

- **comment.** Exactly what its name suggests. Set this to whatever you wish.

- **path.** Set this to the directory where printer data files will be spooled. If you have a lot of users who print large files, make sure you have plenty of disk space for this directory.

- **browseable.** By default, printers are not visible in a browser (such as Network Neighborhood) or NET VIEW command output. To change this behavior, set this to **yes.**

- **guest ok.** By default, printer services are not available to guest users who do not have passwords. To change this behavior, set this to **yes.**

- **printable.** By default, this parameter permits printing. If this is set to no, printing is completely disabled.

The default configuration includes many commented configuration parameters and additional sections. Carefully investigate these options and enable anything that you want to use. However, if you are using Samba for the first time, first get it working using the default configuration.

Managing Samba via the Web

Using the new Web-based configuration tool, SWAT, shipped with Samba, you can manage Samba using a standard Web browser. Here is how you can use SWAT.

1. Verify that your /etc/services file has the following line:

   ```
   swat                901/tcp
   ```

   If the above line is not present, add this line and save the /etc/services file.

2. Verify that your /etc/xinetd.d/swat file has the following line:

   ```
   disable = no
   ```

If the above line is missing, commented out, or set to yes, add or uncomment it such that disable is set to no. In such a case, reconfigure the xinetd daemon using the killall -USR1 xinetd command.

3. Next, run your favorite Web browser to access your Samba server. Enter the following URL:

    http://your-samba-server:901/

4. You will be asked to enter a username and password. Enter root as the username and the password. If you have entered an appropriate username/password pair, you'll see the SWAT welcome screen.

5. Click on the available links to manage various aspects of Samba.

Testing the /etc/samba/smb.conf configuration

Any time you change a Samba configuration file, run the testparm utility, which is bundled with the Samba package. When you run this nifty utility from the command line, it checks the syntax of the /etc/samba/smb.conf file and gives you useful warning and error messages. Because a misconfigured /etc/samba/smb.conf file can be a security hole, use this utility whenever you modify this file.

Starting, stopping, and restarting the Samba service

After you make sure that your /etc/samba/smb.conf file is error-free, you are ready to start Samba. Two daemons come with the Samba package. The smbd daemon is the Samba server, and the nmbd daemon is the NetBIOS name server. To start the daemons, run the following command as root:

/etc/rc.d/init.d/smb start

You can then start accessing the Samba server from your Windows computers. To stop the Samba server, run the same command with a stop argument. You can also restart the daemons by using the same command with a restart argument.

If you want to start the Samba service at boot time, create a symbolic link as follows:

```
ln -s /etc/rc.d/init.d/smb   /etc/rc.d/rc3.d/S91smb
```

This starts the Samba service when your Red Hat Linux server enters run level 3, which is the default run level for all multiuser systems.

If you use an X Window System–based login (using XDM) and want to start Samba automatically, create the following link:

```
ln -s /etc/rc.d/init.d/smb   /etc/rc.d/rc5.d/S91smb
```

Using a Linux File Server on Windows

Using a Linux file server on Windows probably is the most common reason why a Linux administrator in a Linux/Windows shop may consider using Samba. For example, suppose you want to make a Linux partition (or directory) called intranet available to a group of Windows users (john, jennifer, and chad) on your LAN. Here is what you do:

1. If you set the security parameter in the [global] configuration section to user or share, create three user accounts (john, jennifer, and chad) on your Linux system. These user accounts need to be set up so that the password for each account matches its Windows counterpart. For example, if jennifer's password on her Windows system is set to tsk#tsk, then you must set her Linux account with the same password. Also, create a group called intranet in /etc/group that includes users john, jennifer, and chad as the only members.

2. Modify the /etc/samba/smb.conf file to add the following:

```
[Intranet]
    comment = Intranet Directory
    path = /intranet
    public = no
    writable = yes
    write list = @intranet
    printable = no
```

The preceding [Intranet] configuration specifies that /intranet is not publicly accessible, and write permission is given for the intranet group. After you run testparm to make sure that the /etc/samba/ smb.conf file contains no syntax errors, you can restart the Samba service.

Now you can have john, jennifer, and chad access the /intranet partition or directory from their Windows machines. If you want to create a read-only file server, set the writable parameter to no and remove the write list parameter from the preceding configuration. To force the file permissions in this shared partition (or directory) to remain the same, use the force create mode parameter. For example

```
force create mode 0750
```

ensures that all files created in the shared space have full access (read, write, and execute) for the owner, and read and execute access for everyone in the group. Anyone outside the group will not have any access to these files.

Using a Windows File Server on Your Linux System

If you have a Windows file server that you want to make available to your Linux users, use smbfs (SMB file system) to mount Windows disks and directories onto your Linux system. For example, to mount the default drive (c:\ drive) of a Windows NT/2000 Server called PLUTO on a Linux Samba server, do the following:

1. On the Windows NT/2000 system, double-click the My Computer icon to open the My Computer window. Select the c:\ drive icon and then right-click it. In the pop-up window that displays, select the Sharing option. This opens the Properties dialog box with the Sharing tab selected.

2. Click the Shared As radio button and select a name for the share from the drop-down Share Name list. In this example, the share name is C. Write a comment line to help identify the share when browsed from other computers.

3. Click Apply and exit the window.

You've just enabled SMB sharing for the C:\ drive. Now, simply mount this share on your Linux system. The smbfs file system comes with a command called smbmount that enables you to mount an SMB share. The common syntax is shown here:

```
smbmount //WINDOWS_SERVER/path  /mount_point  \
-o username=WindowsUser,password=WindowsUserPassword
```

//WINDOWS_SERVER is the Windows system with the share (path); /mount_point is the mount directory on the Linux system; WindowsUser is a user on the Windows system that has at least read access to the share; and WindowsUserPassword is the password for that user. If your Windows NT/2000 is set up correctly, only the Administrator user (or an equivalent user) should have full access to the entire drive. So, this example uses the Administrator user to mount the C drive. Here is an example of smbmount that mounts the C:\ drive from PLUTO:

```
smbmount //PLUTO/c /mnt/pluto-c  \
-o username=Administrator,password=gowent
```

If you get an error message when you run your version of the preceding command, make sure you have entered the proper password. Also, try the -I option to specify the IP address of the Windows NT/2000 server, just in case it does not advertise its IP address. When the command is successful, you will see /mnt/pluto-c in your df listing and will be able to access all the files from the C:\ drive of your Windows system. If you prefer to mount the C:\ drive such that only certain users and groups on the Linux system can access the drive, use the uid=UID and gid=GID options, as in the following example:

```
smbmount //PLUTO/c /mnt/pluto-c  \
-o username=Administrator,password=gowent,\
uid=root,gid=admin
```

Here, only root and anyone in group admin have access to PLUTO's C:\ drive, which is mounted on the Linux system under /mnt/pluto-c.

Also, note that you if you wish to mount a Samba file system (smbfs) automatically you can add a line such as the following in your /etc/fstab file.

```
//WINDOWS-SERVER/path  /mount_point  smbfs \
username=WinUser,password=WinUserPasswd,uid=UID,gid=GID
```

Here the *//WINDOWS_SERVER/path* is the physical file system under a Windows system, /mount-point is the mount point where the Windows file system will be mounted on, smbfs is the type of file system, the user-name and password parameters are credentials needed to access the remote Windows file system, and the uid and gid parameters are needed to tell Linux which local user and group have access to the mounted file system. For example:

```
LABEL=/          /               ext2    defaults        1 1

/dev/fd0         /mnt/floppy     auto    noauto,owner    0 0

LABEL=/usr       /usr            ext2    defaults        1 2

LABEL=/opt       /www            ext2    defaults        1 2

none             /proc           proc    defaults        0 0

none             /dev/pts        devpts  gid=5,mode=620  0 0

/dev/hda2        swap            swap    defaults        0 0

/dev/cdrom       /mnt/cdrom      iso9660 noauto,owner,kudzu,ro 0 0

//eclipse/c$     /mnt/eclipse    smbfs   \
username=winguy,password=1dI0t,uid=admin,gid=root 0 0
```

Here an example /etc/fstab is shown that allows the user to mount the C drive (c$) of a Windows system called eclipse on the /mnt/eclipse mount point. This file system can be automatically mounted when Linux boots up, or you can mount it using mount /mnt/eclipse like any other Linux file system.

To unmount or remove an SMB file system from the Linux system, run the smbumount command. For example, the following command unmounts the //PLUTO/c share from the Linux system:

```
smbumount /mnt/pluto-c
```

Sharing printers between Linux and Windows

Sharing printers is a common benefit of a LAN environment. Using Samba, you can share printers between Linux and Windows.

Sharing a Windows printer with Linux

On your Windows system attached to the printer, create an account that can use the printer and that doesn't require a password. For example, on a Windows NT/2000 workstation or server, follow these steps to create such an account:

1. Use the User Administrator program to create an account called printeruser. Do not assign any password for this user and assign the user to the regular user group only.

2. Select your printer from the My Computer folder and right-click it to open the Printer Properties window. Select the Security tab and click Permissions. If Everyone has print access, you don't need to do anything. If Everyone does not have print access, add printeruser to the list, with the privilege to print to the selected printer. After you configure the Windows NT/2000 account to print, you are ready to test it.

3. From the Linux system, use the smbclient program to connect to the printer, as follows:

```
smbclient //WINDOWS_SYSTEM/SharedPrinter -U
printeruser -N -P
```

Replace *WINDOWS-SYSTEM* with your Windows system name, and replace *SharedPrinter* with the printer name. If you have white space characters in the name you should double quote printer name. For example, if your printer's share name is HP4100 PS, use //WINDOWS_SYSTEM/"HP4100 PS". The -N and -P options are used to instruct the smbclient program to use the null password for connection.

4. At the smbclient program prompt, enter the printmode text command to set print mode to text and enter a command such as print /path/to/a/linux/textfile to print the file. If your printer prints the file, you're halfway done.

5. Configure the Linux side. The easiest way to configure an SMB-based printer is to use the X–based `printtool` utility, which comes with Red Hat Linux. Run `printtool` from an xterm and click Add. In the dialog box that appears, select the SMB/Windows 9*x*/NT Printer option. You will see a warning message about a remote SMB/Windows printer's possibly requiring a username/password. The warning window will recommend that if your remote printer requires a username/password, you should make sure the account used is not a real user account. In other words, use an unprivileged user account on your SMB/Windows server for your printer. Click OK to continue.

6. If this is your first printer, the name will be set to `lp`, which you can change to whatever you want. This name is used by print commands, such as `lpr`, to identify this printer. The spool directory should also be set to `/var/spool/lpd/lp`. If you change the printer name, make sure that you also change the spool directory path to reflect the name change. The File Limit option should be left as is, unless you are setting up the printer in an environment in which users can send large files. In such a case, use a reasonable limit, such as 2048K (2MB). The host name of the printer should be set to the Windows NT/2000 to which the printer is attached. The IP address of this host is optional. The printer name is the share name you created for the printer. The username should be the printer user (`printuser`) you created earlier. The password field should be left blank, because you have not assigned a password to this user.

7. Click Input Filter Select to modify the input filter. The Configure Filter dialog box appears. Select the printer type and printer options as appropriate. Click OK to complete the filter configuration, and click OK to add the new printer.

8. Test the printer. From the Red Hat Linux Print System Manager screen, select the newly created printer and then click the Tests menu and select a test option to test your printer. If you get output on the printer, your configuration is working. However, if your output is pretty much garbage, go back to the Input Filter configuration dialog box and make changes to get better or more appropriate output.

If you successfully test-printed in the last step, you are done with the printer configuration and can use the printer from your Linux applications. For example, to use the printer to print a text file from the command line, use the lpr command as follows:

```
lpr -Pprintername /path/to/file
```

If the printer name is lp and you want to print the /etc/samba/ smb.conf file, use the following command:

```
lpr -Plp /etc/samba/smb.conf
```

Use the lpq command to see the print queue, and use the lprm command to remove print jobs from the queue. Note that when the file being printed is transferred to the Windows print spooler, its status is no longer available to you.

Sharing a Linux printer with Windows

To share a Linux printer with Windows, modify your /etc/samba/ smb.conf file as follows:

1. In the [global] configuration section, set the following:

    ```
    printcap name = /etc/printcap
    load printers = yes
    ```

2. In your [printers] configuration section, set the following:

    ```
    comments = All Printers
    path = /var/spool/lpd
    writable = no
    printable = yes
    browseable = no
    guest ok = no
    ```

If you want the printer list to appear in the browser list, set the browseable parameter to yes in the preceding configuration. Similarly, if you want to allow the guest account to use the printer, set guest ok to yes in the [printers] configuration.

That's all that is required to set up all of your printers. However, if you prefer to make one or more printers privately available to one or more users, you can specify a separate section for each of these users. For example, if I want to create private printer (`fancyjet`) access for a user called `bigboss`, I can create a configuration such as the following:

```
[fancyjet]
comment = Big Boss Only Printer
valid users = bigboss
path = /home/bigboss/fancyjet
guest ok = no
browseable = no
writable = no
printable = yes
```

The `valid users` parameter enables you to specify a space-separated list of users who have access to the printer.

After you modify and test the `/etc/samba/smb.conf` file, restart the Samba service and you should be able to access the Linux printers from your Windows computers.

Using an interactive Samba client

`smbclient` also enables you to access a Samba resource interactively. For example, if you want to access a disk share on a Windows system from your Linux system, use `smbclient` as follows:

```
smbclient //WINDOWS-SERVER/resource  -U username -P password
```

In the following example, `smbclient` is used to access the `C:\` drive on PLUTO as user `kabir`:

```
smbclient //PLUTO/c -U kabir -P foobar
```

If the authentication is successful (in other words, PLUTO allows connection), `smbclient` displays an FTP client–like prompt and allows you to perform many FTP client commands. Typing `help` or `?` at any time provides more information about the commands.

You can use `smbclient` to list the available Samba resources on a remote computer. In the following example, the **-L** option specifies that the Samba server be interrogated using username `kabir`:

```
smbclient -L reboot -U kabir
```

The example output is shown in Listing 16-2.

Listing 16-2 *Example output of smbclient*

```
Server time is MOn Jul 30 19:48:03 2001

Timezone is UTC-8.0

Password:

Domain=[EVOKNOW] OS=[Windows NT/2000 4.0] Server=[NT LAN Manager 4.0]

security=user


Server=[REBOOT] User=[] Workgroup=[EVOKNOW] Domain=[]


        Sharename       Type        Comment

        ---------       ----        -------

        ADMIN$          Disk        Remote Admin

        C               Disk        C Drive on PLUTO

        C$              Disk        Default share

        F               Disk

        home            Disk

        IPC$            IPC         Remote IPC

        Okidata0        Printer     Okidata OL-600e

        print$          Disk        Printer Drivers

        sheila          Disk

        TEMP            Disk



This machine has a browse list:


        Server                  Comment

        ---------               -------

        PICASO                  Picaso Samba Server
```

Continued

Listing 16-2 *Continued*

```
    PLUTO


    R2D2              EVOKNOW Laptop (r2d2)
    REBOOT


This machine has a workgroup list:


    Workgroup         Master
    ---------         -------
    EVOKNOW           PLUTO
```

As you can see, the smbclient program can be used to determine what resources are being shared by other Samba-compliant systems.

The smbclient program also allows you to send Windows pop-up messages to Windows computers that have enabled this service. For example, when you run

```
smbclient -M reboot
```

smbclient enables you to type text messages that it displays as pop-up messages on the target Windows computer.

Securing Your Samba Server

If used correctly, Samba can turn a mixed environment (Linux/Windows) into a smoother computing environment. However, like any other useful service, Samba can be a potential source of security holes when it is misconfigured. This is especially true if your Samba server is connected to the Internet. I recommend that you do not connect a Samba server to the Internet or enable Samba services over the Internet. This section discusses a few security measures you can take to reduce risks involving Samba.

See the "Setting the [global] parameters" section earlier in this chapter for info on how to enable plain-text passwords on later versions of Windows 9x and Windows NT/2000 systems. This works well for those systems, but it might not be suitable for a LAN or WAN environment, where a potential exists for illegal TCP/IP packet sniffers. In other words, if you believe that your network might be vulnerable to packet sniffers, implement encrypted passwords. The encrypted password–based authentication that the SMB protocol permits never transmits any passwords between a Samba client and server. This ensures a higher degree of security and hence is very desirable in high-risk scenarios in which security and confidentiality are of utmost importance. Two ways exist to use encrypted passwords, both of which are described next.

Using a Windows NT/2000 server as a password server

A Windows NT/2000 server, by default, can provide encrypted password services. So, if you have a Windows NT/2000 server on your network, consider making it your password server. You can centralize all of your user accounts on the Windows NT/2000 server so that Samba services can be enabled using encrypted passwords. To use a Windows NT/2000 server as your encrypted password server, do the following:

1. Create a Windows NT/2000 server account for each user who needs Samba access.

2. Modify the `/etc/samba/smb.conf` file so that you have the password server parameter set to the name of the Windows NT/2000 server. Also, set the `security` parameter to `server`.

3. Run the `testparm` command to ensure that all configuration lines are syntactically correct in the `/etc/samba/smb.conf` file.

4. Restart the Samba service.

To test your new configuration, use one of the Windows NT/2000 server user accounts to access the Samba server.

Using encrypted passwords on your Samba server

The Samba package shipped with Red Hat is precompiled with encrypted password support, so you don't need to download the Samba source code and compile it with encrypted password support. To enable encrypted passwords, take these steps:

1. Use the `mksmbpasswd.sh` script supplied with the Samba package to create a replacement password file for `/etc/passwd`. Run the following command:

```
cat /etc/passwd | /usr/bin/mksmbpasswd.sh >
/etc/samba/smbpasswd
```

This creates a special password file that has lines such as the following:

```
root:0:XXXXXXXXXXXXXXXXXXXXXXXXXXXXXXXX:XXXXXXXXXXX
XXXXXXXXXXXXXXXXXXXX:root:/root:/bin/tcsh: [U
]:LCT-00000000:root
```

2. Use the `smbpasswd` program to create an encrypted Samba password for each user. For example, to create an encrypted Samba password for a user called `sheila`, run the following command:

```
smbpasswd sheila
```

3. Modify the `/etc/samba/smb.conf` file so that the following line appears in the `[global]` configuration section:

```
encrypt passwords = yes
```

4. Test your new configuration by running the `testparm` program; if the test is successful, restart the Samba service. On the other hand, if `testparm` shows errors, review and modify your configuration as needed.

Test the Samba service from your Windows systems. If you have modified your Windows Registry to use plain-text passwords, remove the Registry entry you created so that encrypted passwords can be used.

Part IV

Appendixes

The appendixes will introduce you to the most commonly used command-line Linux commands, the basics of IP networking, and such Internet resources as USENET news groups, Web sites, and mailing lists that are available for Linux. I also show you how to recover from a system crash using your Red Hat Linux CD-ROM.

Appendix

A   Common Linux Commands

B   IP Networking Basics

C   Internet Resources for Linux

D   Recovering from a System Crash

Appendix A

Common Linux Commands

Red Hat Linux is very rich in command-line tools and graphical tools. However, in alignment with other Unix or Unix-clone systems out there, the power of Red Hat Linux still lies with the command-line tools. In this appendix I will show you the common use of many command line tools that you can use frequently.

Before learning about the tools, you should know how to get online help information from Red Hat Linux about any tool. The Red Hat Linux system comes with online manual page (called *man pages* for short) that you can access using the man command. The man pages are categorized in different sections as shown in Table A-1.

Table A-1 *Sections of man Pages*

Section	Topic
1	Executable programs or shell commands
2	System calls (functions the kernel provides)
3	Library calls (functions within system libraries)
4	Special files (usually in /dev)
5	File formats (that is, /etc/passd)
6	Games
7	Miscellaneous information
8	Maintenance commands

The man command allows you to view the online manuals. The syntax for this command is as follows:

```
man [-k] [section] keyword
```

The keyword is usually the name of the program, utility, or function. The default action is to search in all of the available sections following a predefined order and to show only the first page found, even if the keyword exists in several sections.

Because commands may appear in several sections, the first page found might not be the man page you are looking for. The command `printf` is a good example.

Say you are writing a program and would like to know more about the ANSI C library function printf (). Just by typing

```
man printf
```

you get information about printf. However, the man pages for this printf are for the shell command `printf`. Obviously, this is the wrong information. A reasonable solution is to list all of the sections covering `printf` (if it exists in multiple sections) and to select the correct one. You can search the keywords of the man pages with the `-f` option:

```
man -k printf
fprintf      printf (3)    - formatted output conversion
fprintf      printf (3)    - print formatted output
printf       printf (1)     - write formatted output
printf       printf (3)    - formatted output conversion
printf       printf (3)    - print formatted output
```

The `printf` you are interested in in this example is a library function that can be found in section 3 (from Table B-4) or, more specifically, in section 3b or 3s (as you can see from the preceding output). To specify a particular section of a man page, you pass it to man at the command line to find the correct information you are looking for:

```
man 3b printf
```

General File and Directory Commands

In this section, you will learn about file- and directory-specific commands that you're likely to use on a daily basis.

cat

Syntax: `cat file [>|>] [destination_file]`

The `cat` command displays the contents of a file to the standard output, enabling you to examine the contents of a file. The argument you pass to `cat` is the file you wish to view. To view the total content of a file called name, you'd use the following command (the command is shown with the sample output below it):

```
cat name
Kiwee
Joe
Ricardo
Charmaine
```

`cat` can also merge existing multiple files into one:

```
cat name1 name2 name3 > allnames
```

This example combines the files name1, name2, and name3 to produce the final file allnames. You establish the order of the merge by the order in which you enter the files at the command line.

Using `cat`, you can append a file to another file. For example, if you forgot to add the file name4 in the previous command, you can add it to the allnames file by executing the following command:

```
cat name4 >> allnames
```

chmod

Syntax: `chmod [-R] permission_mode file_or_directory`

Use this command to change the permission mode of a file or directory. The permission mode is specified as a three- or four-digit octal number. For example:

```
chmod 755  myscript.pl
```

The preceding command changes the permission of `myscript.pl` script to 755 (rwxr-xr-x), which allows the file owner to read, write, and execute and allows only read and execute privileges for everyone else. Here is another example:

```
chmod -R 744 public_html
```

The preceding command changes the permissions of the `public_html` directory and all its contents (files and subdirectories) to 744 (rwxr — r —), which is a typical permission setting for personal Web directories you access using `http://server/~username` URLs with an Apache server. The `-R` option tells `chmod` to recursively change permissions for all files and directories under the named directory.

chown

Syntax: `chown  [ -fhR ]  owner  [ :group ]  { file . . .  | directory. . . }`

The `chown` command changes the owner of the file the File parameter specifies to the user the Owner parameter specifies. The value of the Owner parameter can be a user ID or a login name in the `/etc/passwd` file. Optionally, you can also specify a group. The value of the group parameter can be a group ID or a group name in the `/etc/group` file.

Only the root user can change the owner of a file. You can change the group of a file only if you are a root user or if you own the file. If you own the file but are not a root user, you can change the group only to a group of which you are a member. Table A-2 discusses the details of the `chown` options.

Table A-2 *chown Options*

Option	Description
-f	Suppresses all error messages except usage messages.
-h	Changes the ownership of an encountered symbolic link but not that of the file or directory the symbolic link points to.
-R	Descends directories recursively, changing the ownership for each file. When a symbolic link is encountered and the link points to a directory, the ownership of that directory is changed, but the directory is not further traversed.

The following example changes the owner of the file to another user:

```
chown bert hisfile.txt
```

clear

Syntax: `clear`

The `clear` command clears your terminal and returns the command-line prompt to the top of the screen.

cmp

Syntax: `cmp [-ls] file 1 file2`

This command compares the contents of two files. If there are no differences within the two files, `cmp` by default is silent.

To demonstrate, say that `file1.txt` contains the following:

```
this is file 1
the quick brown fox jumps over the lazy dog.
```

and `file2.txt` contains the following:

```
this is file 2
the quick brown fox jumps over the lazy dog.
```

The only difference between the two files is the last character of the first line. In one file, the character is a "1," and the other file has a "2." Now use cmp to compare the files as follows:

```
cmp file1.txt file2.txt
file1.txt file2.txt differ: char 14, line 1
```

As you can see in the preceding, the results of cmp correctly identify character 14, line 1 as the unequal character between the two files. The −1 option prints the byte number and the differing byte values for each of the files.

```
cmp −l file1.txt file2.txt
14 61 62
```

The results of the preceding example show us that byte 14 is different, with the first file having an octal 61 and the second file having an octal 62.

Finally, the -s option displays nothing. The -s option only returns an exit status indicating the similarities between the files. It returns a 0 (zero) if the files are identical and a 1 if the files are different. Lastly, the -s option returns a number >1 (greater than 1) when an error occurs.

cp

Syntax: cp [-R] *source_file_or_directory file_or_directory*

Use the cp command to make an exact copy of a file. The cp command requires at least two arguments: the first argument is the file you wish to copy, and the second argument is the location or filename of the new file. If the second argument is an existing directory, cp copies the source file into the directory.

```
cp main.c main.c.bak
```

The preceding example copies the existing file main.c file and creates a new file called main.c.bak in the same directory. These two files are identical, bit for bit.

cut

Syntax: cut [-cdf *list*] *file*

The cut command extracts columns of data. The data can be in bytes, characters, or fields from each line in a file. For example, a file called names contains information about a group of people. Each line contains data pertaining to one person:

```
Fast  Freddy:Sacramento:CA:111-111-1111
Joe   Smoe:Los Angeles:CA:222-222-2222
Drake Snake:San Francisco:CA:333-333-3333
Bill  Steal:New York:NY:444-444-4444
```

To list the names and telephone numbers of all individuals in the file, use the -f and -d options as follows:

```
cut -f 1,4 -d : names
Fast  Freddy:111-111-1111
Joe   Some:222-222-2222
Drake Snake:333-333-3333
Bill  Steal:444-444-4444
```

The -f list option specifies the fields you elect to display. The -d options define each field. In the preceding example, -d : indicates that a colon separates each field. Using : as the field delimiter makes fields 1 and 4 the name and phone number fields.

To display the contents of a particular column, use the -c list option. The following example shows how to list columns 1 through 5 in the filename names and nothing else:

```
cut -c 1-5 names
Fast
Joe
Drake
Bill
```

diff

Syntax: diff [-iqb] *file1* *file2*

You use the diff command to determine differences between files and/or directories. The diff command is different from the cmp command in the way it compares the files. The diff command is used to report differences between two files, line by line. The cmp command reports differences between two files character by character, instead of line by line. As a result, it is more useful than diff for comparing binary files. By default, diff does not produce any output if the files are identical.

For text files, cmp is useful mainly when you want to know only whether two files are identical.

To illustrate the difference between considering changes character by character and considering them line by line, think of what happens if you add a single newline character to the beginning of a file. If you compare that file with an otherwise identical file that lacks the newline at the beginning, diff reports that a blank line has been added to the file, and cmp reports that the two files differ in almost every character.

The normal output format consists of one or more hunks of differences; each hunk shows one area where the files differ. Normal format hunks look like this:

```
change-command
< from-file-line
< from-file-line. . .
--
> to-file-line
> to-file-line. . .
```

There are three types of change commands. Each consists of a line number or comma-separated range of lines in the first file, a single character indicating the kind of change to make, and a line number or comma-separated range of lines in the second file. All line numbers are the original line numbers in each file. The types of change commands are:

- 'lar' — Add the lines in range r of the second file after line l of the first file. For example, '8a12,15' means append lines 12–15 of file 2 after line 8 of file 1; or, if changing file 2 into file 1, delete lines 12–15 of file 2.

- `'fct'` — Replace the lines in range f of the first file with lines in range t of the second file. This is like a combined add and delete but more compact. For example, '5,7c8,10' means change lines 5–7 of file1 to read as lines 8–10 of file2; or, if changing file2 into file1, change lines 8–10 of file2 to read as lines 5–7 of file1.

- `'rdl'`: Delete the lines in range r from the first file; line l is where they would have appeared in the second file had they not been deleted. For example, '5,7d3' means delete lines 5–7 of file 1; or, if changing file 2 into file 1, append lines 5–7 of file 1 after line 3 of file 2.

For example, a.txt contains

```
a
b
c
d
e
```

and b.txt contains

```
c
d
e
f
g
```

The diff command produces the following output:

```
1,2d0
< a
< b
5a4,5
> f
> g
```

The diff command produces output that shows how the files are different and what you need to do for the files to be identical. First, notice how 'c' is the first common character between the two files. The first line reads 1,2d0. This is interpreted as deleting lines 1 and 2 of the first file, lines a and b. Next, the third line reads 5a4,6. The 'a' signifies append. If you append lines 4 through 6 of the second file to line 5 of the first file, the files are identical.

The `diff` command has some common options. The `-i` option ignores changes in case. `diff` considers upper- and lowercase characters equivalent. The `-q` option gives a summary of information. Simply put, the `-q` option reports if the files differ at all.

```
diff -q a.txt b.txt
Files a.txt and b.txt differ
```

The `-b` option ignores changes in whitespace. The phrase "the foo" is equivalent to "the foo" if you use the `-b` option.

du

Syntax: `du [-ask]` *filenames*

This command summarizes disk usage. If you specify a directory, du reports the disk usage for that directory and any directories it contains. If you do not specify a filename or directory, du assumes the current directory. `du -a` breaks down the total and shows the size of each directory and file. The `-s` option will just print the total. Another useful option is the `-k` option. This option prints all file sizes in kilobytes. Here are some examples of the various options:

```
du -a
247     ./util-linux_2.9e-0.1.deb
130     ./libncurses4_4.2-2.deb
114     ./slang1_1.2.2-2.deb
492     .

du -s
492     .
```

fgrep

The `fgrep` command is designed to be a fast-searching program (as opposed to `grep`). However, it can search only for exact characters, not for general specifications. The name fgrep stands for "fixed character grep."

These days, computers and memory are so fast that there is rarely a need for `fgrep`.

file

Syntax: file *filename*

The `file` command determines the file's type. If the file is not a regular file, this command identifies its file type. It identifies the file types directory, FIFO, block special, and character special as such. If the file is a regular file and the file is zero-length, this command identifies it as an empty file.

If the file appears to be a text file, `file` examines the first 512 bytes and tries to determine its programming language. If the file is an executable a.out, `file` prints the version stamp, provided it is greater than 0.

```
file main.C
main.C:        c program text
```

find

Syntax: find *[path]* *[-type fdl]* *[-name pattern]* *[-atime [+-]number of days]* *[-exec command {} \;]* *[-empty]*

The `find` command finds files and directories. For example:

```
find . -type d
```

The `find` command returns all subdirectory names under the current directory. The `-type` option is typically set to d (for directory) or f (for file) or l (for links). Following are a few of the things you can do with `find`:

- Find all text files (ending with .txt extension) in the current directory, including all its subdirectories:

  ```
  find . -type f -name "*.txt"
  ```

- Search all text files (ending with the .txt extension) in the current directory, including all its subdirectories for the keyword "magic," and return their names (because -l is used with grep):

```
find . -type f -name "*.txt" -exec grep -l 'magic' {} \;
```

- Find all GIF files that have been accessed in the past 24 hours (one day) and display their details using the `ls -l` command.

  ```
  find . -name "*.gif" -atime -1 -exec ls -l {} \;
  ```

- Display all empty files in the current directory hierarchy.

  ```
  find . -type f -empty
  ```

grep

Syntax: `grep [-viw] pattern file(s)`

The `grep` command allows you to search for one or more files for particular character patterns. Every line of each file that contains the pattern is displayed at the terminal. The `grep` command is useful when you have lots of files and you want to find out which ones contain particular words or phrases.

Using the `-v` option, you can display the inverse of a pattern. Perhaps you want to select the lines in `data.txt` that do not contain the word "the," you could use the following :

```
grep -vw 'the' data.txt
```

If you do not specify the `-w` option, any word containing "the" matches, such as "toge[the]r." The `-w` option specifies that the pattern must be a whole word. Finally, the `-i` option ignores the difference between uppercase and lowercase letters when searching for the pattern.

Much of the flexibility of `grep` comes from the fact that you can specify not only exact characters but also a more general search pattern. To do this, use what you describe as "regular expressions."

See Chapter 9 for details on regular expression.

head

Syntax: head [-*count* | -n *number*] *filename*

This command displays the first few lines of a file. By default, it displays the first ten lines of a file. However, you can use the preceding options to specify a different number of lines. The following example illustrates how to view the first two lines of the text file doc.txt.

```
head —2 doc.txt
# Outline of future projects
# Last modified:  02/02/99
```

ln

Syntax: ln [-s] *sourcefile target*

ln creates two types of links: hard and soft. Think of a link as two names for the same file. After you create a link, you cannot distinguish it from the original file. You cannot remove a file that has hard links from the hard drive until you remove all links. You create hard links without the -s option.

```
ln ./www ./public_html
```

However, a hard link does have limitations. A hard link cannot link to another directory, and a hard link cannot link to a file on another file system. Using the -s option, you can create a soft link, which eliminates these restrictions. For example, the following command creates a soft link between the directory www on file system 2 and a newly created file public_ html on file system 1:

```
ln —s /dev/fs02/jack/www /dev/fs01/foo/public_html
```

locate

Syntax: locate *keyword*

The locate command finds the path of a particular file or command. locate finds an exact or substring match. For example:

```
locate foo
/usr/lib/texmf/tex/latex/misc/footnpag.sty
/usr/share/automake/footer.am
/usr/share/games/fortunes/food
/usr/share/games/fortunes/food.dat
/usr/share/gimp/patterns/moonfoot.pat
```

The output of `locate` contains the keyword "foo" in the absolute path or does not have any output.

ls

Syntax: `ls [-laRl] file or directory`

The `ls` command allows you to list files (and subdirectories) in a directory. It is one of the most popular programs used in Linux. The following Table A-3 shows some of the more popular options for `ls`.

Table A-3 *Popular Options for ls*

Option	What It Displays
-1	Only the file and directory names in the current directory
-l	A long listing containing file and directory permission information, size, modification date, and so on
-a	All files and directories (including the ones that have a leading period in their names) within the current directory
-R	Displays the contents of the subdirectories (if any) recursively

mkdir

Syntax: `mkdir directory . . .`

To make a directory, use the `mkdir` command. You have only two restrictions when choosing a directory name: (1) File names can be up to 255 characters long, and (2) directory names can contain any character except the /. For example, the following example creates three subdirectories in the current directory:

```
mkdir dir1 dir2 dir3
```

mv

Syntax: `mv [-if]sourcefile targetfile`

Use the `mv` command to move or rename directories and files. The command performs a move or rename depending on whether the target file is an existing directory. To illustrate, say you want to give a directory called `foo` the new name of `foobar`.

```
mv foo foobar
```

Because `foobar` does not already exist as a directory, `foo` becomes `foobar`. If you issue the following command

```
mv doc.txt foobar
```

and `foobar` is an existing directory, you perform a move. The file `doc.txt` now resides in the `foobar` directory.

The `-f` option removes existing destination files and never prompts the user. The `-i` option prompts the user whether to overwrite each destination file that exists. If the response does not begin with "y" or "'Y," the file is skipped.

pico

Syntax: `pico [filename]`

This full-screen text editor is very user-friendly and highly suitable for users who migrate from a Windows or MS-DOS environment.

pwd

Syntax: `pwd`

This command prints the current working directory. The directories displayed show the absolute path. None of the directories displayed are hard or soft symbolic links.

```
pwd
/home/usr/charmaine
```

rm

Syntax: rm [-rif] *directory/file*

To remove a file or directory, use the rm command. Here are some examples:

```
rm doc.txt
rm ~/doc.txt
rm /tmp/foobar.txt
```

To remove multiple files with rm, you can use wildcards or type each file individually. For example,

```
rm doc1.txt doc2.txt doc3.txt
```

is equivalent to:

```
rm doc[1-3].txt
```

rm is a powerful command that can cause chaos if you use it incorrectly. For example, say you have your thesis that you've worked so hard on for the last six months saved in your current working directory. You decide to rm all of the docs in the directory, thinking you are in another directory altogether. After finding out a backup file does not exist (and you are no longer in denial), you would wonder if there had been any way you could have prevented this.

The rm command has the -i option that allows rm to be interactive. This tells rm to ask your permission before removing each file. For example, if you entered:

```
rm -i *.doc
rm: remove thesis.doc (yes/no)? n
```

The -i option gives you a parachute. It's up to you to either pull the cord (answer no) or suffer the consequences (answer yes). The -f option is completely the opposite; the -f (force) option tells rm to remove all the files you specify, regardless of the file permissions. Use the -f option only when you are 100 percent sure you are removing the correct file(s).

To remove a directory and all files and directories within it, use the -r option. rm -r will remove an entire subtree, as follows:.

```
rm -r documents
```

If you are not sure what you are doing, combine the -r option with the -i option, as follows:

```
rm —ri documents
```

The preceding example asks for your permission before it removes every file and directory.

sort

Syntax: `sort [-rndu] [-o outfile] [infile/sortedfile]`

The obvious task this command performs is to sort files. However, sort also merges files. The sort command reads files that contain previously sorted data and merges them into one large, sorted file. The simplest way to use sort is to sort a single file and display the results on your screen. If the file a.txt contains the following:

```
b
c
a
d
```

To sort a.txt and display the results to the screen:

```
sort a.txt
a
b
c
d
```

To save sorted results, use the -o option: `sort -o sorted.txt a.txt` saves the sorted a.txt file in sorted.txt. To use sort to merge existing sorted files and to save the output in sorted.txt, you use the following command:

```
sort -o sorted.txt a.txt b.txt c.txt
```

The -r option for this command reverses the sort order. Therefore, a file that contains the letters of the alphabet on a line is sorted from z to a if you use the -r option.

The -d option sorts files based on dictionary order. The sort command considers only letters, numerals, and spaces, and ignores other characters.

The -u option looks for identical lines and suppresses all but one. Therefore, sort produces only unique lines.

stat

Syntax: stat *file*

This program displays various statistics on a file or directory. For example:

```
stat foo.txt
```

This command displays the following output:

```
  File: "foo.txt"
  Size: 4447232      Filetype: Regular File
  Mode: (0644/-rw-r-r-)  Uid: ( 0/root)  Gid: (0/root)
Device: 3,0    Inode: 16332     Links: 1
Access: Mon Mar  1 21:39:43 1999(00000.02:32:30)
Modify: Mon Mar  1 22:14:26 1999(00000.01:57:47)
Change: Mon Mar  1 22:14:26 1999(00000.01:57:47
```

You can see the following displayed: file access; modification; change date; size; owner and group information; permission mode; and so on.

strings

Syntax: strings *filename*

The strings command prints character sequences at least four characters long. You use this utility mainly to describe the contents of nontext files.

tail

Syntax: `tail [-count | -fr]` *filename*

The `tail` command displays the end of a file. By default, `tail` displays the last 10 lines of a file. To display the last 50 lines of the file `doc.txt`, you issue the following command:

```
tail -50 doc.txt
```

The `-r` option displays the output in reverse order. By default, `-r` displays all lines in the file, not just 10 lines. For example, to display the entire contents of the file `doc.txt` in reverse order, use the following command:

```
tail -r doc.txt
```

To display the last 10 lines of the file `doc.txt` in reverse order, use the following command:

```
tail -10r doc.txt
```

TIP
The `-f` option is useful when you are monitoring a file. With this option, `tail` waits for new data to be written to the file by some other program. As new data is added to the file by some other program, `tail` displays the data on the screen. To stop tail from monitoring a file, press Ctrl+C (the interrupt key) because the `tail` command does not stop on its own.

touch

Syntax: `touch` *file or directory*

This command updates the timestamp of a file or directory. If the named file does not exist, `touch` creates it as an empty file.

umask

See the section on default file permissions for users in Chapter 4.

uniq

Syntax: uniq [-c] *filename*

The uniq command compares adjacent lines and displays only one unique line. When used with the -c option, uniq counts the number of occurrences. For example, a file that has the following contents

```
a
a
a
b
a
```

produces the following result when you use it with uniq:

```
uniq test.txt
a
b
a
```

Notice how the adjacent *a*s are removed, but not all of the *a*s in the file. This is an important detail to remember when using uniq. If you would like to find all the unique lines in a file called test.txt, you can run the following command:

```
sort  test.txt  | uniq
```

This command sorts the test.txt file and puts all similar lines next to each other, allowing uniq to display only unique lines. For example, say that you want to quickly find how many unique visitors come to your Web site; you can run the following command:

```
awk '{print $1}' access.log | sort | uniq
```

This displays the unique IP addresses in a CLF log file, which is what Apache Web server uses to log visitors.

vi

The vi program is a powerful full-screen text editor you can find on almost all Unix systems. The vi editor does not require much in the way of resources to utilize its features. In addition to the basic edit functions, vi can search, replace, and concatenate files. vi even has its own macro language, in addition to a number of other features.

There are two modes in vi. It is important to learn and understand these modes; learning them makes your life a whole lot easier. The first mode is the *input mode*. In input mode, text is entered in the document. You can insert or append text. The second mode is the *command mode*. When vi is in command mode, you can move within the document, merge lines, search, and so on. You can carry out all functions of vi from command mode except entering text. You can enter text only in input mode.

A typical vi newbie assumes he is in input mode and begins typing his document. He expects to see his typed text, but instead what he sees is his current document mangled because he is in command mode.

When vi starts, it is in command mode. You can go from command mode to input mode by pressing I. To return to command mode, press the Esc key for normal exit, or press Interrupt (the Ctrl+C key sequence) to end abnormally. Table A-4 shows a summary of common vi commands and their effects in command mode.

Table A-4 *Summary of Common vi Commands*

Commands	Effects
Ctrl+D	Moves window down by half a screen
Ctrl+U	Moves window up by half a screen
Ctrl+F	Moves window forward by a screen
Ctrl+B	Moves window back by a screen
K or up arrow	Moves cursor up one line
J or down arrow	Moves cursor down one line
L or right arrow	Moves cursor right one character
H or left arrow	Moves cursor left one character
Enter	Moves cursor to beginning of next line
– (minus)	Moves cursor to beginning of previous line
w	Moves cursor to beginning of next word
b	Moves cursor to beginning of previous word
^ or 0	Moves cursor to beginning of current line

Continued

Table A-4 *Continued*

Commands	Effects
$	Moves cursor to end of current line
A	Inserts text immediately after the cursor
o	Opens a new line immediately after the current line
O (note this is an uppercase letter o, not a zero)	Opens a new line immediately before the current line
x	Deletes character under the cursor
dw	Deletes a word (including space after it)
D or d	Deletes from the cursor until the end of line
d^ character to the left of the cursor	Deletes from the beginning of the line to the space or
dd	Deletes the current line
U undo; that is, nothing changes)	Undoes last change (note that two undos will undo the
:w editing	Writes the changes for the current file and continues
:q!	Quits **vi** without saving any changes
:ZZ	Saves current file and exits **vi**

WC

Syntax: wc [-lwc] *filename*

The wc (word count) command counts lines, characters, and words. If you use the wc command without any options, the output displays all statistics of the file. The file test.txt contains the following text:

```
the quick brown fox jumps over the lazy dog
wc test.txt
        1       9      44 test.txt
```

These results tell us there is one line with nine words containing 44 characters in the file test.txt. To display only the number of lines, you use the -l option. The -w option displays only the number of words. Finally, the -c option displays only the total number of characters.

whatis

Syntax: whatis `keyword`

This command displays a one-line description for the keyword entered in the command line. The whatis command is identical to typing man -f. For example, if you want to display the time but you are not sure whether to use the time or date command, enter

```
whatis time date
```

to get results like the following:

```
time          time (1)        - time a simple command
date          date (1)        - print the date and time
```

Looking at the results, you can see that the command you want is date. The time command actually measures how long it takes for a program or command to execute.

whereis

The whereis command locates source/binary and manuals sections for specified files. The command first strips the supplied names of leading pathname components and any (single) character file extension, such as .c, .h, and so on.

```
whereis ls
ls: /bin/ls /usr/man/man1/ls.1.gz
```

The preceding example indicates the location of the command in question. The ls command is in the /bin directory, and its corresponding man pages are at /usr/man/man1/ls.1.gz.

which

Syntax: which `command`

The which command displays the path and aliases of any valid, executable command.

```
which df
/usr/bin/df
```

The preceding example shows us that the df command is in the /usr/ bin directory. which also displays information about shell commands.

```
which setenv
setenv: shell built-in command.
```

File Compression and Archive-Specific Commands

When working with files of any kind, at some point you're likely to want to make your files smaller (so that you can more easily send them over the Internet, for example), to back them up in archive form, or to package them such that they're easier to install. The commands that I discuss in this section all deal with compressing, archiving, and packaging files.

compress

Syntax: compress [-v] file(s)

The compress command attempts to reduce the size of a file using the adaptive Lempel-Ziv coding algorithm. A file with a .Z extension replaces an uncompressed file. Using any type of compression for files is significant because smaller file sizes increase the amount of available disk space. Also, transferring smaller files across networks reduces network congestion.

The -v (verbose) option displays the percentage of reduction for each file you compress and tells you the name of the new file. Here is an example of how to use the compress command:

```
ls -alF inbox
```

Here's the resulting output:

```
-rw----   1 username cscstd    194261 Feb 23 20:12 inbox
compress -v inbox
inbox: Compression: 37.20%-replaced with inbox.Z

ls -alF inbox.Z
-rw----   1 username cscstd    121983 Feb 23 20:12 inbox.Z
```

See uncompress for details on how to uncompress the compressed file.

gunzip

Syntax: `gunzip [-v] file(s)`

To decompress files to their original form, use the `gunzip` command. `gunzip` attempts to decompress files ending with the following extensions: .gz, -gz, .z, -z, _z, .Z, or tgz.

The -v option displays a verbose output when decompressing a file.

```
gunzip -v README.txt.gz
README.txt.gz:          65.0%-replaced with README.txt
```

See `gzip` for details on how to compress a file that can be uncompressed by gunzip.

gzip

Syntax: `gzip [-rv9] file(s)`

The `gzip` command is a compression program that's known for having one of the best compression ratios, but at a price: `gzip` can be considerably slow. Files compressed with `gzip` are replaced by files with a .gz extension and can be unzipped with the `gunzip` command (which is discussed in the previous section).

The -9 option yields the best compression, but sacrifices speed. The -v option is the verbose option: the size, total, and compression ratios are listed for each file. Also, the -r option recursively traverses each directory, compressing files along the way.

```
ls -alF README.txt
-rw-r-r-  1 root     root      16213 Oct 14 13:55 README.txt


gzip -9v README.txt
README.txt:          65.0%-replaced with README.txt.gz


ls -alF README.txt.gz
-rw-r-r-  1 root     root       5691 Oct 14 13:55 README.txt.gz
```

See `gunzip` for details on how to uncompress a `gzipped` file.

rpm

Syntax: `rpm   -[ivhqladefUV]   [-force]   [-nodeps]`
`[-oldpackage] package list`

This is the Red Hat Package Manager program. It allows you to manage RPM packages, making it very easy to install and uninstall software.

To install a new RPM package called `precious-software-1.0.i386.rpm`, for example, run the following command:

```
rpm -i precious-software-1.0.i386.rpm
```

You can make `rpm` a bit more verbose by using `-ivh` instead of just the `-i` option. If you have installed the package and for some reason would like to install it again, you need to use the `--force` option to force `rpm`.

If you are upgrading a software package, you should use the `-U` option. For example:

```
rpm -Uvh precious-software-2.0.i386.rpm
```

This command upgrades the previous version of the precious-software package to version 2.0. However, if you have installed a newer version and want to go back to the previous version, `rpm` detects this condition and displays an error message saying that the installed version is newer than the one you are trying to install. In such a case, should you decide to proceed anyway, use the `--oldpackage` option with the `-U` option to force `rpm` to downgrade your software.

To uninstall a package such as sendmail, run:

```
rpm -e sendmail
```

If you find that removing a package or program breaks other programs because they depend on it or its files, you have to decide if you want to break these programs or not. If you decide to remove the package or the program, you can use the `--nodeps` option with the `-e` option to force `rpm` to uninstall the package.

Other common uses you'll find for the `rpm` command include:

- **Find a list of all available packages installed on your system:**
  ```
  rpm -qa
  ```
- **Find out which package a program such as sendmail belongs to:**
  ```
  rpm -q sendmail
  ```

This returns the RPM package name you use to install sendmail.

- **Find out which package a specific file such as /bin/tcsh belongs to:**

```
rpm -qf /bin/tcsh
```

This displays the package name of the named file.

- **Find the documentation that comes with a file:** Use the -d option along with the -qf options.

- **List all files associated with a program or package, such as sendmail, use the -l option:**

```
rpm -ql sendmail
```

- **Ensure that an installed package has not been modified in any way:** Use the -V option. This option becomes very useful if you learn that you or someone else could have damaged one or more packages. For example, to verify that all installed packages are in their original state, run the following command:

```
rpm -Va
```

tar

Syntax: tar [c] [x] [v] [z] [f *filename*] *file_or_directory_ names*

The tar command allows you to archive multiple files and directories into a single .tar file. It also allows you to extract files and directories from such an archive file. For example:

```
tar cf source.tar *.c
```

This command creates a tar file called source.tar, which contains all C source files (ending with extension .c) in the current directory.

```
tar cvf source.tar *.c
```

Here, the v option allows you to see which files are being archived by tar.

```
tar cvzf backup.tar.gz  important_dir
```

Here, all the files and subdirectories of the directory called important_
dir are archived in a file called backup.tar.gz. Notice that the z option
is compressing this file; hence, you should give the resulting file a .gz
extension. Often, the .tar.gz extension is shortened by many users to be
.tgz as well.

To extract an archive file called backup.tar, you can run the following
command:

```
tar xf backup.tar
```

To extract a compressed tar file (such as backup.tgz or backup.tar.gz),
you can run the following command:

```
tar xzf backup.tgz
```

uncompress

Syntax: uncompress [-v] *file(s)*

When you use the compress command to compress a file, the file is no
longer in its original form. To return a compressed file to its original form,
use the uncompress command.

> **TIP**
> The uncompress command expects to find a file with a .Z
> extension, so the command line "uncompress inbox" is equiv-
> alent to "uncompress inbox.Z."

The -v option produces verbose output.

```
uncompress -v inbox.Z
inbox.Z: —replaced with inbox
```

unzip

Syntax: unzip *file(s)*

This command decompresses files with the .zip extension (the single
most popular Windows compression format). You can compress these files
with the unzip command, Phil Katz's PKZIP, or any other PKZIP-
compatible program.

uudecode

Syntax: uudecode *file*

The uudecode command transforms a uuencodeed file into its original form. uudecode creates the file by using the "target_name" the uuencode command specifies, which you can also identify on the first line of a uuencodeed file.

To convert our uuencodeed file from the following entry back to its original form:

uudecode a.out.txt

As a result, you create the executable file a.out from the text file a.out.txt.

uuencode

Syntax: uuencode *in_file target_name*

The uuencode command translates a binary file into readable form. You do this by converting the binary file into ASCII printable characters. One of the many uses of uuencode is transmitting a binary file through e-mail. A file you have uuencoded appears as a large e-mail message. The recipient can then save the message and use the uudecode command to retrieve its binary form.

The *target_name* is the name of the binary file you create when you use the uuencode.

The following example uuencodes the executable program a.out. The target name that uudecode creates is b.out. You save the uuencoded version of a.out in the file a.out.txt.

uuencode a.out b.out > a.out.txt

zip

Syntax: zip [-ACDe9] *file(s)*

This compression utility compresses files in a more popular format, enabling compatibility with systems such as VMS, MS-DOS, OS/2, Windows NT, Minix, Atari, Macintosh, Amiga, and Acorn RISC OS. This is mainly because of zip's compatibility with Phil Katz's PKZIP program. Files compressed with zip have the .zip extension.

The zip command has an array of options that are toggled by its switches. This command can create self-extracting files, add comments to ZIP files, remove files from an archive, and password-protect the archive.

These are a few of the features zip supports. For a more detailed description, see your local zip man page.

File Systems – Specific Commands

The commands that I discuss in this section deal with file systems. Using these commands you can create and format file systems, check disk usage, and so on.

dd

Syntax: dd if=*input file* [conv=*conversion type*] of=*output file* [obs=*output block size*]

This program allows you to convert ASCII and EBCDIC (IBM) file formats. For example:

```
dd if=/tmp/uppercase.txt   conv=lcase of=/tmp/lowercase.txt
```

This command takes the /tmp/upppercase.txt file and writes a new file called /tmp/lowercase.txt and converts all characters to lowercase (lcase). To do the reverse, you can use conv=ucase option. However, dd is most widely used to write a boot image file to a floppy disk that has a file system that mkfs has already created. For example:

```
dd if=/some/boot.img   conv=lcase of=/dev/fd0 obs=16k
```

This command writes the /some/boot.image file to the first floppy disk (/dev/fd0) in 16K blocks.

df

Syntax: df [-k] FileSystem | File

The df command summarizes the free disk space for the drives mounted on the system. Hard drive space is an important resource in a computer, and you should monitor it carefully. Mismanagement of hard drive space can cause a computer to crawl on its knees and result in some unhappy users.

```
df
```

```
Filesystem   512-blocks     Free %Used   Iused %Iused Mounted on
/dev/hd4         49152     25872  48%    2257   19% /
/dev/hd2       1351680    243936  82%   19091   12% /usr
/dev/hd9var      49152     12224  76%    2917   48% /var
/dev/hd3         57344     52272   9%     125    2% /tmp
/dev/lv00        57344     55176   4%      19    1% /tftpboot
/dev/hd1        163840     16976  90%    1140    6% /home
/dev/fs01      8192000   6381920  23%   20963    3% /home/fs01
/dev/fs02      8192000   1873432  78%      72    1% /home/fs02
```

To view the disk space summary for the current file system:

```
df .
Filesystem   512-blocks     Free %Used   Iused %Iused Mounted on
/dev/fs01      8192000   6381920  23%   20963    3% /home/fs01
```

Notice that the df output is printed in 512-byte blocks. It may seem odd to think of blocks with this size if you are used to 1K blocks, or, more precisely, 1,024-byte blocks. The -k option displays the summary with 1,024-byte blocks instead:

```
df -k .
```

```
Filesystem   1024-blocks    Free %Used   Iused %Iused Mounted on
/dev/fs01      4096000   3190960  23%   20963    3% /home/fs01
```

With the -k option in mind, the results are very different. If you interpret the output incorrectly, you may run out of disk space sooner than you think.

edquota

See the section on assigning disk quotas to users in Chapter 7 for details.

fdformat

Syntax: fdformat   *floppy-device*

This program does a low-level format on a floppy device. For example, the following command formats the first floppy disk (/dev/fd0) as a high-density 1.44MB disk:

```
fdformat /dev/fd0H1440
```

fdisk

See Chapter 2 for details on fdisk.

mkfs

Syntax: mkfs   [-t   *fstype*]   [-cv]   *device-or-mount-point* [*blocks*]

This command allows you to make a new file system. For example, the following command creates an ext2-type file system on the /dev/hda3 partition of the first IDE hard drive:

```
mkfs -t ext2   /dev/hda3
```

The -c option allows you instruct mkfs to check bad blocks before building the file system; the -v option produces verbose output.

mkswap

See Chapter 2 for details on mkswap.

mount

Syntax: mount -a [-t *fstype*] [-o *options*] *device directory*

This command mounts a file system. Typically, the mount options for commonly used file systems are stored in /etc/fstab. For example:

```
/dev/hda6   /intranet   ext2   defaults 1 2
```

If the preceding line is in `/etc/fstab`, you can mount the file system stored in partition /dev/hda6 as follows:

```
mount   /intranet
```

You can also mount the same file system as follows:

```
mount   -t ext2 /dev/hda6 /intranet
```

You use the `-t` option to specify file system type. To mount all the file systems specified in the `/etc/fstab`, use the `-a` option. For example:

```
mount   -a -t ext2
```

The preceding command mounts all ext2 file systems. Commonly used options for `-o` option are `ro` (read-only) and `rw` (read/write). For example:

```
mount   -t ext2 -o ro /dev/hda6 /secured
```

The preceding command mounts `/dev/hda6` on `/secured` as a read-only file system.

quota

See the section on monitoring disk usage in Chapter 7 for details.

quotaon

See the section on configuring your system to support disk quotas in Chapter 7 for details.

swapoff

Syntax: `swapoff -a`

This command allows you to disable swap devices. The `-a` option allows you to disable all swap partitions specified in `/etc/fstab`.

swapon

Syntax: `swapon -a`

This command allows you to enable swap devices. The -a option allows you to enable all swap partitions specified in /etc/fstab.

umount

Syntax: umount   -a [-t *fstype*]

This command unmounts a file system from the current system. For example:

```
umount  /cdrom
```

The preceding command unmounts a file system whose mount point is /cdrom and the details of whose mount point are specified in /etc/fstab.

The -a option allows you to unmount all file systems (except for the proc file system) specified in the /etc/fstab file. You can also use the -t option to specify a particular file system type to unmount. For example, the following command unmounts all iso9660-type file systems, which are typically CD-ROMs:

```
umount  -a -t iso9660
```

DOS-Compatible Commands

If you need access to MS-DOS files from your Linux system, you need to install the Mtools package. Mtools is shipped with Red Hat Linux as an RPM package, so installing it is quite simple. See the rpm command for details on how to install an RPM package.

Mtools is a collection of utilities that allow you to read, write, and move around MS-DOS files. It also supports Windows 95–style long filenames, OS/2 Xdf disks, and 2m disks. The following section covers the common utilities in the Mtools package.

 Do not use the Windows-style back slash (\) in path names when using the commands discussed below. Use the forward slash (/) instead.

mcopy

Syntax: mcopy [-tm] *source_file_or_directory destination_file_or_directory*

You use the mcopy utility to copy MS-DOS files to and from Linux. For example:

```
mcopy  /tmp/readme.txt   b:
```

The preceding command copies the readme.txt file from the /tmp directory to the b: drive. The -t option enables you to automatically translate carriage return/line feed pairs in MS-DOS text files into new line feeds. The -m option allows you to preserve the existing file modification time.

mdel

Syntax: mdel *MS-DOS_file*

This utility allows you to delete files on an MS-DOS file system.

mdir

Syntax: mdir [-/] *MS-DOS_file_or_directory*

This utility allows you to view an MS-DOS directory. The −/ option allows you to view all the subdirectories as well.

mformat

Syntax: mformat [-t cylinders] [-h heads] [-s sectors]

This utility allows you to format a floppy disk to hold a minimal MS-DOS file system.

TIP

I find it much easier to format a disk by using an MS-DOS machine than to use mformat and have to specify cylinders, heads, sectors, and so on.

mlabel

Syntax: mlabel [-vcs] *drive:[new label]*

This utility displays the current volume label (if any) of the name drive and prompts for the new label if you do not enter it after the drive: in the command line. The -v option prints a hex dump of the boot sector of the named drive; the -c option clears the existing volume label, and the -s shows the existing label of the drive.

System Status – Specific Commands

The commands that I discuss in this section deal with status information on system resources. Here you can find out about boot-time kernel messages, free memory space, system information such as amount of time system has been up and running since last reboot, and so on.

dmesg

Syntax: dmesg

This program prints the status messages the kernel displays during bootup.

free

Syntax: free

This program displays memory usage statistics. An example of output looks like this:

```
               total    used    free    shared  buffers  cached
Mem:           127776   124596  3180    30740   2904     107504
-/+ buffers/cache: 14188   113588
Swap:          129900   84      129816
```

shutdown

Syntax: shutdown [-r] [-h] [-c] [-k]   [-t *seconds*] *time* [*message*]

This command allows a superuser or an ordinary user listed in the /etc/shutdown.allow file to shut the system down for a reboot or halt. To reboot the computer now, run the following command:

```
shutdown -r now
```

To halt the system after the shutdown, replace the -r with -h. The -k option allows you to simulate a shutdown event. For example, the following command sends a fake shutdown message to all users:

```
shutdown -r -k now System going down for maintenance
```

The -t option allows you to specify a delay in seconds between the warning message and the actual shutdown event. In such a case, if you decide to abort the shutdown, run shutdown again with the -c option to cancel it.

Note that you can use the HH:MM format to specify the time. For example:

```
shutdown -r 12:55
```

This reboots the system at 12:55. You can also use +*minutes* to specify time. For example:

```
shutdown -r +5
```

This starts the shutdown process five minutes after you print the warning message.

uname

Syntax: uname [-m] [-n] [-r] [-s] [-v] [-a]

This command displays information about the current system. For example:

```
uname -a
```

This command displays a line such as the following:

```
Linux picaso.evoknow.com 2.0.36 #1 Tue Oct 13 22:17:11 EDT 1998 i586 unknown
```

The -m option displays the system architecture (for example, i586); the -n option displays the host name (for example, picaso.evoknow.com); the -r option displays the release version of the operating system (for example, 2.0.36); the -s option displays the operating system name (for example, Linux); and the -v option displays the local build version of the operating system (for example, #1 Tue Oct 13 22:17:11 EDT 1998).

uptime

Syntax: uptime

This command displays the current time, how long the system has been up since the last reboot, how many users are connected to the server, and the system load in the last 1, 5, and 15 minutes.

User Administration Commands

The commands that I discuss in this section deal with user administration. Using this command you can add, modify, delete user, or change a user's finger information, default shell, group affiliations, password, and so on.

chfn

See the section on modifying an existing user account in Chapter 7.

chsh

See the section on modifying an existing user account in Chapter 7.

groupadd

See the section on creating a new group in Chapter 7.

groupmod

See the section on modifying an existing group in Chapter 7.

groups

Syntax: groups [*username*]

This command displays the list of group(s) the named user currently belongs to. If no username is specified, this command displays the current user's groups.

last

Syntax: last [*-number*] [*username*] [reboot]

This command displays a list of users who have logged in since /var/log/wtmp was created. For example, the following command shows the number of times user julie has logged in since the last time /var/log/wtmp was created:

last julie

This command shows only the last 10 logins by julie:

last -10 julie

This last command displays the number of times the system has been rebooted since the /var/log/wtmp file was created:

last reboot

passwd

Syntax: passwd *username*

This command allows you to change a user's password. Only a superuser can specify a username; everyone else must type passwd without any argument, which allows the user to change his or her password. A superuser can change anyone's password using this program.

su

Syntax: su [-] [*username*]

You can use the su command to change into another user. For example:

su john

This command allows you to be the user john as long as you know john's password, and this account exists on the server you use.

The most common use of this command is to become root. For example, if you run this command without any username argument, it assumes that you want to be root and prompts you for the root password. If you enter the correct root password, su runs a shell by using the root's UID (0) and GID (0). This allows you effectively to become the root user and to perform administrative tasks.

This command is very useful if you have only Telnet access to the server. You can telnet into the server as a regular user and use it to become root to perform system administrative tasks. If you supply the − option, the new shell is marked as the login shell. Once you become the root user, you can su to other users without entering any password.

useradd

See the section on creating new user accounts in Chapter 7.

userdel

See the section on deleting or disabling a user account in Chapter 7.

usermod

See the section on modifying an existing user account in Chapter 7.

who

Syntax: who

This command displays information about the users who are currently logged into a system. You can also use the w command for the same purpose.

whoami

Syntax: whoami

This command displays your current username.

User Commands for Accessing Network Services

The commands that I discuss in this section allow you to access various network services. You can use these tools to get finger information on a user, transfer files, browse Web pages, read and send e-mails, Telnet to other systems, and so on.

finger

Syntax: finger user@host

This program allows you to query a finger daemon at the named host. For example, the following command requests a finger connection to the finger daemon running on the blackhole.integrationlogic.com server:

```
finger kabir@blackhole.integrationlogic.com
```

If the named host does not allow finger connections, this attempt fails. On success, the finger request displays information about the named user. If the user has a .plan file in the home directory, most traditional finger daemons display this file. Because finger has been used by hackers to cause security problems, most system administrators disable finger service outside their domains.

ftp

Syntax: `ftp ftp hostname or IP address`

This is the default FTP client program. You can use this to FTP to an FTP server. For example:

```
ftp  ftp.cdrom.com
```

This opens an FTP connection to `ftp.cdrom.com` and prompts you to enter a username and a password. If you know the username and password, you can log into the FTP server and upload or download files. Once you're at the FTP prompt, you can enter **help** or **?** to get help on FTP commands.

lynx

Syntax: `lynx [-dump] [-head] [URL]`

This is the most popular interactive text-based Web browser. For example, the following command displays the top page of the site:

```
lynx http://www.integrationlogic.com/
```

This is a very handy program to have. For example, say you want quickly to find what kind of Web server the site uses without asking the Webmaster. You can run the following command:

```
lynx -head http://www.integrationlogic.com/
```

This displays the HTTP header the lynx browser receives from the Web server. An example of output is shown here:

```
HTTP/1.1 302 Moved
Date: Tue, 02 Mar 1999 06:47:27 GMT
Server: Apache/1.3.3 (Unix)
Location: http://www.integrationlogic.com/index.shtml
Connection: close
Content-Type: text/html
```

As you can see, this header shows that `www.integrationlogic.com` runs on the Apache 1.3.3 Web server on a Unix platform. Note that not all Web sites give their Web server platform information, but most do. If you would like to avoid the interactive mode, you can use the -dump option to dump the page on the screen. For example,

```
lynx -dump -head http://www.integrationlogic.com/
```

This dumps the header to the screen. The -dump feature can be quite handy. For example:

```
lynx -dump -head http://webserver/new.gif > new.gif
```

This allows you to save new.gif on the Web server host on a local file called new.gif.

The interactive mode (i.e., without -dump) allows you to browse a text browser-friendly site in a reasonably nice manner.

mail

Syntax: mail user@host [-s *subject*]   [< *filename*]

This is the default SMTP mail client program. You can use this program to send or receive mail from your system. For example, if you run this program without any argument, it displays an & prompt and shows you the currently unread mail messages by listing them in a numeric list. To read a message, enter the index number and the mail is displayed. To learn more about mail, use the ? command once you are at the & prompt.

For example, to send a message to a user called kabir@evoknow.com with the subject header "About your Red Hat book," you can run:

```
mail  kabir@evoknow.com  -s "About your Red Hat book"
```

You can then enter your mail message and press Ctrl+D to end the message. You can switch to your default text editor by entering ~v at the beginning of a line while you are in the compose mode.

If you have already prepared a mail message in a file, you can send it using a command such as:

```
mail  kabir@evoknow.com  -s "About your Red Hat book" <<
feedback.txt
```

This sends a message with the given subject line; the message consists of the contents of the feedback.txt file.

pine

Syntax: `pine`

This is a full-screen SMTP mail client that is quite user-friendly. If you typically use mail clients via telnet, you should definitely try this program. Because of its user-friendly interfaces, it is suitable for your Linux users who are not yet friends with Linux.

rlogin

Syntax: `rlogin [-l username] host`

This command allows you to log remotely into a host. For example, to log into a host called `shell.myhost.com`, you can run:

```
rlogin shell.myhost.com
```

The `-l` option allows you to specify a username to use for authentication. If you would like to log remotely into a host without entering a password, create a `.rhosts` file in the user's home directory. Add the host name or IP address of the computer you use to issue the `rlogin` request.

 Because `rlogin` is not safe, I recommend that you use it only in a closed LAN environment.

talk

Syntax: `talk username [tty]`

If you need to send a message to another user, e-mail works just fine. But if you need to communicate with another user in real-time, like a telephone conversation, use the `talk` command.

To talk to another user who is logged in, use the following command:

```
talk ronak@csus.edu
```

The user you request has to accept your `talk` request. Once the user accepts your `talk` request, you can begin talking (or typing) to each other. The `talk` program terminates when either party presses Ctrl+C (the program interrupt key combination). Also, note that if the user is logged in multiple time you have to specify the tty device name to talk to a specific instances of the user login. You can run w or who command to find the tty names for each user login.

telnet

Syntax: telnet *hostname_or_IP_address* [*port*]

This is the default Telnet client program. You can use this program to connect to a Telnet server. For example:

```
telnet shell.myportal.com
```

This command opens a Telnet connection to the shell.myportal.com system if the named host runs a Telnet server. Once a connection is opened, the command prompts you for a username and password and, on successful login, allows you to access a local user account on the Telnet server.

wall

Syntax: wall

This command allows you to send a text message to everyone's terminal as long as he or she has not disabled write access to the tty via the mesg n command. After you type wall, you can enter a single or multiline message and can send it by pressing Ctrl+D.

Network Administrator's Commands

The commands that I discuss in this section allow you to gather information on network services and on the network itself. Using these commands you can get a host name by IP, display or set host name of the system you are on, configure network interfaces, perform network queries, and so on.

host

Syntax: host [-a] *host IP address*

By default, this program allows you to check the IP address of a host quickly. If you use the -a option, it returns various sorts of DNS information about the named host or IP address.

hostname

Syntax: hostname

This program displays the host name of a system.

ifconfig

Syntax: ifconfig [*interface*] [up | down] [netmask mask]

This program allows you to configure a network interface. You can also see the state of an interface using this program. For example, if you have configured your Red Hat Linux for networking and have a preconfigured network interface device eth0, you can run the following command:

```
ifconfig eth0
```

You should see output similar to the following:

```
eth0 Link encap:Ethernet HWaddr 00:C0:F6:98:37:37
inet addr:206.171.50.50  Bcast:206.171.50.63 Mask:255.255.255.240
UP BROADCAST RUNNING MULTICAST  MTU:1500  Metric:1
RX packets:9470 errors:0 dropped:0 overruns:0 frame:0
TX packets:7578 errors:0 dropped:0 overruns:0 carrier:0 collisions:0
Interrupt:5 Base address:0x340
```

Here ifconfig reports that network interface device eth0 has an Internet address (inet addr) 206.171.50.50, a broadcast address (Bcast) 206.171.50.63, and network mask (255.255.255.240). The rest of the information shows the following: how many packets this interface has received (RX packets); how many packets this interface has transmitted (TX packets); how many errors of different types have occurred so far;

what interrupt address line this device is using; what I/O address base is being used; and so on.

You can run `ifconfig` without any arguments to get the full list of all the up and running network devices.

You can use `ifconfig` to start an interface. For example:

```
ifconfig eth0 206.171.50.50 netmask 255.255.255.240 broadcast 206.171.50.63
```

The preceding command starts `eth0` with IP address 206.171.50.50. You can also quickly take an interface down by using the `ifconfig` command. For example, the following command takes the eth0 interface down:

```
ifconfig eth0 down
```

netcfg

See the section on using `netcfg` to configure a network interface card in Chapter 9.

netstat

Syntax: `netstat [-r] [-a] [-c] [-i]`

This program displays the status of the network connections both to and from the local system. For example, the following command displays all the network connections on the local system:

```
netstat -a
```

To display the routing table, use the `-r` option. To display network connection status on a continuous basis, use the `-c` option. To display information on all network interfaces, use the `-i` option.

nslookup

Syntax: `nslookup [-query=DNS record type] [hostname or IP] [name server]`

This command allows you to perform DNS queries. You can choose to query a DNS server in an interactive fashion or just look up information immediately. For example, the following command immediately returns the MX records for the `integrationlogic.com` domain:

```
nslookup -query=mx evoknow.com
```

The following command does the same, but instead of using the default name server specified in the /etc/resolv.conf file, it uses `ns.evoknow.com` as the name server.

```
nslookup -query=mx evoknow.com ns.evoknow.com
```

You can also use -q instead of -query. For example:

```
nslookup -q=a www.evoknow.com
```

This command returns the IP address (Address record) for the named host name.

You can run `nslookup` in interactive mode as well. Just run the command without any parameters, and you will see the `nslookup` prompt. At the `nslookup` prompt, you can enter "?" to get help. If you are planning on performing multiple DNS queries at a time, interactive mode can be very helpful. For example, to query the NS records for multiple domains such as `evoknow.com` and `mobidac.com`, you can just enter the following command:

```
set query=ns
```

Once you set the query type to ns, you can simply type `evoknow.com` and wait for the reply; once you get the reply, you can try the next domain name; and so on. If you would like to change the name server while at the nslookup prompt, use the `server` command. For example:

```
server ns.evoknow.com
```

This will make nslookup use `ns.evoknow.com` as the name server. To quit interactive mode and return to your shell prompt, enter `exit` at the `nslookup` prompt.

ping

Syntax: ping [-c *count*] [-s *packet size*] [-I *interface*]

This is one of the programs network administrators use most often. You use `ping` to see if a remote computer is reachable via the TCP/IP protocol. Technically, this program sends an Internet Control Message Protocol (ICMP) echo request to the remote host. Because the protocol requires a response to an echo request, the remote host is bound to send an echo response. This allows the `ping` program to calculate the amount of time it takes to send a packet to a remote host. For example:

```
ping blackhole.evoknow.com
```

This command sends `ping` messages to the `blackhole.evoknow.com` host on a continuous basis. To stop the `ping` program, press Ctrl+C, which causes the program to display a set of statistics. Here is an example of output of the `ping` requests the preceding command generates:

```
PING blackhole.evoknow.com (209.63.178.15): 56 data bytes

64 bytes from 209.63.178.15: icmp_seq=0 ttl=53 time=141.5 ms

64 bytes from 209.63.178.15: icmp_seq=1 ttl=53 time=162.6 ms

64 bytes from 209.63.178.15: icmp_seq=2 ttl=53 time=121.4 ms

64 bytes from 209.63.178.15: icmp_seq=3 ttl=53 time=156.0 ms

64 bytes from 209.63.178.15: icmp_seq=4 ttl=53 time=126.4 ms

64 bytes from 209.63.178.15: icmp_seq=5 ttl=53 time=101.5 ms

64 bytes from 209.63.178.15: icmp_seq=6 ttl=53 time=98.7 ms

64 bytes from 209.63.178.15: icmp_seq=7 ttl=53 time=180.9 ms

64 bytes from 209.63.178.15: icmp_seq=8 ttl=53 time=126.2 ms

64 bytes from 209.63.178.15: icmp_seq=9 ttl=53 time=122.3 ms

64 bytes from 209.63.178.15: icmp_seq=10 ttl=53 time=127.1 ms

-- blackhole.evoknow.com ping statistics--

11 packets transmitted, 11 packets received, 0% packet loss

round-trip min/avg/max = 98.7/133.1/180.9 ms
```

The preceding output shows 10 `ping` requests to the `blackhole.evoknow.com` host. Because the program is interrupted after the eleventh request, the statistics show that `ping` has transmitted 11 packets and has also received all the packets, and therefore no packet loss has occurred. This is good: packet loss is a sign of poor networking between the `ping` requester and the `ping` responder. The other interesting statistics are the round-trip minimum (`min`) time, the average (`avg`) time, and the maximum (`max`) time. The lower these numbers are, the better the routing is between the involved hosts. For example, if you `ping` a host on the same LAN, you should see the round-trip numbers in the 1-millisecond range.

If you would like to have `ping` stop automatically after transmitting a number of packets, use the `-c` option. For example:

```
ping -c 10 blackhole.evoknow.com
```

This sends 10 `ping` requests to the named host. By default, `ping` sends a 64-byte (56 data bytes + 8 header bytes) packet. If you are also interested in controlling the size of the packet sent, use the `-s` option. For example:

```
ping -c 1024 -s 1016 reboot.evoknow.com
```

This command sends a packet 1,024 (1016 + 8) bytes long to the remote host.

By sending large packets to a remote host running weak operating systems (you know what they are), you might cause the host to become very unusable to the user(s) on the remote host. This could be considered as an attack by many system administrators and therefore is very likely to be illegal in most parts of the world. So, be very careful when you start experimenting with `ping` and someone else's computer.

route

Syntax 1: `route add -net` *network_address netmask* `dev` *device*

Syntax 2: `route add -host` *hostname_or_IP* `dev` *device*

Syntax 3: `route add default gw` *hostname_or_IP*

This command allows you to control routing to and from your computer. For example, to create a default route for your network, use the route command as follows:

```
route add -net network_address netmask    device
```

To create a default route for 206.171.50.48 network with a 255.255.255.240 netmask and eth0 as the interface, you can run the following command:

```
route add -net 206.171.50.48 255.255.255.240 eth0
```

To set the default gateway, you can run the route command as follows:

```
route add default gw gateway_address device
```

For example, to set the default gateway address to 206.171.50.49, you can run the following command:

```
route add default gw 206.171.50.49 eth0
```

You can verify that your network route and default gateway are properly set up in the routing table by using the following command:

```
route -n
```

Here is an example of output of the preceding command:

```
Kernel IP routing table
Destination    Gateway Genmask        Flags Metric Ref Use Iface
206.171.50.48 0.0.0.0 255.255.255.240 U     0      0   6   eth0
127.0.0.0      0.0.0.0 255.0.0.0       U     0      0   5   lo
0.0.0.0        206.171.50.49  0.0.0.0 UG    0      0   17  eth0
```

> **TIP**   Make sure that you have IP forwarding turned on in /etc/sysconfig/network and also in the kernel to allow routing packets between two different network interfaces.

tcpdump

Syntax: tcpdump *expression*

This is a great network debugging tool, allowing you to debug a network problem at a low level. If you are experiencing a problem in using a service between two hosts, you can use tcpdump to identify the problem. For example, to trace all the packets between two hosts brat.evoknow.com and reboot.evoknow.com, you can use the following command:

```
tcpdump host brat.evoknow.com and reboot.evoknow.com
```

This command makes `tcpdump` listen for packets between these two computers. If `reboot.nitec.com` starts sending `ping` requests to `brat.nitec.com`, the output looks something like the following:

```
tcpdump: listening on eth0
09:21:14.720000 reboot.evoknow.com> brat.nitec.com: icmp: echo request
09:21:14.720000 brat.evoknow.com> reboot.nitec.com: icmp: echo reply
09:21:15.720000 reboot.evoknow.com> brat.nitec.com: icmp: echo request
09:21:15.720000 brat.evoknow.com> reboot.nitec.com: icmp: echo reply
09:21:16.720000 reboot.evoknow.com> brat.nitec.com: icmp: echo request
09:21:16.720000 brat.evoknow.com> reboot.nitec.com: icmp: echo reply
09:21:17.730000 reboot.evoknow.com> brat.nitec.com: icmp: echo request
09:21:17.730000 brat.evoknow.com> reboot.nitec.com: icmp: echo reply
```

If you're having a problem connecting to an FTP server, you can use `tcpdump` on your LAN gateway system to see what is going on. For example:

```
tcpdump port ftp or ftp-data
```

This displays the FTP-related packets originating and arriving in your network.

traceroute

Syntax: `traceroute host or IP address`

This program allows you to locate network routing problems. It displays the routes between two hosts by tricking the gateways between the hosts into responding to an ICMP TIME_EXCEEDED request. Here is an example of `traceroute` from my local system to the `blackhole.evoknow.com` host:

```
traceroute to blackhole.evoknow.com (209.63.178.15), 30 hops max, 40 byte
packets
 1 router (206.171.50.49)  4.137 ms  3.995 ms  4.738 ms
 2 PM3-001.v1.NET (206.171.48.10) 32.683 ms  33.295 ms  33.255 ms
 3 HQ-CS001.v1.NET (206.171.48.1) 42.263 ms  44.237 ms  36.784 ms
 4 ix.pxbi.net (206.13.15.97) 106.785 ms  63.585 ms  101.277 ms
 5 ix.pxbi.net (206.13.31.8) 86.283 ms  64.246 ms  69.749 ms
 6 ca.us.ixbm.net (165.87.22.10) 71.415 ms  72.319 ms  85.183 ms
```

```
 7 mae.elxi.net (198.32.136.128) 101.863 ms   80.257 ms   67.323 ms

 8 y.exli.net (207.173.113.146) 71.323 ms   104.685 ms   110.935 ms

 9 z.exli.net (207.173.113.217) 69.964 ms   137.858 ms   85.326 ms

10 z1.exli.net (207.173.112.251) 81.257 ms   107.575 ms   78.453 ms

11 209.210.249.50 (209.210.249.50) 90.701 ms   91.116 ms   109.491 ms

12 209.63.178.15 (209.63.178.15) 83.052 ms   76.604 ms   85.406 ms
```

Each line represents a hop; the more hops there are, the worse the route usually is. In other words, if you have only a few gateways between the source and the destination, chances are that packets between these two hosts are going to be transferred at a reasonably fast pace. However, this won't be true all the time because it takes only a single, slow gateway to mess up delivery time. Using traceroute, you can locate where your packets are going and where they are perhaps getting stuck. After you locate a problem point, you can contact the appropriate authorities to resolve the routing problem.

Process Management Commands

The commands that I discuss in this section show you how to manage processes, i.e., running programs in your system. Using these commands you can send processes to the background or foreground, query the running background jobs, send signals to running processes, and so on.

bg

Syntax: bg

This built-in shell command is found in popular shells and allows you to put a suspended process into background. For example, say that you decide to run du –a / | sort –rn > /tmp/du.sorted to list all the files and directories in your system according to the disk usage (size) order and to put the result in a file called /tmp/du.sorted. Depending on the number of files you have on your system, this can take a while. In such a case, you can simply suspend the command by using Ctrl+Z and type bg to send all the commands involved in the command line to background, thus returning your shell prompt for other use.

TIP

If you wish to run a command in the background from the start, you can simply append "&" to the end of the command line.

To find out what commands are running in the background, enter the jobs and you see the list of background command lines. To bring a command from the background, use the fg command (discussed in the next section).

fg

Syntax: fg [%*job-number*]

This built-in shell command is found in popular shells. This command allows you to put a background process into foreground. If you run this command without any argument, it brings up the last command you put in the background. If you have multiple commands running in the background, you can use the jobs command to find the job number and can supply this number as an argument for fg to bring it to the foreground. For example, if jobs shows that you have two commands in the background, you can bring up the first command you put in the background by using the following command:

```
fg %1
```

jobs

Syntax: jobs

This built-in shell command is found in popular shells and allows you to view the list of processes running in the background or currently suspended.

kill

See the section on signaling a running process in Chapter 8.

killall

See the section on signaling a running process in Chapter 8.

ps

See the section on using ps to get process status in Chapter 8.

top

See the section on monitoring processes and system load in Chapter 8.

Task Automation Commands

The commands that I discuss in this section show you how to run unattended tasks. Using these commands you can schedule a program to run at a later time.

at

See the section on scheduling processes section in Chapter 8.

atq

See the section on scheduling processes in Chapter 8.

atrm

See the section on scheduling processes in Chapter 8.

crontab

See the section on scheduling processes in Chapter 8.

Productivity Commands

The commands that I discuss in this section help you increase your productivity.

bc

Syntax: bc

This is an interactive calculator that implements a calculator-specific language as well. Personally, I am not all that interested in learning the language, but I find this tool very useful in doing quick calculations. When you run the command without any arguments, it takes your input and interprets it as calculator programming statements. For example, to multiply 1,024 by 4, you can simply enter 1024*4 and the result is displayed. You can reuse the current result by using the period character. For example, if you want to multiply the last result (4096) with 10, you can simply type .*10.

cal

Syntax: cal [month] [year]

This nifty program displays a nicely formatted calendar for the month or year specified in the command line. If you do not specify anything as an argument, the calendar for the current month is displayed. To see the calendar for an entire year, enter the year in 1–9999 range. For example, cal 2001 displays the following calendar for the year 2001:

ispell

Syntax: ispell filename

This program allows you to correct spelling mistakes in a text file in an interactive fashion. If you have a misspelling in the file, the program suggests a spelling and gives you options to replace it with a correctly spelled word. This is the spell checker for text files.

mesg

Syntax: mesg [y | n]

This program allows you to enable or disable public write access to your terminal. For example, the following command enables write access to your terminal so that another user on the same system can use the write command to write text messages to you:

```
mesg y
```

The n option allows you to disable write access. If you do not wish to be bothered by anyone at any time, you can add mesg n to your login script (.login) file in your home directory.

write

Syntax: write *username tty*

This program allows you to write text messages to the named user if he or she has not disabled write access to her tty. For example:

```
write  shoeman
```

This command allows you to type a text message on screen, and when you finish the message by pressing Ctrl+D, the message is displayed on the user shoeman's terminal. If the user is logged in more than once, you have to specify the terminal name as well. For example:

```
write  shoeman ttyp0
```

This allows you to write to shoeman and to display the message on terminal ttyp0. If someone has multiple terminals open, you might want to run the w or who command to see which tty is most suitable.

Shell Commands

In this section, you will find some very basic shell commands. These commands allow you to create alias names for other commands, recall commands that you have executed earlier in the current session, set and view environment information, and so on.

alias

Syntax: alias *name of the alias = command*

This is a built-in shell command available in most popular shells that lets you create aliases for commands. For example, the following command creates an alias called dir for the ls —l command:

```
alias dir  ls -l
```

To see the entire alias list, run alias without any argument.

history

Syntax: history

This is a built-in shell command available in most popular shells. history displays a list of commands you have recently entered at the command line. The number of commands that history displays is limited by an environment variable called history. For example, if you add set history = 100 to your .login file in the home directory, whenever you log on, you allow the history command to remember up to 100 command lines. You can easily rerun the commands you see in the history by entering their index number with an exclamation point. For example, say that when you enter the history command, you see the following listings:

```
1  10:25   vi irc-bot.h
2  10:25   vi irc-bot.c
3  10:26   which make
```

To run the vi irc-bot.c command again, you can simply enter !2 at the command line.

set

Syntax: set var = value

This is a built-in shell command available in most popular shells that allows you to set environment variables with specific values. For example, in the following command a new environment variable foo is set to have bar as the value:

```
set foo = bar
```

To see the list of all environment variables, run set by itself. To view the value of a specific environment variable, such as path, run:

```
echo $path
```

This shows you the value of the named environment variable. If you use this command quite often to set a few special environment variables, you can add it to .login or .profile or to your shell's dot file in your home directory so that the special environment variables are automatically set when you log in.

source

Syntax: source *filename*

This is a built-in shell command available in most popular shells. This command lets you read and execute commands from the named file in the current shell environment.

unalias

Syntax: unalias *name of the alias*

This is a built-in shell command that's available in most popular shells that lets you remove an alias for a command. For example, the following command removes an alias called dir:

```
unalias dir
```

To remove all aliases, use "*" as the argument.

Printing-Specific Commands

This section discusses commands that help you print from your Linux system. Using these commands you can view the print queue status, print files, or remove print jobs from the current print queue.

lpq

Syntax: lpq [-al] [-P *printer*]

The `lpq` command lists the status of the printers. If you enter `lpq` without any arguments, information about the default printer is displayed.

```
lpq
Printer: lp@rembrandt  'Generic dot-matrix printer entry'
Queue: no printable jobs in queue
Status: server finished at 21:11:33
```

The `-P` option specifies information about a particular printer. The `-a` option returns the status of all printers. With the `-1` option, `lpq` reports the job identification number, the user name that requests the print job, the originating host, the rank in queue, the job description, and the size of the job.

lpr

Syntax: `lpr [-i indentcols] [-P printer] [filename]`

This command sends a file to the print spool to be printed. If you give no filename, data from standard input is assumed. The `-i` option allows the option of starting the printing at a specific column. To specify a particular printer, you can use the `-P printer` option.

```
lpr main.c
```

The preceding example attempts to print the file `main.c`.

lprm

Syntax: `lprm [-a] [jobid] [all]`

The `lprm` command sends a request to the print daemon `lpd` to remove an item from the print queue. You can specify the print jobs by the job ID or usernames to remove it, or you can remove all print jobs by specifying the `all` option.

To remove all jobs in all print queues:

```
lprm -a all
```

To remove all jobs for the user `kiwee` on the printer `p1`:

```
lprm -Pp1 kiwee
```

Appendix B

IP Networking Basics

Currently, Ipv4 (which uses 32-bit IP addresses) IP addresses are in use on the Internet. A 32-bit IP address is divided into two parts: the network-prefix and the host-number. Traditionally, each IP address belongs to an IP class. The class breakdown is identified by a self-encoded key in each IP address. For example, if the first bit of an IP address is set to 0 it is considered a Class A IP address; if the first 2 bits are 10 then it is considered to be a Class B IP address, and similarly if the first 3 bits are 110 then it is considered to be a Class C IP address.

Class A IP Networks

Each Class A network address has the highest bit set to 0 and a 7-bit network number followed by a 24-bit host-number. Class A networks are now referred as /8 networks.

Since only the first 8 bits are used in defining the network-prefix, the maximum number of Class A (/8) networks possible are 128. However, 0.0.0.0 (entire IP space or default route) and 127.0.0.0 (loopback network) are special addresses that need to be excluded from the list of valid Class A (/8) networks. This means that there are only 126 ($2^7 - 2$) Class A (/8) networks available.

Each Class A network can have 2^{24} hosts. However, we need to exclude x.0.0.0 and x.1.1.1 host addresses where x is the 8-bit network-prefix with first bit set to 0. The address with all 0s is considered as the network address, and the one with all 1s is considered the broadcast address. So a total of 16,777,214 ($2^{24} - 2$) host addresses are available per Class A (/8) network.

Class B IP Networks

Each Class B network address has the two highest-order bits set to 10. The network-prefix is 14-bit long and the host-number is 16-bit long. A Class B network is referred as a /16 network. A total of 16,384 (2^{14}) networks are possible in Class B, and each of such networks has a possible 65,534 | ($2^{16} - 2$) hosts.

Class C IP Networks

Each Class C network address has the three highest-order bits set to 110. The network-prefix is 21-bit long and the host-number is 8-bit long. A Class C network is referred as a /24 network. A total of 2,097,152 (2^{21}) networks are possible in Class C, and each such network has 254 ($2^8 - 2$) hosts.

Each of these classes can be summarized as shown in Table A-1.

Table B-1 *IP Class Networks*

Address Class	Starting IP Address (in Decimal Dotted Notation)	Ending IP Address (in Decimal Dotted Notation)
A (/8)	1.xxx.xxx.xxx	126.xxx.xxx.xxx
B (/16)	128.0.xxx.xxx	191.255.xxx.xxx
C (/24)	192.0.0.xxx	223.255.255.xxx

Subnetting IP Networks

Each of the IP classes (A, B, or C) can be broken into smaller networks which are called subnets. When you divide up any of the IP classes into subnets you accomplish two things: (a) you are helping to minimize the routing table for your outmost router and also hiding details of your networked organization. For example, say you have a Class B network, 130.86.32.0. Your router to the Internet is responsible for receiving all IP packets for this entire network. However, once the packets enter your network you can use several subnets to route the IP packets to different divisions of your organization.

In the absence of subnetting you would either use a large Class B network or multiple Class C networks to support multiple divisions of your organization. In the latter case the number of routes in your router table will increase, which will effectively slow down the performance of the network.

To create a subnet, you divide the host-number portion of the IP address into a subnet-number and a new host-number. So subnet is a shift from the two-level class hierarchy to a three-level subnet hierarchy. Let's take a look at an example of subnetting a Class C network called 192.168.1.0. Say that we want to create six subnets for this network in which the largest subnet has 20 hosts.

The very first step is to determine how many bits are necessary to create six subnets from the host-number part, which is 8 bit. Because each bit can be a 1 or a 0, you must divide your subnet along binary boundaries. Therefore, the possible subnets are 2 (2^1), 4 (2^2), 8 (2^3), 16 (2^4), 32 (2^5), 64 (2^6), and 128 (2^7). Because we need six subnets, the best choice for us is 8 (2^3), which gives us two additional subnets for the future. If we use a 3-bit subnet number we are left with 5 bits in the new host-number. So the maximum subnet mask would be 255.255.255.224 or in binary it would be 11111111. 11111111. 11111111. 11100000. Now the last subnet mask 255.255. 255.224 can be also represented as /27, which is called an extended network-prefix. Here we have subnetted a class C (/24) network using /27 (3-bit extended). Table A-2 shows all the subnets for this network.

Table B-2 Subnets of 192.168.1.0/24 Network

Network (Subnet)	Subnet Mask (Dotted-decimal notation)	Subnet Mask (Binary)	Maximum Hosts
192.168.1.0/27	255.255.255.0	11111111. 11111111. 11111111.00000000	30
192.168.1.32/27	255.255.1.32	11111111. 11111111. 11111111.00100000	30
192.168.1.64/27	255.255.1.64	11111111. 11111111. 11111111.01000000	30
192.168.1.96/27	255.255.1.96	11111111. 11111111. 11111111.01100000	30
192.168.1.128/27	255.255.1.128	11111111. 11111111. 11111111.10000000	30
192.168.1.160/27	255.255.1.160	11111111. 11111111. 11111111.10100000	30
192.168.1.192/27	255.255.1.192	11111111. 11111111. 11111111.11000000	30
192.168.1.224/27	255.255.1.224	11111111. 11111111. 11111111.11100000	30

Appendix C

Internet Resources for Linux

This appendix provides you with a list of Linux resources. Many Linux-oriented newsgroups, mailing lists, and Web sites are available on the Internet. Although you are likely to discover many more new Linux resources as time passes and as Linux's popularity increases, the following resources are likely to remain in good health at all times. I personally use these resources on an almost daily basis.

Usenet Newsgroups

The following Usenet newsgroups can be a great place to learn about advances in Linux, to engage in Linux-specific discussions, and also to find answers to questions you might have.

The comp.os.linux hierarchy

Linux has its own hierarchy of Usenet newsgroups. These groups are strictly Linux only. Before you post an article or a question in any of these newsgroups (or any Usenet newsgroup), make sure you know the charter of the group. In particular, when you are looking for answers to questions or solutions to problems, make sure you have read the available frequently asked questions, man pages, and HOW-TO documentation. If you post a question that has been answered in a FAQ or a HOW-TO document, chances are that some people who participate in that group might not take it kindly. Also, be careful when you post the same question in multiple groups (known as cross-posting) in the hope that you are increasing your chances of getting answers. As long as your post is relevant to the group, you should be okay.

comp.os.linux.advocacy (unmoderated)

This newsgroup is intended for discussions of the benefits of Linux compared with other operating systems.

comp.os.linux.announce (moderated)

This newsgroup is intended for all Linux-specific announcements. You will find information on new Linux software, bug and security alerts, and user group information here.

comp.os.linux.answers (moderated)

The Linux FAQ, HOW-TO, README, and other documents are posted in this newsgroup. If you have a question about Linux, check this newsgroup before posting your question in any Linux newsgroup.

comp.os.linux.development.apps (unmoderated)

This newsgroup is intended for Linux developers who want to discuss development issues with others.

comp.os.linux.hardware (unmoderated)

This newsgroup is intended for hardware-specific discussions. If you have a question about a piece of hardware you are trying to use with Linux, look for help here.

comp.os.linux.m68k (unmoderated)

This newsgroup is intended for Motorola 68K architecture-specific Linux development.

comp.os.linux.alpha (unmoderated)

This newsgroup is intended for Compaq/Digital Alpha architecture-specific discussions.

comp.os.linux.networking (unmoderated)

This newsgroup is intended for networking-related discussions.

comp.os.linux.x (unmoderated)

This newsgroup is intended for discussions relating to the X Window System (version 11), and compatible software such as servers, clients, libraries, and fonts running under Linux.

comp.os.linux.development.system (unmoderated)

This newsgroup is intended for kernel hackers and module developers. Here you will find ongoing discussions on the development of the Linux operating system proper: kernel, device drivers, loadable modules, and so forth.

comp.os.linux.setup (unmoderated)

This newsgroup is intended for discussions on installation and system administration issues.

comp.os.linux.security (unmoderated)

This newsgroup is intended for discussion of Linux security issues.

comp.os.linux.powerpc (unmoderated)

This newsgroup is intended for discussion of Linux on power pc platform.

comp.os.linux.misc (unmoderated)

This is the bit-bucket for the comp.os.linux hierarchy. Any topics not suitable for the other newsgroups in this hierarchy are discussed here.

Miscellaneous Linux newsgroups

The following newsgroups are mainstream Linux newsgroups. Most of these groups are geographically oriented and typically used for local Linux-related announcements for Linux user group meetings and events.

- `alt.uu.comp.os.linux.questions`
- `aus.computers.linux`
- `dc.org.linux-users`
- `de.alt.sources.linux.patches`
- `de.comp.os.linux.misc`

- de.comp.os.linux.networking
- de.comp.os.x
- ed.linux
- fido.linux-ger
- fj.os.linux
- fr.comp.os.linux
- hannet.ml.linux
- hannet.ml.linux.680x0
- it.comp.linux
- it.comp.linux.setup
- it.comp.linux.development
- it.comp.linux.announci
- no.linux
- okinawa.os.linux
- tn.linux
- tw.bbs.comp.linux
- ucb.os.linux
- umich.linux

Unix security newsgroups

The following newsgroups are mainstream Unix security newsgroups. They often discuss current security matters that might also apply to Linux.

- comp.security.announce
- comp.security.misc
- comp.security.pgp.announce
- comp.security.ssh
- comp.security.unix

Mailing Lists

Mailing lists provide a good way of getting information directly to your e-mail account. If you are interested in Linux news, announcements, and other discussions, mailing lists can be quite helpful. This is especially true of mailing lists that provide a digest option. Such mailing lists send a digest of all daily or weekly messages to your e-mail address.

General lists

The following Linux mailing lists provide good general discussions of Linux news and helpful information for beginning Linux users.

linux-announce

Subscribe to Linux-Announce by sending an e-mail to `linux-announce-request@ redhat.com` with the word "subscribe" in the subject line of the message.

linux-list

To subscribe, send an e-mail to `linux-list-request@ssc.com` with the word "subscribe" in the body of the message.

linux-newbie

To subscribe, send an e-mail to `majordomo@vger.rutgers.edu` with the words "subscribe linux-newbie" in the body of the message.

linuxusers

To subscribe, send an e-mail to `majordomo@dmu.ac.uk` with the words "subscribe linux users" in the body of the message.

Security alert lists

The following mailing lists deal with Linux and computer security issues.

bugtraq

Although BugTraq is not specific to Linux, it is a great bug alert resource. To subscribe, send an e-mail to `listserv@netspace.org` with the following as the body of the message: "SUBSCRIBE bugtraq *your_firstname your_lastname.*"

 I strongly recommend that you subscribe to the bugtraq mailing list immediately.

linux-security

Red Hat Software, Inc. hosts this mailing list. To subscribe, send e-mail to `linux-security-request@redhat.com` with the words "subscribe linux-security" in the subject line.

Special lists

The following mailing lists deal with two issues: Linux as a server platform and Linux as a desktop platform.

SERVER-LINUX

To subscribe, send an e-mail to `listserv@netspace.org` with the words "subscribe SERVER-LINUX" in the subject line.

WORKSTATION-LINUX

To subscribe, send an e-mail to `listserv@netspace.org` with the words "subscribe WORKSTATION-LINUX" in the subject line.

Web Sites

Many Web sites provide Linux-oriented information. Here are a few good ones.

Red Hat Network

The Red Hat Network, located at `www.redhat.com/products/network`, is a great Web site for getting information on the latest bug fixes, package enhancements, and security alerts.

General resources

The following Web sites are general. Most of these sites act as portal sites:

- www.redhat.com/
- www.linux.com/
- www.linuxresources.com/
- linuxcentral.com/
- www.linuxcare.com/

Publications

The following Web sites are official Web sites for various Linux publications:

- www.linuxworld.com/
- www.linuxgazette.com/
- www.linuxjournal.com/

Software stores

The following Web sites offer commercial Linux software:

- www.linuxmall.com/
- www.cheapbytes.com/
- www.lsl.com/

Security resources

The following Web sites deal with computer security:

- www.cert.org/
- www.securityfocus.com/
- www.rootshell.com/

User Groups

A local Linux user group could be just the help you need for finding information on Linux. You can locate or even register a new user group of your own in your area at the following Web site:

`www.linuxresources.com/glue/index.html`

Appendix D

Recovering from a System Crash

The official Red Hat CD-ROM (disk 1) can serve as a bootable emergency disk for most modern PCs with BIOS that can boot from CD-ROMs. It includes file system tools for emergency system administration. Using this disc you can attempt to recover from file system-related crashes.

When your system crashes due to a power failure or any other dire reasons, you may find your file system to be corrupt, and Red Hat Linux might refuse to boot as normal. In such a case do the following:

1. Insert the official Red Hat CD-ROM (disc 1) in your CD-ROM and boot your computer.

2. After the system starts booting from the CD-ROM you will see a screen that displays a boot prompt. Enter `linux rescue` at the boot prompt to boot the system in rescue mode.

3. You will be asked to select the language, which defaults to English. Select the appropriate language and press OK to continue.

4. You will be asked to select the keyboard type, which defaults to us (USA). Select the appropriate keyboard type and press OK to continue.

5. Linux notes that the rescue mode will attempt to mount your existing partitions under `/mnt/sysimage` directory. You should select the Skip button because you are trying to fix a file system problem (most file system tools do not work on mounted file systems for security reasons).

597

6. Once you are at the shell prompt, run the `fsck` `partition_name` command to perform a file system check for your hard drive. For example, to check the first partition of your first IDE/EIDE disk, run the `fsck` `/dev/hda1` command. Similarly, to check the first partition of your first SCSI disk run the `fsck` `/dev/sda1` command. This will display errors that the `fsck` program finds in the named partition and ask you to take an action. If you are not interested in getting prompted for one or more file system errors and want the `fsck` program to fix whatever it can, you can run this same command with a `-p` option. For example, the `fsck` `-p` `/dev/hda1` command runs the `fsck` program on the first IDE/EIDE hard drive partition and tries to fix everything it can.

7. If your disk has bad blocks, you can locate bad blocks in a disk by running the `badblocks` `device_name` command. For example, to find bad blocks on the second partition of the first IDE/EIDE disk run the `badblocks` `/dev/hda2` command.

8. Repeat the previous steps as many times necessary to check all your file system partitions.

TIP

If you have a problem accessing the partition, try the `rescuept` `device_name` command to restore the partition.

9. Press Ctrl+Alt+Del to reboot the system and make sure to remove the CD-ROM so that your system can boot from your hard drive.

Index

Continued

Continued